The Institute of Chartered Accountants in England and Wales

FINANCIAL MANAGEMENT

For exams in 2016

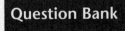

Question Bank

www.icaew.com

ICAEW

Financial Management
The Institute of Chartered Accountants in England and Wales

ISBN: 978-1-78363-217-6

Previous ISBN: 978-0-85760-997-7

First edition 2007
Ninth edition 2015

The content of this publication is intended to prepare students for the ICAEW
examinations, and should not be used as professional advice.

British Library Cataloguing-in-Publication Data
A catalogue record for this book is available from the British Library

Originally printed in the United Kingdom by Polestar Wheatons on paper
obtained from traceable, sustainable sources.

Polestar Wheatons
Hennock Road
Marsh Barton
Exeter
EX2 8RP

ICAEW

Contents

The following questions are exam-standard. Unless told otherwise, these questions are the style, content and format that you can expect in your exam.

Title		Marks	Time allocation Mins		
37	Turners plc (June 14)	35	52.5	44	193
38	Middleham plc (Sample paper)	35	52.5	45	196
39	Better Deal plc (Mar 10)	35	52.5	46	198
40	Havant Hall Ltd (June 11)	35	52.5	47	201
41	Puerto plc (Dec 13)	35	52.5	48	204
42	Efficient markets hypothesis	12	18	49	207
43	Abydos plc	16	24	50	208
44	Wiggins plc (Dec 14)	35	52.5	51	210
45	Perryfield Paper plc (Mar 15)	35	52.5	52	214

Business valuations, plans, dividends and growth

46	Worsley plc (June 10)	32	48	54	217
47	Wentworth plc (Dec 06)	22	33	56	220
48	Biddaford Lundy plc (Mar 12)	35	52.5	57	222
49	Duofold plc (Mar 04)	17	25.5	57	225
50	Portico plc (Dec 04)	16	24	58	227
51	Cern Ltd (Dec 12)	31	46.5	59	229
52	Wexford plc (Dec 08)	30	45	61	231
53	Loxwood (Mar 14)	35	52.5	62	234
54	Arleyhill Redland plc (Sept 13)	35	52.5	64	237
55	Sennen plc (June 14)	35	52.5	65	240
56	Megagreat plc (June 02)	17	25.5	66	243
57	Printwise UK plc (Mar 10)	30	45	67	245
58	Tower Brazil plc (Sept 14)	35	52.5	68	247
59	Hildes and Heimer	25	37.5	70	249
60	Pinky and Perky	20	30	71	253
61	Brennan plc	20	30	71	255
62	Lipton plc (Dec 10)	35	52.5	72	256

Risk management

63	Fratton plc (June 11)	30	45	73	259
64	Dayton plc (Dec 11)	28	42	74	262
65	Sunwin plc (Dec 12)	26	39	75	264
66	Atherton plc and Tyldesley Inc (June 10)	26	39	76	267
67	Strauss Cook plc (Mar 10)	23	34.5	77	269
68	Springfield plc and Woodhouse plc (Dec 10)	25	37.5	78	271
69	Padd Shoes Ltd (Mar 14)	30	45	79	273
70	Stelvio Ltd (June 14)	30	45	80	275
71	JEK Computing Ltd (Sept 14)	30	45	81	278
72	Mayo plc (Dec 08)	22	33	82	281
73	Brampton plc (June 13)	27	40.5	83	284
74	Lambourn plc (Sample paper)	30	45	84	286
75	Clifton Bernard Ltd (Sept 13)	30	45	86	288
76	American Adventures Ltd (Dec 13)	30	45	87	291

Question Bank

Your exam will consist of

3 or 4 written test questions   100 marks

Time available   2.5 hours

1 Stakeholders

Requirements

1.1 In the following situations, identify the stakeholders that could be involved in potential conflicts.

    (a) A large conglomerate 'spinning off' its divisions by selling them or setting them up as separate companies.

    (b) A private company converting into a public company.

    (c) A Japanese car manufacturer building new plants in other countries. **(9 marks)**

1.2 'I get paid to make the owners of the Coca-Cola Co. increasingly wealthy with each passing day. Everything else is just fluff.' Roberto Goizueta, Former CEO of Coca-Cola.

    Discuss the argument that maximisation of shareholder wealth should be the only objective of a company. **(8 marks)**

Total: 17 marks

2 Stoane Gayte Sounds plc

Stoane Gayte Sounds plc (SGS) manufactures audio equipment and has a financial year end of 31 March. Its directors are considering making use of SGS's cash reserves to finance an investment of £4.9 million in a new range of high specification audio speakers for cars, to be marketed under the brand name of Inca. However, two of SGS's directors are of the opinion that this money should be used for an ordinary dividend payment instead, as they feel that this would help to increase the company's share price.

You work in SGS's finance team and have been asked to advise the SGS board. You have been given the following information:

Sales

£80,000 of market research work for SGS's has been done by Etchingham Tyce Marketing Ltd (ETM) in the past two months and the payment for this work has yet to be made. The results of the research suggest that, although it is a very competitive market, Inca speakers would be popular amongst young drivers for at least three years. ETM's estimated figures for Inca sales over the next four years, based on a selling price of £190 per unit (at 31 March 20X3 prices), are shown below:

	Units
Year to 31 March 20X4	65,000
Year to 31 March 20X5	110,000
Year to 31 March 20X6	55,000
Year to 31 March 20X7	15,000

As a result of these estimates SGS' directors are concerned about the riskiness of the proposal and so wish to appraise the investment in Inca speakers over a three-year period only (ie to 31 March 20X6).

Costs

The estimated variable costs (at 31 March 20X3 prices) of manufacturing one Inca unit are:

	£
Raw materials	43
Variable overheads	45
Skilled labour (£9/hour)	18

Because of a lack of skilled labour, SGS will have to transfer all of the skilled production hours required to manufacture the Inca away from the manufacture of another, lower specification speaker, the Boom-Boom. Thus a proportion of the Boom-Boom production would have to cease. Current production details for the Boom-Boom (at 31 March 20X3 prices) are shown below:

	Per unit
	£
Selling price	99
Raw materials	28
Variable overheads	35
Skilled labour (£9/hour)	9

SGS' directors estimate that the company's total fixed overheads are unlikely to change as a result of manufacturing the Inca, but will nonetheless apportion a share of SGS' existing fixed costs at a rate of £27 per Inca unit (at 31 March 20X3 prices). However this does not include the depreciation charge (to be spread evenly over the three financial years ending 31 March 20X6) that will be incurred as a result of the capital expenditure for the Inca (see details below).

Capital expenditure

In order to manufacture the Inca speakers, new machinery costing £4.9 million would be purchased on 31 March 20X3. SGS's production director estimates that this could be sold on 31 March 20X6 for £980,000 (at 31 March 20X6 prices).

This machinery will attract 20% (reducing balance) capital allowances in the year of expenditure and in every subsequent year of ownership by the company, except the final year. In the final year, the difference between the machinery's written down value for tax purposes and its disposal proceeds will be treated by the company either:

- As an additional tax relief, if the disposal proceeds are less than the tax written down value, or
- As a balancing charge, if the disposal proceeds are more than the tax written down value.

Working capital

SGS's directors estimate that a net investment of £750,000 for additional working capital to support the Inca will be required on 31 March 20X3 and that this will be fully recoverable on 31 March 20X6.

Inflation

Revenues, costs and working capital are all expected to increase in line with the general rate of inflation, which is estimated at 3% pa.

Taxation

SGS's directors wish to assume that the corporation tax rate will be 28% pa for the foreseeable future and that tax flows arise in the same year as the cash flows which gave rise to them.

Cost of capital

For investment appraisal purposes SGS uses a money cost of capital of 11% pa.

Other information

- SGS's ordinary dividends have been rising steadily over the past five years and in the financial year to 31 March 20X2 they totalled £3.4 million.

- Unless otherwise stated, all cash flows occur at the end of the relevant trading year.

Requirements

2.1 Calculate the net present value of the Inca proposal at 31 March 20X3 and, based on this calculation alone, advise SGS's directors whether they should proceed with it. **(17 marks)**

2.2 Calculate the internal rate of return of the Inca proposal at 31 March 20X3 and advise SGS's directors as to the usefulness of this figure. **(6 marks)**

2.3 Discuss, with reference to relevant theories, the view that SGS should, as an alternative to the Inca proposal, pay an ordinary dividend in order to increase the company's share price. **(6 marks)**

Total: 29 marks

3   Profitis plc

Profitis plc has a continuing need for a machine. At the level of intensity of use by the company, after four years from new the machine is not capable of efficient working. It has been the company's practice to replace it every four years. The production manager has pointed out that in the fourth year the machine needs additional maintenance to keep it working at normal efficiency. The question has therefore arisen as to whether to replace it after three years instead of the usual four years.

Relevant information is as follows.

(1)   The machine costs £80,000 to buy new. If it is retained for four years, it will have a zero scrap value at the end of the period. If it is retained for three years, it will have an estimated disposal value of £10,000.

The machine will attract capital allowances. For the purposes of this analysis assume that it will be excluded from the general pool. This means that it will attract a 18% (reducing balance) tax allowance in the year of acquisition and in every subsequent year of being owned by the company, except the last year. In the last year the difference between the machine's written-down value for tax purposes and its disposal proceeds will either be allowed to the company as an additional tax relief if the disposal proceeds are less than the written-down value, or be charged to the company if the disposal proceeds are more than the tax written-down value.

Assume that the machine will be bought and disposed of on the last day of the company's accounting year.

(2)   The company's corporation tax rate is 21%. Tax is payable on the last day of the accounting year concerned.

(3)   During the first year of ownership the supplier takes responsibility for any necessary maintenance work. In the second and third years maintenance costs average £10,000 a year. During the fourth year these rise to £20,000. Maintenance charges are payable on the first day of the company's accounting year and are allowable for tax.

(4)   The company's cost of capital is estimated at 15%.

Requirements

3.1   Prepare calculations to show whether it would economically be more desirable to replace the machine after three years or four years.   **(13 marks)**

3.2   Discuss any other issues that could influence the company's replacement decision. This should include any weaknesses in the approach taken in 3.1.   **(4 marks)**

Total: 17 marks

4   Harrow plc

Harrow plc (Harrow) manufactures a range of electric hand tools which are sold to specialist retailers and tool hire companies. The company's accounting year end is 31 December. For investment appraisal purposes, the directors currently use a discount rate of 10% pa, which the finance director has calculated using the capital asset pricing model. The company's principal objective is to maximise shareholder value.

For some years the company has been successfully selling a heavy duty circular saw, the RotoEdge, but last year the company's two major competitors introduced innovative new products which threatened the market share of the RotoEdge. In view of this, the directors of Harrow are considering two strategic options:

Option 1

To cease production and sale of the RotoEdge on 31 December 20X0 and replace it from 1 January 20X1 with a new product, the Diamond, which has been developed during the last six months. Full product development costs amounted to £325,000, of which £100,000 is still to be paid on 31 December 20X0.

If production and sale of the RotoEdge ceases on 31 December 20X0, sales of the Diamond in subsequent years are expected to be as follows:

	Units
20X1	12,000
20X2	18,000
20X3	24,000
20X4	18,000
20X5	12,000

The marketing director has calculated that these projected sales figures could be achieved at a selling price of £120 per unit, with variable production costs expected to be £48 per unit, incremental fixed costs £300,000 pa and allocated head office fixed costs £50,000 pa.

Option 2

To introduce the Diamond on 1 January 20X1 and retain the RotoEdge as the marketing director believes that there will still be demand in certain market segments for the cheaper RotoEdge for a maximum of three years.

If the RotoEdge is retained for three years, then based on a selling price of £96 per unit, sales are forecast to be 4,800 units in 20X1, 3,600 units in 20X2 and 2,400 units in 20X3. However, the marketing director has also pointed out that retention of the RotoEdge would diminish sales of the Diamond in those three years by one unit for every two units of the RotoEdge sold.

The RotoEdge has an estimated £54 per unit variable cost element and has associated incremental fixed costs of £20,000 pa.

Machinery

If the Diamond were to be introduced, then to achieve the minimum efficient scale of production, Harrow would need to invest £1.5 million in new machinery, payable when the machinery is delivered on 31 December 20X0. This machinery would be expected to operate for five years and then be scrapped at the end of 20X5, by which time the value of the machinery is expected to be negligible.

The machinery currently used to manufacture the RotoEdge has been owned by Harrow for many years and whenever it is disposed of its market value will be negligible. The tax written-down value of the machinery is currently close to zero and can, therefore, be ignored.

Redundancies

Any decision made by the directors will result in redundancies:

Option 1

If the directors decide to cease production and sale of the RotoEdge and introduce the Diamond, redundancy payments of £144,000 would be due to production staff on 31 December 20X0.

Option 2

If the directors decide to introduce the Diamond and retain the RotoEdge, redundancy payments would be as follows (all at 31 December):

	£
20X0	60,000
20X1	48,000
20X2	48,000
20X3	24,000

All redundancy payments would attract corporation tax relief.

Working capital

The finance director has also highlighted the need for working capital equal to 10% of the following year's sales value to be in place by the start of each relevant year. No such working capital is currently in place and this requirement will be reduced to zero by the end of 20X5, at which time the directors will undertake a further strategic review of the company's product range. The directors are assuming that these working capital requirements will have no tax effect.

Taxation

The company's corporation tax rate is expected to be 21% for the foreseeable future, and it can be assumed that tax payments occur at the end of the accounting year to which they relate. The directors are also assuming that the new machinery will attract full capital allowances at 18% pa on a reducing balance basis commencing in the year of purchase and continuing throughout the company's ownership of the machinery. A balancing charge or allowance will arise on disposal of the new equipment which is expected to be on 31 December 20X5.

Requirements

4.1 Calculate the incremental cash flows associated with Option 1 (ignoring any opportunity cash flows associated with Option 2) and use these to calculate the net present value of Option 1 at 31 December 20X0. **(11 marks)**

4.2 Calculate the incremental cash flows associated with Option 2 (ignoring any opportunity cash flows associated with Option 1) and use these to calculate the net present value of Option 2 at 31 December 20X0 and recommend which of the two options the company should pursue. **(8 marks)**

4.3 Explain the two major weaknesses of the assumptions of the capital asset pricing model when using it to calculate a discount factor for investment appraisal purposes. **(2 marks)**

4.4 Identify **six** value drivers which could be managed by the directors in this scenario to increase shareholder value, explaining briefly, for each driver, how improvements in shareholder value might be achieved. **(6 marks)**

4.5 Identify and discuss three areas where the interests of shareholders and directors may conflict leading the directors to pursue objectives other than maximising shareholder wealth. **(8 marks)**

Total: 35 marks

Notes Ignore inflation

5 Tidefrost plc

Tidefrost plc (Tidefrost) is a printing firm and has a financial year end of 30 June. Its senior management is considering two investment opportunities, which are mutually exclusive:

(1) **Three year contract with Collins Morrison Limited**

Tidefrost has been invited to make a tender bid for a three year contract with Collins Morrison Limited ('Collins') which would commence on 30 June 20X8. The following information has been prepared with regard to the contract:

Year to 30 June	20X8	20X9	20Y0	20Y1
	£'000	£'000	£'000	£'000
Purchase of machinery for contract (note 1)	940			
Trade-in value of machinery (at 20Y1 prices)				100
Annual costs (notes 2 & 5)		440	510	580

Notes

1 The machinery would be purchased just before the end of the financial year to 30 June 20X8 and the trade-in price would be fixed at £100,000 on 30 June 20Y1.

2 The annual cost figures are specific to the Collins contract and include a charge for depreciation of the machinery using the straight-line method.

3 If Tidefrost takes on the contract then it will have to reduce its scale of operations in other parts of the business. The company's management estimates that Tidefrost will lose an annual contribution of £150,000 because of this.

4 The contract would also require an investment of £160,000 in additional working capital from 30 June 20X8. This will be recovered in full at the end of the contract.

5 Unless otherwise stated, all figures above are stated at 30 June 20X8 prices. Tidefrost's annual income, costs and working capital investment will increase at 5% per annum, in line with general price inflation.

6 The tender price would be received at the end of the contract on 30 June 20Y1.

The machinery would qualify for writing down allowances at the rate of 18% per annum on a reducing balance basis. The allowances would commence in the year in which the machinery was acquired. As at 30 June 20Y1, a balancing charge or allowance would arise equal to the difference between any disposal proceeds and the machinery's tax written down value.

You should assume that all cash flows occur on the last day of each financial year. Tidefrost pays corporation tax at a rate of 21% on its taxable profits and which is payable at the end of the financial year in which profits are earned.

Tidefrost uses a money cost of capital figure of 10% for the appraisal of capital projects.

However Tidefrost's marketing director has commented that:

'Waiting until 20Y1 for our money is too risky. We should be asking for £2 million cash in total – £1 million receivable at the start of the contract (for tax reasons I suggest July 20X8), and the balance in July 20X9.'

(2) **Acquisition of Barryfinn plc**

Tidefrost is considering the acquisition of Barryfinn plc ('Barryfinn'), another printing company.

The most recent relevant financial details for the two companies are shown below:

	Tidefrost	Barryfinn
Earnings per share	£0.26	£0.15
Price earnings ratio	18	8
Shares in issue	20 million	14 million

Tidefrost's board estimates that the acquisition would generate total after tax annual savings of £1.8 million across the two companies. It is believed that the stock market would apply a P/E ratio of 16 to the combined entity. The board is unsure as to whether (a) a cash offer or (b) a share-for-share exchange would be the best method of settlement.

Requirements

5.1 Calculate the minimum tender price that Tidefrost could submit for the Collins contract that would leave its shareholders' wealth unchanged. **(14 marks)**

5.2 Determine whether the marketing director's opinion is reasonable. **(4 marks)**

5.3 Outline in general terms the potential advantages of a business combination with Barryfinn. **(3 marks)**

5.4 Calculate the maximum price that Tidefrost should offer for Barryfinn. **(3 marks)**

5.5 Outline the advantages and disadvantages for Tidefrost of (a) a cash offer and (b) a share-for-share exchange. **(3 marks)**

Total: 27 marks

6 Horton plc

6.1 The objective of the directors of Horton plc (Horton) is the maximisation of shareholder wealth. The directors are currently considering Horton's capital investment strategy for 20Y0. Five potential investment projects have been identified, each one having an expected life of four years. However, at this stage the directors are uncertain of the precise financial situation the company will be in on 31 December 20X9 when it will actually make its chosen investments. The company accountant has already undertaken net present value calculations for each of the five potential investment projects as follows:

	Initial Investment (31.12.X9) £	Net Present Value (31.12.X9) £
Project 1	(2,400,000)	2,676,600
Project 2	(2,250,000)	(461,700)
Project 3	(3,000,000)	4,111,500
Project 4	(2,630,000)	2,016,250
Project 5	(3,750,000)	(45,250)

Whilst these net present value calculations include the impact of corporation tax, which the company pays at 21%, they do not include the effect of capital allowances. Project 3 is the only project that will attract capital allowances and these allowances will apply just to the initial £3m investment. The allowances will be at a rate of 18% per annum on a reducing balance basis, commencing in the year of initial investment, with either a balancing charge or allowance arising in the final year of the project. The directors are confident that the company will be able to use all capital allowances in full.

The company's cost of capital is 10%. The cashflows used by the company accountant to calculate the original net present values of the projects were as follows:

	T_0	T_1	T_2	T_3	T_4
Project 1	(2,400,000)	(750,000)	300,000	4,200,000	3,450,000
Project 2	(2,250,000)	(750,000)	1,800,000	900,000	450,000
Project 3	(3,000,000)	(1,500,000)	3,750,000	3,750,000	3,750,000
Project 4	(2,630,000)	750,000	1,650,000	2,100,000	1,500,000
Project 5	(3,750,000)	1,050,000	1,350,000	1,950,000	250,000

Project 3's T_4 cashflow of £3.75m includes disposal proceeds of £1m relating to the assets originally purchased on 31 December 20X9 for £3m.

To reflect the uncertainty regarding Horton's financial position at the end of 20X9, four potential scenarios have been identified for consideration:

Scenario 1: Horton will face no capital rationing and the five projects will be independent and divisible.

Scenario 2: Horton's available capital for investment at T_0 will be limited to £4.5m; the five projects will be independent and divisible and none of the projects can be delayed.

Scenario 3: Horton's available capital for investment at T_0 will not be limited, but its available capital for investment at T_1 will be limited to £0.3m; the five projects will be independent and divisible and none of the projects can be delayed.

Scenario 4: Horton's available capital for investment at T_0 will be limited to £5.25m, and whilst the five projects will be independent and none of the projects can be delayed, they will be indivisible.

One director has indicated that he wishes to discuss the possibility of leasing some of the assets that would be required as a result of these investment projects in preference to outright purchase of the assets. He is, however, a little uncertain as to the leasing options available to the company.

Requirements

(a) Calculate the revised net present value of Project 3 at 31.12.X9 taking account of the capital allowances attributable to that project. **(4 marks)**

(b) For each of the four scenarios, prepare calculations which show the proportion of each project that should be undertaken. **(12 marks)**

(c) Summarise the different characteristics of finance leases and operating leases and discuss the potential attractions of lease finance over outright purchase of an asset. **(8 marks)**

6.2 The managing director of one of Horton's subsidiary companies has approached Horton's finance director for advice. On 31 December 20X9 the subsidiary company will be replacing its three existing company cars with brand new vehicles. The managing director wishes to know whether to replace these new vehicles every one, two or three years from now on. He has provided the following background information:

(1) Each new car will cost £11,000.

(2) Resale values for each car (assumed to be received in cash on the last day of the year to which they relate) are estimated to be £7,000 after one year, £4,200 after two years and £1,800 after three years.

(3) Annual running costs for each car (assumed to be paid on the last day of the year to which they relate) are estimated at £6,600 in the first year of ownership, £7,600 in the second year and £9,200 in the third year.

(4) The subsidiary company uses a discount rate of 10% in its appraisal of such investments.

(5) For the purposes of the advice to be given to the managing director, taxation and inflation can be ignored.

Requirements

(a) Using appropriate calculations, advise the managing director of the optimal replacement policy for these new company cars. **(5 marks)**

(b) Outline the limitations of the method used in answering 6.2(a) above. **(6 marks)**

Total: 35 marks

7 Oxidian plc

In December 20X0 Oxidian plc (Oxidian) successfully completed the development of a new product, the SeaGuard, a mobile alarm for use with yachts and small boats. The development costs of this new product have totalled £120,000, of which half has already been paid and half is due to be paid on 31 December 20X0, although the amount of this second instalment will fall to £40,000 if the SeaGuard is not launched onto the market. All development costs attract tax relief in the year in which the payment is made.

The firm's marketing director has indicated that a market research report (previously commissioned at a cost of £3,500, payable in 20X1) indicates that the SeaGuard should have a life of four years. The report has confirmed that the superior functionality of the SeaGuard, compared to existing products, means that it is highly likely to be a commercial success, but that this success will lead to lost sales for Oxidian's current product for the yacht market, the Mobilok.

In light of the market research report, the marketing director has estimated that the loss of Mobilok sales revenue will equate to 30% of the projected sales revenue of the SeaGuard in each year of the SeaGuard's life. Mobilok will generate a contribution of 60p per £1 of sales during those four years.

Production and sales of the SeaGuard could start on 1 January 20X1, with sales expected to be as follows:

Year ending 31 December	Units
20X1	7,500
20X2	12,000
20X3	15,000
20X4	7,500

The projected selling price will be £100 per unit with a contribution of £55 per unit.

Product management of the SeaGuard will be undertaken by two managers at a total annual employment cost of £45,000 each. Both of these managers are currently due to leave the company on 31 December 20X0, but have expressed a willingness to manage the product and will leave the company four years later. Were they to leave at the end of 20X0 they would each be entitled to receive, at that time, redundancy payments from the company of £30,000. By the end of 20X4, this will have increased to £40,000 each. Redundancy payments are fully allowable for corporation tax in the year in which the expenditure is incurred. These management costs have not been included in calculating the SeaGuard's unit contribution figure above.

Oxidian always budgets for a working capital requirement for all of its products at the rate of 10% of annual sales revenue and the company ensures that this is in place at the start of each year. Working capital will have no tax impact and will be released in full at the end of the SeaGuard's estimated life.

The launch of the SeaGuard will require investment on 31 December 20X0 in new production machinery at a cost of £900,000. This will be expected to have a market value of £150,000 on disposal at the end of the project, although the directors are uncertain whether it will be most advantageous for Oxidian to dispose of the machinery on 31 December 20X4 or 1 January 20X5.

The company's corporation tax rate is expected to be 21% for the foreseeable future, and it can be assumed that tax payments occur at the end of the year to which they relate. The directors are also assuming that the new machinery will attract full capital allowances at 18% pa on a reducing balance basis commencing in the year of purchase and continuing throughout the company's ownership of the machinery. A balancing charge or allowance will arise on disposal of the new equipment.

In appraising the SeaGuard the directors are assuming that all operating revenues and expenses arise on 31 December of the year concerned and that the company's cost of capital is 10% pa.

Requirements

7.1 Prepare capital allowance calculations for the SeaGuard production machinery on the following two bases:

(a) Disposal of the machinery on 31 December 20X4
(b) Disposal of the machinery on 1 January 20X5

and, without undertaking any further calculations, state whether Oxidian would be best advised to sell this machinery on 31 December 20X4 or on 1 January 20X5. **(5 marks)**

7.2 Taking account of the decision reached in 7.1, produce a schedule of annual net cash flows and use it to indicate whether, on the basis of their net present value at 31 December 20X0, production of the SeaGuard should proceed. **(14 marks)**

7.3 Identify the areas in which conflicts of interest might occur between the directors and shareholders of Oxidian. **(6 marks)**

Total: 25 marks

Notes

1   Ignore inflation
2   Work to the nearest £

8   Broadham Hotels Ltd

Broadham Hotels Ltd (BH) owns and manages a hotel in a major Midlands city. The hotel has 500 identical, twin-bedded rooms for which a standard rate of £50 per night is charged, whether the room is occupied by one or two people. Occupancy rates have fallen below those which were envisaged when the hotel was built five years ago.

Septo, a Japanese-owned business, which is shortly to open a local manufacturing plant, has approached the hotel's management with a proposal that it takes over 100 of the rooms, in effect the whole of the top two floors of the hotel, to accommodate its staff and guests when they visit the plant. Septo wishes to take over the rooms for a five-year period starting on 1 July 20X2. Septo would employ its own staff to service and manage the rooms.

On the basis of past experience and taking account of future developments in the market, the hotel's management believes that future average nightly demand will be as follows.

Rooms	Probability (%)
380	20
400	20
420	30
440	20
460	10

The hotel is open for 360 nights each year.

It is estimated that the variable costs of having a room occupied is on average 10% of the room rate. All staff costs are effectively fixed costs, and no staff cost savings are expected to be made by the hotel should the Septo proposal be accepted. The total fixed costs of running the hotel are estimated at £4 million a year.

Under the proposal Septo would pay a fixed fee annually on 1 July from 20X2 to 20X6 inclusive.

There is expected to be a general annual rate of inflation of 3% throughout the five-year period. This will affect the room rate, the variable costs and the fixed costs, all of which are stated above at 1 July 20X2 prices.

BH has a corporation tax rate of 21% and an accounting year ending on 30 June. Tax will be payable on the last day of the accounting year in which the relevant transactions occur. You should assume that all operating cash flows occur on the last day of the relevant accounting year, except for any receipt from Septo, which will be received on the first day.

BH's cost of capital, in real terms, is 10% per annum.

Requirements

8.1 Determine, on the basis of net present value and the information given in the question, the minimum fixed annual payment that Septo must make so that BH is as well off in expected value terms as it would be without the Septo proposal.

Notes

1   Work in 'money' terms.

2   Assume for this requirement that neither Septo's new plant nor the proposal to BH would affect the projected nightly demand figures given in the question.   **(13 marks)**

8.2 State and explain any other items of information, not mentioned in the question, that should have been brought into the determination of the minimum annual payment in 8.1.   **(4 marks)**

8.3 Discuss briefly whether in principle from Septo's perspective the planned provision of accommodation seems a good idea.   **(5 marks)**

Total: 22 marks

9   ProBuild plc

ProBuild plc (ProBuild) runs a network of builders' merchants in northern England. The company has a small subsidiary, Cabin Ltd (Cabin) that hires out various types of portable cabin used on building sites. In recent years, Cabin's performance (relative to that of ProBuild's core business) has been disappointing and the directors of ProBuild have decided that they should focus resources on their core operations and dispose of Cabin.

Having advertised the business for sale, ProBuild has now been approached by the directors of Brixham plc (Brixham) with an offer to buy Cabin on 31 December 20X3. Brixham has agreed, in principle, to pay ProBuild the net present value (as at 31 December 20X3) of the projected incremental net cash flows of Cabin over the four-year period to 31 December 20X7.

You have been asked by Brixham's directors to calculate an appropriate purchase price using the following information which has been provided by ProBuild and verified by independent accountants:

(1) All cash flows can be assumed to occur at the end of the relevant year unless otherwise stated.

(2) Inflation is expected to average 2% pa for all costs and revenues.

(3) The real discount rates applicable to the appraisal of this investment are:

20X4:	5%
20X5:	6%
20X6:	7%
20X7:	7%

(4) During the past five years, Cabin's annual revenue (at 31 December 20X3 prices) has been extremely volatile, having peaked at £2 million in one year, whilst falling to a low of £1.2 million in another year.

(5) During the past five years, Cabin's variable costs have been similarly volatile, being as low as 25% of annual revenue in one year, whilst having been as high as 30% of annual revenue in another year. There has been no direct correlation between annual revenue and variable costs during the past five years.

(6) It has been estimated that under Brixham's ownership, annual fixed costs will be £0.6 million (at 31 December 20X3 prices), including a share of Brixham's existing head office costs equal to £0.25 million.

(7) Working capital equal to 8% of Cabin's annual revenue for that year must be in place by the start of the year concerned and, for the purposes of the calculation of a purchase price, it can be assumed to be released in full on 31 December 20X7.

(8) Cabin has an existing commitment (which Brixham would have to honour as a condition of its purchase of Cabin) to make a substantial investment of £1.5 million in new plant and equipment on 31 December 20X3. This equipment is expected to have a useful working life of four years, at which time it is estimated that it will be disposed of for a sum of £100,000 (at 31 December 20X7 prices).

This new plant and equipment will attract capital allowances of 20% pa on a reducing balance basis commencing in the year of purchase and continuing throughout Brixham's ownership of the equipment. A balancing charge or allowance will arise on disposal of the equipment on 31 December 20X7.

It can be assumed that sufficient profits would be available for Brixham to claim all such tax allowances in the year they arise. It can also be assumed that the corporation tax rate will be 28% for the foreseeable future, and that tax payments will occur at the end of the accounting year to which they relate.

Requirements

9.1 Using money cash flows, calculate the net present values at 31 December 20X3 of the Cabin business for both the 'worst case' and 'best case' scenarios. **(17 marks)**

9.2 Distinguish between the terms 'uncertainty' and 'risk' in the context of investment decision-making and describe how the directors of Brixham might adjust the calculations made in 9.1 from calculations made under conditions of uncertainty to calculations made under conditions of risk. **(6 marks)**

9.3 Explain what is meant by the term 'real options' and suggest two real options that might be relevant to Brixham's purchase of Cabin. **(6 marks)**

Total: 29 marks

10   Frome Lee Electronics Ltd

Frome Lee Electronics Ltd (Frome Lee) makes small portable radios. Frome Lee's board has been considering the financial implications of launching a new radio, which it would call 'The Pink 'Un'. You have recently been appointed on a short term contract at Frome Lee following the sudden resignation of the company's chief accountant and have received this memo from the managing director:

To: A Newman
From: Diana Marshall

As you are aware, our chief accountant, John Smith, left Frome Lee earlier this week following a disagreement over company policy.

As a result we desperately need financial advice from you. We are considering the purchase of capital equipment for the manufacture of a new radio, The Pink 'Un. Our marketing team feels that we would have a competitive advantage with this new radio for three years. Mr Smith had prepared some estimated figures which we were going to consider at our next meeting on Monday and he left some of them behind. You will find my summary of them (with some of my notes) in the Appendix below. We would want to purchase the equipment at the end of our financial year on 30 September, commence production very soon after and sell the equipment at the end of September 20Y1.

The board would like to consider a complete set of figures and your recommendations over the weekend so that we can reach a prompt decision on Monday. Apologies for giving you so little time, but we don't want to miss what could be a valuable investment opportunity for the company.

Diana Marshall

Friday 5 September

Appendix – summary of information available

Year to 30 September	20X8 £'000	20X9 £'000	20Y0 £'000	20Y1 £'000
Equipment cost	(400.000)			
Equipment scrap value				60.000
Working capital increment	(32.000)	(Note 1)	(3.000)	40.000
Direct material costs		(52.000)	(64.000)	(70.000)
Other variable costs		(12.000)	(14.000)	(16.000)
Incremental fixed costs		(11.000)	(11.800)	(12.700)
Sales (Note 1)			Figures to be calculated	
Direct labour costs (Note 2)			Figures to be calculated	

Notes

1   As you can see, I don't know the estimated sales figures, but we always make sure that we have sufficient working capital, based on 10% of the annual sales, in place at the beginning of the relevant year. All working capital will be recovered at the end of September 20Y1. We need to know the missing figures for (a) annual sales (for 20X9-20Y1) and (b) working capital (for 20X9) from this information.

2   We always estimate labour costs at 50% of material costs.

3   When discounting, we use a real cost of capital figure of 5% and make adjustments for inflation when necessary. The figures in the appendix above are all in money terms and I'd like you to use the following annual rates of general price inflation when working out the present values of the estimated cash flows:

	%
Year to 30 September 20X9	3
Year to 30 September 20Y0	3
Year to 30 September 20Y1	4

I'm not sure how accurate our cost of capital is, but I did read the other day that if a business uses the wrong cost of capital figure, 'it destroys shareholder value'.

Capital allowances

The equipment would attract capital allowances, but would be excluded from the general pool. Assume that this means that it attracts 18% (reducing balance) tax allowances in the year of expenditure and in every subsequent year of ownership by the company, except the final year. In the final year, the difference between the machinery's written down value for tax purposes and its disposal proceeds will be either:

(1)   Allowed to the company as an additional tax relief, if the disposal proceeds are less than the tax written down value; or

(2)   Be charged to the company, if the disposal proceeds are more than the tax written down value

The corporation tax rate can be assumed to be 21% over the next three years.

Requirements

10.1 Calculate the net present value at 30 September 20X8 of proceeding with production of The Pink 'Un and advise the board as to whether it should purchase the equipment. **(15 marks)**

10.2 Explain your approach to the effects of inflation in your calculation in 10.1 above. **(3 marks)**

10.3 In response to Diana Marshall's Note (3), discuss the view that a business, by using the wrong cost of capital figure, 'destroys shareholder value'. **(4 marks)**

10.4 Explain, in the context of the proposed investment, the nature and importance of follow-on and abandonment real investment options. **(4 marks)**

Total: 26 marks

11   Farmshoppers Ltd

You have been recently appointed as the accountant/finance manager of Farmshoppers Ltd, a firm of agricultural suppliers located in Herefordshire. You are the only member of the staff with any real understanding of accounting and financial issues. The directors are considering making a major investment in providing a new service for their farmer customers. You have helped with estimating the potential cash flows from this investment. You have also, with the help of the directors, looked at the range of feasible outcomes for each of the items of input data and ascribed probabilities to various outcomes for each of these input data. Using all of this information you have

- Carried out a net present value (NPV) assessment of the best estimates of the cash flows and have found a significant positive outcome

- Carried out a sensitivity analysis on the positive NPV

- Derived the expected NPV using the expected values of each of the items of input data

You are due to present this information to the directors, but you feel that it would be a good idea to include some notes for them.

Requirement

Draft the notes for the directors explaining why you have used the NPV approach, what a sensitivity analysis is and what the expected value means. Your notes should also discuss how useful the results of these three analyses are in helping the directors to make a decision and how the analyses might be extended to provide more useful information. **(13 marks)**

12   CAPM and project appraisal

You were recently appointed by a major manufacturing company as the senior accountant at one of the divisions of the company, which is located in Cardiff. You have received the following memorandum from the divisional manager.

'I tried to see you today, but you were tied up with the auditors.

I have to go to a meeting at head office on Friday about the robotics project. We sent head office the projected cash flow figures for it before you arrived.

Apparently one of the head office finance people has discounted our figures, using a rate which was calculated from the capital asset pricing model. I do not know why they are discounting the figures, because inflation is predicted to be negligible over the next few years – I think that this is all a ploy to stop us going ahead with the project and let another division have the cash.

I looked up capital asset pricing model in a finance book which was lying in your office, but I could not make head nor tail of it, and anyway it all seemed to be about buying shares and nothing about our project.

We always use payback for the smaller projects which we do not have to refer to head office. I am going to argue for it now because the project has a payback of less than five years, which is our normal yardstick.

I am very keen to go ahead with the project because I feel that it will secure the medium-term future of our division.

I will be tied up all day tomorrow, so again I will not be able to see you. Could you please make a few notes for me which I can read on the train on Friday morning?

I want to know how the capital asset pricing model is supposed to work, plus any other things which you feel I ought to know for the meeting. I do not want to look a fool or lose the project because they blind me with science.

As you have probably discovered I do not know much about finance, so please do not use any technical jargon or complicated maths.'

Requirements

12.1 Prepare notes for the divisional manager which will provide helpful background for the meeting.

(14 marks)

12.2 Critically comment on the following statement, explaining the reasons for your comments and clearly defining any technical terms that you use.

'The capital asset pricing model is a device for deriving the guaranteed return for an equity share in a particular company. Some people misguidedly seek to use it to estimate the cost of capital to be used in a net present value assessment of an investment in a non-current asset.'   **(4 marks)**

Total: 18 marks

13   Nuts and Bolts Ltd

Nuts and Bolts Ltd (NBL) manufactures parts for motor cars and the majority of its customers are UK-based. Its financial year end is 31 March. Its management team is considering the purchase of machinery that would produce a new type of catalytic converter (model number NBL 1114). However, NBL's management team, mindful of the current weakness of the UK economy, is uncertain as to the level of demand for NBL 1114. As a result it commissioned a market research report from Ashford Hume Research and that report showed two alternative overall levels of demand for NBL 1114 – pessimistic throughout the project's life or optimistic throughout the project's life. The report concluded that these alternative overall levels of demand were equally likely to occur.

For each of the overall levels of demand (pessimistic or optimistic), demand for NBL 1114 varies in the first year of the project as shown here in Table 1:

Table 1

Pessimistic		Optimistic	
Annual demand (units)	Probability	Annual demand (units)	Probability
6,000	25%	10,000	25%
10,000	50%	14,000	37.5%
14,000	25%	20,000	37.5%

Demand in each subsequent year of the project's life would remain at the first year's expected level.

Financial information about the new machinery and NBL 1114 is shown here in Table 2:

Table 2

NBL 1114's period of competitive advantage (1 April 20X1 to 31 March 20X4)	3 years
Maximum annual output of new machinery (units of NBL 1114)	12,800
Cost of new machinery (payable on 31 March 20X1)	£480,000
Scrap value of new machinery (at end of three year period, ie 31 March 20X4)	£nil
NBL 1114's contribution per unit (based on a selling price per unit of £65)	£33
Additional annual fixed costs incurred (including annual depreciation charge of £160,000)	£300,000
Extra working capital required at 31 March 20X1 (recoverable in full on 31 March 20X4)	£50,000

Working capital

The working capital requirement for each year must be in place at the start of the relevant year.

Capital allowances

NBL's machinery and equipment attracts capital allowances, but is and will be excluded from the general pool. The equipment attracts 18% (reducing balance) capital allowances in the year of expenditure and in every subsequent year of ownership by the company, except the final year. In the final year, the difference between the machinery's written down value for tax purposes and its disposal proceeds will be either (a) treated by the company as an additional tax relief, if the disposal proceeds are less than the tax written down value, or (b) be treated as a balancing charge to the company, if the disposal proceeds are more than the tax written down value.

Inflation

All of the above figures are stated at 31 March 20X1 prices. NBL's management is unsure of the rate of inflation and would like to consider the impact of either 0% or 5% annual inflation.

Other relevant information:

(1)   NBL's directors would like to assume that the corporation tax rate will be 21% for the foreseeable future and the tax will be payable in the same year as the cash flows to which it relates.

(2)   Unless otherwise stated all cash flows occur at the end of the relevant trading year.

(3)   NBL uses a real post-tax cost of capital of 10% for appraising its investments.

Requirements

13.1 Assuming that the annual rate of inflation is zero, calculate the expected net present value of the NBL 1114 project at 31 March 20X1 and advise NBL's management whether it should purchase the new machinery. **(18 marks)**

13.2 Assuming that the annual rate of inflation is 5%, explain, with supporting calculations, what the impact will be on the expected net present value at 31 March 20X1 of this proposed investment if the effects of inflation on pre-tax contribution and working capital are taken into account.

(6 marks)

Total: 24 marks

14 Newmarket plc

Newmarket plc (Newmarket), a listed company, has recently developed a new lawnmower, the NL500. Development of the NL500 was supported by market research which was undertaken by an external agency who agreed that their £10,000 fee would only be payable if the NL500 was actually launched, with payment due at the end of the NL500's first year on the market.

Newmarket's directors estimate that the market life of the NL500 will be five years but they would be willing to launch the NL500 only if they were satisfied that the required investment would generate a net present value of at least £300,000, using a discount factor of 10% pa.

Production and sale of the NL500 would commence on 1 July 20X3 and would require investment by Newmarket in new production equipment costing £750,000, payable on 30 June 20X3. On 30 June 20X8 it is expected that this equipment could be sold back to the original vendor for £50,000. Newmarket depreciates plant and equipment in equal annual instalments over its useful life.

The company's directors would like to assume that the corporation tax rate will be 21% for the foreseeable future, and it can be assumed that tax payments would occur at the end of the accounting year to which they relate. The directors are also assuming that the new production facilities would attract capital allowances of 18% pa on a reducing balance basis commencing in the year of purchase and continuing throughout the company's ownership of the equipment. A balancing charge or allowance would arise on disposal of the equipment on 30 June 20X8. It can be assumed that sufficient profits would be available for Newmarket to claim all such tax allowances in the year they arise.

Purchase of the new production equipment would be financed by a five-year fixed rate bank loan which will be drawn down on 30 June 20X3 at an interest rate of 6% pa. Interest on the loan would be payable annually, with repayment of the capital being made in full on 30 June 20X8.

Newmarket's marketing director has estimated annual demand for the NL500 to be 2,000 units and on that basis the finance department has estimated the unit cost of the NL500 as follows:

	£
Labour (4 hours @ £12 per hour)	48.00
Components	32.00
Loan interest	22.50
Depreciation	70.00
Variable energy costs	5.00
Share of Newmarket's fixed costs	20.00
	197.50

If the NL500 is launched, a manager already employed by Newmarket would be moved from his present position to manage production and sale of the NL500. This existing manager's position would consequently have to be filled by a new recruit, specifically employed to replace him, on a five-year contract at a fixed annual salary of £35,000. The launch of the NL500 would have a negligible impact on both Newmarket's working capital requirements and on its fixed costs.

Newmarket's accounting year end is 30 June and it can be assumed that all cash flows would occur at the end of the year to which they relate.

Requirements

14.1 Calculate (to the nearest £) the minimum price per unit that Newmarket should charge for the NL500 if a net present value of at least £300,000 is to be achieved. **(15 marks)**

14.2 Identify and describe **two** quantitative techniques that Newmarket could use to assess and adjust for the various risks to which launching the NL500 would expose the company. **(6 marks)**

14.3 Distinguish between systematic risk and non-systematic risk and explain, using examples, how each of these types of risk might apply to the launch of the NL500. **(6 marks)**

14.4 Identify and explain, in the context of the proposed investment in the NL500, the nature and importance of the real options available to Newmarket. **(8 marks)**

Total: 35 marks

15   Grimpen McColl International Ltd

Grimpen McColl International Ltd (GMI) specialises in the construction of hydroelectric dams. It has a financial year end of 31 December. GMI is currently negotiating with the government of a South American country regarding a new dam that the government plans to build on a tributary of the River Amazon. You work for GMI and have been asked to advise its directors during the negotiations. The following information has been collected:

Costs

GMI's estimated costs of constructing the dam (all at 31 December 20X2 prices except where stated otherwise) are shown below:

		31 December		
	20X2	20X3	20X4	20X5
	£'000	£'000	£'000	£'000
Specialist machinery (Note 1)	30,000			
Working capital (Note 2)	5,000			
Materials and labour costs		7,000	8,000	9,000
Overheads (Note 3)		4,000	4,500	5,000
Lost contribution (Note 4)		4,000	4,000	4,000

Notes

1   GMI will need to purchase specialist machinery for the construction of the dam. This will have an estimated resale value at the end of the construction period of £5 million (at 31 December 20X5 prices).

2   The initial working capital required will increase by £1 million pa (in 31 December 20X2 prices), but will be fully recoverable on 31 December 20X5.

3   The overhead costs include a share of GMI head office costs which have been allocated to this project at a rate of £1.5 million pa.

4   South America would be a new market for GMI and its directors are keen to win this contract. If GMI were successful then it would be necessary to transfer resources from other projects – typically service contracts for existing GMI dams in Europe and North America. The directors estimate that this would result in a loss of contribution in each year of the construction period.

Inflation rates and cost of capital

GMI's directors propose using the following inflation rates:

Materials, labour and overhead costs	4% pa
Working capital	4% pa
Lost contribution	5% pa

GMI's directors plan to use a money cost of capital of 8% when appraising this investment. However, one of GMI's directors has commented 'I think that our hurdle rate may be wrong. Inflation rates may actually be higher than those used in our estimates, which should be adjusted to take account of this.'

Capital allowances

The specialist equipment attracts 18% (reducing balance) capital allowances in the year of expenditure and in every subsequent year of ownership by the company, except the final year. In the final year, the difference between the plant and equipment's written down value for tax purposes and its disposal proceeds will be treated by the company either:

- As an additional tax relief, if the disposal proceeds are less than the tax written down value, or
- As a balancing charge, if the disposal proceeds are more than the tax written down value.

Contract price

GMI's board is keen that the contract price is not too high and has tendered a price of £95 million. £10 million would be receivable on 31 December 20X2 when the specialist equipment is purchased. The second instalment of £85 million (in 31 December 20X5 prices) would be receivable on completion of the dam.

Taxation

GMI's directors wish to assume that the corporation tax rate will be 21% pa for the foreseeable future and that tax flows arise in the same year as the cash flows which gave rise to them.

Maintenance contract

The South American government has also proposed that, were GMI to build the dam, then GMI should also provide annual maintenance in perpetuity from completion of the dam on 31 December 20X5. GMI's directors estimate that this would cost GMI £3 million pa (in 31 December 20X5 prices) and feel that it would be reasonable to charge a price of £5 million pa (in 31 December 20X5 prices). Costs and revenues for the maintenance contract are expected to rise by 3% pa after 31 December 20X5. However, they are concerned about such a long-term commitment and would like to investigate the price at which GMI could sell this maintenance contract to another company.

Other information

- Unless otherwise stated, all cash flows occur at the end of the relevant trading year.
- Ignore all foreign currency issues.

Requirements

15.1 Ignoring the maintenance contract, calculate the net present value of the dam project at 31 December 20X2 and advise GMI's directors whether they should proceed with it.　(13 marks)

15.2 Calculate the minimum value of the second instalment of the contract price (receivable on 31 December 20X5) that would be acceptable to the GMI board, assuming that it wishes to enhance shareholder value.　(3 marks)

15.3 With reference to the GMI director's concerns about the rates of inflation being more than the original estimates, discuss the potential effect of this on the project's cash flows, cost of capital and net present value.　(5 marks)

15.4 Advise the GMI board, showing supporting calculations, of the minimum selling price on 31 December 20X2 that it should set were it to sell the maintenance contract.　(4 marks)

15.5 Discuss the types of political risk that GMI may encounter were its proposed investment in South America to proceed.　(5 marks)

Total: 30 marks

16　Wicklow plc

Wicklow plc (Wicklow) is a manufacturer of prestige cast iron cookers, having a long-standing reputation for selling distinctive high price, high quality cookers to an increasingly global market. In the face of growing competition from firms offering slightly more modern style cookers at much lower prices, Wicklow's recent strategy has been to introduce a 'Heritage' version of some of its major product lines. The aim has been to emphasise the original design features of the brand and to differentiate itself further from its competitors.

Wicklow is currently considering the introduction of a 'Heritage' version of its existing 'Duo' product, a standard two-oven cooker. Wicklow has recently spent £375,000 developing the new version of the product, to be known as the Duo Heritage (DH).

Production of the DH would require Wicklow to invest £2m in new machinery and equipment on 31 December 20X8. Based on past experience, the directors are assuming that this machinery and equipment will have a disposal value on 31 December 20Y2 of £200,000.

Sales of the DH would be expected to commence during the year ending 31 December 20X9. Based on a unit selling price of £7,000, Wicklow's marketing director has estimated that unit sales in 20X9 will be either 1,500 (0.65 probability) or 2,000 (0.35 probability). In view of the uncertainty of unit demand in the first year of production, the marketing director has also forecast that if 20X9 sales were to be 1,500 units, then 20Y0 sales would be estimated at either 1,800 units (0.7 probability) or 2,000 units (0.3 probability). However, if 20X9 sales were to be 2,000 units, 20Y0 sales would be estimated at either 2,200 units (0.6 probability) or 2,500 units (0.4 probability). In 20Y1 and 20Y2 unit sales would be 110% of the expected unit sales in 20Y0. In each year production will equal sales, which can be assumed to occur on the last day of each year.

As with other similar 'Heritage' product launches, the company invariably experiences a consequent loss of sales on the original product line. In this particular case, the expectation is that for every two DHs sold, the sale of one standard Duo oven will be lost. This effect would be expected to continue throughout the four years over which the directors have decided to appraise this potential project. As a result, it can be assumed that sales of both cookers will not continue beyond 20Y2.

The unit selling price and cost structure of the standard Duo product are as follows:

	£
Selling price	6,500
Materials	3,516
Labour (8 hours)	200
Fixed overheads (on a labour hour basis)	480

Launch of the DH is not expected to impact on the company's total fixed overheads.

The material cost per unit of the DH will be £3,800. Production of each DH will require eight hours of labour. The reduced levels of production on the Duo product line would mean that part of this labour requirement will be met from labour transferred from that product, but to the extent that this would provide insufficient hours, additional labour will be recruited at the company's standard labour rate of £25 per hour.

Each major product line within Wicklow is currently managed by a dedicated team of managers. However, should the DH be launched, one additional manager would need to be recruited to the Duo team. Wicklow has identified this new manager. He is currently employed by the company and had recently accepted voluntary redundancy but would now be asked to stay on until 31 December 20Y2. He was due to leave Wicklow on 31 December 20X8 and to receive a lump sum of £35,000 at that time. He will be paid an annual salary of £40,000 together with a lump sum bonus of £20,000 payable on 31 December 20Y2.

Working capital to support production of the DH would be expected to run at a rate of 15% of sales value, although this would be off-set to some extent by reduced working capital commitments in respect of the standard Duo product which also requires working capital equal to 15% of sales value. The working capital would need to be in place by the beginning of each year and can be assumed to be released in full on 31 December 20Y2. The working capital flows will have no tax effects.

Regarding tax, the directors are assuming that if Wicklow buys the new machinery and equipment it will attract capital allowances of 18% per annum on a reducing balance basis, commencing in the year of acquisition, with either a balancing charge or allowance arising at the end of the equipment's useful life. The company can be assumed to be in a position to claim all tax allowances in full as soon as they become available and to pay corporation tax at a rate of 21% per annum over the life of the DH project. All tax is payable at the end of the year to which it relates.

At the present time the company is financed entirely by equity and it has been decided that this will continue even if the DH is launched, with internal funds being used to finance the investment. The decision on whether or not to introduce the DH is to be based on the expected net present value of the relevant cash flows, discounted at the company's cost of equity capital of 8%.

However, the finance director had argued strongly that if Wicklow did decide to introduce the DH, then the company should partly finance the project with a four-year loan of £2m (at an interest rate of 5% per annum), which would be well within Wicklow's current debt capacity.

Requirements

16.1 Calculate the expected net present value at 31 December 20X8 of the introduction of the DH product and advise the directors whether or not Wicklow should proceed with its introduction.

(18 marks)

16.2 Calculate the sensitivity of the decision to invest in DH to changes in:

    (a)   The DH selling price (For the purpose of this calculation, assume working capital does not change.)
    (b)   The cost of equity.   **(7 marks)**

16.3 Calculate the adjusted present value of the introduction of the DH product if Wicklow had decided to inject debt on the basis proposed by the finance director.   **(4 marks)**

16.4 Explain the weaknesses of the adjusted present value methodology used in 16.3 above.   **(6 marks)**

                                                                                  Total: 35 marks

Note. Ignore inflation.

17   Beaters Ltd

Beaters Ltd makes plastic kits for building model sailing ships. The company's designer has just developed a new product, a kit for making a model of the *Golden Hind*, the ship in which Drake circumnavigated the world. To make the kits a new plastic moulding machine will have to be bought for £50,000.

A net present value appraisal has been carried out that indicates a positive net present value (NPV) of £2,983. This appraisal was followed up with an assessment of the riskiness of the project. This was achieved by taking each of the input factors in turn and estimating the value for it at which the project would have a zero NPV. In looking at each input factor it was assumed that the other factors would be as originally estimated.

Data on the original estimates and on the values of each of them that generate a zero NPV are as follows.

	Original estimate	Value to generate a zero NPV
Cost of moulding machine	£50,000	£52,983
Selling price (per unit)	£20	£19.60
Material cost (per unit)	£6	£6.40
Labour cost (per unit)	£5	£5.40
Variable overheads (per unit)	£2	£2.40
Sales life	6 years	5.5 years

The above assessment is based on the assumptions of a discount rate of 15% and of constant sales of 2,000 units per annum. It has been reliably established that the new production would not affect fixed costs or working capital to any significant extent. There are no other input factors for the decision.

The risk-free rate of interest over the six years has been estimated to be 6%.

Requirements

17.1 To generate a zero NPV estimate the values for:

    (a)   The discount rate
    (b)   The annual sales volume   **(5 marks)**

17.2 Comment on the results of both the NPV appraisal and the subsequent quantitative analysis. Discuss how the managers might proceed to put themselves in a position to reach a decision on whether to go ahead with the new product. Your discussion should include some consideration of the usefulness of the quantitative analysis already undertaken and how this might usefully be extended.   **(11 marks)**

Note. Ignore taxation and inflation.   **Total: 16 marks**

18   Air Business Ltd

Air Business Limited (ABL) is a UK airline company that offers flights between London and European cities. All six of its aircraft are four-seaters and the company offers an exclusive travel service for business customers. ABL has a financial year end of 30 September and has been trading since 1992. Historically it has not tried to compete with cheaper competitors. However, the company has now endured two years of stagnant sales.

ABL's board is considering changing its business strategy. It will reduce ticket prices and, to accommodate the expected increase in demand, buy three larger aircraft to replace two of its existing aircraft. You work in ABL's finance team and have been asked to help the board with their decision regarding this proposed investment. You have been given the following information:

Life of investment

You have been informed that, because of the volatility of the airline market, the board wishes to set a three-year time limit on this investment appraisal.

Sales and costs

Table 1 below (with notes) is a summary of recent and estimated sales and costs prepared by ABL's management accounting team:

Table 1

	Current strategy Sales and costs (year to 30 September 20X3)				Proposed strategy Annual sales and costs (three years to 30 September 20X6)			
		25%	Fixed			22%	Fixed	
	Sales	margin	costs	Profit	Sales	margin	costs	Profit
	£'000	£'000	£'000	£'000	£'000	£'000	£'000	£'000
	4,150	1,038	(50)	988	7,350	1,617	(90)	1,527

Notes

1   '% margin' represents the contribution to sales ratio.

2   All figures in Table 1 are in 30 September 20X3 prices.

3   Sales and costs, in 30 September 20X3 prices, can be assumed to remain constant for the next three years if no change in strategy occurs.

Capital expenditure

On 30 September 20X3 ABL will purchase three larger aircraft for £1 million each. Management estimates that these would have a trade-in value of £200,000 each (in 30 September 20X6 prices) on 30 September 20X6.

These three new aircraft will replace two of its existing aircraft, which have a current tax written down value of zero and will be traded in for £380,000 each on 30 September 20X3.

The aircraft will attract 18% (reducing balance) capital allowances in the year of expenditure and in every subsequent year of ownership by the company, except the final year. In the final year, the difference between the aircrafts' written down value for tax purposes and their disposal proceeds will be treated by the company either:

• As an additional tax relief, if the disposal proceeds are less than the tax written down value, or
• As a balancing charge, if the disposal proceeds are more than the tax written down value.

Working capital

ABL currently has a working capital investment of £140,000 on 30 September 20X3. The proposed strategy is expected to increase this to £220,000 on 30 September 20X3 and any incremental working capital will be fully recoverable on 30 September 20X6.

Inflation

ABL's sales, costs and working capital are all expected to increase in line with the general rate of inflation, which is estimated at 5% pa.

Taxation

ABL's directors wish to assume that the corporation tax rate will be 21% pa for the foreseeable future and that tax flows arise in the same year as the cash flows which gave rise to them.

Cost of capital

For investment appraisal purposes ABL uses a money cost of capital of 8% pa.

Other information

Unless otherwise stated, all cash flows occur at the end of the relevant trading year.

In addition to this investment appraisal, ABL's directors are aware that there have been a number of takeovers and mergers in the airline industry in the past three years. They are concerned that the company might be the subject of a takeover bid and wish to explore how they could make use of Shareholder Value Analysis to value the company.

Requirements

18.1 Calculate the net present value of the proposed investment in the three new aircraft on 30 September 20X3 and advise ABL's directors whether they should proceed with the investment.

(16 marks)

18.2 Calculate the sensitivity of your advice in 18.1 to:

    (a)   Changes in the estimated trade-in value of the new aircraft at 30 September 20X6. **(4 marks)**
    (b)   Changes in the estimated incremental annual profits arising from the new strategy. **(5 marks)**

18.3 Explain the theory underpinning the Shareholder Value Analysis method of valuing a business and advise ABL's directors as to what extent your calculations in 18.1 above could be used to calculate a valuation of ABL using this method were it to be subject to a takeover bid.   **(10 marks)**

Total: 35 marks

19   Investment portfolios

In connection with the selection and holding of investments, discuss *each* of the following points of view.

19.1 An investor holding only one security need be concerned only with the unsystematic risk of that security.

19.2 However, an investor who holds a number of securities should take account of total risk.

19.3 An investor should never add to a portfolio an investment that yields a return less than the market rate of return.   **Total: 12 marks**

20   Sunday newspaper article

Recently a director of a client company said the following to you.

> 'Over the weekend I was reading an article on finance in a Sunday newspaper. It said that as shareholder wealth maximisation is the generally accepted corporate objective, net present value is the most logical approach to investment appraisal. It then went on to say that the 'capital asset pricing model' is the best way to find the appropriate discount rate to use. This is apparently because you can use the average rate of return from other businesses; also it ignores the specific risk of the investment concerned.
>
> This all seems nonsense to me. These days corporate management needs to be concerned with more than just the shareholders. What about all of the other groups who contribute to the business? They can't be ignored. Even if shareholders' wealth were the key issue, I don't see how NPV fits in. Surely internal rate of return is more to the point because it favours investments that get the best returns and cover financing costs. Those investments will make the shareholders richer. As for CAPM, it seems to defy all logic. It can't be correct to ignore the returns that the investing business seeks and just concentrate on other businesses. Risk must be taken into account. In our business we compare weighted average cost of capital with the IRR and this seems more logical than using CAPM.'

The director went on to say:

> 'The article also said that, in theory, it doesn't make any difference to the shareholders whether new finance is raised from a share issue or a loan stock issue as they both cost the same. We raise all of our new finance from retained earnings, which doesn't cost anything, but loan finance has a cost.'

Requirement

Draft a reply to the director, bearing in mind that he is clearly not very well informed on finance.

Total: 19 marks

21 Daniels Ltd

Daniels Ltd (Daniels) is a large civil engineering company and it has a financial year end of 31 May. Much of Daniels' work involves long-term contracts for the railway industry. You work for Daniels and have been asked for advice by the board on the following problems:

Problem 1

Daniels is considering a major investment involving five possible projects in the West of England and South Wales which have been put out to tender. Daniels' board of directors has prepared the following estimated cash flows (and resultant net present values at 31 May 20X7) for the five projects:

Project	Location	Investment on 31/5/X7 £'000	Year to 31/5/X8 £'000	Year to 31/5/X9 £'000	Year to 31/5/Y0 £'000	NPV £'000
B	Bristol	(4,150)	(1,290)	530	7,270	577
C	Cardiff	(3,870)	(1,310)	3,130	1,550	(1,309)
G	Gloucester	(6,400)	1,770	2,160	3,160	(632)
S	Swansea	(5,000)	(2,610)	6,450	6,520	2,856
T	Tiverton	(4,600)	1,290	2,870	3,620	1,664

You can assume that the net present values shown in the table above are accurate.

Due to financial constraints, the company, if successful with its tenders, would be unable to take on all five projects. The board is prepared to release £8 million for initial investment (on 31 May 20X7) into one or more of the projects, but might increase this figure to £9 million if there are grounds for doing so. An alternative scenario which has been considered would be to make available sufficient funds to start all five projects in May 20X7, but this would limit the capital available in the year to 31 May 20X8 to a maximum of only £500,000.

Problem 2

Daniels runs a fleet of vans to support its operations. Currently it replaces those vans every three years, but the board is not sure whether this is in the company's best interests. Vans cost, on average, £12,400 each. Daniels' transport manager has prepared the following schedule of costs and resale values for the vans:

	Maintenance and running costs £		Resale value £
In first year of van's life	4,300	After one year	9,800
In second year of van's life	4,800	After two years	7,000
In third year of van's life	5,100	After three years	5,000

Problem 3

About a year ago (March 20X6) Daniels completed construction of a factory for Kithill Ltd (Kithill). This cost Daniels £720,000 to construct and Kithill is paying £190,000 a year for eight years. Daniels will, therefore, ultimately make a profit of £800,000, which gives a return on the investment of over 100%. When Kithill sent its first annual instalment last week, it indicated that rather than make annual payments it would prefer to settle the outstanding balance by making a one-off payment of £925,000 in a year's time (March 20X8). One of Daniels' directors is keen on this proposal stating 'I know that this is less than we would receive over the full eight years, but my calculations show that the internal rate of return would be much better.'

General information

(1) Daniels uses a cost of capital of 10% when appraising possible investments.
(2) You should assume that all cash flows take place at the end of the year in question.
(3) All projects are independent.

Requirements

21.1 For Problem 1, assuming that all of the projects are divisible and:

   (a) Assuming that Daniels has no capital rationing, advise its directors as to which projects should be accepted. **(2 marks)**

   (b) Assuming that the directors are prepared to spend a maximum of £8 million on 31 May 20X7, advise them as to which projects should be accepted. **(3 marks)**

   (c) Assuming that the directors are prepared to make available sufficient funds to start all five projects on 31 May 20X7, but only £500,000 on 31 May 20X8, advise them as to which projects should be accepted. **(5 marks)**

21.2 For Problem 1, **assuming that none of the projects are divisible** and that the directors are prepared to spend a maximum of £9 million on 31 May 20X7, advise them as to which projects should be accepted. **(4 marks)**

21.3 For Problem 2, advise the directors as to the optimal replacement period for Daniels' vans and comment on the limitations of the approach used. **(6 marks)**

21.4 For Problem 3, advise the directors as to whether they should accept Kithill's proposal. **(5 marks)**

Total: 25 marks

Note. Ignore taxation.

22 Adventurous plc

Adventurous plc (Adventurous) is a UK listed company that manufactures and sells global positioning system (GPS) devices worldwide. Following favourable market research that cost £20,000, Adventurous has developed a new GPS based bicycle computer (BC). It intends to set up a manufacturing facility in the UK, although the board of Adventurous had contemplated setting up in an overseas country. The BC project will have a life of four years.

The selling price of the BC will be £295 per unit and sales in the first year to 31 December 20X4 are expected to be 10,000 units per month, increasing by 5% pa thereafter. Relevant direct labour and materials costs are expected to be £170 per unit and incremental fixed production costs are expected to be £3 million pa. The selling price and costs are stated in 31 December 20X3 prices and are expected to increase at the rate of 3% pa. Research and development costs to 31 December 20X3 amounted to £1 million.

Investment in working capital will be £1.5 million on 31 December 20X3 and this will increase in line with sales volumes and inflation. Working capital will be fully recoverable on 31 December 20X7.

Adventurous will need to rent a factory for the life of the project. Annual rent of £1 million will be payable in advance on 31 December each year and will not increase over the life of the project.

Plant and machinery will cost £50 million on 31 December 20X3. The plant and machinery is expected to have a resale value of £15 million (in 31 December 20X7 prices) at the end of the project. The plant and machinery will attract 18% (reducing balance) capital allowances in the year of expenditure and in every subsequent year of ownership by the company, except the final year. In the final year, the difference between the plant and machinery's written down value for tax purposes and its disposal proceeds will be treated by the company either:

•   As an additional tax relief, if the disposal proceeds are less than the tax written down value; or
•   As a balancing charge, if the disposal proceeds are more than the tax written down value.

Adventurous' directors wish to assume that the rate of corporation tax will be 21% pa for the foreseeable future and that tax flows arise in the same year as the cash flows which gave rise to them.

The project will be financed from the company's pool of funds and there will be no change in current gearing levels. An appropriate weighted average cost of capital for the project is 10% pa.

Adventurous' directors are concerned that there are rumours in the industry of research by a rival company into a much cheaper alternative to the GPS devices currently available. However, the rumours that the directors have heard suggest that this research will take another year to complete and, if it is successful, it will be a further year before any new devices are operational.

Requirements

22.1 Calculate, using money cash flows, the net present value of the BC project on 31 December 20X3 and advise Adventurous' board as to whether it should proceed. **(15 marks)**

22.2 Calculate and comment upon the sensitivity of the project to a change in each of the following:

 (a) The annual rent of the factory
 (b) The weighted average cost of capital **(7 marks)**

22.3 Assume now that the project had been financed entirely by debt and that this had caused the gearing of Adventurous to change materially. Describe how you would have appraised the project in such circumstances. **(3 marks)**

22.4 If the board of Adventurous decided to set up the manufacturing facility overseas, advise the board on how political risk could change the value of the project and how it might limit its effects. **(5 marks)**

22.5 Identify and discuss the real options available to Adventurous in relation to the BC project. **(5 marks)**

Total: 35 marks

23 Headington Ltd

Headington Ltd operates a private members' club, known as the Eaton Club, in central London. The directors of the company have, for some time, been conscious of the increasing age profile of its fee-paying membership. Recently, therefore, the directors have been considering a number of potential strategies for attracting and retaining younger members. One such strategy is the possible installation of gymnasium facilities in a part of the club's premises which is currently rented out to a financial recruitment company at an annual rent, receivable in arrears, of £85,000 (at 20X6 prices).

The club's income is made up primarily of membership fees and revenues from bar and restaurant facilities. As part of their consideration of this potential new strategy, the directors commissioned a market research firm, at a cost of £7,500 (paid in full last month), to assess the likely impact of the installation of gymnasium facilities on the club's income. The summarised findings of the market researchers were somewhat inconclusive. Whilst it was felt that the most likely impact would be an increase in annual revenues of £760,000 (0.6 probability), the researchers also suggested that, dependent on the prevailing economic climate, additional annual revenue could be as high as £1m (0.2 probability) or as low as £608,000 (0.2 probability). The club generates a contribution of 50% on revenues. The market researchers have also suggested that all costs and revenues associated with this project (other than the initial investment) are likely to be subject to an inflation rate of 5% per annum from the start of the first year that the facilities will be operational, ie from 1 January 20X7.

In order to pursue this strategy the company would need to spend £750,000 on building costs and gymnasium equipment in 20X6. It is also expected that the equipment will be disposed of for £100,000 (at 20X6 prices) after five years of use. In addition, the directors estimate that the operation of the gymnasium will add £85,000 per annum (at 20X6 prices) to the company's fixed costs.

The company has also made the following assumptions:

- The corporation tax rate will be 21% for the next five years

- The company's money cost of capital will be 10% for the next five years

- The capital cost of the project will qualify for writing down allowances at the rate of 18% per annum on a reducing balance basis. The allowances will commence in the year in which the initial investment is made. As at 31 December 20Y1, a balancing charge or allowance will arise equal to the difference between any residual value and the written down value

- All cash flows will arise at the end of the year to which they relate.

Requirements

23.1 Use the net present value model to assess the project over a five-year assessment horizon and, on the basis of this, make a suitable recommendation to the directors. **(11 marks)**

23.2 Calculate the sensitivity of the net present value of the project to changes in the expected annual contribution. **(5 marks)**

23.3 Describe any reservations you might have concerning the figures used in assessing the project in 23.1 above. **(3 marks)**

Total: 19 marks

24 Hawke Appliances Ltd

24.1 Hawke Appliances Ltd (Hawke) is a UK-based manufacturer of household appliances. It has a financial year end of 31 December. You work for Hawke and have been asked to advise the company's board on the viability of a proposed new product.

The company is considering the development of a new vacuum cleaner, the JH143. This will be more expensive than Hawke's other vacuum cleaners but it contains a number of innovative design features that Hawke's board believes will be attractive in an increasingly competitive market. Because of these market conditions, Hawke's board wishes to evaluate the JH143 over a three-year time horizon.

Selling price, materials and unskilled labour

You have obtained the following information on the budgeted price and costs per unit for the JH 143 (in 31 December 20X4 prices):

	£
Selling price	155
Materials	53
Unskilled labour	28

Fixed costs are not expected to increase as a result of producing the JH143.

Skilled labour

Each JH143 will require one hour of skilled labour that is in short supply. Hawke will need to transfer some of its skilled labour away from making another older vacuum cleaner (the JH114), which requires half the skilled labour time per unit of the JH143. The current selling price of the JH114 is £96 and its materials and unskilled labour costs total £74 per unit (in 31 December 20X4 prices). Hawke's skilled labour is paid £8.80 per hour (in 31 December 20X4 prices).

Inflation

Revenues and costs are expected to inflate at a rate of 4% pa.

Sales volumes

Hawke commissioned market research at a cost of £55,000 for the JH143 project, half of which remains unpaid and is due for settlement on 31 December 20X4. An extract from the results of that market research is shown here:

	20X5	20X6	20X7
Estimated annual sales of the JH143 (units)	50,000	95,000	45,000

Machinery

Specialised new production machinery will be required in order to make the new vacuum cleaner. This machinery will cost £4.5 million to buy on 31 December 20X4 and will have an estimated scrap value of £1 million on 31 December 20X7 (in 31 December 20X7 prices). If production of the existing JH114 is reduced then some of Hawke's older machinery could be sold on 31 December 20X4. This machinery had a tax written down value of £80,000 on 1 January 20X4 and Hawke estimates that it could be sold for £220,000.

The machinery will attract 18% (reducing balance) capital allowances in the year of expenditure and in every subsequent year of ownership by the company, except the final year. In the final year, the difference between the machinery's written down value for tax purposes and its disposal proceeds will be treated by the company either:

- As an additional tax relief, if the disposal proceeds are less than the tax written down value, or
- As a balancing charge, if the disposal proceeds are more than the tax written down value.

Corporation tax

Assume that the corporation tax rate will be 21% pa for the foreseeable future.

Working capital

Hawke will invest in working capital at a rate of 10% of the JH143's annual sales revenue, to be in place at the start of each year. It expects to recover the working capital in full on 31 December 20X7.

Cost of capital

Hawke uses a money cost of capital of 12% pa for investment appraisal purposes.

Requirements

(a) Using money cash flows, calculate the net present value on 31 December 20X4 of the proposed development of the JH143 and advise the company's board whether it should proceed with the investment. **(16 marks)**

(b) **Ignoring the effects on working capital**, calculate the sensitivity of your advice in part (a) to:

- Changes in the selling price of the JH 143 **(3 marks)**
- Changes in the volume of sales of the JH 143. **(4 marks)**

24.2 Hawke's board is also investigating the possibility of buying another company, Durram Electricals Ltd (Durram) which is a successful retailer of electrical goods. The board has obtained the following information about Durram:

Earnings and cash flows for the year ended 31 August 20X4	£700,000
Expected growth of earnings and cash flows	5% pa
Book value of equity at 31 August 20X4	£3,600,000
Average industry P/E ratio	11
Cost of capital	12% pa

Hawke's board has no experience of buying another company and you have been invited to the next board meeting to answer these questions:

(1) What range of values is reasonable for Durram on 31 August 20X4?
(2) Why do many acquisitions not benefit the bidding firm?
(3) Would it be better to pay for Durram in cash or with Hawke's shares?

Requirement

Prepare calculations and notes that will enable you to answer these questions at the next board meeting. **(12 marks)**

Total: 35 marks

25 Rossendale Hotels plc

You should assume that the current date is 31 December 20X4

Rossendale Hotels plc (Rossendale) operates a chain of city centre and country hotels in the UK. Rossendale set up a division, Inside&Out, which carries out the maintenance, cleaning and gardening at all its own hotels and the hotels of some other companies in the industry.

At a recent meeting the board of Rossendale were discussing a possible restructuring of the company by divesting of Inside&Out. However, the board is not certain about the best way to achieve the divestment in order to maximise the wealth of Rossendale's shareholders. The Chief Executive (CE) feels that a demerger would be the most appropriate method, but also feels that the existing management team of Inside&Out should be given the opportunity to buy the division. One of the other board members feels that a sell-off to a third party would be most beneficial for Rossendale's shareholders. At the meeting the CE stated that the first thing to do is to put a value, at 31 December 20X4, on Inside&Out. He has now asked Rossendale's finance director to value the division and prepare notes regarding how and why the restructuring should be undertaken before a final decision is made.

Rossendale's finance director intends to value the division using net present value at 31 December 20X4. However, one difficulty that he has is that sales are hard to predict. After analysing data for the past ten years he has estimated that sales (in 31 December 20X5 prices) and associated probabilities for the year ended 31 December 20X5 will be:

Sales	Probability
£m	%
25	40
105	20
130	40

Sales in the following three years would remain at the first year's expected level, adjusted for volume and price changes.

Additional cost and revenue information:

- After 31 December 20X5, sales volume growth is expected to be 10% pa for three years and sales prices are expected to rise by 5% pa. Contribution is 15% of sales.

- Incremental fixed costs will be £5m for the year ended 31 December 20X5 and will increase subsequently by the general level of inflation.

- Currently the vehicles and equipment of Inside&Out are leased. It is now the intention to buy new vehicles and equipment. Investment in new vehicles and equipment on 31 December 20X4 will be £10m. The vehicles and equipment will have a value of £2m on 31 December 20X8 (in 31 December 20X8 prices). The vehicles and equipment will attract 18% (reducing balance) capital allowances in the year of expenditure and in every subsequent year of ownership by the company, except the final year. In the final year, the difference between the plant and machinery's written down value for tax purposes and its disposal proceeds will be treated by the company either:

  (1) As an additional tax relief, if the disposal proceeds are less than the tax written down value; or
  (2) As a balancing charge, if the disposal proceeds are more than the tax written down value.

- Assume that the rate of corporation tax will be 21% pa for the foreseeable future and that tax flows arise in the same year as the cash flows which gave rise to them.

- An appropriate real weighted average cost of capital for the division is 7% pa and the general level of inflation is expected to be 3% pa.

- On 31 December 20X4 Inside&Out requires an additional investment of £5m in working capital, which will increase at the start of each year in line with sales volume growth and sales price increases. Working capital will be fully recoverable on 31 December 20X8.

- The finance director intends to include in the valuation of the division a continuing value at the end of four years that will represent the value of the net cash flows beyond the fourth year after tax. This will be calculated as a multiple of 10 times the after tax operating cash flows for the year ended 31 December 20X8.

- Unless otherwise stated you should assume that all cash flows arise at the end of the year to which they relate.

Requirements

25.1 Calculate, using money cash flows, the expected net present value of Inside&Out on 31 December 20X4. **(16 marks)**

25.2 **Ignoring the effects on working capital**, calculate the sensitivity of the valuation of Inside&Out to changes in sales revenue and discuss this sensitivity with reference to the sales and associated probability estimates provided by the finance director. **(5 marks)**

25.3 Outline another valuation method that would be appropriate for placing a value on Inside&Out. **(3 marks)**

25.4 Explain and justify the possible reasons for the divestment of Inside&Out from Rossendale. **(5 marks)**

25.5 Discuss the advantages and disadvantages of Rossendale divesting itself of Inside&Out by:

(a) A demerger (also known as a spin-off) into two listed companies
(b) A sell-off
(c) A management buyout (MBO) **(6 marks)**

Total: 35 marks

26 Premier Transport Group plc

Premier Transport Group plc (Premier) is a UK transport operator that has two divisions – (1) bus services and (2) express coach services. It has a financial year end of 30 April. Premier's board is investigating capital investment proposals for each of its divisions.

26.1 Bus division

The bus division is bidding for a three-year contract to operate a number of bus routes in a large tourist resort in the south of England. This contract covers the period from 1 May 20X5 to 30 April 20X8. Your colleagues in Premier's finance team have produced estimates of the incremental income and expenses (in 30 April 20X5 prices) for the period of the contract as shown below:

Years to 30 April	20X6	20X7	20X8
	£	£	£
Fares	918,400	2,250,000	3,450,000
Fuel costs	(432,000)	(446,400)	(489,600)
Other costs (see note)	(755,000)	(840,000)	(905,000)
Profit/(Loss) before taxation	(268,600)	963,600	2,055,400

Note. Premier is considering hiring eight extra buses to operate on this new contract. The annual hire cost per bus is £45,000 (which is allowable for tax) and this has been included in the 'other costs' figure above.

Bus purchase

As an alternative to the plan to hire the eight new buses, Premier's directors are considering whether it would be preferable to purchase them instead. These would cost £200,000 each on 30 April 20X5 and would have a market value of £50,000 each (in 30 April 20X8 prices) at the end of the contract. It is company policy to write off buses using the straight-line depreciation method.

The buses will attract 18% (reducing balance) capital allowances in the year of expenditure and in every subsequent year of ownership by the company, except the final year. In the final year, the difference between the buses' written down value for tax purposes and their disposal proceeds will be treated by the company either:

- As a balancing allowance, if the disposal proceeds are less than the tax written down value; or
- As a balancing charge, if the disposal proceeds are more than the tax written down value.

Inflation

Premier's directors estimate that all costs (except for hiring and depreciation) will increase by 3% pa, but they will cap fare increases at 2% pa.

Corporation tax

Assume that the rate of corporation tax will be 21% pa for the foreseeable future and that tax flows arise in the same year as the cash flows which gave rise to them.

Cost of capital

Premier uses a money cost of capital of 10% pa for investment appraisal purposes.

Cash flows

Assume that, unless otherwise instructed, all cash flows occur at the end of a financial year.

Requirements

(a) Using money cash flows, calculate the net present values on 30 April 20X5 of the two proposals   bus hiring or bus purchase – and advise Premier's board which of the two proposals it should accept. **(16 marks)**

(b) Calculate how sensitive your decision in (a) above is to the market value of the buses on 30 April 20X8. **(4 marks)**

(c) Estimate the internal rate of return of the bus purchase proposal and explain the advantages and disadvantages of this method of investment appraisal. **(5 marks)**

26.2 Express coach division

Premier's fleet of medium-sized express coaches operates on long distance routes across the UK. Its board wishes to establish the most cost effective method of replacing its coaches. Your colleagues in Premier's finance team have produced the following estimates of capital and running costs:

Coach type	Deluxe	Mid-Range	Economy
Purchase price	£260,000	£210,000	£160,000
Annual running costs (in money cash flows)	£57,000	£54,000	£70,000
Estimated life (in years)	6	4	3

The expected life of the Economy coach could be doubled to six years, but this would mean that the coach would require £90,000 of refurbishment costs at the end of the third year and that its annual running costs for years 4 to 6 would be £85,000.

It can be assumed that all costs are paid at the end of the year to which they relate, with the exception of the initial purchase price which is paid at the time of purchase. Premier's directors would like to assume that the market value of each type of coach at the end of its life will be nil.

Requirement

Advise Premier's board (showing supporting workings) as to which coach type should be purchased, assuming that Premier wishes to minimise the present value of its costs. **(10 marks)**

Note. Ignore inflation and taxation when answering 26.2

Total: 35 marks

27 Bluesky Entertainments plc

You should assume that the current date is 30 June 20X5

Bluesky Entertainments plc (Bluesky) is a company listed on the London Stock Exchange (LSE) which operates entertainment facilities throughout the UK. Bluesky is seeking to diversify and expand its activities by opening a new aquatic adventure park called Waterworld and has asked a market research company, for a fee of £100,000, to estimate the number of visitors in the first year of operation and the potential for growth. The Waterworld project would be a major undertaking for Bluesky and, subject to a satisfactory project appraisal, the details will be made public in an announcement to the LSE. One of the Bluesky board members has suggested that it would be a good idea to advise their close family members to buy shares in Bluesky shortly before any public announcement is made.

It has come to the attention of the board that a competitor, Underseaworld, which specialises in sea-based entertainment facilities in the USA, is considering expanding into the UK. Underseaworld has identified a suitable location in the UK and has applied for planning permission to develop the site. However, it will be a year before the planning decision is made as to whether Underseaworld will be allowed to start development of the site.

The market research company has produced a report that gives an indication of the forecast numbers of visitors to Waterworld in the first year of operations to 30 June 20X6, together with associated probabilities and the forecast growth in the number of visitors for the next three years. The estimated visitor numbers in the first year are:

Number of visitors	Probability
12,000,000	50%
9,000,000	30%
6,000,000	20%

Visitor numbers in the following three years to 30 June 20X9 would remain at the first year's expected level adjusted for growth of 5% pa.

You are an ICAEW Chartered Accountant and the finance director of Bluesky. You intend to appraise the Waterworld project at 30 June 20X5 using net present value analysis.

Additional cost and revenue information relating to the Waterworld project:

- The estimated sales revenue per visitor will be £34 in the first year of operations. After 30 June 20X6 sales revenue per visitor is expected to increase by the general rate of inflation of 2.5% pa. Contribution is 40% of sales.

- Incremental selling and administration expenses in the year to 30 June 20X6 are estimated to be £90 million and will increase at the rate of 4% pa thereafter.

- On 30 June 20X5 the project requires an investment in working capital of £35 million, which will increase at the start of each year in line with sales volume growth and sales price increases. Working capital will be fully recoverable on 30 June 20X9.

On 30 June 20X5 the project will require an investment in land of £40 million and plant and equipment of £500 million. It is estimated that on 30 June 20X9 (in 30 June 20X9 prices) the land will have a value of £80 million after tax and the plant and equipment will have a value of £120 million before tax. The plant and equipment will attract 18% (reducing balance) capital allowances in the year of expenditure and in every subsequent year of ownership by the company, except the final year.

In the final year, the difference between the plant and equipment's written down value for tax purposes and its disposal proceeds will be treated by the company either:

(1) As a balancing allowance, if the disposal proceeds are less than the tax written down value; or
(2) As a balancing charge, if the disposal proceeds are more than the tax written down value.

- Assume that the rate of corporation tax will be 21% pa for the foreseeable future and that tax flows arise in the same year as the cash flows that gave rise to them.

- Bluesky has a money weighted average cost of capital (WACC) of 8% pa. However, because of the nature and size of the Waterworld project the managing director of Bluesky feels that the rate should be increased by 2%, to 10% pa.

- You intend to include in the net present value analysis a continuing value at the end of four years that will represent the value of the net cash flows after tax beyond the fourth year. This will be calculated as a multiple of nine times the expected after tax operating cash flows for the year ended 30 June 20X9.

- Unless otherwise stated you should assume that all cash flows arise at the end of the year to which they relate.

Information relating to Bluesky excluding the Waterworld project:

- Issued 10p ordinary shares with a total nominal value of £9 million.
- Ex-div share price at 30 June 20X5 is £12 per share.

Requirements

27.1 Using money cash flows, calculate the expected net present value of the Waterworld project on 30 June 20X5 and advise Bluesky's board whether it should accept the project. **(16 marks)**

27.2 **Ignoring the effects on working capital**, calculate the sensitivity of the Waterworld project to changes in sales revenue and discuss this sensitivity with reference to the visitor numbers and associated probability estimates provided by the market research company. **(5 marks)**

27.3 Identify and explain **two** real options associated with the Waterworld project. **(4 marks)**

27.4 Discuss whether the managing director of Bluesky is justified in simply adding 2% to the company's current WACC when appraising the Waterworld project and outline an alternative way of arriving at a discount rate for the project. **(4 marks)**

27.5 Assuming the Waterworld project goes ahead, explain and calculate the likely effect on Bluesky's share price after it makes the public announcement to the LSE. **(3 marks)**

27.6 Outline the ethical and legal issues for you as an ICAEW Chartered Accountant, regarding the suggestion by the board member that their close family members should be advised to buy shares in Bluesky shortly before the announcement of the Waterworld project. **(3 marks)**

Total: 35 marks

28 Silverdale plc

Silverdale plc (Silverdale) is a listed manufacturer of domestic and commercial cleaning products. Silverdale sustained losses for several years but has recently returned to profit. It is now 31 May 20X5 and the board is currently planning the company's expansion over the next two financial years to 31 May 20X6 and 31 May 20X7.

Silverdale has secured a contract to supply a new range of domestic cleaning products to a large chain of supermarkets. To fulfil the contract Silverdale will need to purchase additional plant and machinery on 1 June 20X5 at a cost of £75 million and will raise this amount on that date from one of the following two sources of finance:

- A rights issue at a discount of 20% on the current ex-div market price of Silverdale's shares of 586p.

- An issue of debentures at par. These would have a coupon equal to the gross redemption yield of Silverdale's existing 7% coupon debentures, which are now trading at £95 ex-interest and have three years until redemption at par.

The board notes that the industry in which Silverdale operates has an average gearing ratio (debt/equity by book values) of 50% and an interest cover of 20.

It is anticipated that expansion in the year to 31 May 20X7 will be financed from cash surpluses accumulated at the end of the year to 31 May 20X6. However, the board is concerned about the company's current ratio and would like to ensure that, at 31 May 20X6, it is approaching the industry average of 2:1.

The finance director of Silverdale has established the following information regarding the impact of the new contract on Silverdale's management accounts in the year to 31 May 20X6:

- The company's revenue is expected to increase by 15%.

- Capital allowances can be assumed to be equal to the depreciation charged in a particular year.

- It is expected that direct costs, other than depreciation, will increase by 16%.

- Indirect costs are expected to increase by £12 million.

- Inventory is expected to increase by £15 million.

- The ratio of receivables to sales and payables to direct costs (excluding depreciation) will remain the same as in the year to 31 May 20X5.

- Depreciation of existing and new plant and machinery is 20% pa on a reducing balance basis.

- Tax is payable at a rate of 21% pa in the year in which the liability arises.

- Dividends are payable in the year following their declaration and the board of directors has confirmed its intention to maintain the company's current dividend payout ratio of 50% for the foreseeable future.

Extracts from Silverdale's most recent management accounts are shown below:

Income Statement for the year ended 31 May 20X5

	£'000
Revenue	780,000
Direct costs (including depreciation of £36 million)	(468,000)
Indirect costs	(225,000)
Operating profits	87,000
Interest	(4,200)
Profit before tax	82,800
Taxation	(17,388)
Profit after tax	65,412
Dividend (declared)	32,706

Balance Sheet at 31 May 20X5

	£'000	£'000
Plant and machinery (net book value)		144,000
Current assets: Inventory	60,000	
Trade receivables	130,000	190,000
		334,000
50p Ordinary shares		40,000
Retained earnings		81,000
7% Debentures at par value		60,000
Current liabilities: Trade payables	95,000	
Bank overdraft	25,294	
Dividends payable	32,706	153,000
		334,000

Requirements

28.1 **For each of the financing alternatives being considered**, prepare a forecast Income Statement for the year ended 31 May 20X6 and a forecast Balance Sheet at 31 May 20X6. **(18 marks)**

Note. Ignore transaction costs on the issuing of new capital and returns on surplus cash invested in the short term.

28.2 Write a report to Silverdale's board that includes:

(a) Calculations of Silverdale's gearing (debt/equity by book values), interest cover and earnings per share at 31 May 20X5 and at 31 May 20X6 for the two potential methods of financing the purchase of the new plant and machinery. **(4 marks)**

(b) With reference where appropriate to your calculations in 28.2(a), an evaluation of the two potential methods of financing the purchase of the new plant and machinery. **(10 marks)**

(c) An evaluation of whether the expansion in the year to 31 May 20X7 can be financed from the forecast cash resources at 31 May 20X6. **(3 marks)**

Total: 35 marks

29 Bradford Bedwyn Medical plc

Bradford Bedwyn Medical plc (BBM) is a UK company that manufactures a range of medical equipment for use in hospitals and doctors' surgeries. BBM has a year end of 28 February and it has been trading since 1993.

Extracts from BBM's most recent management accounts are shown below:

Income Statement for the year ended 28 February 20X4

	£'000
Profit before interest and taxation	6,816
Debenture interest	(516)
Profit before taxation	6,300
Taxation (21%)	(1,323)
Profit after taxation	4,977
Dividends	(1,493)
Retained profit	3,484

Balance Sheet at 28 February 20X4

	£'000
Ordinary share capital (£1 shares)	34,600
Retained earnings	31,384
	65,984
6% Redeemable debentures (redeemable 20X9)	8,600
	74,584

BBM's ordinary shares had a market value of £2.45 each (ex-div) and a beta of 0.9 on 28 February 20X4. The return on the market is expected to be 8.6% pa and the risk free rate 2.1% pa.

BBM's debentures had a market value of £110 (cum interest) per £100 nominal on 28 February 20X4 and they are redeemable at par on 28 February 20X9.

BBM's board is now considering diversifying its operations by expanding into a new market. The average equity beta for companies already operating in this market is 1.9 with an average ratio of equity to debt (by market values) of 83:17

This diversification will cost BBM approximately £25 million. However, there is disagreement amongst BBM's directors as to how the diversification should be funded and whether it should happen at all. There are three proposals that are being considered:

Proposal 1

BBM proceeds with the diversification. It would raise the additional funding required from equity and debt sources in such a way as to leave its existing equity: debt ratio (by market values) unchanged following the diversification. The additional debt raised would be in the form of 8% redeemable debentures issued at par.

Proposal 2

BBM proceeds with the diversification. It would raise all of the additional funding required in the form of 8% redeemable debentures issued at par.

Proposal 3

BBM does not proceed with the diversification. The funds, raised as in proposal 2, are used instead to buy back some of its ordinary shares.

Assume that the corporation tax rate will be 21% pa for the foreseeable future.

Requirements

29.1 Ignoring the diversification plans, calculate BBM's WACC (weighted average cost of capital) on 28 February 20X4, using:

    (a)   The Gordon growth model   **(10 marks)**
    (b)   The CAPM   **(3 marks)**

29.2 Explain the limitations of the Gordon growth model.   **(3 marks)**

29.3 Assuming that Proposal 1 is accepted and using the CAPM, calculate the WACC that BBM should use when appraising its diversification plans and explain your reasoning.   **(9 marks)**

29.4 Assuming that Proposal 2 is accepted, discuss the issues that BBM faces when trying to determine an appropriate WACC for appraising its diversification plans.   **(5 marks)**

29.5 Assuming that Proposal 3 is accepted, explain why BBM would wish to buy back its shares and the implications for its shareholders.   **(5 marks)**

Total: 35 marks

30   Liteform plc

The finance director of Liteform plc (Liteform) has been asked to calculate a discount factor for use in appraising all the firm's potential investment projects in the forthcoming year. He has gathered the following information, which he has passed on to you, the firm's finance manager, with the request that you use the information provided to calculate the firm's weighted average cost of capital, which will then be used as the required discount factor.

(1)   The current cum-dividend price of a Liteform ordinary share is £4.58 and an annual dividend of £1,134,000 is due to be paid in the near future. Dividends have represented a constant proportion of profits after interest and tax over the last few years.

(2)   The current price of the firm's loan stock is £85.10 per £100 of stock. The loan stock is redeemable in ten years' time at a premium of 5% compared to the nominal value of the loan stock. Annual interest on the loan stock has just been paid.

(3)   The current rate of corporation tax is 21% and the current basic rate of income tax is 20%.

(4)   Extracts from Liteform's most recent financial statements:

	£'000
Issued ordinary share capital (£1 shares)	4,200
Retained profits	9,159
Shareholders' funds	13,359
7% loan stock	1,819
	15,178

	£'000
Profit after interest and tax	2,106
Dividend	1,134
Retained profit for the year	972

Requirements

30.1 Using the information provided, calculate Liteform's weighted average cost of capital (WACC).   **(10 marks)**

30.2 Discuss the underlying assumptions and weaknesses of the approach you have employed in calculating the cost of equity in 30.1.   **(8 marks)**

30.3 Discuss any reservations you may have regarding the use of the WACC as a discount factor in appraising Liteform's potential investment projects next year.   **(5 marks)**

Total: 23 marks

31 Seager Forest Scientific plc

Seager Forest Scientific plc (SFS) is a large listed pharmaceutical company with a financial year end of 30 April. Its management accounts on 30 April 20X1 are expected to show the following:

Extract from SFS Balance Sheet at 30 April 20X1

	£m
Issued ordinary share capital (50p shares)	300.00
Retained earnings	118.98
Shareholders' funds	418.98
7% Redeemable debentures (redeemable at par in 20X4)	120.00
9% Irredeemable debentures	80.00
	618.98

Extract from SFS Income Statement for the year to 30 April 20X1

	£m
Profit before interest and taxation	84.10
Less debenture interest	(15.60)
Profit before taxation	68.50
Less taxation (21%)	(14.39)
Profit after taxation	54.11
Less dividends	(12.00)
Retained profit	42.11

Ignoring any effect of the new funds and investment discussed below, the prices of SFS equity and debt on 30 April 20X1 are expected to be:

Ordinary shares	£1.24 each, ex-div
7% Redeemable debentures (20X4)	£96.00 each, ex-int
9% Irredeemable debentures	£94.00 each, ex-int

SFS has not increased its issued share capital figure since 20W8. Its dividend per share for the year to 30 April 20X0 was 3.7% of the 50p par value and the dividend growth rate anticipated for the year to 30 April 20X1 is expected to continue for the foreseeable future.

New funds and investment

SFS's board is discussing how to raise £110 million on 1 May 20X1 and is unsure whether this should be via an issue of equity or debt. This additional funding will enable SFS to expand its product range and establish a foothold in new geographical markets and, according to the board's estimates, next year's profit before interest figure (to 30 April 20X2) will increase by 8% over the previous year.

> **Equity issue** – it is planned to raise the £110 million by a 1 for 6 rights issue. However one of the directors is concerned that this will have an adverse effect on the company's earnings per share figure and has suggested that 'a higher multiple (ie 1 for 8 or even 1 for 10) would be better.'

> **Debt issue** – alternatively the £110 million would be raised by an issue of 6% irredeemable debentures at par.

SFS's directors would like to assume that the corporation tax rate will be 21% for the foreseeable future.

Requirements

31.1 Calculate SFS's weighted average cost of capital on 30 April 20X1 ignoring the new funds and investment. **(11 marks)**

31.2 Discuss whether:

(a) The weighted average cost of capital figure from 31.1 above; or

(b) The individual cost of whichever new source of funding (ie equity or debt) is selected would be a suitable hurdle rate to appraise the planned new investment. **(4 marks)**

31.3 Calculate SFS's earnings per share figure for the year to 30 April 20X2 if, for the new funding, the board chooses:

(a) A 1 for 6 rights issue; or
(b) An issue of 6% irredeemable debt. **(6 marks)**

31.4 Comment on the director's assertion that, regarding the rights issue, 'a higher multiple (ie 1 for 8 or even 1 for 10) would be better.' **(5 marks)**

31.5 Based on your knowledge of the UK stock market, discuss, with reference to the efficient market hypothesis, whether the decision by SFS's board to proceed with raising the new funds and the new investment would affect the price of SFS's ordinary shares. **(4 marks)**

31.6 Discuss whether behavioural effects mean that the UK stock market is no longer efficient. **(5 marks)**

Total: 35 marks

32 Penny Rigby Fashions plc

Penny Rigby Fashions plc (PRF) is a UK-based fashion clothes retailer. It has a financial year end of 31 May. A friend of yours is a PRF shareholder and has e-mailed you recently following his attendance at PRF's annual general meeting (AGM) in August. An extract from his e-mail is shown here:

At the AGM a sheet of 'Key Figures' was distributed to PRF shareholders. However they weren't explained very well and I wondered if you could help. Here they are:

Penny Rigby Fashions plc – Key Figures at 31 May 20X1			
Type of Capital	Total Nominal Value (£m)	Market Value	Post-tax Cost of Capital
Ordinary shares (50p)	4.0	£2.00/share ex-div	10.50% (k_e)
Preference shares (25p)	0.8	£0.80/share ex-div	8.75% (k_p)
Irredeemable debentures (£100)	1.4	£110% ex-int	4.17% (k_d)
Weighted Average Cost of Capital (WACC) at 31 May 20X1			9.791%
Retained profits for trading year to 31 May 20X1			£300,000
Dividend growth in the last 3 years			0% pa

PRF's managing director said that when calculating these figures, PRF's directors had taken account of taxation where appropriate, assuming that the corporation tax rate will be 21% for the foreseeable future and that tax will be payable in the same year as the cash flows to which it relates.

PRF's managing director also made these statements at the AGM:

(1) The WACC of 9.791% represented the total return to the company's providers of finance ie, the total of the after-tax interest and dividends for the trading year to 31 May 20X1.

(2) Unless the company exceeds the WACC 'hurdle rate' when investing in new projects then shareholder value will be destroyed.

(3) It is possible to calculate, using the 'Key Figures' provided, the following for PRF for the trading year to 31 May 20X1 – earnings per share, price earnings ratio, gearing ratio and profit before interest and tax. He said something about 'working backwards' to get these but I'm not sure what he meant.

Requirements

32.1 Show, with workings, how PRF's WACC figure of 9.791% has been calculated.

Assume that the figure of 9.791% is correct. **(4 marks)**

32.2 Calculate PRF's total after-tax interest and dividends for the year to 31 May 20X1 and show how these relate to its WACC figure of 9.791%. **(5 marks)**

32.3 Explain the managing director's statement regarding the WACC as a 'hurdle rate' in your friend's email. **(4 marks)**

32.4 Calculate the following for PRF for the year to/at 31 May 20X1:

(a) Earnings per share
(b) Price earnings ratio
(c) Gearing ratio (based on market values)
(d) Profit before interest and tax. **(8 marks)**

32.5 Explain in general terms how the rate of dividend growth can be calculated and the significance of PRF's dividend growth figure of 0%. **(6 marks)**

Total: 27 marks

33 Personal investment

A friend has recently spoken to you about personal investment. She said

'I've always played safe and put my savings into bank and building society savings accounts, but recently the interest rates have been so tiny that it doesn't seem worth it. Everyone seems to be saying that investing in companies' shares is a much better bet. I must admit that I can't really see the difference between the two.

I think that I am right in saying that, with shares you get dividends instead of interest, but I was reading the other day that sometimes companies don't pay a dividend for a particular year. Surely they have to or no one will invest money with them. How do they decide on the size of each year's dividend?

My newspaper says that shares in Sainsco, the supermarket, are cheap at the moment and I'm thinking about taking my money out of the savings accounts and buying Sainsco shares. I do most of my food shopping at Sainsco and I find them very good, so I can believe that their shares are pretty good value.'

You have made it plain that you are not in a position to offer advice about specific investments, but that you will try to clarify the issues that she has raised and to warn her of any risks inherent in her plans.

Requirement

Draft some notes of the points that you will make in reply to your friend. You should bear in mind, as is obvious from what she has said, that she has little understanding of financial matters. **Total: 14 marks**

Note. Ignore taxation.

34 Sheridan plc

Sheridan plc (Sheridan) is a listed company involved in the UK commercial carpet and floor-covering market. It is presently financed by a mix of ordinary share capital and loan stocks, and has grown rapidly since its flotation two years ago.

During that period, retained earnings have consistently been ploughed back into the business to fund its growth, but this has left Sheridan short of funds at the present time, although its current debt to equity ratio of 60% is below the 75% average for firms in this market.

The company has recently identified an investment opportunity involving the acquisition of a competitor company, Vernon Ltd (Vernon). Negotiations have been successfully concluded with the directors of Vernon for a cash purchase at a price which amounts to approximately 35% of Sheridan's current market capitalisation.

A board meeting has been called to consider the question of financing the purchase of Vernon. Sheridan has already ruled out the possibility of a further public issue of new shares so soon after its flotation, but the following short list of other possibilities has been drawn up:

(1) A rights issue
(2) A further issue of loan stock
(3) Bank loan finance.

Before the board meeting various comments have been made by some of the directors.

Director A: 'We do not want to make a rights issue at the present time, given the current low level of our share price which will mean issuing a relatively high number of shares to raise the funds required.'

Director B: 'I would not favour a further issue of loan stock as that would increase financial gearing in excess of the sector average and would not, therefore, help our share price.'

Director C: 'I seem to remember from my business school days that it doesn't make any difference to the existing shareholders whether new finance is raised from a share issue or from some form of borrowing.'

Director D: 'I am not keen on going to our bankers for loan finance. We have done well to avoid dependence on bank lending and all the restrictions that the bank may impose on us.'

Requirement

You have been asked to prepare briefing notes for the board meeting that will address all the relevant issues regarding the potential funding arrangements for the acquisition, as well as the specific points made by each of the four directors. None of the directors is a financial expert, so your notes should be expressed in language that will be understood by them.　　　　　　　　　　　　　**(12 marks)**

35 Nash Telecom

An uncle of yours, who has a comparatively small holding of shares in Nash Telecom, has sent you a newspaper report that contains the following commentary.

'Nash Telecom raised a record €9 billion after the banks underwrote a rights issue intended to resolve concerns about the €40 billion debt mountain. Shareholders will be able to buy 16 new Nash Telecom shares at €15.5 each for every 20 existing Nash Telecom shares held.

Nash Telecom's share price fell 1.5% to €20. Shares will start trading on an ex-rights basis today with a theoretical ex-rights price of €18.'

Requirements

35.1 Explain the terms 'rights issue', 'ex-rights' and 'underwriting'.　　　　　　　　　　**(3 marks)**

35.2 Explain how the 'theoretical ex-rights price of €18' is calculated and why the actual price might be different.　　　　　　　　　　　　　　　　　　　　　　　　　　　　　　　　**(4 marks)**

35.3 Explain to your uncle the effect on his wealth of:

- Subscribing; or
- Not subscribing for the rights issue.　　　　　　　　　　　　　　　　　　　**(4 marks)**

35.4 Explain to your uncle two other ways in which Nash Telecom might raise money in order to reduce its debt mountain, setting out the differing impacts on the shareholders and debt holders involved.
　　　　　　　　　　　　　　　　　　　　　　　　　　　　　　　　　　　　(5 marks)

35.5 Discuss the possible effects on Nash Telecom's weighted average cost of capital of increasing equity and reducing borrowings in this way.　　　　　　　　　　　　　　**(3 marks)**

Total: 19 marks

36 Battlesbridge Roberts plc

You should assume that the current date is 31 March 20X3

You are employed in the finance team of Battlesbridge Roberts plc (BR) a company that owns a number of holiday centres in the UK.

To date BR's directors have used the payback method to appraise investment opportunities. However they are now considering a number of large scale investments and wish to use the NPV approach instead.

BR's directors are proposing to use a cost of capital of 5.5% pa in their NPV calculations on the basis that this represents the average nominal cost of BR's preference shares and debentures (ie, [7% + 4%]/2).

The company's long-term capital comprises the following:

	Total nominal value	Market value (each)
£0.50 Ordinary shares (Note 1)	£13.5 million	£4.80 (cum div)
7% £1 Irredeemable preference shares	£2.8 million	£1.18 (ex div)
4% Redeemable debentures (Note 2)	£4.6 million	£97 (cum interest)

Notes

1   The next ordinary dividend of £6.48 million will be paid shortly. Ordinary dividends have been growing at a rate of 6% pa for a number of years.

2   The debentures are redeemable at par in three years' time (ie, 31 March 20X6).

BR's directors wish to assume that the corporation tax rate will be 28% pa for the foreseeable future.

Two matters recorded in the minutes of BR's most recent board meeting are shown below:

- 'Susanna Eaton (BR production director) noted that she had read an online financial blog which predicted that by 31 March 20X4 the average post-tax return for redeemable debentures will rise to 7% pa.'

- 'Nigel Hurst (BR marketing director) asked whether the board should be considering an alternative to the NPV approach and that perhaps we should be considering the capital asset pricing model (CAPM) instead. The meeting agreed that, as Gill Buss (BR finance director) is on holiday for a further ten days, we should take advice from her finance team'.

Requirements

36.1 Calculate BR's WACC at 31 March 20X3.   **(11 marks)**

36.2 Explain to BR's directors why it would be preferable to use the WACC that you have calculated in 36.1, rather than the proposed cost of capital of 5.5%, in their NPV calculations.   **(6 marks)**

36.3 Assuming that the online financial blog prediction is correct, calculate the ex-interest price of BR's redeemable debenture stock at 31 March 20X4.   **(3 marks)**

36.4 Advise BR's directors of the reasoning underpinning the CAPM and whether it is appropriate to use it as an alternative to the NPV approach as suggested.   **(8 marks)**

Total: 28 marks

37 Turners plc

Turners plc (Turners) is a listed company in the food retailing sector and has large stores in all the major cities in the UK. Turners' board is considering diversifying by opening holiday travel shops in all of its stores.

At a recent board meeting the directors were discussing how the holiday travel shops project ('the project') should be appraised. The sales director insisted that Turners' current weighted average cost of capital (WACC) should be used to appraise the project as the majority of its operations will still be in food retailing. The finance director disagreed because the existing cost of equity does not take into account the systematic risk of the new project. The finance director also said that the company's overall WACC, which reflects all of the company's activities, would change as a result of the project's acceptance. The board were also concerned about the market's reaction to their diversification plans. A further board meeting was scheduled at which Turners' advisors would be asked to make a presentation on the project.

You work for Turners' advisors and have been asked to prepare information for the presentation. You have established the following:

Turners intends to raise the capital required for the project in such a way as to leave its existing debt:equity ratio (by market values) unchanged following the diversification.

Extracts from Turners' most recent management accounts are shown below:

Balance Sheet at 31 May 20X4

	£m
Ordinary share capital (10p shares)	233
Retained earnings	5,030
	5,263
6% Redeemable debentures at nominal value (redeemable 20X8)	1,900
Long term bank loans (interest rate 4%)	635
	7,798

On 31 May 20X4 Turners' ordinary shares had a market value of 276p (ex-div) and an equity beta of 0.60. For the year ended 31 May 20X4 the dividend yield was 4.2% and the earnings per share were 25p. The return on the market is expected to be 8% pa and the risk free rate 2% pa.

Turners' debentures had a market value of £108 (ex-interest) per £100 nominal value on 31 May 20X4 and they are redeemable at par on 31 May 20X8.

Companies operating solely in the holiday travel industry have an average equity beta of 1.40 and an average debt: equity ratio (by market values) of 3:5. It has been estimated that if the project goes ahead the overall equity beta of Turners will be made up of 90% food retailing and 10% holiday travel shops.

Assume that the corporation tax rate will be 21% pa for the foreseeable future.

Requirements

37.1 Ignoring the project, calculate the current WACC of Turners using:

    (a)   The CAPM   **(8 marks)**

    (b)   The Gordon growth model   **(6 marks)**

37.2 Using the CAPM, calculate the cost of equity that should be included in a WACC suitable for appraising the project and explain your reasoning. **(6 marks)**

37.3 By calculating an overall equity beta and using the CAPM, estimate the overall WACC of Turners assuming that the project goes ahead and comment upon the implications of a permanent change in the overall WACC. **(6 marks)**

37.4 Discuss whether Turners should diversify its operations and how the stock market might react to the proposed project. **(5 marks)**

37.5 Identify the appropriate project appraisal methodology that should be used when a project's financing results in a major increase in a company's market gearing ratio and, using the data relating to Turners, calculate the project discount rate that should be used in these circumstances.

(4 marks)

Total: 35 marks

38 Middleham plc

Middleham plc (Middleham) is a company involved in the production of printing inks used in a wide range of applications in the food packaging industry. The directors of Middleham are currently considering a £2 million investment in new production facilities. At the present time, the company's finance director is seeking to establish an appropriate cost of capital figure for use in the appraisal of the proposed investment. Extracts from Middleham's most recent financial statements for the year ended 31 March 20X3 are shown below:

	£'000
Ordinary share capital (50p shares)	3,200
5% irredeemable preference share capital (50p shares)	1,400
Reserves	7,000
	11,600
7% debentures (at nominal value)	1,500
	13,100
Current liabilities	3,700
Total equity and liabilities	16,800

	£'000
Profit before taxation	3,000
Taxation	(800)
Preference share dividends	(70)
Ordinary share dividends	(1,088)

The market prices for the company's shares and debentures on 31 March 20X3 were:

(1)   Ordinary shares: £1.42 each (cum-div)
(2)   5% irredeemable preference shares: £0.20 each (ex-div)
(3)   7% debentures: £105.00 (per £100 nominal)

The ordinary dividend for the year ended 31 March 20X3 is due to be paid shortly. This is the first dividend paid since the year ended 31 March 20W9, when the dividend payout ratio was 40% and the earnings per share were £0.35. Middleham's directors expect future dividends to grow at the annual growth rate implied by the dividends paid in 20W9 and 20X3. The number of ordinary shares in issue has not changed since March 20W8.

The annual debenture interest has recently been paid. The 7% debentures are redeemable at par in 10 years' time.

Shares in the industrial sector in which Middleham operates typically have an equity beta of 1.3 with a debt to equity ratio of 1:1. The risk free rate is 6% pa and the return from the market portfolio is 14% pa.

The company's finance director has proposed that, if the investment is undertaken, then an issue of redeemable debentures is used to finance it. However, Middleham's chief executive has expressed concerns about the possible use of redeemable debentures. His view is that increasing the number of debentures issued by the company will increase the company's gearing dramatically and the increased financial risk associated with this could easily lead to a fall in the company's share price and, therefore, its market value.

The directors wish to assume a rate of corporation tax of 21% for the foreseeable future.

Requirements

38.1 Calculate (using the dividend growth model) a weighted average cost of capital that could be used to appraise Middleham's proposed investment.   **(13 marks)**

38.2 Explain the underlying assumptions and any other relevant factors that may mean it is inappropriate to use the cost of capital figure calculated in requirement 38.1 in the appraisal of Middleham's proposed investment.   **(5 marks)**

38.3 (a)   Estimate Middleham's cost of equity using the capital asset pricing model.

   (b)   Explain **two** key assumptions that would underpin the use of this cost of equity in the calculation of the weighted average cost of capital.   **(7 marks)**

38.4 Comment on the views expressed by Middleham's chief executive.   **(5 marks)**

38.5 Explain, with reference to the efficient market hypothesis, when news of the proposed investment in the new production facilities would be reflected in Middleham's share price on the London Stock Exchange.   **(5 marks)**

Total: 35 marks

39 Better Deal plc

Better Deal plc (Better Deal) is a UK supermarket chain which has a financial year end of 28 February. An extract from its Balance Sheet at 28 February 20Y0 is shown below:

	£m
Ordinary shares (50p each)	82.5
Retained earnings	391.5
	474.0
8% debentures (at nominal value; redeemable at par in 20Y4)	340.0
	814.0

Additional information about Better Deal:

Current market value of one ordinary share (ex div)	£2.65
Current market value of one 8% debenture (ex int)	£98
Dividends paid on 28 February 20Y0	£29.5m
Dividends paid on 28 February 20X6	£25.2m
Equity beta	1.1
Market return	11.4% pa
Risk free rate	5.2% pa

Notes

1 There have been no changes in the number of issued shares over the period 20X6 – 20Y0. Better Deal's annual dividend payments have risen steadily since 20X6.

2 Better Deal's management is considering diversifying its product range and opening petrol outlets at a number of its stores. The finance for this capital investment would be raised in such a way as not to alter the current gearing ratio of Better Deal (measured by market values). The debt element of the finance raised will come from a new issue at par of 9% irredeemable debentures.

3 Better Deal's finance team has undertaken research into the company's competitors in the UK petroleum market and has calculated that the equity beta for this market is 1.5 and companies in that market have, on average, long term funds in the ratio of 64:31 for equity:debt by market value.

4 You should assume that the corporation tax rate is 21% pa and is payable in the same year as profits are earned.

Requirements

39.1 Calculate Better Deal's current weighted average cost of capital based on:

   (a)   The dividend growth model.
   (b)   The CAPM model.
   (10 marks)

39.2 Calculate the cost of capital that Better Deal should use when appraising the proposed investment in petrol outlets and explain the reasoning for your approach.
   (11 marks)

39.3 Compare and contrast multiple factor models with the CAPM model as a means of dealing with risk.
   (8 marks)

39.4 Advise Better Deal's management as to what extent the company's dividend policy will affect the market value of its shares.
   (6 marks)

Total: 35 marks

40 Havant Hall Ltd

Havant Hall Ltd (HH) is a small private company that runs a residential activity centre from a stately home, Havant Hall, and its 125-acre estate in southern England. The company's client base comprises principally of local government bodies who send groups of disadvantaged children for residential stays at the estate and private firms who send employees on people development programmes centred on all aspects of leadership, team-building and management development.

Since HH was established almost 15 years ago, all of its shares have been owned by members of the Elliot family. In addition, the residential courses on offer and the range of activities included in them have been restricted by the level of accommodation available in Havant Hall itself and by the fact that HH has never used long-term external finance to invest in developing the available facilities.

However, following the recent appointment of Andrew Elliot as chief executive in succession to his father, John Elliot, who has retired, the family is now keen to expand both the accommodation on the estate and the range of activities on offer to clients. A recently commissioned report by a firm of management consultants has estimated that HH's proposed expansion plans will cost £2.8 million.

The most recent management accounts for HH can be summarised as follows:

Income Statement for the year ended 31 May 20X1

	£'000
Revenue	11,024
Profit from operations	1,167
Tax	(245)
Profit after tax	922
Dividends	(433)
Retained profit for the year	489

Balance Sheet as at 31 May 20X1

	£'000
Non-current assets	4,228
Current assets	616
Current liabilities	(594)
	4,250
Share capital (ordinary £1 shares)	2,000
Retained profits	2,250
	4,250

Returns on invested funds and the proportion of profits retained are consistent with previous years. Within its current assets HH has only a small cash balance and within its current liabilities it has no borrowings.

Upon his retirement, the former chief executive, John Elliot, sold his shares to other members of the family. At the time, the consideration paid for these shares was based on an estimated valuation provided by HH's auditors of £4 per share.

There has been much debate among the directors regarding the source of finance for the firm's proposed expansion, with some directors wishing to continue with the policy of no long-term debt and others believing that debt finance should be the preferred option.

Requirements

40.1 Calculate HH's cost of capital, stating and justifying the assumptions and methodology you employ. **(7 marks)**

40.2 Discuss the underlying assumptions and weaknesses of the approach you have used in calculating the cost of equity in 40.1. **(7 marks)**

40.3 Discuss the advantages and disadvantages of a rights issue to fund the proposed expansion, and, as an alternative to a rights issue, whether a listing on the Alternative Investment Market (AIM) would be appropriate, given HH's particular circumstances. **(8 marks)**

40.4 If debt finance were to be used:

    (a)   explain the benefits that might accrue to HH if the proposed expansion was financed by convertible loans rather than an ordinary bank loan; and

    (b)   explain the implicit assumptions underlying the use of HH's resultant weighted average cost of capital as a discount factor in appraising the proposed expansion. **(7 marks)**

40.5 Without using calculations, identify the methods that the company's auditors might have used to value HH's shares. **(6 marks)**

Total: 35 marks

41 Puerto plc

You should assume that it is now 1 December 20X3.

Puerto plc (Puerto) is listed on the UK stock market and operates in the vehicle leasing industry. During a period of expansion from 20W3 to 20W7 the company funded growth by way of convertible loans obtained from an investment bank, SM Capital (SMC). As a result of the global economic downturn Puerto has experienced a number of trading difficulties, and the company ceased to pay dividends to its ordinary shareholders in 20W8. Since 20W9 Puerto has embarked on a significant restructuring of its business. Although in the current year to 30 November 20X3 the company has sustained losses, industry conditions have stabilised giving both the board of Puerto and SMC confidence in the company's future. This confidence is also shared by the UK stock market as Puerto's share price has been increasing over the last six months to 10p per ordinary share on 30 November 20X3.

Extracts from Puerto's most recent management accounts are shown below:

Income statement for the year ended 30 November 20X3

	£'000
Operating profit	2,280
Interest	(2,460)
Profit/(loss) before tax	(180)
Taxation	0
Profit/(loss) after tax	(180)

The board of Puerto is now considering a further restructuring that includes the purchase on 1 December 20X3 of another vehicle leasing business that in the last financial year achieved a pre-tax operating profit of £3 million. The purchase price for this business is £24 million. The board is confident it will be able to raise the additional borrowings required for this purchase on 1 December 20X3, particularly as SMC, as part of the restructuring, has agreed to exercise its option to convert its convertible loans into equity on that date in order to participate in Puerto's future growth potential. The board and SMC believe that Puerto's share price will increase immediately on 1 December 20X3 by 35% as a result of the restructuring.

Additional information:

- The SMC convertible loans amount to £68 million and the rate of interest on these loans is 3% pa. The market value of these loans, on 30 November 20X3, is equal to their nominal value of £68 million.

- SMC has the option to convert its loans into thirty ordinary shares for every £4 of loan.

- Puerto also has non-convertible secured bank loans amounting to £6 million that carry an interest rate of 7% pa.

- On 30 November 20X3 Puerto had 492 million ordinary shares in issue.

- £24 million of new secured borrowings at an interest rate of 6% pa will be raised from Risky Bank plc (Risky) to finance the purchase of the vehicle leasing business. A covenant attached to this loan requires that the gearing (debt/equity by market values) immediately after the restructuring is not more than the industry average of 25%.

- Corporation tax is 21% pa on current year profits.

- Puerto has an equity beta of 2.13 which reflects Puerto's gearing on 30 November 20X3.

- The risk free rate is 2.8% pa.

- An appropriate market risk premium is 5% pa.

Requirements

41.1 Prepare Puerto's forecast income statement for the year ended 30 November 20X4 assuming that the restructuring goes ahead and that both the existing and newly acquired leasing businesses earn similar operating profits to those in the year to 30 November 20X3. **(3 marks)**

41.2 Calculate Puerto's gearing ratio (debt/equity) by market values on 30 November 20X3 and on 1 December 20X3 immediately after the restructuring. **(5 marks)**

41.3 Using your answer to 41.1 and 41.2, comment on the financial health of Puerto both before and after the restructuring and whether the covenant imposed by Risky would be met if Puerto's share price remains at 10p on 1 December 20X3. **(5 marks)**

41.4 Calculate (using the capital asset pricing model) the weighted average cost of capital of Puerto on 30 November 20X3 and on 1 December 20X3 immediately after the restructuring. **(10 marks)**

41.5 Discuss, with reference to relevant theories, whether the change in Puerto's capital structure following the restructuring on 1 December 20X3 will bring about a permanent change in its weighted average cost of capital. **(6 marks)**

41.6 Advise the board of Puerto on the likely reaction of the various stakeholders in the company to the restructuring. **(6 marks)**

Total: 35 marks

42 Efficient markets hypothesis

You are presented with the following different views of stock market behaviour.

(1) If a company publishes an earnings figure higher than the market expects, the shares of that company will usually experience an abnormally high return, both on the day of the earnings announcement and over the two or three days following.

(2) The return on professionally managed portfolios of equities is likely to be no better than that which could be achieved by a naive investor who holds the market portfolio.

(3) Share prices usually seem to rise sharply in the first few days of a new fiscal year. However, this can be explained by the fact that many investors sell losing stocks immediately prior to the fiscal year end in order to establish a tax loss for capital gains tax purposes. This causes abnormal downward pressure which is released when the new fiscal year begins.

Requirements

42.1 Briefly describe the three forms of the efficient markets hypothesis. **(4 marks)**

42.2 Consider what each of the above three statements tells you about the efficiency of the stock market. Where appropriate, relate your comments to one or more forms of the efficient markets hypothesis. **(8 marks)**

Total: 12 marks

43   Abydos plc

Abydos plc is considering a large strategic investment in a significantly different line of business to its existing operations. The scale of the new venture is such that a significant injection of £12.5 million of new capital will be required.

The current gearing of Abydos is 80% equity and 20% debt by market value.

The new project will require outlays immediately as follows:

	£'000
Plant and equipment (purchased on first day of financial year)	10,000
Working capital	1,500
Equity issue costs (not tax allowable)	700
Debt issue costs (not tax allowable)	300
	12,500

Other details are as follows:

- Estimates of relevant cash flows and other financial information associated with the possible new investment. These are shown below.

	Year 1 £'000	Year 2 £'000	Year 3 £'000	Year 4 £'000
Pre-tax operating cash flows	3,000	3,400	3,800	4,300

- The directors have examined similar quoted companies operating in the same sector as the new investment and have determined that a suitable equity beta is 1.4, using average industry gearing of 60% equity, 40% debt by market values.

- The risk free rate is 5% and the market return 12%.

- £5 million of debt (an 8% fixed rate debenture) will be raised to fund part of the investment. The remainder will be equity.

- Capital allowances are at 18% per year on a reducing balance basis.

- Tax is payable at 21% in the year that the taxable cash flow arises.

- The after tax realisable value of the investment (including any balancing allowance/charge on the equipment) as a continuing operation is estimated to be £4 million (including working capital) at the end of Year 4.

- Working capital may be assumed to be constant during the four years.

The board of directors of Abydos plc is discussing how the company should appraise the new investment. There is a difference of opinion between two directors.

The sales director believes that net present value at the current weighted average cost of capital should be used as positive NPV investments should be quickly reflected in increases in the company's share price.

The finance director states that NPV is not good enough as it is only valid in potentially restrictive conditions, and should be replaced by APV (adjusted present value).

Requirements

43.1 Calculate the expected APV of the proposed investment.   **(10 marks)**

43.2 Discuss briefly the validity of the views of the two directors. Use your calculations in 43.1 to illustrate and support the discussion.   **(6 marks)**

Total: 16 marks

44 Wiggins plc

You should assume that the current date is 30 November 20X4

Wiggins plc (Wiggins) provides engineering and production support to the power generation industry. Wiggins is planning its capital expenditure programme and, on 1 December 20X4, intends to raise £200m to invest in projects during 20X5. Some of these projects will be in a different industry sector to current operations. The board is discussing how the additional £200m should be raised.

The finance director of Wiggins has presented the board with two alternative sources of finance as follows:

Debt issue – the £200m would be raised by an issue of 3% coupon debentures, redeemable at par on 1 December 20Y4. The bond markets would currently expect a gross redemption yield for such an issue of 5% pa.

Equity issue – the £200m would be raised by a 1 for 8 rights issue, priced at a discount on the current market value of Wiggins's ordinary shares.

The board has expressed a number of concerns regarding the raising of the £200m and the hurdle rate that should be used to appraise the projects in which the funds will be invested. The sales director is concerned that the hurdle rate will increase and that some of the new projects may be unviable and will be rejected. The Chief Executive has read that, whatever the hurdle rate, the Capital Asset Pricing Model (CAPM) has severe weaknesses and that other models should be used to calculate the company's cost of equity. The production director is concerned about the issue price of the debentures and, if a rights issue is used, whether the rights will be fully subscribed.

An extract from Wiggins' most recent management accounts is shown below:

Income statement for the year ended 30 November 20X4

	£m
Operating profit	239
Interest on debentures	12
Profit before tax	227
Taxation	48
Profit after tax	179

Wiggins' financial structure at 30 November 20X4

£300m 4% debentures, redeemable at par on 30 November 20X8, with a current market value of £108 cum-interest per £100 nominal debenture.

360m ordinary shares with a current ex-dividend market value of £5.60 per share.

Additional information:

- Wiggins has an equity beta of 1.20

- The risk free rate is 2.0% pa

- An appropriate market risk premium is 5% pa

- The corporation tax rate can assumed to be 21% pa for the foreseeable future

- The power generation industry average cover is 11 and average gearing (debt/equity by market values) is 30%.

Requirements

44.1 **Ignoring the new finance and investments**, calculate (using the CAPM) Wiggins' weighted average cost of capital on 30 November 20X4. **(6 marks)**

44.2 Assuming debt is issued on 1 December 20X4, calculate the issue price and the total **nominal** value of new debt that will have to be issued to give a gross redemption yield of 5% pa and discuss the reasons why this yield is different to the yield on Wiggins' existing debentures. **(5 marks)**

44.3 Assuming a 1 for 8 rights issue is made on 1 December 20X4:

    (a)   Calculate both the discount the rights price represents on Wiggins' current share price and the theoretical ex-rights price

    (b)   Discuss whether the actual share price is likely to be equal to the theoretical ex-rights price.

        (5 marks)

44.4 Outline the advantages and disadvantages of the two alternative sources for raising the £200m and, using the industry average interest cover and gearing information, advise Wiggins' board on which source should be used.
    (10 marks)

44.5 Discuss whether the hurdle rate to appraise the planned new investments should be either:

    (a)   The weighted average cost of capital figure calculated in 44.1 above; or

    (b)   The individual cost of whichever new source of funding (ie equity or debt) is selected.

        (5 marks)

44.6 Explain how multiple factor models might overcome the weaknesses of the CAPM.   **(4 marks)**

        Total: 35 marks

45   Perryfield Paper plc

You should assume that the current date is 31 March 20X5.

You work in the finance team at Perryfield Paper plc (PP) a listed UK paper manufacturer which has a financial year end of 31 March.

PP currently has a very healthy level of liquid funds (approximately £8.5m) in its bank accounts. At the company's most recent board meeting the following issues were discussed:

- Should the firm's current weighted average cost of capital (WACC) figure of 6.5% be amended? This figure has been used for many years and the directors are concerned that this rate does not represent current market conditions.

- Should the dividend growth model or the capital asset pricing (CAPM) model be used to calculate the WACC?

- Should PP's long-term funding be restructured?

Cost of capital

The figures below have been given to you for the year ended/at 31 March 20X5:

Type of capital (nominal value)	Total dividends/interest	Total market value	Total nominal value
Ordinary shares (25p)	£4,976,400	£63,800,000	£14,500,000
Preference shares (50p)	£313,200	£5,400,000	£2,000,000
Irredeemable debentures (£100)	£405,000	£14,175,000	£13,500,000

Notes

1   All dividends have been paid for the year ended 31 March 20X5. Ordinary dividends have been growing at a steady rate of 2% pa for the past five years.

2   All debenture interest payable for the year to 31 March 20X5 has been paid.

Restructuring the long-term funding

Two mutually-exclusive proposals have been made to restructure PP's capital:

(1)   Purchase and cancel all of PP's irredeemable debentures at their current market value. Issue 4% coupon debentures with a nominal value of £9 million, redeemable in four years' time at par.

(2)   Buy back 10% of PP's ordinary shares.

Assume that the corporation tax rate will be 21% pa for the foreseeable future.

ICAEW

Requirements

45.1 Using the dividend growth model, calculate PP's current WACC on 31 March 20X5.   **(8 marks)**

45.2 Giving reasons, advise PP's directors whether they should use the WACC figure from 45.1 when appraising potential investments rather than the current figure of 6.5%.   **(4 marks)**

45.3 Discuss the logic underpinning the CAPM and explain how the CAPM can be used to calculate the WACC.   **(7 marks)**

45.4 For proposal (1), if, at their issue date, the market gross redemption yield for similar redeemable debentures is 5% pa, calculate the issue price of the new redeemable debentures and the total funds raised.   **(4 marks)**

45.5 For proposal (2), explain how a share buy-back works and the implications of a buy-back for PP's individual shareholders, ignoring any impact on PP's gearing.   **(5 marks)**

45.6 Making reference to relevant theories, discuss how the share buy-back would affect PP's gearing and its WACC.   **(7 marks)**

Total: 35 marks

46 Worsley plc

46.1 Worsley plc (Worsley) is a supplier of specialist engineering components to the UK defence and airline industries. In spite of the impact of the global recession, demand for the company's products has held up well in recent times and is expected to pick up further in the next two years.

As part of a recent strategic review, the directors have made the following projections for the years ending 31 March 20X1 and 31 March 20X2:

(1) An anticipated increase in annual revenues of 8% pa in each of the years.

(2) An anticipated increase in operating costs (excluding depreciation) of 4% pa in each of the years.

(3) The directors are assuming that for the next two years tax will continue to be paid at a rate of 21% and be payable in the year in which the liability arises.

(4) The ratio of trade receivables to revenue will remain the same in each of the next two years as will the ratio of trade payables to operating costs (excluding depreciation).

(5) An anticipated increase in inventory levels of 10% in the year ending 31 March 20X1, but remaining stable thereafter.

(6) The non-current assets in the company's balance sheet are Worsley's headquarters and main factory complex, both of which are freehold premises. The company's accounting policy is that these assets are not depreciated. Capital allowances on these assets are negligible and can be ignored.

(7) The directors foresee no change in the company's annual dividend growth rate of 6% pa. Annual dividends are declared at the year end and paid in full during the following financial year.

(8) To cope with the anticipated increase in business levels, Worsley will shortly be purchasing new machinery at a cost of £8 million. All existing machinery is rented and its rental costs are included in operating costs. The company is not intending to seek any equity or long-term debt financing in respect of this machinery purchase, as it intends to accommodate the purchase within existing overdraft facilities available to the company. The new machinery will be depreciated on a straight-line basis over 8 years (assuming a residual value of £1 million) with a full year's depreciation to be charged in the year the machinery is purchased. Capital allowances on a reducing balance basis at a rate of 18% pa will be available on the new machinery from the year of acquisition.

(9) As a result of this machinery purchase, there will be an anticipated increase in finance costs of 50% in the year ending 31 March 20X1, but remaining stable in the following year.

Extracts from the company's most recent financial statements are provided below:

Income Statement for the year ended 31 March 20X0

	£'000
Revenue	60,240
Operating costs	(49,500)
Operating profit	10,740
Finance costs	(800)
Profit before tax	9,940
Tax	(2,286)
Profit after tax	7,654

Balance Sheet as at 31 March 20X0

ASSETS	£'000	£'000
Non-current assets		28,850
Current assets		
Inventories	9,020	
Trade receivables	9,036	
Cash and cash equivalents	396	
		18,452
		47,302
EQUITY AND LIABILITIES		
Equity		
Ordinary share capital	16,700	
Retained earnings	12,482	
		29,182
Non-current liabilities		
6% Debentures 20X8		8,000
Current liabilities		
Trade payables	7,336	
Dividends	2,784	
		10,120
		47,302

Requirement

Prepare forecast financial statements (comprising income statement, balance sheet and cash flow statement) for each of the years ending 31 March 20X1 and 31 March 20X2. **(21 marks)**

Note. All calculations should be undertaken to the nearest £'000.

46.2 Looking beyond 31 March 20X2, the directors are considering a suggestion made by the finance director that one of Worsley's smaller UK subsidiaries be disposed of because, relative to most of the other UK operations, it is trading poorly, albeit still profitably. Whilst the directors are broadly supportive of the finance director's suggestion, they are keen to avoid liquidation of the subsidiary as they are acutely conscious of the industrial relations problems that might arise from the redundancies that would inevitably be involved.

Requirements

(a) Describe **four** methods, other than liquidation, that the firm might consider to effect the divestment of this subsidiary company. **(6 marks)**

(b) Assuming that the same firm of accountants acts for both Worsley and a potential purchaser of the UK subsidiary, explain how any conflicts of interest could be managed. **(5 marks)**

Total: 32 marks

47 Wentworth plc

The shares of Wentworth plc are listed on the London Stock Exchange. The current distribution of the company's shareholders is as follows:

	%
Institutional investors	60
Directors	30
Private individuals	10

Wentworth plc is a long established printing company operating in the highly competitive UK magazine market. In recent years growth has been steady rather than spectacular, although the company has maintained its high dividend pay-out ratio.

Competitive pressures in the industry demand that players keep pace with technological developments in printing processes if they are to survive. The company currently has the opportunity of tendering for a large contract with a national publishing company, but in order to tender the company will need to purchase a new laser-based printing machine at significant cost in terms of purchase price, installation and staff training. At the present time, the company is unlikely to be able to raise further external finance. The finance director has, therefore, highlighted the fact that this significant investment will place some immediate pressure on the company's liquidity and has forewarned that the current high dividend pay-out ratio may need to be reduced in at least the next two years to allow the company to cope with the strain on its finances.

The finance director's comments have received a mixed reception amongst the other directors. Some directors have expressed indifference to the possible change and feel that the company's shareholders should also be indifferent, whilst other directors have expressed grave concern that the dividend policy might change in the way suggested and feel that many of the company's shareholders will share their concerns.

Requirements

47.1 Discuss the potential reasons why the directors of Wentworth plc might choose to adopt a high dividend pay-out policy. **(5 marks)**

47.2 Explain the theory that might justify the opinion of those directors who feel that the shareholders should be indifferent to the proposed change in dividend policy. **(6 marks)**

47.3 Identify and discuss the risks faced by a company when deciding to change its dividend policy which might justify the opinion of those directors who feel that the proposed change in dividend policy is a cause for concern. **(6 marks)**

47.4 Explain how shareholders who might be unhappy with any future pattern of dividend payments adopted by the company can respond to achieve their own income preferences and explain one dividend strategy the company might employ to address the potential liquidity issues facing it. **(5 marks)**

Total: 22 marks

48 Biddaford Lundy plc

Biddaford Lundy plc (BL) is a large UK engineering company. Its ordinary shares are quoted on the London Stock Exchange.

BL's board is concerned that the company's gearing level is too high and that this is having a detrimental impact on its market capitalisation. As a result the board is considering a restructuring of BL's long term funds, details of which are shown here as at 29 February 20X2:

	Total par value £m	Market value
Ordinary share capital (50p)	67.5	£2.65/share ex-div
7% Preference share capital (£1)	60.0	£1.44/share ex-div
4% Redeemable debentures (£100)	45.0	£90% ex-int

The debentures are redeemable in 20X7. BL's earnings for the year to 29 February 20X2 were £32.4 million and are expected to remain at this level for the foreseeable future. Retained earnings at 29 February 20X2 were £73.2 million.

The board is considering a 1 for 9 rights issue of ordinary shares and this additional funding would be used to redeem 60% of BL's redeemable debentures at par. However, some of BL's directors are concerned that this issue of extra ordinary shares will cause the company's ordinary share price and its earnings per share (EPS) to fall by an excessive amount, to the detriment of BL's shareholders. Accordingly, they are arguing that the rights issue should be designed so that the EPS is not diluted by more than 5%.

The directors wish to assume that the corporation tax rate will be 21% for the foreseeable future and that tax will be payable in the same year as the cash flows to which it relates.

Requirements

48.1 Calculate BL's gearing ratio using both book and market values and discuss, with reference to relevant theories, why BL's board might have concerns over the level of gearing and its impact on BL's market capitalisation. **(9 marks)**

48.2 Assuming that a 1 for 9 rights issue goes ahead, calculate the theoretical ex-rights price of a BL ordinary share and the value of a right. **(4 marks)**

48.3 Discuss the directors' view that the rights issue will cause the share price and the EPS to fall by an excessive amount, to the detriment of BL's ordinary shareholders. Your discussion should be supported by relevant calculations. **(10 marks)**

48.4 Calculate and comment on the rights issue price that would cause a 5% dilution in the current EPS figure. **(6 marks)**

48.5 Discuss the factors to be considered when making a rights issue. **(6 marks)**

Total: 35 marks

49 Duofold plc

You are a shareholder in Duofold plc, a listed company with an issued share capital of 10m ordinary £1 shares with a current market price of £1.80 per share at the close of business yesterday afternoon. Today you are to attend the company's annual general meeting, and just before the meeting begins you are in conversation with a number of fellow shareholders.

(1) The first shareholder is Alan Jones who owns 2,000 shares in Duofold plc. He expresses great concern that before the market opened this morning the company announced its intention to pursue a 1-for-2 rights issue at £1.00 per share to raise funds for a new project that it claimed has a net present value of £2m. 'This massive discount to the market price is atrocious, and the consequent fall in the share price will be bad news for me.'

(2) The second shareholder, Peter Atkins, produces a recent investment bank report that hints at a possible acquisition by Duofold plc of its principal UK competitor. The report states that the annual cash flows of Duofold are currently £4.2m and that 'an appropriate discount rate for these cash flows is 12%'. The report goes on to estimate that combined annual cash flows would total £6.8m and that 'the appropriate discount rate for these cash flows is 10%'. Peter's concern is that he does not know what would be a reasonable price for the directors to pay in such circumstances, as the report makes no reference to a likely purchase price.

(3) The final shareholder is Norma Benbow, who is concerned by rumours that Duofold plc might be about to cut its dividend, because she has read that a cut in dividend by another company adversely affected that company's share price. At the same time, however, Norma mentions that a friend has suggested that a company's dividend policy is irrelevant. She is confused.

Requirements

49.1 Advise Mr Jones of his various options in such a scenario, making clear to him the expected ex-rights price of the company's ordinary shares, how much he could reasonably sell his rights for (if he chose to) and provide calculations to illustrate to him the effect on his wealth of each of the options available to him.

(6 marks)

49.2 Calculate for Mr Atkins the maximum price the directors of Duofold plc should consider paying for this acquisition, and advise him of the potential reasons why the directors of Duofold plc might recommend an acquisition to their shareholders.

(5 marks)

49.3 Outline to Mrs Benbow the theoretical and practical positions regarding the relevance or otherwise of a company's dividend policy.

(6 marks)

Total: 17 marks

50 Portico plc

Portico plc (Portico) has recently become a listed company. Prior to its flotation this previously family-owned private company made dividend decisions each year to suit the particular requirements at the time of both the company and the small number of family shareholders who held substantially all of the company's equity. There was no long-term, stable dividend policy in place.

Following flotation, the family is no longer involved in the day-to-day management of the firm but has retained 45% of the equity, which currently represents the largest single block of shares owned. None of the family members is any longer a director of the firm, but one member has been retained as a non-executive director. The new board of directors consists of a group of young professional managers who are all keen to grow the business rapidly.

Now that it is a listed company, the question of establishing a more formal dividend policy has arisen and a forthcoming board meeting will address the issue. As the company's finance director you have been approached by two directors who have made the following observations.

Director A

'The value of the company's shares is tied to the level of the company's dividend, so we should pay the maximum dividend possible. If at any time this policy places pressure on finances, then raising further equity will be that much easier, given the policy of maximum dividends the company will have established'.

Director B

'What strikes me is the variety of different views on this issue among our shareholders. Some shareholders tell me they want us to maximise the dividends as they depend so much on the income and are not primarily concerned with capital growth. Others say they would prefer the company to retain much of its profits to invest in new projects so as to maximise the share price'.

Both these directors have limited financial knowledge.

Requirement

Prepare briefing notes for the forthcoming board meeting that

- Set out the key considerations for a company in Portico's position when formulating a dividend policy.

- Address the specific points made by the two directors and how Portico might address the fact that particular groups of investors may have different preferences in respect of dividends.

- Explain to the board the relationship between a company's dividend policy and the 'agency problem' in business finance.

Total: 16 marks

51 Cern Ltd

51.1 Cern Ltd (Cern) is an unquoted company that manufactures a range of products used in the construction industry. Extracts from the most recent management accounts of Cern are set out below:

Income statement for the year ended 30 September 20X2

	£
Profit before interest and tax	1,080,000
Interest	(180,000)
Profit before tax	900,000
Tax (21%)	(189,000)
Profit after tax	711,000

Dividends declared and paid:	
Preference dividend	43,200
Ordinary dividend	180,000

Balance sheet at 30 September 20X2

Non-current assets		
Intangibles	900,000	
Freehold land and property	1,800,000	
Plant and equipment	3,600,000	
Investments	900,000	
		7,200,000
Current assets		
Inventory	540,000	
Receivables	1,080,000	
Cash	180,000	
	1,800,000	
Current liabilities	(1,080,000)	
		720,000
		7,920,000
Equity and non-current liabilities		
Ordinary share capital (£1 shares)	3,600,000	
6% Preference shares (£1 shares)	720,000	
Retained earnings	1,800,000	
		6,120,000
10% Debentures		1,800,000
		7,920,000

The following information is also available:

(1) In the two previous financial years the profit before interest and tax was:

- Year ended 30 September 20X1: £440,000
- Year ended 30 September 20X0: £1,800,000

(2) The current market value of the preference shares has been estimated at £0.90 per preference share.

(3) The current market value of the debentures has been estimated at £110 per £100 of debentures.

(4) The current rental value of the freehold land and property is £270,000 pa and this represents a 6% return.

(5) The current market value of the investments is £1,350,000.

(6) The most recent P/E ratios of two comparable quoted companies operating in the same sector as Cern are 9.6 and 7.0, and their most recent dividend yields are 4% and 3.4% respectively.

(7) Cern's directors wish to assume that for the foreseeable future the corporation tax rate will be 21%.

The directors have recently received an approach from Fenton Holdings plc (Fenton), a conglomerate company, whose directors have expressed an interest in making an offer to buy the whole of Cern. Fenton's directors have confirmed that if an acquisition goes ahead, they will purchase the debentures at their market value and Fenton's bank has agreed to buy the preference shares at their market value. Cern's directors have sought your advice as an external consultant.

Requirements

(a) Using the available information, calculate the minimum price per ordinary share that the shareholders of Cern should be willing to accept from Fenton using each of the following methods of valuation:

- Net assets
- Dividend yield
- P/E ratio

(13 marks)

(b) Comment on the values you have calculated and any issues you think should be brought to the attention of Cern's directors.

(4 marks)

(c) Identify the motives that might lie behind Fenton's possible acquisition of Cern. (4 marks)

51.2 Cern has an annual cost of capital of 10%. One of its most successful products is Hadtone, a mortar colouring agent. Hadtone is made using a single processing machine which mixes the raw ingredients and dispenses the completed product into five-litre cartons.

A five-litre carton of Hadtone sells for £12.00 and estimated maximum annual demand at this price is 300,000 cartons. At this level of demand, Cern can justify the operation of only one processing machine, which Cern currently replaces every three years, although the processing machine has a productive life of four years.

In the first year of its life the processing machine has a productive capacity in line with the maximum annual demand for the product, but each year thereafter this productive capacity falls at a rate of 15,000 units pa. Annual maintenance costs in the first year of operating the processing machine are estimated at £12,000. Thereafter, the directors expect the annual maintenance costs to increase by £2,000 pa regardless of the actual number of five-litre cartons produced. Cern incurs variable costs, excluding depreciation and maintenance costs, of £8.00 in producing each five-litre carton. Cern provides for depreciation on all its non-current assets using the straight-line method.

If Cern were to dispose of the processing machine after one year, the directors estimate sale proceeds of £320,000, but these would fall by £120,000 pa in each of the following two years. Once the machine has reached the end of its four-year productive life its residual value will be £10,000.

Following a recent increase in the cost of a processing machine to £480,000, Cern's directors are reconsidering their current replacement policy with a view to maximising the present value of the company's cash-flows. It can be assumed that all revenues and costs are received or paid in cash at the end of the year to which they relate, with the exception of the initial price of the processing machine which is paid in full at the time of purchase.

Requirement

Assuming that the processing machine is used to maximum capacity, and showing all your supporting calculations, advise Cern's directors how often they should replace the processing machine.

(10 marks)

Total: 31 marks

Note. Ignore inflation and taxation when answering 51.2.

52 Wexford plc

Wexford plc (Wexford) is a listed manufacturer of dairy products. In recent years the company has experienced only modest levels of growth, but following the recent retirement of the chief executive, his replacement is keen to expand Wexford's operations.

It is currently December 20X8 and the board of directors has recently agreed to support a proposal by the new chief executive that the company purchase new manufacturing equipment to enable it to expand its range of yoghurt-based products. The new equipment will cost £25m and the company is seeking to raise new finance to fund the expenditure in full. However, the board of directors is undecided as to how the new finance is to be raised. The directors are considering either a 1 for 5 rights issue at a price of 250p per share or a floating rate loan of £25m at an initial interest rate of 8% per annum. The company's bank has agreed to provide the £25m loan. The loan would be for a term of five years, with interest paid annually in arrears and with the capital being repaid in full at maturity. The loan would be secured against the company's freehold land and buildings.

You are employed by Wexford as a company accountant and have been able to obtain the following additional information:

- As a result of the investment in the new machinery, the directors aim to increase the company's revenue by 15% per annum for the foreseeable future.

- It is expected that direct costs, other than depreciation, will, on average, increase by 18% during the year ending 30 November 20X9 due to the 'learning curve' effects associated with the new machinery.

- Indirect costs are expected to increase by £10m in the year to 30 November 20X9.

- The ratios of receivables to sales and payables to direct costs (excluding depreciation) will remain the same as in the year to 30 November 20X8.

- Depreciation on assets existing at 30 November 20X8 is forecast to be £18m in the year ending 30 November 20X9.

- Depreciation on the new machinery will be 20% per annum on a straight line basis commencing in the year of purchase.

- Capital allowances can be assumed to be equal to the depreciation charged in a particular year.

- The company's inventory levels are expected to increase by £10m as a result of the increased levels of business.

- Tax is payable at a rate of 21% per annum in the year in which the liability arises.

- Dividends are payable the year following their declaration and the board of directors has confirmed to the bank its intention to maintain the company's current dividend payout ratio for the foreseeable future.

A summary of Wexford's most recent draft financial statements is shown below:

Income Statement for the year ended 30 November 20X8

	£'000
Revenue	270,000
Direct costs (Note)	171,000
Indirect costs	40,000
Operating profit	59,000
Interest	5,000
Profit before tax	54,000
Taxation	11,340
Profit after tax	42,660

Note. Includes depreciation of £19m.

The company has declared a dividend that will cost £22,680,000.

Balance Sheet at 30 November 20X8

	£'000	£'000
Non-current assets (carrying amount)		152,590
Current assets		
Inventory	35,000	
Trade receivables	49,000	
Cash at bank	10,500	
		94,500
		247,090
Capital and reserves		
£1 Ordinary shares		50,000
Retained earnings		81,410
		131,410
Non-current liabilities		
10% Debentures (repayable 20Y5)		50,000
Current liabilities		
Trade payables	43,000	
Dividends payable	22,680	
		65,680
		247,090

Requirements

52.1 For each of the financing alternatives being considered, prepare a forecast Income Statement for the year ending 30 November 20X9 and a forecast Balance Sheet at 30 November 20X9.

(16 marks)

Note. Transaction costs on the issuing of new capital and returns on surplus cash invested in the short term can both be ignored.

52.2 Write a report (including appropriate calculations) to Wexford's board of directors that fully evaluates the two potential methods of financing the company's expansion plans. **(14 marks)**

Total: 30 marks

53 Loxwood

Loxwood is a firm of ICAEW Chartered Accountants. You work in its Business Valuations Unit (BVU) which advises clients wishing either (a) to sell their own business or (b) to purchase a new business. You are currently advising three of Loxwood's clients:

Client One

Walton plc (Walton) is considering making takeover bids for two of its competitors, Hampton plc (Hampton) and Richmond Ltd (Richmond). Loxwood has been asked to advise Walton as to what value it should place on these target companies. You have obtained the following financial data:

	Walton	Hampton	Richmond
Profit before interest and tax (year ended 28 February 20X4)	£36.2m	£5.5m	£4.8m
Average annual growth in profit after tax (years ended 28 February 20X0-20X4)	5%	7.5%	9%
Average dividend pay-out ratio (years ended 28 February 20X0-20X4)	30%	35%	45%
P/E ratio (at 28 February 20X4)	16.5	15.2	Not available
Cost of equity (estimated)	5.0%	9%	10.5%

Balance Sheet extracts at 28 February 20X4

	Walton £m	Hampton £m	Richmond £m
Non-current assets (Note 1)	177.0	32.7	22.4
Current assets (Note 1)	146.5	22.8	33.3
Current liabilities	(96.5)	(11.3)	(13.7)
Non-current liabilities (Note 2)	(70.0)	(22.5)	(19.3)
	157.0	21.7	22.7
Ordinary share capital (£1 shares)	62.0	17.6	9.8
Retained earnings	95.0	4.1	12.9
	157.0	21.7	22.7

Notes

1   These assets have been professionally valued on 28 February 20X4 as follows:

	Hampton £m	Richmond £m
Non-current assets	45.2	24.1
Current assets	25.1	35.2

2   The non-current liabilities are all debentures, redeemable within the next six years, with coupon rates as follows: Hampton, 7%; Richmond, 8%.

Assume that the corporation tax rate will be 21% pa for the foreseeable future.

Client Two

Jackie Wight has run a very successful fashion business, Regent Spark Ltd, for many years and is now considering selling it and taking early retirement. She has read a recent article in the financial press and is concerned that she won't get a fair price for her company. As a result she has contacted Loxwood for guidance. Extracts from the article appear below:

'Angel Ventures (AV) recently bid for biometrics company Praed Bio (PB), offering PB's shareholders £5.20 a share. Maida Money (MM), a hedge fund that owns PB shares, disliked the deal and sought a court's opinion on fair value. MM wanted £10.25 a share. AV countered with £5.10. In court, the judge, using shareholder value analysis (SVA), settled on £5.80 but said there were problems in estimating future cash flows and in calculating the value of the cash flows after the competitive advantage period (the residual value).'

Client Three

Doug Williams owns 60 acres of agricultural land in south west England and is considering accepting an offer from So Lah Energy Ltd (SLE) to install solar panels on his land. SLE would pay Doug £1,000 per acre pa (in 28 February 20X4 prices) at the end of each of the next 10 years for the use of his land, after which time it would revert back to agricultural use. To take account of the general rate of inflation, SLE will increase this payment by 3% pa (compound). One of Doug's neighbours, Bill Etheridge, is very unhappy at the prospect of this solar farm and is prepared to buy Doug's land from him for £500,000 in order to stop it being built. The land has a market value of £120,000 in agricultural use on 28 February 20X4 and this is expected to rise in line with the general rate of inflation, ie, 3% pa. Doug could invest Bill's money in a bank account bearing interest at 4% pa, but he is unsure whether he should accept his offer.

Requirements

53.1 For Client One, prepare a report for Walton's board advising it of a range of suitable prices for both Hampton and Richmond using asset, dividend and earnings based valuations. Your report should include your workings supported by a clear commentary as to the strengths and weaknesses of each of the valuation methods used.   **(20 marks)**

53.2 For Client Two, explain how SVA works and why future cash flows and the residual value are such problems.   **(7 marks)**

53.3 For Client Three, ignoring tax, advise Doug Williams as to whether he should accept Bill's offer. You should support your answer with workings and any assumptions that you make should be clearly stated.   **(5 marks)**

53.4 Loxwood is planning a new marketing campaign for its BVU. Outline the key ethical issues that Loxwood should consider when planning this campaign.   **(3 marks)**

Total: 35 marks

54 Arleyhill Redland plc

Arleyhill Redland plc (AR) is a UK listed manufacturer of domestic kitchen equipment. AR's directors are planning to expand and update the company's product range through a mixture of organic growth and the acquisition of smaller competitors. These plans would require an additional £12 million of funding (to be raised in September 20X3) and you, as a project analyst at AR, have been asked to prepare working papers to aid the directors' decision as to which source of finance to use. AR's financial year ends on 31 August and extracts from its most recent management accounts are shown below:

Income Statement for the year to 31 August 20X3

	£'000
Sales	54,400
Variable costs	(32,640)
Fixed costs	(8,200)
Profit before interest	13,560
Debenture interest	(930)
Profit before tax	12,630
Taxation (@ 21%)	(2,652)
Profit after tax	9,978
Dividends	(1,728)
Retained profit	8,250

Balance Sheet at 31 August 20X3

	£'000
Ordinary share capital (£1)	28,800
Revenue reserves	30,850
6% debentures	15,500
	75,150
Total assets less current liabilities	75,150

Market research commissioned by AR's directors has estimated that the £12 million of additional funding would increase annual turnover from September 20X3 by one fifth and that this expansion of the company's operations would also lead to an additional £0.5 million of annual fixed costs. The directors also expect AR's contribution to sales ratio to remain unchanged. Two methods of raising the additional funding have been suggested:

(1)   A rights issue at £2.50 per share; or
(2)   An issue of 7% debentures at par.

The most recent board meeting was held on 2 September 20X3 and an extract from the minutes of that meeting is shown here:

'Martin Cotham (Finance Director) suggested that AR should raise the £12 million via a rights issue. The current share price is £3.10. If the issue was priced at £2.50 per share, he thought this was sufficient a discount to be attractive to shareholders and should guarantee a successful outcome. He said it's also good as it reduces AR's gearing and so will send the shareholders a positive message. He felt if, after the rights issue, AR could get its share price up above its current level, even if it's only a £0.20 per share increase, then the rights issue looks like the best method.'

'Amy Wills (Managing Director) said that we should issue more debentures as (1) the rights issue will dilute the value of AR's shares and (2) AR is not making enough use of the tax shield. She also said that a rights issue might upset the shareholders, as, if they can't afford it and don't take up the rights, they would lose money. The debentures would also put less pressure on AR to maintain annual dividend levels and, thereby, maintain investors' confidence in us. A slightly higher coupon rate of 7% would make the debentures more attractive than those currently in issue. She also said we should consider other types of debt such as convertibles and loan stock with warrants.'

Requirements

54.1 Aside from the factors already identified by Martin Cotham and Amy Wills, outline the other factors that should be considered by a company contemplating a rights issue as a means of raising finance. **(4 marks)**

54.2 Using the market research estimates above, and assuming that AR's dividend per share remains unchanged, prepare AR's forecast Income Statement for the year to 31 August 20X4 if it uses:

- A rights issue at £2.50 per share; or
- An issue of 7% debentures at par to raise the £12 million of additional funding required. **(9 marks)**

54.3 Calculate AR's earnings per share for the year to 31 August 20X3 and, for both financing methods, its estimated earnings per share for the year to 31 August 20X4. **(5 marks)**

54.4 Calculate AR's gearing ratio (in book and market value terms) on 31 August 20X3 and similarly, for both financing methods, its gearing ratio on 31 August 20X4. You should assume that on 31 August 20X4 AR's ordinary share price is £3.30 per share and that its debentures are quoted at par on 31 August 20X3 and 31 August 20X4. **(8 marks)**

54.5 Using the calculations undertaken in 54.2, 54.3 and 54.4, advise AR's directors of the key issues to consider en deciding whether to raise the required funds via a rights issue or a debenture issue. **(5 marks)**

54.6 Explain the differences between convertible loan stock and loan stock with warrants. **(4 marks)**

Total: 35 marks

55 Sennen plc

You should assume that the current date is 31 May 20X4.

Sennen plc (Sennen) is a UK listed company in the chemical industry. Morgan plc (Morgan) is a UK listed company that has a policy of expanding by way of acquisition. As a result of financing its acquisitions with borrowings, Morgan's gearing is high compared to its competitors.

Morgan has identified Sennen as a potential takeover target and intends to make an offer for all of the ordinary shares of the company. The finance director of Morgan wishes to value Sennen's ordinary shares including any synergistic benefits that may arise following the acquisition. He is also considering the advantages and disadvantages of the different methods that can be used to pay for the ordinary shares. The intended offer for Sennen is not public knowledge.

The finance director of Morgan has asked North West Corporate Finance (NWCF) to give him advice regarding the intended offer for the ordinary shares of Sennen. You work for NWCF and a partner in the firm has asked you to prepare a report for a meeting that he is due to attend with the board of Morgan. You have established the following data relating to Sennen:

Sales revenue for the year ended 31 May 20X4	£20 million
Competitive advantage period	3 years
Estimated sales revenue growth for the next three years	5% pa
Estimated sales revenue growth thereafter in perpetuity	2% pa
Operating profit margin	15%
Additional working capital investment at the start of each year	1% of that year's sales revenue
Additional non-current asset investment at the end of each year	2% of that year's sales revenue
After tax synergies at the end of each year	2.5% of that year's sales revenue
Number of ordinary shares in issue	17,000,000
Current share price	160p
Appropriate weighted average cost of capital	7% pa
Price earnings (p/e) multiple used to value recent takeovers in the chemical industry	17

You may assume that replacement non-current asset expenditure equals depreciation in each year.

On 31 May 20X4 Sennen had short-term investments with a market value of £2 million currently yielding 3% pa and irredeemable debt with a market value of £10 million. The current gross yield on Sennen's debt is 5% pa.

Assume that corporation tax will be 21% of operating profits for the foreseeable future and that there are no other tax issues that need to be considered.

The management team of Sennen, which includes a member of the ICAEW, has been preparing a business plan to present to potential financial backers of a management buyout (MBO) that they intend to launch for the ordinary shares of the company. The intended MBO is not public knowledge.

Requirements

55.1 Prepare a report for the partner in NWCF which includes:

(a) The estimated value of the ordinary shares of Sennen calculated using Shareholder Value Analysis (SVA) and an explanation of the strengths and weaknesses of this valuation method.

(13 marks)

(b) The sensitivity of the total value of Sennen (debt plus the value of equity calculated in (a) above) to a change in the after tax synergies.

(3 marks)

(c) The value of the ordinary shares of Sennen using the p/e method and an explanation of the strengths and weaknesses of this valuation method.

(5 marks)

(d) A discussion of whether Morgan should offer the shareholders of Sennen a premium over its current share price given the valuations calculated in parts (a) and (c).

(3 marks)

(e) Advice on the suitability of each of the following methods that Morgan could use to pay for the ordinary shares of Sennen:

- Cash
- A share for share exchange
- A loan stock for share exchange
- Part cash and part share for share exchange

(8 marks)

55.2 Identify and briefly discuss the ethical issues faced by the MBO team should Morgan make an offer for the ordinary shares of Sennen.

(3 marks)

Total: 35 marks

56 Megagreat plc

Megagreat plc has recently announced a takeover bid for Angelic plc. The offer is that for every four Angelic plc ordinary shares the owner would receive three ordinary shares in Megagreat plc plus £6 in cash. Both companies are listed.

According to published estimates, if Angelic plc were to remain independent the company would pay its next dividend in one year's time at 37p per share. Subsequently dividends are expected to grow by an average 5% pa. Angelic plc has an equity cost of capital of 12% pa.

Estimates for Megagreat plc, assuming that the takeover goes ahead, suggest that a dividend of 43p per share will be paid in one year's time and the same amount in two years' time. In three years' time the dividend paid will be 7% higher than the 43p to be paid next year and the year after. This rate of growth is expected to continue indefinitely. The expanded Megagreat plc is expected to have a cost of equity of 11% pa.

Requirements

56.1 Show calculations that indicate whether, on the basis of the published estimates, Angelic plc shareholders would be advised to accept the offer from Megagreat plc.

(6 marks)

56.2 Discuss reasons why any particular shareholder might look beyond the result of the calculations in 56.1 when deciding whether to accept the offer.

(4 marks)

56.3 Suggest the possible effect on Angelic plc's ordinary share price of the announcement of the bid, stating and explaining any assumptions made in reaching your conclusion.

(4 marks)

56.4 Suggest and explain any other strategies that Megagreat plc could use to achieve growth, apart from taking over other businesses.

(3 marks)

Total: 17 marks

57 Printwise UK plc

You are employed by Printwise UK plc (Printwise), a very large printing firm with retail outlets across the UK. Its board is considering making an offer to buy 100% of the shares of Leyton Stratford Limited (LSL), a competitor of Printwise in the south east of England. LSL's financial year end is 28 February and its most recent financial statements are summarised below:

LSL Income Statement for the year ended 28 February 20X0

	£m
Revenue	17.3
Profit before interest and tax	5.9
Interest	(0.3)
Profit before taxation	5.6
Corporation tax at 21%	(1.2)
Profit after taxation	4.4
Dividends declared	1.1

LSL Balance Sheet at 28 February 20X0

	£m	£m	£m
Non-current assets:			
Freehold land and buildings (original cost £4.1m)			3.5
Machinery (original cost £8.8m)			5.3
			8.8
Current assets:			
Inventories		3.0	
Receivables		0.5	
Cash and bank		2.8	
		6.3	
Current liabilities:			
Trade payables	3.5		
Dividends	1.1		
Taxation	1.2		
		(5.8)	
			0.5
			9.3
Non-current liabilities:			
10% debentures (redeemable 20Y0)			(3.0)
			6.3
Equity:			
Ordinary shares of £1 each			2.1
Retained earnings			4.2
			6.3

Additional information

LSL's management had some of the company's assets independently revalued in January 20X0. Those values are shown below:

	£m
Freehold land and buildings	8.3
Machinery	4.1
Inventories	3.1

The average price/earnings ratio for listed businesses in the printing industry is 9 and the average dividend yield is 6% pa.

The cost of equity of businesses in the printing industry, taking account of the industry average level of capital gearing, is 14% pa.

LSL's finance department has estimated that the company's pre-tax net cash inflows (after interest) for the next four trading years ending 28 February, before taking account of capital allowances, will be:

	£m
Year to 20X1	4.6
Year to 20X2	4.3
Year to 20X3	5.2
Year to 20X4	5.7

LSL's machinery pool for taxation purposes had a written-down value of £3.6 million at 28 February 20X0. The pool attracts 18% (reducing balance) tax allowances in every year of ownership by the company, except the final year. In the final year, the difference between the machinery's written-down value for tax purposes and its disposal proceeds will be either (a) treated by the company as an additional tax relief, if the disposal proceeds are less than the tax written-down value, or (b) be treated as a balancing charge to the company, if the disposal proceeds are more than the tax written-down value. You should assume that LSL will not be purchasing or disposing of any machinery in the years 20X1-20X4 and that it would dispose of the existing pool of machinery on 28 February 20X4 at its tax written-down value.

Printwise's board estimates that in four years' time, ie 28 February 20X4, it could, if necessary, dispose of LSL for an amount equal to four times its after-tax cash flow (ignoring the effects of capital allowances and the disposal value of the machinery) for the year to 28 February 20X4.

Assume that the corporation tax rate is 21% pa.

Requirements

Using the information provided, prepare a report for Printwise's board which:

57.1 Calculates the value of one share in LSL based on each of these methods:

    (a)   Net asset basis (historic cost).
    (b)   Net asset basis (revalued).
    (c)   Price/earnings ratio.
    (d)   Dividend yield.
    (e)   Present value of future cash flows.

(16 marks)

57.2 Explains the advantages and disadvantages of using each of the five valuation methods in 57.1.

(8 marks)

57.3 Identifies and explains the different methods by which the LSL shareholders could be remunerated for their shares.

(6 marks)

Total: 30 marks

58 Tower Brazil plc

You are an ICAEW Chartered Accountant and work in the finance team at Tower Brazil plc (Tower). The company manufactures wallpaper and paint for major UK homeware retailers and has been trading since 2001. It has a financial year end of 31 August. Extracts from its most recent management accounts are shown below.

Income Statement for the year ended 31 August 20X4

	£'000
Profit before interest	9,356
Debenture interest	(2,338)
Profit before tax	7,018
Tax at 21%	(1,474)
Profit after tax	5,544
Dividends - preference shares	(480)
Dividends - ordinary shares	(4,509)
Retained profits	555

Balance Sheet at 31 August 20X4

	£'000
£1 ordinary share capital	16,500
Retained earnings	26,420
	42,920
6% £1 preference shares	8,000
5% debentures at nominal value (redeemable 20X6)	46,750
	97,670

The market values of Tower's long-term finance on 31 August 20X4 are shown below:

£1 ordinary share capital	£4.20/share
6% £1 preference shares	£0.80/share
5% debentures	£110%

Extracts from the minutes of Tower's board meeting, 1 September 20X4

AB (Production Director) once again raised the issue of Tower's 'gearing problem' and said that gearing was now over 50%. DB (Marketing Director) and WR (Sales Director) concurred. All three felt that gearing should be reduced as a matter of urgency, otherwise, according to AB, it's very risky and the company's share price (and cost of capital) will be adversely affected which will make new projects difficult to justify.

It was agreed to investigate the implications of using a rights issue to address the gearing problem. The rights issue would enable ordinary shareholders to significantly increase their investment and so reward them for their loyalty. It was proposed that a one for two rights issue would be made, but concerns were raised that this would reduce the company's earnings per share figure by more than 10%.

WR raised the point that dividends have increased 3% pa on average over the past five years. He suggested that rather than raising more capital the company could change its dividend policy. As a result it would retain more of its profits for re-investment. He thought this would not be popular with shareholders, but that, if they **did** react badly to the change then Tower could always pay a one-off special dividend to make up for any shortfall.

As a result of these discussions the board decided to explore the implications of making a 1 for 2 rights issue which would raise sufficient funds to purchase and cancel 60% of Tower's debentures by market value.

In advance of the next board meeting, you have been asked by your manager, Luke Cleeve, to prepare calculations and advice for Tower's directors. Luke pointed out to you that you should 'be careful with this information as it's potentially price sensitive and not in the public domain.'

Assume that the corporation tax rate will be 21% pa for the foreseeable future.

Requirements

58.1 Calculate Tower's theoretical ex-rights share price if a 1 for 2 rights issue were made on 1 September 20X4. **(3 marks)**

58.2 (a) Calculate Tower's earnings per share figure for the year ended 31 August 20X4 and for the year ended 31 August 20X5 after the proposed rights issue (assuming no change in profit before interest).

(b) Calculate and comment on the terms of the rights issue required if the earnings per share figure is not to worsen by more than 10% for the year ended 31 August 20X5. **(11 marks)**

58.3 Calculate Tower's gearing (debt/debt + equity) at 31 August 20X4 using both book and market values and advise its board as to whether it has a 'gearing problem' and how its gearing level could affect its share price. Where relevant, make reference to theories regarding the impact of capital structure on share price. **(9 marks)**

58.4 Advise Tower's board as to whether the suggested change in dividend policy would have a negative impact on the company's share price. Where relevant, make reference to theories regarding the impact of dividend policy on share price. **(9 marks)**

58.5 Explain the ethical implications for an ICAEW Chartered Accountant of having access to 'price-sensitive information'. **(3 marks)**

Total: 35 marks

59 Hildes and Heimer

Hildes and Heimer have each owned 50% of the issued share capital of Kelly Ltd since its incorporation 45 years ago and are its only directors. Kelly Ltd supplies computer hardware and software and during the past few years has grown significantly. It now operates through four divisions, each of which has its own manager who is responsible for the day-to-day operations of his division.

Heimer now wishes to retire and sell his shares in Kelly Ltd; if possible, Hildes wishes to continue to run Kelly Ltd as a private company.

The directors have asked you to determine the value of Kelly Ltd's shares and advise on possible ways in which Heimer may be able to realise his investment in Kelly Ltd.

Kelly Ltd's recent trading results and its forecast results for the coming year are

	Year to 30 November	
	20X7	20X8
	£'000	£'000
Sales	4,000	4,500
Profit before taxation	350	400
Taxation @ 21%	74	84
Profit after taxation	276	316

You also ascertain the following information about Kelly Ltd.

(1) Its balance sheet at 30 November 20X7, prepared on an historical cost basis, showed total net assets as follows:

	£'000
Land and buildings	300
Plant and equipment	150
Net current assets	280
Net assets	730

The above amounts reflect the current market value of the assets with the exception of land and buildings, the value of which is £500,000.

(2) Both Hildes and Heimer received directors' emoluments of £75,000 during the year ended 30 November 20X7 and have included similar amounts in the forecast for the coming year. If Heimer retires, an accountant would have to be employed at an annual cost of £25,000.

(3) Your review of Kelly Ltd's corporate plan reveals that its future growth in earnings is expected to be 8% per annum.

(4) No dividends have been paid in the past five years.

You have researched comparable quoted companies and found one such company whose cum div market value is £6.05 per share, has a dividend growth rate of 7%, a proposed dividend of £0.70 per share and a price earnings ratio of 14. Your research has led you to conclude that the cost of equity of Kelly Ltd would be 4% lower than this company's.

Requirements

59.1 Prepare a report to the directors of Kelly Ltd covering

- The maximum amount that a potential purchaser should be prepared to pay for Heimer's shares

- The minimum amount Heimer should be prepared to accept

Your report should include an explanation of the valuation bases you have used to arrive at your recommendations and any assumptions you have made. **(20 marks)**

59.2 Discuss the ways in which Heimer may be able to realise his investment whilst also enabling Hildes to continue to run Kelly Ltd as a private company. **(5 marks)**

Total: 25 marks

Note. Assume a corporation tax rate of 21% throughout.

60 Pinky and Perky

Pinky plc and Perky plc operate in the same field, manufacturing children's clothes and toys although Perky plc also has interests in sportswear and equipment. Pinky plc is planning to take over Perky plc and the shareholders of Perky plc do not regard it as a hostile bid.

The following information is available about the two companies.

	Pinky plc	Perky plc
Current earnings	£650,000	£240,000
Number of shares	5,000,000	1,500,000
Percentage earnings retained	20%	80%
Return on new investment	15%	15%
Return required by ordinary shareholders	21%	24%

Dividends have just been paid and the retained earnings have already been reinvested in new projects. Pinky plc plans to adopt a policy of retaining 35% of earnings after the takeover and expects to achieve a 17% return on new investment.

Savings due to economies of scale are expected to be in the region of £85,000 per annum.

Required return to ordinary shareholders will fall to 20% due to portfolio effects. Neither company is quoted.

Requirements

60.1 Calculate the existing share values of Pinky plc and Perky plc.   (4 marks)

60.2 Find the value of Pinky plc after the takeover.   (6 marks)

60.3 Advise Pinky plc on the maximum amount it should pay for Perky plc.   (3 marks)

60.4 What reasons might a company have for buying another company?   (7 marks)

Total: 20 marks

Note. Ignore taxation.

61 Brennan plc

Brennan plc is a family run business, which obtained a stock market listing around three years ago. The board is comprised of 75% of members of the founding family. Brennan plc has a current stock market capitalisation of £250 million and the board owns 45% of the issued shares. The net book value of assets held by Brennan plc is £300 million.

Brennan currently enjoys competitive advantage through being a low cost producer and the board feels that this competitive advantage is likely to continue for the next six years. The following information relating to Brennan and the period of competitive advantage is available.

Current sales revenue	£200 million
Estimated sales growth	6%
Operating profit margin after depreciation	15%
Additional working capital investment	7% of sales increase
Additional non-current asset investment	12% of sales increase

Following the end of the period of competitive advantage, cash flows are expected to remain constant for the foreseeable future.

Brennan plc currently has no long-term debt and holds short-term investments worth £2.5 million. The corporation tax rate is expected to be 21% for the foreseeable future.

Brennan plc has an equity beta of 0.75, the risk free rate of interest is 3% and the return on the market portfolio is 11%.

Brennan plc has a policy of paying out 10% of its post-tax earnings as dividends.

Requirements

61.1 Calculate the value of Brennan plc using SVA methodology and comment on the results.

(13 marks)

61.2 Discuss the reasons why Brennan plc has a market capitalisation lower than its net book value of assets.

(7 marks)

Total: 20 marks

62 Lipton plc

Lipton plc (Lipton) is a listed company which operates in the pharmaceutical sector, manufacturing a broad range of drugs under licence in a number of countries. Around 75% of the book value of Lipton's non-current assets comprises factories situated across Europe. In recent years the company has grown organically but a proposal has now been put forward by the company's investment bank that the company might consider the acquisition of a smaller firm, Becal Ltd (Becal), as a route to both further expansion and diversification of the company's activities.

Becal is involved in a different area of the pharmaceutical sector from Lipton as it is primarily a research-driven company involved in the development of new drugs arising from the latest academic research, often working with research departments of universities and teaching hospitals to turn the research into commercial reality.

The majority of Becal's shares are owned by members of the three founding families, many of whom still work for the company. They are now considering selling Becal if a suitable price can be agreed.

The following financial information has been obtained for Lipton, along with comparative information for Becal:

	Lipton	Becal
Forecast earnings in next financial year (£ million)	7.50	2.00
Shares in issue (million)	12.50	0.75
Current earnings per share (pence)	56.25	76.50
Current dividend per share (pence)	25.30	50.00
Share price (pence)	618.50	n/a
Book value of equity (£ million)	175.00	22.50
Gearing ratio (debt as a % of market value)	25.00	0
Forecast dividend growth rate pa	3%	6%
Cost of equity	7%	n/a

Becal does not calculate a cost of equity, but the average for listed companies operating in the same sector is 8%. At this stage, the directors of Lipton have identified either a rights issue or a floating rate term loan as the most likely method by which they might finance the purchase of Becal.

Requirements

62.1 In your role as a corporate finance manager at Lipton, prepare a report to Lipton's directors which provides valuations of Becal using:

    (a) Net assets

    (b) Dividends

    (c) Current and forecast earnings (using Lipton's current price-earnings ratio)

    and, for each valuation calculated, identify any specific reservations or other issues that you might wish to bring to the attention of Lipton's directors.

(16 marks)

62.2 Evaluate (without undertaking any calculations) the two potential methods of financing the purchase of Becal.

(8 marks)

62.3 Discuss the relative advantages of organic growth and growth by acquisition.

(6 marks)

62.4 As a Chartered Accountant working for Becal, explain how you would deal with a request from the three founding families to provide Lipton with forecasts of earnings and dividend growth far in excess of those stated in the table above.

(5 marks)

Total: 35 marks

63 Fratton plc

63.1 Fratton plc (Fratton) trades extensively in Europe. The firm is due to receive €2,960,000 in three months' time. The following information is available:

(1) The spot exchange rate is currently €1.1845 – 1.1856/£.

(2) The three-month forward rate of exchange is currently at a 0.79 – 0.59 cent premium.

(3) The prices of three-month sterling traded option contracts (premiums in cents per £ are payable up front, with a standard contract size of £62,500) are as follows:

Exercise price	Calls	Puts
€1.18	2.40	3.60

(4) Annual interest rates at the present time are as follows:

	Deposit	Borrowing
UK	1.15%	2.40%
Eurozone	0.75%	1.60%

Requirements

(a) Calculate the net sterling receipt that Fratton can expect in three months' time if it hedges its foreign exchange exposure using:

- The forward market
- The money market
- The options market, assuming the spot exchange rate in three months is:

  - €1.1185 - 1.1200/£
  - €1.1985 - 1.2000/£ **(14 marks)**

(b) Discuss the advantages and disadvantages of using futures contracts as opposed to forward contracts when hedging foreign currency exposure. **(7 marks)**

63.2 In addition, in three months' time Fratton will be drawing down a three-month £2.5 million loan facility which is granted each year by its bank to see the firm through its peak borrowing period. The following information is available:

(1) The quotation for a '3-6' forward rate agreement is currently 2.60 – 1.35.

(2) The spot rate of interest today is 2.40% pa and the relevant three-month sterling interest rate futures contract (standard contract size £500,000) is currently trading at 97.20.

Requirements

(a) Explain how Fratton could use a forward rate agreement to resolve the uncertainty surrounding its future borrowing costs and show the effect if, in three months' time, the spot rate of interest is 3% pa. **(4 marks)**

(b) Explain how Fratton could use sterling interest rate futures to hedge its exposure to interest rate risk and show the effect if, in three months' time, the spot rate of interest is 3% pa and the price of the interest rate futures contract has fallen to 97. **(5 marks)**

Total: 30 marks

64 Dayton plc

Assume throughout this question that the current date is 31 December 20X1

64.1 Dayton plc (Dayton) is a UK manufacturer of thermal insulation products and does a significant amount of business in mainland Europe. The company has just delivered a major export order to a customer in Luxembourg at a price of €35 million payable in six months' time and as the company's finance director you are concerned about the potential impact of currency volatility on the profitability of this particular order. You have obtained the following exchange rate and interest rate data at the close of business today:

Spot rate (€/£)   1.1735 - 1.1760
6-month forward rate   0.34 cent - 0.26 cent premium

Annual interest rates:	Deposit	Borrowing
UK	2.25%	2.50%
Eurozone	1.75%	2.00%

Dayton's bank has quoted a premium of £100,000 (payable up-front) for a €35 million six-month over-the-counter currency put option with an exercise price of €1.17/£. Dayton has the £100,000 available on deposit at the current time and would leave it on deposit for the next six months if it was not used to purchase the currency put option.

Requirements

(a) Calculate the unhedged sterling value of the €35 million receivable if, in six months' time, sterling has depreciated by 5%. **(2 marks)**

(b) Calculate the hedged sterling value of the €35 million receivable if Dayton chooses to use a forward exchange contract. **(2 marks)**

(c) Calculate the hedged sterling value of the €35 million receivable if Dayton chooses to use a money market hedge and calculate the effective forward exchange rate achieved. **(2 marks)**

(d) Calculate the hedged sterling value of the €35 million receivable if Dayton chooses to use an over-the-counter currency put option and the spot exchange rate in six months' time is:

    (1) €1.14/£
    (2) €1.20/£   **(3 marks)**

(e) Discuss how the principle of interest rate parity explains the difference between the spot and forward rates of exchange quoted above. **(3 marks)**

(f) With regard to a firm's exposure to exchange rate movements, distinguish between economic exposure and translation exposure. **(2 marks)**

(g) Discuss the long-term strategies a firm may adopt to hedge its economic exposure. **(4 marks)**

64.2 Dayton's employee pension fund currently holds a portfolio of FTSE 100 shares with a value of £48 million. The pension fund trustees are worried that by the end of September 20X2, when they plan to liquidate much of the portfolio, share prices will have fallen. They are considering the use of FTSE 100 index futures to hedge against the risk of capital loss. The current value of the FTSE 100 index is 5,000. The index value for contracts to be completed at the end of September 20X2 is 4,900 and the price of futures is £10 per full index point.

Requirements

(a) Assuming that at the end of September 20X2 the portfolio value has dropped to £46.98 million, and the September 20X2 future is quoted at 4,800, illustrate how a FTSE 100 index futures hedge could protect the pension fund against a drop in share prices, showing the value of each contract and the required number of contracts to effect the hedge. **(4 marks)**

(b) Calculate and explain the hedge efficiency achieved by the FTSE 100 index futures hedge. **(2 marks)**

64.3 Dayton has a subsidiary, Fulton Energy Ltd (Fulton), a manufacturer of domestic heating products. Fulton's business tends to be highly seasonal. From September to March the business tends to be highly cash generative but in the other six months of the year the business needs to borrow to cover its outgoings.

At the end of March 20X2 Fulton will move into its six-month borrowing period and will need to borrow £3m for the entire six months. Fulton's directors are concerned that interest rates are expected to increase over the next few months. Annual interest rates and forward rate agreements (FRAs) are currently quoted as follows:

Spot   2.50 – 2.25%
3-6 FRA   2.57 – 2.34%
3-9 FRA   2.69 – 2.39%

Requirement

By calculating the interest cash flows, demonstrate the result of using a forward rate agreement and state the effective loan rate achieved if on 31 March 20X2 the relevant spot interest rate has moved to:

(a)   3.5%
(b)   1.5%   **(4 marks)**

Total: 28 marks

65   Sunwin plc

65.1 The finance director of Sunwin plc (Sunwin) is a trustee of the firm's employee pension fund. The vast majority of the fund's assets are currently invested in a portfolio of FTSE 100 shares. It is 1 December 20X2 and the trustees are concerned that FTSE 100 share prices will fall over the next month and they wish to hedge against this possibility by using FTSE index options. The current market value of the pension fund's portfolio of shares is £5.6 million. The FTSE 100 index stands at 5,000 on 1 December 20X2 and the directors wish to protect the current value of the portfolio. The trustees have obtained the following information as at 1 December 20X2:

FTSE 100 INDEX OPTIONS: £10 per full index point (points per contract)

	4,900		4,950		5,000		5,050		5,100	
	Call	Put	Call	Put	Call	Put	Call	Put	Call	Put
December	139	34	104	48	74	70	49	99	34	134
January	214	94	184	114	154	134	124	159	104	189
February	275	135	245	155	220	180	190	200	165	225

Requirement

Demonstrate how FTSE 100 index options can be used by the trustees to hedge the pension fund's exposure to falling share prices and show the outcome if, on 31 December 20X2, the portfolio's value:

(a)   Rises to £6.608 million and the FTSE index rises to 5,900;
(b)   Falls to £4.592 million and the FTSE index falls to 4,100.   **(8 marks)**

65.2 It is 1 December 20X2 and Sunwin's board of directors has recently agreed to purchase machinery from a UK supplier on 28 February 20X3. The firm's cash flow forecasts reveal that the firm will need to borrow £4 million on 28 February 20X3 for a period of nine months. The directors are concerned that short-term sterling interest rates may rise between now and the end of February and are considering the use of either sterling short-term interest rate futures or traded interest rate options on futures to hedge against the firm's exposure to interest rate rises.

The spot rate of interest on 1 December is 3% pa and March three-month sterling interest rate futures with a contract size of £500,000 are trading at 96. Information regarding traded interest options on futures on 1 December 20X2 is as follows:

Strike Price	Calls			Puts		
	March	June	September	March	June	September
96.25	0.20	0.23	0.25	0.18	0.96	1.66
96.50	0.09	0.10	0.11	0.32	1.19	1.89
96.75	0.05	0.06	0.07	0.53	1.43	2.14

Premiums are in annual % terms.

Requirements

(a) Demonstrate how sterling short-term interest rate futures can be used by Sunwin to hedge against interest rate rises, and show the effective loan rate achieved and the hedge efficiency if, on 28 February 20X3, the spot rate of interest is 4.5% pa and the March interest rate futures price has fallen to 95.

(6 marks)

(b) Demonstrate how traded interest rate options on futures can be used by Sunwin to hedge against the interest rate rising above 3.75% pa and show the effective loan rate achieved if, on 28 February 20X3:

(1) The spot price is 4.4% pa and the futures price is 95.31.
(2) The spot price is 2.1% pa and the futures price is 97.75.

(9 marks)

(c) Identify three factors that will affect the time value of an option.

(3 marks)

Total: 26 marks

66 Atherton plc and Tyldesley Inc

66.1 Atherton plc (Atherton) is a UK manufacturer of trains, which it sells to many EU countries as well as to countries further afield. In three months' time, Atherton is due to receive €8 million from a Belgian customer. At a board meeting today, the directors will be discussing whether or not there is a need to hedge the foreign exchange exposure associated with this transaction and, if so, how best this might be achieved. At the board meeting, three possible alternatives will be considered:

(1) Not to hedge this transaction.

(2) Use a forward contract. Exchange rates quoted by Atherton's bank today are:

Spot	€1.1648 – 1.1708/£
3-months forward	€0.0110 – 0.0100 premium

(3) Use an over-the-counter currency option on euro which is available through Atherton's bank. Current premiums at an exercise price of €1.1750/£ are £1.10 per €100 for a call option and £1.25 per €100 for a put option.

Requirements

(a) Discuss why a firm might reasonably choose not to hedge its exposure to exchange rate risk.

(5 marks)

(b) Show the effect of each of the three alternatives being considered, assuming that the spot exchange rate in three months' time is either (a) €1.1950 – 1.1980/£ or (b) €1.1395 – 1.1420/£.

(7 marks)

(c) Describe **four** methods available to firms to reduce their exposure to foreign exchange risk which do not involve the use of financial contracts.

(4 marks)

66.2 Tyldesley Inc (Tyldesley) is a US company which provides parts and maintenance services to both public and private sector transport operations throughout the US. In order to broaden its geographical reach, Tyldesley has recently entered into negotiations to buy Remedia plc, a company jointly owned by a group of local authorities in the UK. A price of £20 million has been agreed, but conclusion of the deal must await the approval of the local authorities who must each consult their elected bodies to have the deal ratified. Unanimous support from all the local authorities will be required and Tyldesley is aware that there has been some resistance to the sale of this company to an overseas firm. However, the vendors have agreed that, subject to ratification, the deal will be finalised in six months' time.

In light of these developments, the company accountant at Tyldesley is proposing to hedge the company's foreign exchange exposure by using futures contracts. The relevant £ futures contracts are currently priced at $1.6436/£. The £ futures contract size is £62,500. The current spot rate is $1.6520/£.

Requirement

(a) Calculate the cost of the purchase if futures contracts are used and if in six months' time the following scenarios occurred:

    (1) A spot rate of $1.6630/£ and a £ futures price of $1.6610/£

    (2) A spot rate of $1.6420/£ and a £ futures price of $1.6400/£   **(8 marks)**

(b) In light of your answers to part (a), discuss the weaknesses of futures contracts as a means of hedging in this scenario.   **(2 marks)**

Total: 26 marks

67 Strauss Cook plc

You should assume for all parts of this question that today's date is 1 February 20X0.

67.1 Strauss Cook plc (Strauss Cook) has a portfolio of large company UK shares which is worth £6.3 million on 1 February 20X0 and the spot value of the FTSE100 index on that date is 4,200. Strauss Cook's board wishes to explore the implications of hedging the company against a potential fall in share prices in the next month. Accordingly, it is considering the use of traded FTSE100 index options. The following information from Euronext.Liffe has been gathered:

FTSE 100 INDEX OPTION (£10 per full index point)

Exercise price	4,100		4,150		4,200		4,250		4,300	
	Call	Put	Call	Put	Call	Put	Call	Put	Call	Put
March	137	31	101	46	72	67	46	97	32	131
April	211	92	181	111	151	132	122	156	101	187
May	272	131	241	152	217	176	186	197	162	221

Assume that the board decides to use options to protect the current value of the portfolio in one month's time.

Requirement

Explain, with supporting workings, what will happen in one month's time if:

(a) The portfolio's value rises to £6.375 million and the FTSE100 index rises to 4,250

(b) The portfolio's value falls to £6.15 million and the FTSE100 index falls to 4,100   **(7 marks)**

67.2 As an alternative to hedging the £6.3 million portfolio with options, Strauss Cook's board is considering using FTSE100 stock index futures. At 1 February 20X0 the quote on Euronext.Liffe for FTSE100 stock index futures in one month is 4,130 and the face value of a FTSE100 index contract is £10 per index point.

Requirements

(a) Calculate the outcome of this hedge if in one month's time the portfolio's value falls to £6.15 million and the FTSE100 index and the FTSE100 stock index futures contract both fall to 4,100.

(b) Comment on whether this hedge has been effective.   **(5 marks)**

67.3 Strauss Cook has also identified the need to invest £2.5 million in the spot market for a six month period from 1 March 20X0. The current spot interest rate is 5.5% pa and Strauss Cook's board wants to protect the company from interest rates falling below 5% pa and is considering the use of traded interest rate options on 3 month sterling futures. These have a contract size of £500,000 and current prices (option premiums are in annual % terms) are:

Strike price	Calls			Puts		
	March	June	Sept	March	June	Sept
94.50	0.18	0.20	0.23	0.15	0.94	1.63
94.75	0.06	0.08	0.09	0.30	1.16	1.87
95.00	0.03	0.04	0.05	0.51	1.40	2.12

Requirements

(a) Calculate the outcome of the hedge if interest rates on 1 March 20X0 are 4.5% pa and the futures price is 95.80.

(b) Explain the implications of using a Forward Rate Agreement rather than options as a means of hedging this investment.

(11 marks)

Total: 23 marks

68 Springfield plc and Woodhouse plc

68.1 Springfield plc (Springfield) wishes to borrow £20 million for five years to finance the purchase of new non-current assets. The preference of the company's directors is that these funds are borrowed at a fixed rate of interest. The company's long-term debt is currently rated BBB, meaning that Springfield would have to pay 6.50% pa for fixed rate borrowing. Alternatively, Springfield could borrow at a floating rate of LIBOR + 2.25% pa at the present time.

The directors of Springfield have recently been informed by its bank that Faversham plc (Faversham) is also currently looking to borrow £20 million for five years at a floating rate of interest and its AA rating gives it access to floating rate borrowing at LIBOR + 1.50% pa. Faversham would pay 5.50% pa for fixed rate borrowing at the present time.

Requirements

(a) State **five** reasons that a company might have for entering into an interest rate swap.

(5 marks)

(b) Show how an interest rate swap could be used to the **equal** benefit of both companies assuming that the terms of the swap agreement are such that Springfield's swap payment to Faversham is to be 5.50% fixed pa.

(5 marks)

(c) Identify, with a supporting explanation, which of the two companies would be disadvantaged if LIBOR were to fall consistently over the five year term of the interest rate swap. **(2 marks)**

(d) Identify **two** risks that the two companies both face should they decide to enter into the interest rate swap agreement.

(2 marks)

68.2 Woodhouse plc (Woodhouse) is planning to borrow £6 million at a fixed rate of interest in March for six months and wishes to protect itself against interest rates rising above 4.75% pa. It is now 15 December and the current interest rate is 4% pa. The following data has been obtained by the company's finance director:

Traded £ options on 3-month futures contracts (contract size £500,000)

Strike Price	Calls			Puts		
	March	June	September	March	June	September
95.25	0.14	0.17	0.19	0.12	0.90	1.60
95.50	0.03	0.04	0.05	0.26	1.13	1.83
95.75	0.01	0.02	0.03	0.47	1.37	2.08

Option premiums are in annual % terms.

Requirements

Demonstrate the outcome of a traded interest rate options hedge (indicating the effective rate of interest achieved by the company on its borrowing) if the interest rate and futures prices on the date the company draws down the loan from its bank are:

(a)   5.4% pa and 94.30 respectively
(b)   3.1% pa and 96.70 respectively   **(11 marks)**

Total: 25 marks

69   Padd Shoes Ltd

You should assume that the current date is 31 March 20X4

You work in the finance team at Padd Shoes Ltd (Padd), a footwear manufacturer and retailer based in the UK. You have been given two tasks to deal with:

Task 1

Padd's chief executive has been contacted by the managing director of a large Indian retailer, DS, who feels that Padd's footwear would sell well in India because, in her words, 'Padd's styles are attractive to our consumers, UK brands are generally highly regarded here in India and our country has a growing middle class with enhanced spending power.'

It has been agreed that, to test the market, Padd will send a large consignment of footwear to DS for sale in its shops across India. The price for this consignment is 200 million Indian rupees (INR), which will be payable by DS on 30 June 20X4.

Padd's board is aware that the Indian rupee has weakened against sterling by almost 2% in the past six months and so it wishes to explore whether to hedge this sale to DS. In addition, because Padd has not traded outside of the UK before, its board has some more general concerns about trading abroad.

You have been asked to prepare advice for the board and have obtained the following information at the close of business on 31 March 20X4:

Spot rate (INR/£)	94.0625 - 95.4930
Sterling interest rate (lending)	3.2% pa
Sterling interest rate (borrowing)	4.0% pa
INR interest rate (lending)	4.2% pa
INR interest rate (borrowing)	4.8% pa
Three-month OTC currency call option on INR – exercise price	INR 94.7500/£
Three-month OTC currency put option on INR – exercise price	INR 95.5500/£
Three-month forward rate discount (INR/£)	0.0195 - 0.2265
Cost of relevant OTC currency option	£8,000
Cost of forward contract	£4,500

Task 2

On 1 April 20X3 Padd borrowed £8.5 million over a four year period at LIBOR + 1% pa to finance an expansion of its production capacity and the refurbishment of a number of its larger stores. Padd's board is now investigating whether it should hedge against adverse interest rate movements over the next 12 months. Its bank has offered either (a) an option at 4% pa plus a premium of 0.75% of the sum borrowed or (b) a Forward Rate Agreement (FRA) at 4.5% pa.

Requirements

69.1 Calculate Padd's sterling receipt from the sale to DS if it:

(a)   Does not hedge the receipt and the Indian rupee weakens by 1% by 30 June 20X4
(b)   Uses an OTC currency option
(c)   Uses a forward contract
(d)   Uses a money market hedge   **(10 marks)**

69.2 With reference to your calculations in 69.1 above, advise Padd's board whether it is worth hedging the DS receipt.   **(8 marks)**

69.3 Advise Padd's board as to the risks, **other than currency risk**, that should be considered if the company is to continue to trade abroad in future.

(5 marks)

69.4 By preparing suitable interest payment calculations, recommend to Padd's board whether it is worth hedging against interest rate movements over the next twelve months if LIBOR is either (a) 3% pa or (b) 6% pa.

(7 marks)

Total: 30 marks

70 Stelvio Ltd

70.1 **You should assume that the current date is 31 May 20X4.**

Stelvio Ltd (Stelvio) imports climbing equipment from suppliers in the USA. In the past Stelvio has not hedged its foreign exchange rate risk and has purchased foreign currency on the spot market as and when required. The managing director of Stelvio, Fred Hughes, has recently been reading about hedging techniques that might assist his company; in particular he has read about the use of forwards, futures and over the counter options. Fred is not convinced about the merits of hedging as he is of the opinion that the forward rate is a good indication of the future spot rate. He believes he can estimate the sterling cost of the company's future foreign currency payments with confidence, without having to use complex derivative instruments.

Stelvio currently has a bank overdraft that costs 6% pa. It has a payment to make of $940,000 on 30 September 20X4.

The following information is available at the close of business on 31 May 20X4:

Exchange rates:

Spot rate ($/£) 1.6025 - 1.6027

Four month forward premium ($/£) 0.0021 - 0.0020

September currency futures price (standard contract size £62,500) $1.5995/£

Over the counter currency option

A September call option to buy $ has an exercise price of $1.6100/£. The premium is 4p per $ and is payable on 31 May 20X4.

Requirements

Produce a report for Fred Hughes which should include:

(a) A calculation of Stelvio's sterling payment if it uses each of the following to hedge its foreign exchange rate risk:

- A forward contract
- Currency futures contracts
- An over the counter currency option.

You should assume that on 30 September 20X4 the spot exchange rate will be $1.5002 – 1.5008/£ and that the sterling currency futures price will be $1.5005/£. (11 marks)

(b) A discussion of the relative advantages and disadvantages of using the methods in part (a) above to hedge Stelvio's foreign exchange rate risk.

(9 marks)

(c) An explanation, making reference to relevant theories regarding foreign exchange rates, of whether Fred is correct that he does not need to hedge Stelvio's foreign exchange rate risk.

(4 marks)

70.2 In May 20W9 Stelvio financed the purchase of a warehouse with a £5 million ten year floating rate loan at LIBOR + 3% pa. Fred Hughes believes that interest rates are going to rise over the next five years and he would like to protect the company against interest rate risk. He has been in contact with Zeta Leasing Ltd (Zeta) which has a policy of keeping a certain proportion of their borrowings at a fixed rate. Zeta would like to swap £5 million of its fixed rate loans to a floating rate. A bank has offered to arrange the swap and Fred has agreed that all the benefits from the swap will be shared equally between Stelvio and Zeta. Stelvio can borrow at a fixed rate of 5% pa. Zeta can borrow at a fixed rate of 3% pa and at a floating rate of LIBOR + 2% pa. LIBOR is currently 0.60% pa.

Requirements

(a) Demonstrate how the proposed interest rate swap between Stelvio and Zeta would be implemented. **(4 marks)**

(b) Calculate the initial difference in annual interest rates for Stelvio if it enters into the interest rate swap and calculate the minimum amount by which LIBOR will have to rise for the swap to breakeven for Stelvio. **(2 marks)**

Total: 30 marks

71 JEK Computing Ltd

You should assume that the current date is 30 September 20X4

You work in the finance team at JEK Computing Ltd (JEK), which is a UK-based computer services company. Founded in 2008, it has to date operated exclusively in the UK but its board recently decided to expand its operations by looking overseas for new contracts.

JEK is ready to submit a tender bid for a contract with the government of Estonia. The local currency in Estonia is the euro. As this would the first in a series of possible contracts with this government, and to make the tender bid more competitive, the board is using a lower sales margin than is usual on its UK contracts. The following summary information has been prepared:

Estonian contract

Total costs plus margin	£12.420 million
Tender bid on 30 September 20X4 at the current spot rate of €1.2165/£	€15.109 million

JEK's board understands that the successful bidder will be announced on 31 October 20X4. If JEK wins the bid then work would start on that date and the board estimates that it would be completed on 31 December 20X4 when payment would be received from the Estonian government.

The board is concerned that the €/£ exchange rate has changed quite significantly over the past three months and that if this trend continues then it could have an impact on the profitability of the contract. The board would like, therefore, to consider hedging against exchange rate risk immediately on 30 September 20X4, even though the outcome of the tender bid is not yet decided.

The spot €/£ exchange rate over the past three months is summarised below:

Exchange rate (€/£)	at 30 June 20X4	1.1150 – 1.1463
	at 31 July 20X4	1.1373 – 1.1692
	at 31 August 20X4	1.1600 – 1.1926
	at 30 September 20X4	1.1832 – 1.2165

You have been asked to advise JEK's board and the following information has been made available to you at the close of business on 30 September 20X4:

Sterling interest rate (lending)	3.2% pa
Sterling interest rate (borrowing)	4.2% pa
Euro interest rate (lending)	2.6% pa
Euro interest rate (borrowing)	3.4% pa
Three-month over the counter (OTC) put option on euro, exercise price (€/£)	1.2150
Three-month over the counter (OTC) call option on euro, exercise price (€/£)	1.1818
Three-month forward contract premium (€/£)	0.0025-0.0020
Forward contract arrangement fee (per euro converted)	£0.002
Relevant OTC option premium (per euro converted)	£0.012

Requirements

71.1 Estimate the spot rate on 31 December 20X4 on the assumption that the €/£ exchange rate continues to change at the same rate as for the period 30 June to 30 September 20X4. **(2 marks)**

71.2 On the assumption that JEK's tender bid is successful:

(a) Calculate JEK's sterling receipt on 31 December 20X4 using your answer to 71.1 above.

(b) Calculate JEK's sterling receipt on 31 December 20X4 if it uses

- A forward contract
- A money market hedge
- An OTC currency option

(9 marks)

71.3 With reference to your calculations in 71.2 above, discuss the issues that should be taken account of by JEK's board when considering whether it should hedge the Estonian contract, assuming the tender bid is successful. **(8 marks)**

71.4 Explain the implications for JEK of using each of the hedging instruments in 71.2(b) above if its tender bid is unsuccessful. **(6 marks)**

71.5 Explain the principle of interest rate parity (IRP) and, given the information provided above, calculate the forward rate of exchange on 31 December 20X4 using IRP, commenting on your result. You should use the average current spot and borrowing/lending rates for the purposes of this calculation. **(5 marks)**

Total: 30 marks

72 Mayo plc

Mayo plc (Mayo) is a UK manufacturer of components used in the computer industry. The company is due to complete two major transactions in 20X9 that it has been working on in recent months:

(1) The sale of one of its UK subsidiaries to a private equity company for a consideration of £35m. The sale is due to be completed at the end of March 20X9, when the company expects to receive the sale proceeds in full.

(2) The purchase of a new factory to enable Mayo to expand the manufacturing operations of one of its other UK subsidiaries. The purchase price of the new factory is £65m and completion of the purchase is set for the end of June 20X9.

The proceeds from the sale of the UK subsidiary will initially be placed on deposit with the company's bank for three months at the end of which they will be used towards completion of the factory purchase. The company is keen to ensure that its return on these funds is in line with current rates of interest, but Mayo's finance director has expressed concern that by March 20X9 interest rates might have fallen from their current level. As a result, she is considering using LIFFE 3-month sterling interest rate futures contracts (contract size £500,000) to remove the company's interest rate risk. At the present time, deposit interest rates are 4.75% p.a. and the March 20X9 3-month sterling interest rate futures contract is trading at 95.00.

In order to complete the purchase of the new factory in June 20X9 and invest in new production equipment, Mayo will also be taking on additional debt finance of £35m, repayable over seven years. Mayo's current credit rating is BBB and its bank has indicated that it would be willing to provide the £35m debt finance at either a fixed rate of 6.00% p.a. or a floating rate of 12-month LIBOR + 1%.

12-month LIBOR is currently 5.75%.

Mayo's finance director has decided that a floating rate interest obligation in respect of the new debt finance is the company's preferred choice and she is currently exploring the possibility of using an interest rate swap to lower the company's floating rate borrowing cost.

Mayo's bank has agreed to act as intermediary swap bank in a seven-year interest rate swap agreement for a fee of 0.20%. The bank has also confirmed that it has already identified a suitable counterparty, Clare plc (Clare), a UK company that has a credit rating of B and can raise fixed rate debt finance at 7.10% p.a. and floating rate debt finance at 12-month LIBOR + 1.4%. Clare is currently looking to raise fixed rate debt finance.

Following negotiations with the bank, Mayo and Clare have agreed to receive, or pay, 12-month LIBOR from/to the bank as appropriate (as the floating leg of the swap) and to share the benefits of the swap agreement (after the swap bank's fee) as follows: Mayo 60%, Clare 40%. These savings will be achieved by the fixed leg payment to/receipt from the bank after allowing for its fee.

It can be assumed that interest payments under the interest rate swap will be made annually.

Requirements

72.1 Advise the finance director of the key characteristics of a LIFFE 3-month sterling interest rate futures contract and explain (without calculations) how such a contract might be used by the company to remove its interest rate risk, specifying whether the company should buy or sell contracts in this particular scenario. **(6 marks)**

72.2 Assuming that by the end of March 20X9 annual interest rates had fallen by 1.25%, illustrate (with calculations) how the use of the interest rate futures contracts selected in 72.1 will enable Mayo to hedge its interest receipts in line with its stated requirements. **(4 marks)**

72.3 (a) Show how an interest rate swap agreement can be established that will meet the requirements of both Mayo and Clare, **setting the floating rate payment to/from the swap bank by both companies at 12-month LIBOR;** and in light of these figures.

   (b) Calculate the actual amount of the cash flows (interest payments and receipts) of the two companies in the first year of the swap agreement. **(8 marks)**

72.4 (a) Calculate the actual amount of the annual cash flows (interest payments and receipts) of the two companies if, by the start of the second year of the agreement, 12-month LIBOR has fallen by 1.4% compared to a year ago and remains at this lower rate for the remainder of the agreement; and

   (b) Evaluate the swap agreement from the perspective of each company in the light of this change in interest rate. **(4 marks)**

Total: 22 marks

Note. Ignore taxation.

73 Brampton plc

Assume that the current date is 30 June 20X3.

Brampton plc (Brampton) is a large company in the UK agricultural market, principally involved in the production of crops for both the brewing and food sectors. The business has grown rapidly in recent years through the acquisition of numerous farming businesses.

As this growth has gathered pace, the finance director has become increasingly concerned by the potential negative impact of interest rate movements on the company, which has never previously hedged its exposure to interest rate risk.

Forecast cash position

As the company accountant, you have recently produced a forecast of average cash balances for the company's next financial year which illustrates the extremely seasonal nature of its business, as evidenced by the following projected average cash balances for each half of the next year:

1 October 20X3 – 31 March 20X4   £40 million borrowing
1 April 20X4 – 30 September 20X4   £70 million cash deposit

The finance director has now asked you to explore how either interest rate options or forward rate agreements might be used to manage the company's interest rate risk.

Three-month interest rates are currently 3.25% pa. You have been able to obtain the following information at the close of business on 30 June 20X3:

Sterling Interest Rate Options on 3-month Futures Contracts

Standard Contract Size £500,000

Premiums in annual % terms

Strike price	Calls			Puts		
	Sept	Dec	March	Sept	Dec	March
96.75	0.53	0.74	0.81	0.42	0.69	0.79

Forward Rate Agreements

Term	Rate (% pa)
3v6	3.00
3v9	2.91
6v9	2.72
6v12	2.68
9v15	2.55

It can be assumed that both deposits and borrowings attract the same rate of interest.

Three scenarios

The finance director has requested that you analyse matters in relation to three specific scenarios:

(1) No change in the current three-month interest rate during the next financial year
(2) An increase in the three-month interest rate to 5.00% pa for the next financial year
(3) A decrease in the three-month interest rate to 1.50% pa for the next financial year

Futures

The finance director has also mentioned that he understands that interest rate futures can achieve the same effect as forward rate agreements, although he has no experience of using interest rate futures in practice.

Requirements

73.1 For **each** of the three specific scenarios in turn, calculate Brampton's net interest received or paid, for each half year and for the full year, if the company chooses to:

(a) Remain unhedged
(b) Use interest rate options
(c) Use forward rate agreements   **(20 marks)**

73.2 Identify for the finance director how hedging interest rate exposure using interest rate futures **differs** from hedging using forward rate agreements.   **(7 marks)**

Total: 27 marks

74 Lambourn plc

Throughout both parts of this question you should assume that today's date is 30 June 20X2.

74.1 Lambourn plc (Lambourn) is a UK company that trades in a range of pharmaceutical products. It buys and sells these products in the UK and also in the USA, where it trades with three companies – Biotron Inc., Hope Inc. and USMed Inc.

In the past, the relatively low level of trading with US companies has meant that Lambourn has not hedged its foreign currency exposure. However, due to increases in the level of trade conducted in the USA, Lambourn's finance director is now considering the use of a variety of hedging instruments.

Receipts and payments in respect of the following exports and imports (designated in the currencies shown) are due in six months' time:

Receipts due from exports to:

Biotron Inc.	$600,000
Hope Inc.	£400,000
USMed Inc.	$200,000

Payments due on imports from:

Biotron Inc.	$1,100,000
Hope Inc.	£900,000
USMed Inc.	$1,250,000

Exchange rates at the present time are as follows:

Spot	$1.6666 - 1.6720/£
3-month forward premium	0.90c - 0.98c
6-month forward premium	2.49c - 2.65c

Sterling currency options (standard contract size £31,250) are currently priced as follows (with premiums, payable up front, quoted in cents per £):

	Calls		Puts	
Strike Price	September	December	September	December
$1.63	3.67	4.59	0.06	1.69
$1.65	2.35	3.07	1.63	3.43
$1.67	1.82	2.65	2.04	5.55

Sterling currency futures (standard contract size £62,500) are currently priced as follows:

September	$1.6555/£
December	$1.6496/£

Annual borrowing and deposit interest rates at the present time are as follows:

Sterling	3.00% - 1.70%
Dollar	1.50% - 0.50%

Requirement

Assuming the spot rate in six months' time will be $1.6400 - 1.6454/£, calculate Lambourn's net foreign currency exposure, and the outcome achieved, using:

(a) A forward market hedge

(b) Exchange-traded currency options (hedging to the nearest whole number of contracts) so as to guarantee no worse an exchange rate than the *current* spot rate

(c) Currency futures contracts (hedging to the nearest whole number of contracts) and assuming the relevant futures contract is trading at $1.6400 in six months' time

(d) A money market hedge   **(17 marks)**

74.2 In six months' time (ie, in December 20X2), Lambourn will need to borrow £1.5 million for a period of six months at a fixed rate of interest. The company's finance director is keen to ensure that the interest rate on the loan does not exceed 3.75% pa. The spot rate of interest is currently 3% pa. The finance director intends to use three-month sterling traded interest rate options on futures to hedge the company's interest rate exposure.

The current schedule of prices (premiums are in annual % terms) for these contracts (standard contract size £500,000) is as follows:

	Calls			Puts		
Strike Price	Sept	Dec	Mar	Sept	Dec	Mar
96.25	0.20	0.23	0.25	0.19	0.96	1.66
96.50	0.09	0.10	0.11	0.32	1.19	1.89
96.75	0.05	0.06	0.07	0.53	1.43	2.14

Requirements

(a) Calculate the outcome of the hedge and the effective annual rate of interest achieved if prices in December 20X2, when Lambourn negotiates the six-month fixed rate loan with its bank, are either:

- A spot interest rate of 4.4% pa and a futures price of 95.31; or
- A spot interest rate of 2.1% pa and a futures price of 97.75. **(10 marks)**

(b) Explain why a hedge using futures contracts may be less than 100% efficient. **(3 marks)**

Total: 30 marks

75 Clifton Bernard Ltd

You should assume that it is now 30 September 20X3

75.1 Clifton Bernard Limited (CB) is a UK engineering firm and specialises in the building of cranes. It has a financial year end of 30 September. Much of CB's trade is in Europe - its main suppliers are based in Germany and a major customer is based in Italy.

CB has two large contracts due for settlement at the end of December 20X3 and, because of the scale of these contracts, its board is considering whether or not to hedge against the possibility of an adverse move of sterling against the euro before the end of 20X3. Details of the two contracts are shown below:

Receipt due from Italian customer on 31 December 20X3	2.600m
Payment due to German supplier on 31 December 20X3	3.350m

You work for CB and have been asked to advise the board on the implications of hedging these two contracts. The information below in Table 1 has been gathered on 30 September 20X3:

Table 1

Spot rate (/£)	1.2080-1.2170
Relevant over the counter (OTC) currency option, exercise price (/£)	1.2070
Three month forward contract – premium (/£)	0.0025-0.0020
OTC currency option cost (per euro converted)	£0.025
Forward contract arrangement fee (per euro converted)	£0.008
Euro interest rate (borrowing)	3.6% pa
Euro interest rate (lending)	2.8% pa
Sterling interest rate (borrowing)	4.4% pa
Sterling interest rate (lending)	3.4% pa

Requirements

(a) Using the information above, and assuming that the spot rate on 31 December 20X3 will be:

(1) Either €1.1850 – €1.1940/£
(2) Or €1.2570 – €1.2660/£

calculate CB's net sterling payment if it uses the following to hedge its foreign exchange transaction risk:

- A forward contract
- A money market hedge
- An over-the-counter currency option. **(11 marks)**

(b) Advise CB's directors of the implications of hedging or not hedging its foreign exchange transactions on 31 December 20X3, showing supporting calculations. **(8 marks)**

(c) Explain the concept of interest rate parity with reference to the information available in Table 1 above. **(5 marks)**

75.2 In June 20W9, CB borrowed £6.3 million at a variable rate of LIBOR plus 2.5% pa to finance the construction of a large new factory. This loan is set to mature in June 20X6 and CB's directors are keen to explore the possibility of an interest rate swap. CB's bank has advised them that Montpelier Neville Industrials plc (MNI) has a similar sized loan with an interest rate of 5% pa. MNI is seeking a variable rate and could borrow at a variable interest rate of LIBOR plus 1.5% pa whilst the best fixed rate available to CB is 6.5% pa. LIBOR on 30 September 20X3 is 5% pa.

Requirement

Suggest a swap arrangement that would be equally fair to both CB and MNI (setting the variable leg of the swap at LIBOR) and, based on the current LIBOR, show the difference in total annual interest payable by CB if the swap goes ahead. **(6 marks)**

Total: 30 marks

76 American Adventures Ltd

You should assume that it is now 30 November 20X3.

76.1 American Adventures Ltd (AA) is a family owned company based in the UK. AA organises walking, cycling and climbing holidays in the United States of America for both British and American customers. AA has the following receipts and payments due in four months' time:

Receipts due from American customers on 31 March 20X4	$2.25 million
Payments due to American suppliers on 31 March 20X4	$3.50 million

You work for Zeta Corporate Finance which has been asked to give advice to AA on hedging its exchange rate risk. You have available the following data on 30 November 20X3:

Exchange rates:

Spot rate ($/£)	1.5154 - 1.5157
4-month forward contract premium ($/£)	0.0012 - 0.0011

March currency futures price (standard contract size £62,500): $1.5148/£

March traded sterling currency options (standard contract size £10,000):

The premiums are quoted in cents per £ and are payable up front.

Strike price	Call premium	Put premium
$1.56	1.04	6.15

Annual borrowing and depositing interest rates:

Sterling	4.70% - 3.50%
Dollar	3.51% - 2.25%

Requirements

(a) Assuming the spot exchange rate on 31 March 20X4 will be $1.5150 – 1.5156/£ and that the sterling currency futures price will be $1.5153/£, calculate AA's net sterling payment if it uses the following to hedge its foreign exchange risk:

- A forward contract
- Currency futures
- A money market hedge
- Currency options **(17 marks)**

(b) Describe the relative advantages and disadvantages of using the methods in part (a) above to hedge AA's foreign exchange risk. **(8 marks)**

76.2 AA intends to take out a £1 million fixed rate loan in four months' time on 31 March 20X4 for a period of three months. The finance director of AA wishes to use a forward rate agreement (FRA) to hedge any unexpected increases in interest rates before the end of March 20X4. The following FRA quotations for annual interest rates have been obtained from AA's bank:

4 v 6	3.55 - 2.50%
4 v 7	3.58 - 2.52%
4 v 8	3.63 - 2.56%

Requirement:

Calculate the receipt from, or payment to, AA's bank arising from the relevant FRA and the net interest that AA will pay on its loan assuming that the actual borrowing rate on 31 March 20X4 is:

(1) Either   3.00% pa
(2) Or   4.00% pa

(5 marks)

Total: 30 marks

77 Northern Risk Management Solutions (NRMS)

77.1 **You should assume that the current date is 30 November 20X4**

Northern Risk Management Solutions (NRMS) is an authorised financial advisor and provides investment and risk management advice to a wide range of clients in Northern England. You are an ICAEW Chartered Accountant employed by NRMS with responsibility for providing risk management advice to two clients, Pared Ltd (Pared) and Spring Gardens Investments (SGI), and investment advice to the owners of Pared.

Pared is an agent for a Spanish wall tile manufacturer and sells tiles to customers in the UK and the Republic of Ireland. In the past Pared has hedged the foreign exchange rate risk on its foreign currency transactions using the money markets (money market hedges). Pared's bank has suggested that it would be better for the company to use either forward contracts or over the counter (OTC) currency options. The owners of Pared are now unsure as to how they should be hedging their currency risk. You have been asked to make a comparison of the results of hedging using the three different techniques.

Pared has the following euro receipts and payments due in three months' time.

Receipts due from Irish customers on 28 February 20X5	€3.4m
Payments due to the Spanish supplier on 28 February 20X5	€2.1m

The following data is available to you at the close of business on 30 November 20X4:

Spot exchange rate (€/£)	1.2184 – 1.2188
Three-month forward contract premium (€/£)	0.0013 – 0.0012

Three-month OTC currency option to buy £ with €:

Exercise price €/£ 1.2180, premium of £0.02 per euro to be converted payable on 30 November 20X4.

Annual borrowing and depositing interest rates are:

Euro   3.60% – 2.80%
Sterling 4.40% – 3.40%

Requirements

(a) Assuming that the spot exchange rate on 28 February 20X5 will be €/£ 1.2179 - 1.2182, calculate Pared's net sterling receipt if it uses the following to hedge its foreign exchange rate risk:

- A money market hedge
- A forward contract
- An OTC currency option

(11 marks)

(b) Discuss the relative advantages and disadvantages of each technique and advise Pared's owners on which would be the most beneficial for hedging its foreign exchange rate risk.

(9 marks)

77.2 One of the supervisors at SGI manages a portfolio of FTSE100 shares. The portfolio is valued at £100m on 30 November 20X4 and the supervisor is convinced that the markets will fall significantly over the next month to 31 December 20X4. He wishes to protect the portfolio against this potential fall in value.

FTSE100 one-month index futures are currently trading at 6,700. Each contract is for a notional value of the futures price multiplied by £10.

Requirements

(a) Demonstrate the result of hedging using index futures over the next month assuming that, on 31 December 20X4, the portfolio value is £95m and the index futures price will be 6,365.

(3 marks)

(b) Identify the disadvantages of a futures hedge and why in practice the hedge may not be totally efficient. (4 marks)

77.3 You have a meeting scheduled for 1 December 20X4 with Yolanda Luz, one of the owners of Pared. She holds some shares in a listed company, Sunshine Holidays plc, and she has asked your advice on whether she should hold or sell them.

During your conversations with the supervisor at SGI he had mentioned to you that he had very reliable information that there is likely to be a takeover of Sunshine Holidays plc.

Requirement

Identify and explain any ethical issues arising for you in advising Yolanda on whether to hold or sell her shares in Sunshine Holidays plc. (3 marks)

Total: 30 marks

78 Chamberlain Jeffries plc

You should assume for all parts of this question that the current date is 1 April 20X5

Chamberlain Jeffries plc (CJ) is a UK-listed international logistics company which started trading in 1982. Its financial year end is 31 March. You are an ICAEW Chartered Accountant who works in CJ"s corporate treasury team. At a recent meeting with your manager it was agreed that you will be involved with three tasks: (1) hedging the interest on a planned loan, (2) hedging CJ"s share portfolio investment using options and (3) hedging CJ"s share portfolio investment using futures.

78.1 Task 1

You have been asked by your line manager to evaluate whether or not CJ should use interest rate futures to hedge against interest rate movements on a loan. CJ"s board is planning to borrow £11.5 million for a nine month period from 1 June 20X5 to 28 February 20X6 and is worried that interest rates will increase from their current level of 8% pa. The current price of June sterling 3-months futures is 91.50 and the standard contract size is £500,000.

Requirement

Demonstrate how sterling interest rate futures can be used by CJ to hedge against interest rate movements, commenting on your results, if by 1 June 20X5:

(a) Interest rates decrease to 6.5% pa and the futures price alters by 1.75%
(b) Interest rates increase to 9% pa and the futures price alters by 1%
(c) Interest rates increase to 10% pa and the futures price alters by 2.25% (10 marks)

78.2 Task 2

CJ has invested in a portfolio of UK FTSE100 shares which is worth £18.225 million on 1 April 20X5. The spot value of the FTSE100 index on that date is 6,750.

CJ"s board wishes to explore the implications of hedging the company against a potential fall in share prices in the next month. Accordingly, it is considering the use of (a) traded FTSE100 index options or (b) FTSE100 stock index futures.

Index options

The following information has been gathered:

FTSE 100 INDEX OPTION (£10 per full index point)

Exercise price	6,650		6,700		6,750		6,800		6,850	
	Call	Put	Call	Put	Call	Put	Call	Put	Call	Put
May	215	95	184	115	154	135	125	159	105	191
June	272	131	241	152	217	176	186	197	162	221

Assume that the board decides to use options to protect the current value of the portfolio in one month's time.

Requirement

Explain, with supporting workings, what will happen in one month's time if:

- The portfolio's value falls to £17.955 million and the FTSE100 index falls to 6,650
- The portfolio's value rises to £18.360 million and the FTSE100 index rises to 6,800   **(8 marks)**

78.3 Task 3

Index futures

As an alternative to hedging the £18.225 million portfolio with options, CJ''s board is considering using FTSE100 stock index futures. At 1 April 20X5 the quote for FTSE100 stock index futures in one month is 6,720 and the face value of a FTSE100 index contract is £10 per index point.

Requirement

Calculate the outcome of this hedge if in one month's time the portfolio's value falls to £17.955 million and the FTSE100 stock index futures contract falls to 6,630. Comment on whether this hedge has been effective and identify the reasons for any inefficiency which may arise when using futures contracts.   **(8 marks)**

78.4 Task 4

Since September 20X4 CJ''s board has held several meetings with the board of another large UK-listed logistics company, Osman Lloyd plc. They have been discussing the potential merger of the two firms. Whilst news of this merger is known only to a few people at both firms, one of your friends in CJ''s corporate treasury team has recently provided financial advice to the board.

Your friend is convinced that CJ''s share price will rise considerably once the news becomes public knowledge. He has told you: 'I know that you can't buy shares, but tell your friends about the merger. They will make a nice profit and so could you, if you're careful.'

Requirement

What are the ethical issues for you as regards this information?   **(4 marks)**

Total: 30 marks

79 Eurocycle plc

You should assume that the current date is 31 May 20X5

Eurocycle plc (Eurocycle) imports high value road bikes from several manufacturers in Europe and sells them to the public in its own stores throughout the UK. On 30 September 20X5 Eurocycle has a payment to make to its suppliers of €8,200,000.

79.1 The following data is available to you at the close of business on 31 May 20X5:

Spot exchange rate (€/£)	1.2789 – 1.2797
Four-month forward rate premium (€/£)	0.0026 – 0.0024

Annual borrowing and depositing interest rates:

Euro	3.90% – 2.90%
Sterling	4.00% – 3.20%

Four-month over the counter (OTC) currency options:

- Call options to buy £ have an exercise price of €/£1.2770 and a premium of £0.005 per € converted.

- Put options to sell £ have an exercise price of €/£1.2765 and a premium of £0.001 per € converted.

Option premiums are payable on 31 May 20X5 and Eurocycle currently has an overdraft.

A foreign currency dealer has provided the finance director of Eurocycle with an estimate of the €/£ spot rate on 30 September 20X5 of €/£ 1.2783 – 1.2793.

Requirements

(a) Calculate Eurocycle's sterling payment and explain, with reasons, which hedging technique is preferable, assuming that it hedges its foreign exchange rate risk using either of the following:

- A forward contract
- A money market hedge **(7 marks)**

(b) Given the estimated spot rate provided by the foreign currency dealer, discuss, with reasons:

- Whether Eurocycle should in fact hedge its euro payment using a forward contract or a money market hedge; and

- The likelihood of the currency dealer being able to outperform the forward market. **(5 marks)**

(c) Explain to the finance director of Eurocycle how an OTC currency option might be used to hedge the company's exposure to foreign exchange rate risk and advise him of what action to take on 30 September 20X5 if the €/£ spot rate is:

- In line with the forward market
- In line with the foreign currency dealer's estimate **(8 marks)**

79.2 Eurocycle is seeking to expand and has recently borrowed £100 million for a period of ten years to purchase a number of properties throughout the UK. The borrowings are at a floating rate of LIBOR +5% pa. LIBOR is currently 0.7% pa. The finance director of Eurocycle believes that interest rates are going to rise over the next ten years and he would like to protect the company against this interest rate risk.

The finance director has been in contact with Netfix plc (Netfix), a company that would like to swap £100 million of its fixed rate loans to a floating rate. It has been agreed that any benefits from the swap will be shared equally between Eurocycle and Netfix. Eurocycle can borrow at a fixed rate of 7.0% pa. Netfix has borrowed at a fixed rate of 5.5% pa and could borrow at a floating rate of LIBOR +4% pa.

Requirements

(a) Demonstrate how the proposed interest rate swap between Eurocycle and Netfix would be implemented with the floating leg of the swap set at LIBOR. **(4 marks)**

(b) Calculate the initial difference in annual interest rates for Eurocycle if it enters into the interest rate swap with Netfix and calculate the minimum amount by which LIBOR will have to rise for the swap to breakeven for Eurocycle. **(2 marks)**

(c) Identify four advantages for Eurocycle of entering into an interest rate swap with Netfix.

(4 marks)

Total: 30 marks

80 Limehouse Ltd

Limehouse Ltd (Limehouse) is a UK-based engineering firm. Its financial year end is 31 August. The company was established by brothers Gordon and Michael Rowe in 1982. They are no longer directors of the company nor are they involved in its day-to-day running. They currently own 60% of its issued ordinary shares between them. The remaining shares are owned by the three directors of Limehouse and two of its senior managers.

Limehouse's external auditors are Chappell White Stepney (CWS), a firm of ICAEW Chartered Accountants. CWS also provides personal tax advice to Gordon and Michael.

The brothers wish to sell their shares in Limehouse to the company's other shareholders and have asked CWS for advice. Limehouse's directors have provided CWS with the following financial information from the company's management accounts:

Balance Sheet at 31 August 2015

	£'000	£'000
Non-current assets		
Land and Buildings		7,400
Plant and Machinery		3,650
Vehicles		585
		11,635
Current assets		
Inventories	2,550	
Trade receivables	1,388	
Bank and cash	82	
	4,020	
Current liabilities		
Trade payables	2,390	1,630
		13,265
Capital and Reserves		
£1 ordinary shares		3,000
Retained earnings		6,115
		9,115
Non-current liabilities		
6% debentures (issued in 2010 and redeemable in 2021)		4,150
		13,265

Income Statement extracts

Year ended 31 August	2012	2013	2014	2015
	£'000	£'000	£'000	£'000
Profit before interest and tax	1,840	1,880	1,875	2,450
Dividends proposed and paid	660	660	660	660

Limehouse's directors had the company's non-current assets independently revalued in April 2015. The values are shown below:

	£'000
Land and Buildings	10,250
Plant and Machinery	4,025
Vehicles	488

Assume that the corporation tax rate has been, and will continue to be, 21% pa.

The price earnings (P/E) ratio and dividend yield figures of four listed UK engineering companies at 31 August 2015 are shown below:

	P/E ratio	Dividend yield
Globe plc	18.5	2.5%
Burdett plc	19.0	3.4%
QM plc	14.4	2.9%
Fieldgate plc	16.5	3.6%

Requirements

80.1 Using the information provided, prepare a report for Gordon and Michael Rowe advising them of a range of suitable prices for their shareholding in Limehouse. Your report should include supporting workings and a clear commentary as to the strengths and weaknesses of each of the valuation methods that you have used. **(23 marks)**

80.2 Discuss how the shareholder value analysis approach to company valuation differs from the valuation methods that you have used in 80.1. **(8 marks)**

80.3 Explain the ethical issues that CWS should consider with regard to its work for Gordon and Michael Rowe. **(4 marks)**

Total: 35 marks

81   Rayner Davies plc

You should assume that the current date is 31 August 2015

Rayner Davies plc ('Rayner') is a UK manufacturer of kitchenware. Its financial year-end is 31 August. Rayner currently sells its products to retail companies which then sell them to the public. It has now decided that it should also sell its products direct to the public online. To do so requires a significant financial investment.

Extracts from Rayner's most recent management accounts are shown below:

Income Statement for the year ended 31 August 2015

	£'000
Sales	25,800
Variable costs	(15,480)
Fixed costs	(4,900)
Profit before interest	5,420
Debenture interest	(410)
Profit before tax	5,010
Taxation (at 21%)	(1,052)
Profit after tax	3,958
Dividends proposed	(3,125)
Retained profit	833

Balance Sheet at 31 August 2015

	£'000
£1 ordinary shares	12,500
Share premium account	2,300
Retained earnings	8,145
	22,945
5% debentures (redeemable in 2017)	8,200
	31,145

Rayner's directors estimate that it would cost the company £6.9 million from either equity or debt sources to finance the proposed investment in online sales. Extracts from the minutes of the company's most recent board meeting are shown below:

Extract 1 - production director: 'We should have a rights issue. I'm sure the shareholders would invest if we priced the shares at £3 each as our shares are currently quoted at £3.45 per share ex-div. Also a rights issue would be better for our gearing level than a debenture issue.'

Extract 2 - marketing director: 'You can't trust the stock market because it's inefficient. Also there are too many irrational investors. I think that our shares are overpriced and that a figure closer to £3 per share is more accurate, so a rights issue at £3 wouldn't be very attractive.'

Extract 3 - human resources (HR) director: 'Why don't we stop paying such a large dividend? If we used this year's proposed dividend plus what we have in the bank, that would give us approximately £3.5 million and so we'd only need to raise an extra £3.4 million rather than the full £6.9 million.'

You are a member of Rayner's finance team. Your manager has asked you to provide relevant workings for her in advance of the next board meeting. She has provided you with the following assumptions for the year ended 31 August 2016:

- Sales will be 20% higher than in the year ended 31 August 2015

- Annual fixed costs attributable to the online investment would be £1.5 million

- Dividends per share would remain unchanged from those proposed for the year ended 31 August 2015

- Rayner's contribution to sales ratio remains constant

Requirements

81.1 Assume that Rayner raises the £6.9 million required by either:

- A rights issue at £3 per share; or
- An issue of 6% redeemable debentures at par.

Using your manager's assumptions, **for each method of finance**:

(a) Prepare a forecast Income Statement for the year ended 31 August 2016.　　(8 marks)

(b) Calculate Rayner's earnings per share for the year ended 31 August 2016.　　(3 marks)

(c) Calculate Rayner's gearing ratio (debt / debt + equity) using book values at August 2016.

(4 marks)

81.2 Evaluate the implications for Rayner of choosing equity or debt as its means of raising the £6.9 million. You should, where possible, make reference to your calculations in part (a) above and the comments of the production director.　　(7 marks)

81.3 Discuss the marketing director's views on the stock market and the assertion that Rayner's shares are overpriced.　　(7 marks)

81.4 Discuss the HR director's view that Rayner should not pay a dividend for the year ended 31 August 2015 to help finance the online investment, making reference to relevant theories.　　(6 marks)

Total: 35 marks

82　IMT Ltd

You should assume that the current date is 30 September 2015

IMT Ltd (IMT) manufactures and distributes scientific instruments for university researchers, pharmaceutical companies and research laboratories. It is based in the UK and has been trading since 2008.

Because IMT's instruments have very high technical specifications they are made to order. Lead times between order and delivery can be as much as six months. Sales were only made in the UK until IMT began exporting to the USA last year. IMT's board has not hedged its exposure to currency risk because most of the American orders were relatively small.

The company has now received an order from a prestigious research laboratory in California and a price of $5.3 million has been agreed. Work will start on the contract in October and the $5.3 million will be received in six months' time on 31 March 2016. IMT's board met recently and three specific issues regarding overseas trade were raised. The minutes included the following:

Issue 1: 'We've seen in the financial press that sterling has strengthened against the US dollar in the past two months. I think that we should consider hedging the Californian contract.'

Issue 2: 'We have longer-term plans to expand our sales market into Europe, South America and Asia. This might involve us in establishing manufacturing and distribution facilities overseas. We need to consider the currency risks that could arise from such an expansion.'

Issue 3: 'As we don't have any specific use for the receipt from the Californian contract until the end of 2016, we ought to consider investing the sterling in a UK deposit account in March 2016. That is six months away. Can we protect against a possible fall in interest rates before then?'

You work in IMT's finance team. To aid the board's decision regarding the possible hedging of the Californian contract, you have been asked to report back to them with relevant workings. The following data has been collected from IMT's bank on 30 September 2015:

Spot rate ($/£)	1.5386 – 1.5398
Sterling interest rate (borrowing)	4.0% pa
Sterling interest rate (lending)	3.6% pa
US dollar interest rate (borrowing)	2.8% pa
US dollar interest rate (lending)	2.4% pa
Six-month forward contract premium ($/£)	0.0096 – 0.0084
Forward contract arrangement fee (per $ converted)	£0.0030
Six-month over the counter (OTC) call option on dollars – exercise price ($/£)	1.5210
Six-month over the counter (OTC) put option on dollars – exercise price ($/£)	1.5280
Relevant OTC option premium (per $ converted)	£0.0050

Requirements

82.1 With reference to Issue 1, calculate IMT's sterling receipt from the Californian contract if it:

    (a)   Does not hedge the dollar receipt and sterling

- Strengthens by 5% by 31 March 2016; or
- Weakens by 5% by 31 March 2016.

    (b)   Uses a money market hedge

    (c)   Uses an OTC currency option

    (d)   Uses a forward contract   **(10 marks)**

82.2 With reference to your calculations in 82.1(a), advise IMT's board whether or not it should hedge its dollar receipt from the Californian contract.   **(9 marks)**

82.3 With reference to Issue 2, explain the different types of currency risk that could arise were IMT to expand its operations overseas as indicated.   **(6 marks)**

82.4 With reference to Issue 3, explain how IMT might hedge its exposure to interest rate risk.   **(5 marks)**

Total: 30 marks

Financial Management: Question Bank

Answer Bank

1 Stakeholders

Marking guide

			Marks
1.1	(a)	Explanation	3
	(b)	Explanation	3
	(c)	Explanation	3
			9
1.2	1–2 marks per argued point		max 8
			17

1.1 (a) A large conglomerate spinning off its divisions

Large conglomerates may sometimes have a market capitalisation which is less than the total realisable value of the subsidiaries ('conglomerate discount'). This arises because more synergy could be found by the combination of the group's businesses with competitors than by running a diversified group where there is no obvious benefit from remaining together.

For many years, Hanson Trust was the exception to this situation, but subsequently it decided to break up the group.

The stakeholders involved in potential conflicts are as follows.

(1) Shareholders

They will see the chance of immediate gains in share price if subsidiaries are sold.

(2) Subsidiary company directors and employees

They may either gain opportunities (eg if their company becomes independent) or suffer the threat of job loss (eg if their company is sold to a competitor).

(b) A private company converting into a public company

When a private company converts into a public company, some of the existing shareholder/managers will sell their shares to outside investors. In addition, new shares may be issued. The dilution of ownership might cause loss of control by the existing management.

Stakeholders involved in potential conflicts

(1) Existing shareholder/managers

They will want to sell some of their shareholding at as high a price as possible. This may motivate them to overstate their company's prospects. Those shareholder/managers who wish to retire from the business may be in conflict with those who wish to stay in control – the latter may oppose the conversion into a public company.

(2) New outside shareholders

Most of these will hold minority stakes in the company and will receive their rewards as dividends only. This may put them in conflict with the existing shareholder/managers who receive rewards as salaries as well as dividends. On conversion to a public company there should be clear policies on dividends and directors' remuneration.

(3) Employees, including managers who are not shareholders

Part of the reason for the success of the company will be the efforts made by employees. They may feel that they should benefit when the company goes public. One way of organising this is to create employee share options or other bonus schemes.

(c) **Japanese car manufacturer building new car plants in other countries**

The stakeholders involved in potential conflicts are as follows.

(1) **The shareholders and management of the Japanese company**

They will be able to gain from the combination of advanced technology with a cheaper workforce.

(2) **Local employees and managers engaged by the Japanese company**

They will gain **enhanced skills** and better **work prospects**.

(3) **The government of the local country, representing the tax payers**

The **reduction** in **unemployment** will ease the taxpayers' burden and increase the government's popularity (provided that subsidies offered by the government do not outweigh the benefits!).

(4) **Shareholders, managers and employees of local car-making firms**

These will be in **conflict** with the **other stakeholders** above as existing manufacturers lose market share.

(5) **Employees of car plants based in Japan**

These are likely to **lose work** if car-making is relocated to lower wage areas. They will need to compete on the basis of **higher efficiency**.

1.2 The concept that the **primary financial objective** of the firm is to **maximise** the **wealth** of shareholders, by which is meant the **net present value** of estimated future cash flows, underpins much of modern financial theory.

Achievement of this goal can be pursued, at least in part, through the setting of specific **subsidiary targets** in terms of items such as return on investment and risk adjusted returns.

A widely adopted approach is to seek to **maximise the present value of the projected cash flows.** In this way, the objective is both made measurable and can be translated into a yardstick for financial decision making. It cannot be defined as a single attainable target but rather as a criterion for the continuing allocation of the company's resources.

There has been some recent debate as to whether wealth maximisation should or can be the only true objective, particularly in the context of the multinational company. The **stakeholder view** of corporate objectives is that **many groups** of people have a stake in what the company does. Each of these groups, which include suppliers, workers, managers, customers and governments as well as shareholders, has its own objectives, and this means that a compromise is required.

The firm has responsibilities towards many groups in addition to the shareholders, including:

- **Employees**: to provide good working conditions and remuneration, the opportunity for personal development, outplacement help in the event of redundancy and so on.

- **Customers**: to provide a product of good and consistent quality, good service and communication, and open and fair commercial practice.

- **The public**: to ensure responsible disposal of waste products.

There are many **other interest groups** that should also be included in the discussion process.

Non-financial objectives may often work indirectly to the financial benefit of the firm in the long term, but in the short term they do often appear to compromise the primary financial objectives.

For example, in the case of the multinational firm with a facility in a politically unstable third world economy, the directors may at times need to place the **interests of local government and economy** ahead of those of its shareholders, in part at least to ensure its own continued stability there.

Conclusion

It is very difficult to find a comprehensive and appropriate alternative primary financial objective to that of **shareholder wealth maximisation** but the definition of non-financial objectives should also be addressed in the context of the overall review of the corporate plan.

2 Stoane Gayte Sounds plc (March 2013)

Marking guide

		Marks
2.1	Machinery	1
	Tax saving	2
	Tax on income	1
	Working capital investment	2
	Discounting and NPV	1
	Recommendation	1
	No market research costs	1
	No fixed costs	1
	Selling price	1
	Raw materials	1
	Variable overheads	1
	Loss of contribution	3
	Labour costs ignored	1
		17
2.2	NPV	1
	IRR	1
	Advice on usefulness	4
		6
2.3	Relevant discussion	6
		29

2.1

	March 20X3 £'000	March 20X4 £'000	March 20X5 £'000	March 20X6 £'000
Machinery	(4,900.000)			980.000
Tax saving (W1)	274.400	219.520	175.616	428.064
Income (W2)		2,008.500	3,500.970	1,803.000
Tax on income (W2)		(562.380)	(980.272)	(504.840)
Working capital investment (W3)	(750.000)	(22.500)	(23.175)	795.675
Total cash flows	(5,375.600)	1,643.140	2,673.139	3,501.899
11% factor	1.000	0.901	0.812	0.731
PV	(5,375.600)	1,480.306	2,169.580	2,560.558
NPV	834.844			

As the NPV is positive SGS should proceed with the investment as this will enhance shareholder wealth.

No market research costs

No fixed costs

WORKINGS

(1)

	March 20X3 £'000	March 20X4 £'000	March 20X5 £'000	March 20X6 £'000
Cost/WDV	4,900.000	3,920.000	3,136.000	2,508.800
WDA (20%)	(980.000)	(784.000)	(627.200)	(1,528.800)
WDV/disposal	3,920.000	3,136.000	2,508.800	980.000
Tax saved (28% x WDA)	274.400	219.520	175.616	428.064

(2)

	March 20X3 £
Contribution/unit	
Selling price	190
Less: Raw materials	(43)
Variable overheads	(45)
Loss of Boom-Boom contribution ([£99-£28-£35] x 2)	(72)
Contribution/unit	30

Labour costs ignored

Contribution adjusted for inflation

	March 20X4	March 20X5	March 20X6
Contribution/unit (real terms)	£30.00	£30.00	£30.00
	×	×	×
Sales volume (units)	65,000	110,000	55,000
	=	=	=
Total contribution	£1,950,000	£3,300,000	£1,650,000
		×	×
Inflation adjustment	1.03	$(1.03)^2$	$(1.03)^3$
	=	=	=
Total contribution (money terms)	£2,008,500	£3,500,970	£1,803,000
Corporation tax on contribution (@ 28%)	£562,380	£980,272	£504,840

(3) **Working capital investment**

	March 20X3	March 20X4	March 20X5	March 20X6
Working capital	£750,000	×1.03 £772,500	×1.03 £795,675	
Increment	(£750,000)	(£22,500)	(£23,175)	£795,675

2.2 IRR calculation

Rework total cash flows at (say) 15%:

Total cash flows	(5,375.600)	1,643.140	2,673.139	3,501.899
15% factor	1.000	0.870	0.756	0.658
PV	(5,375.600)	1,429.532	2,020.893	2,304.250
NPV	**379.074**			

IRR = 15% + [4% × (379.074/(834.844 − 379.074))] = 18.33%

The IRR is approximately 18.3% which exceeds SGS' cost of capital (11%) and so the investment will enhance shareholder wealth. If however the IRR had been less than the cost of capital then shareholder wealth would decline.

IRR and NPV normally give the same result as to whether investment should take place or not. As a percentage return, IRR may be easier to understand for managers and employees. However, IRR does not calculate the change in shareholder absolute wealth. As a result it may provide the wrong result when alternative projects are being ranked. Also non-conventional cash flows can create more than one IRR.

2.3 The traditional school of thought regarding dividends states:

Shareholders would prefer dividends today rather than dividends or capital gains in the future

This is because cash now is more certain than in future

However, this implies that future payments would be discounted at a higher rate to take account of the uncertainty

However does risk increase over time?

Risk is related to the activities and operations of the business and the discount rates applied to dividends should reflect this

Modigliani and Miller (MM)

MM argued that share value is determined by future earnings and the level of risk.

The amount of dividends paid will not affect shareholder wealth providing the retained earnings are invested in profitable investment opportunities and any loss in dividend income will be offset by gains in share price

Shareholders can create home-made dividends and don't have to rely on the company's dividend policy, so if cash is needed, then they can sell some shares instead

Logic difficult to fault, but taxes, share transaction costs and share issue costs will have an effect

Other issues

Informational content – dividends mean that management is confident of the future. The *signalling* view

Clientele effect – investors have a *preferred habitat*. That is they seek a company with a particular dividend policy that suits them. If shares unpopular because of inconsistent policy then share price will suffer.

Agency – separation of ownership from management of firm can lead to sub-optimal decisions being made. Agency costs borne by shareholders. So managers may often make investments that don't increase shareholder wealth. Dividends worsen as a result. However, dividend commitments can reduce agency costs. A high dividend payout and low retentions leads to greater scrutiny of the firm's investment decisions by outsiders (due to the need for external funds).

Tax – some shareholders may prefer income to gains

Overall

Evidence seems to support MM – valuation not closely related to levels of dividends

Clientele effect seems to operate

Dividends don't affect value of shares provided the shareholders know the dividend policy of the company. Establish a consistent policy and stick to it therefore

Lack of consistency means that shareholders will leave habitat and as a result share price likely to fall

Examiner's comments:

This question was generally done very well and had the highest average mark on the paper.

This was a three-part question that tested the candidates' understanding of the investment decisions and valuations element of the syllabus. In addition it tested candidates' understanding of IRR and dividend theory.

In the scenario a company was considering whether or not to proceed with the development of a new range of audio speakers for cars. Part 2.1 for 17 marks was a fairly traditional NPV calculation and required candidates to deal with lost contribution, inflation, working capital and capital allowances. Part 2.2 for six marks asked candidates to calculate the IRR of the proposed investment and explain the usefulness of this figure to the company's directors. In part 2.3, also for six marks, candidates had to discuss whether the company should use company funds to pay a dividend instead of investing in the audio speakers project.

In requirement 2.1, the majority of candidates scored high marks. The most common errors were made with regard to the lost contribution and the non-relevance of skilled labour costs. Also a fair number of candidates were unable to deal correctly with (a) the working capital requirements and/or (b) the correct discount rate.

Most answers to part 2.2 were disappointing. Too few candidates were able to calculate the project's IRR correctly, even allowing for errors made in the NPV calculation in part 2.1. Also it was clear that far too few candidates understood the meaning of the IRR figure and its usefulness to management.

Part 2.3 was answered far better and most candidates demonstrated a good understanding of the theory underpinning dividend policy and thus scored high marks.

3 Profitis plc (December 2001)

Marking guide

		Marks
3.1	Calculations:	
	Time 0	1
	Time 1	1
	Time 2	1.5
	Time 3	2.5
	Time 4	1
	PV	2
	Equivalent annual cost	3
	Conclusion	1
		13
3.2	1½ marks per point, maximum	max 4
		17

3.1 Derivation of the equivalent annual cost: Net present value

Time		3 years PV @ 15% £	£	4 years PV @ 15% £	£
0	Cost	(80,000)		(80,000)	
	Capital allowance (w)	3,024		3,024	
		(76,976)	(76,976)	(76,976)	(76,976)
1	Capital allowance	2,479		2,479	
	Maintenance	(10,000)		(10,000)	
		(7,521)	(6,543)	(7,521)	(6,543)
2	Capital allowance	2,033		2,033	
	Maintenance	(10,000)		(10,000)	
	Tax on maintenance	2,100		2,100	
		(5,867)	(4,436)	(5,867)	(4,436)
3	Capital allowance	7,163		1,667	
	Maintenance	–		(20,000)	
	Tax on maintenance	2,100		2,100	
	Proceeds	10,000		–	
		19,263	12,675	(16,233)	(10,681)
4	Capital allowance	–		7,595	
	Tax on maintenance	–		4,200	
				11,795	6,747
	Present value		(75,280)		(91,889)
	Annuity factor		2.283		2.855
	Equivalent annual cost		£32,974		£32,185

Therefore a four-year life is marginally more economic.

WORKING

Time		@ 21% £	£
0	Cost	80,000	
	Writing-down allowance (18%)	(14,400)	3,024
		65,600	
1	Writing-down allowance (18%)	(11,808)	2,479
		53,792	
2	Writing-down allowance (18%)	(9,683)	2,033
		44,109	
3	Proceeds	(10,000)	
		34,109	7,163
or			
2	Written-down value	44,109	
3	Writing-down allowance (18%)	(7,940)	1,667
		36,169	
4	Proceeds	Nil	
		36,169	7,595

3.2 Discussion of other issues

Relevant issues include the following.

(a) The analysis in 3.1 ignores price changes of all descriptions. A change in the price of a new machine, for example, could easily alter the conclusion. The same would be true for all of the input factors.

(b) The approach taken assumes that replacement will take place with an identical machine. The machine may be technologically superseded. The company may conclude that it no longer has a need for such a machine. In practice it seems unlikely that many such assets are replaced with identical models on a continuing basis.

(c) The timing of the cash outflows on new machines could be an issue in practice, ie making payments every fourth year may cause less of a cash flow problem than every third year.

4 Harrow plc (June 2010)

			Marks
4.1	Option 1:		
	Contribution	2	
	Redundancy	1	
	Fixed costs	1	
	Tax	1	
	Working capital	2	
	Investment	0.5	
	Capital allowances	2	
	Discount factor	1	
	Omission of outstanding committed cost	0.5	
			11
4.2	Option 2:		
	Contribution	2	
	Redundancy	1	
	Fixed costs	1	
	Tax	1	
	Working capital	2	
	Recommendation	1	
			8
4.3	1 mark per weakness identified	max	2
4.4	1 mark per value driver with explanation	max	6
4.5	Up to 3 marks per area discussed	max	8
			35

4.1 Option 1: Introduce the Diamond and drop the RotoEdge

31 December	20X0	20X1	20X2	20X3	20X4	20X5
Unit sales		12,000	18,000	24,000	18,000	12,000
Contribution (£) (72/unit)		864,000	1,296,000	1,728,000	1,296,000	864,000
Redundancy	(144,000)					
Fixed costs		(300,000)	(300,000)	(300,000)	(300,000)	(300,000)
Net cash flow	(144,000)	564,000	996,000	1,428,000	996,000	564,000
Tax (21%)	30,240	(118,440)	(209,160)	(299,880)	(209,160)	(118,440)
Working capital (W1)	(144,000)	(72,000)	(72,000)	72,000	72,000	144,000
Investment	(1,500,000)					
Cap. Allowances (W2)	56,700	46,494	38,125	31,262	25,635	116,783
Net cash flow	(1,701,060)	420,054	752,965	1,231,382	884,475	706,343
df (10%)	1	0.909	0.826	0.751	0.683	0.621
PV	(1,701,060)	381,829	621,949	924,768	604,096	438,639
NPV	1,270,221					

Omission of the outstanding committed cost of £100,000

WORKINGS

1 Working capital

31/12	20X0	20X1	20X2	20X3	20X4	20X5
Sales		1,440,000	2,160,000	2,880,000	2,160,000	1,440,000
Working capital	144,000	216,000	288,000	216,000	144,000	–
Incremental effect	(144,000)	(72,000)	(72,000)	72,000	72,000	144,000

2 Capital allowances

		WDV	Tax saved (21%)
31.12.20X0	Cost	1,500,000	
31.12.20X0	WDA	270,000	56,700
		1,230,000	
31.12.20X1	WDA	221,400	46,494
		1,008,600	
31.12.20X2	WDA	181,548	38,125
		827,052	
31.12.20X3	WDA	148,869	31,262
		678,183	
31.12.20X4	WDA	122,073	25,635
31.12.20X5	Bal.All.	556,110	116,783

4.2 Option 2: Introduce the Diamond and retain the RotoEdge

31/12	20X0	20X1	20X2	20X3	20X4	20X5
Unit sales:						
RotoEdge		4,800	3,600	2,400		
Diamond		9,600	16,200	22,800	18,000	12,000
(£)						
Contribution:						
RotoEdge (42/unit)		201,600	151,200	100,800		
Diamond (72/unit)		691,200	1,166,400	1,641,600	1,296,000	864,000
Redundancy	(60,000)	(48,000)	(48,000)	(24,000)		
Fixed costs		(320,000)	(320,000)	(320,000)	(300,000)	(300,000)
Net cash flow	(60,000)	524,800	949,600	1,398,400	996,000	564,000
Tax (21%)	12,600	(110,208)	(199,416)	(293,664)	(209,160)	(118,440)
Working capital (W1)	(161,280)	(67,680)	(67,680)	80,640	72,000	144,000
Investment	(1,500,000)					
Cap. Allowances	56,700	46,494	38,125	31,262	25,635	116,783
Net cash flow	(1,651,980)	393,406	720,629	1,216,638	884,475	706,343
df (10%)	1	0.909	0.826	0.751	0.683	0.621
PV	(1,651,980)	357,606	595,240	913,695	604,096	438,639
NPV	1,257,296					

WORKINGS

1 Working capital

31/12	20X0	20X1	20X2	20X3	20X4	20X5
Sales		1,612,800	2,289,600	2,966,400	2,160,000	1,440,000
Working capital	161,280	228,960	296,640	216,000	144,000	–
Incremental effect	(161,280)	(67,680)	(67,680)	80,640	72,000	144,000

The recommendation, therefore, should be that Option 1 be pursued.

4.3   1   The firm's shareholders may not be diversified, as assumed by the CAPM.

       2   The shareholders are not the only stakeholders in the firm, as assumed by the CAPM – directors and employees will struggle to be persuaded that they should be unconcerned if the new project has an adverse effect on the risk/return profile of the firm.

4.4   1   Increase the rate of growth of sales
       2   Increase the operating profit margin (increase selling price/decrease variable costs)
       3   Reduce the investment in non-current assets (acquire for less than £1.5m)
       4   Reduce the investment in working capital (less than 10%)
       5   Reduce the firm's cost of capital (change capital structure)
       6   Extend the life of the project

4.5 Takeovers

Directors often devote large amounts of time and money to 'defend' their companies against takeover. However, research has shown that shareholders in companies that are successfully taken over often earn large financial returns. On the other hand, directors of companies that are taken over frequently lose their jobs! This is a common example of the conflict of interest between the two groups.

Time horizon

Directors know that their performance is usually judged on their short-term achievements; shareholder wealth, on the other hand, is affected by the long-term performance of the firm. Directors can frequently be observed to be taking a short-term view of the firm which is in their own best interest but not in that of the shareholders.

Risk

Shareholders appraise risks by looking at the overall risk of their investment in a wide range of shares. They do not have 'all their eggs in one basket', unlike directors whose career prospects and short-term financial remuneration depend on the success of their individual firm.

Examiner's comments:

With an average mark of 71.9%, it is clear that most candidates were well prepared for this standard question on the investment appraisal section of the syllabus.

In the opening section of the question the majority of candidate responses scored highly, although weaker scripts were characterised by errors in the following areas:

1   A failure to omit irrelevant costs, which included the costs to which the firm in the two scenarios was already committed

2   Accurate calculation of the working capital impact of the investment proposals

3   Confusion regarding the correct treatment of fixed costs in the second of the two scenarios outlined in the question.

In part 4.3 of the question, there was some polarisation of performance between those candidates with a clear knowledge of the relevant area of the learning materials and those with none. In addition, many candidates made reference to the issue of a beta calculation, but this was a difficulty associated with the methodology rather than an assumption underpinning its use to calculate a discount factor for investment appraisal purposes.

In part 4.4 of the question, the vast majority of candidates were able to list many, if not all, of the value drivers, although the frequent references to the idea that the firm could simply reduce the rate of corporation tax scored no marks as this is not a variable the firm can directly influence even if the firm can seek to minimise the amount of tax it pays in absolute terms. Another key characteristic of weaker candidates was their failure to follow up the identification of value drivers with an explanation of <u>how</u> improvements in shareholder value might actually be achieved in practice.

5 Tidefrost plc (March 2008)

			Marks
5.1	Tender price		14
5.2	Amended NPV		4
5.3	Advantages	4	Max 3
5.4	Value		3
5.5	Cash and shares	4	Max 3
			27

5.1

	t_0 £'000	t_1 £'000	t_2 £'000	t_3 £'000
Machine	(940.000)			100.000
Tax on machine (W1)	35.532	29.136	23.892	87.840
Annual costs (W2)		(168.000)	(253.575)	(347.288)
Contribution (W3)		(157.500)	(165.375)	(173.644)
Tax on loss		68.355	87.980	109.396
Working capital (W4)	(160.000)	(8.000)	(8.400)	176.400
Total cash flows	(1,064.468)	(236.009)	(315.478)	(47.296)
Discount factor (10%)	1.000	0.909	0.826	0.751
PV	(1,064.468)	(214.532)	(260.585)	(35.519)
NPV	(1,575.104)			

Minimum tender price = £1,575,104 ÷ discount factor, 3 years, 10% ÷ 0.79 (to account for 21% tax)

= £1,575,104 ÷ 0.751 ÷ 0.79

= £2,654,864

Thus in order to at least maintain shareholder wealth the minimum tender price for the contract is £2,654,864.

WORKINGS

(1)

	t_0 £'000	t_1 £'000	t_2 £'000	t_3 £'000
Cost	940.000	770.800	632.056	518.286
WDA @ 18%/bal. allowance	(169.200)	(138.744)	(113.770)	(418.286)
WDV	770.800	632.056	518.286	100.000
Tax on WDA @ 21%	35.532	29.136	23.892	87.840

(2)

	t_1 £'000	t_2 £'000	t_3 £'000
Gross annual costs	440.000	510.000	580.000
Less depreciation (840/3)	(280.000)	(280.000)	(280.000)
Net annual costs	160.000	230.000	300.000
Net annual costs inflated @ 5% p.a.	168.000	253.575	347.288

(3)

	t_1 £'000	t_2 £'000	t_3 £'000
Contribution forgone	150.000	150.000	150.000
Contribution forgone inflated @ 5% p.a.	157.500	165.375	173.644

(4)

	t_0 £'000	t_1 £'000	t_2 £'000	t_3 £'000
Working capital (in money terms)	(160.000)	(168.000)	(176.400)	0
Increment to working capital (in £)	(160,000)	(8,000)	(8,400)	176,400

5.2

	t_0 £'000	t_1 £'000	t_2 £'000	t_3 £'000
Machine	(940.000)			100.000
Tax on machine (W1)	35.532	29.136	23.892	87.840
Income	1,000.000	1,000.000		
Annual costs (W2)		(168.000)	(253.575)	(347.288)
Contribution (W3)		(157.500)	(165.375)	(173.644)
Tax on profit/loss (W5)		(141.645)	(122.021)	109.396
Working capital (W4)	(160.000)	(8.000)	(8.400)	176.400
Total cash flows	(64.468)	553.991	(525.479)	(47.296)
Discount factor (10%)	1.000	0.909	0.826	0.751
PV	(64.468)	503.578	(434.046)	(35.519)
NPV	(30.455)			

The NPV is a negative figure, albeit marginal, and so it would not be worth following the director's suggestion as this will reduce shareholder wealth. If the board agrees with the director and thinks that waiting for the tender monies until 20Y1 is risky then it should increase the discount rate to take account of the risk.

WORKING

(5)

	t_0 £'000	t_1 £'000	t_2 £'000	t_3 £'000
Income (receivable y/e 20X9 & 20Y0)		1,000.000	1,000.000	
Annual costs		(168.000)	(253.575)	(347.288)
Contribution		(157.500)	(165.375)	(173.644)
Taxable	0	674.500	581.050	(520.932)
Tax (payable)/receivable @ 21%	0	(141.645)	(122.021)	109.396

5.3 Advantages of a business combination:

(a) Synergistic savings – administration, economies of scale, use of common investment, leaner management structures, access to under-utilised assets

(b) Risk reduction – more stable cash flows, so less risk, so lower WACC

(c) Reduced competition in the market

(d) Fast way of expanding, compared to organic growth

(e) Vertical integration

5.4

	£m
Current value of Tidefrost = 20m × £0.26 × 18 =	93.6
Value of combined business = ([20m × £0.26]+[14m × £0.15]+£1.8m) × 16 =	145.6
Maximum offer price for Barryfinn	52.0

5.5

Advantages of a cash offer:	More attractive to seller
	Certain amount received
Disadvantages of a cash offer:	Can create liquidity problems – possibility of extra borrowings
	Possible tax implications
Advantages of a share exchange:	Preserves liquidity
	No tax issues
Disadvantages of a share exchange:	Extra shares increases dilution of ownership
	Dealing costs (selling shares)
	Uncertain amount received

ICAEW

Examiner's comments:

This question scored the highest average mark for the paper.

This was based on a business considering two investment opportunities – (1) a contract to supply materials to a customer and (2) the acquisition of another company in the same industry which will lead to significant costs savings. The question was structured around two investment appraisals – (1) an NPV calculation involving a tender bid [parts 5.1 and 5.2] and (2) [parts (5.3) to (5.5)] required analysis using price/earnings (p/e) ratios and earnings figures for both companies.

In part 5.1 most candidates were able to calculate the relevant cash flows and dealt with the effects of inflation correctly. However, a number of candidates did poorly with the working capital figures. The tender bid required candidates to calculate a minimum price, payable at the end of the contract. Disappointingly, few of them properly took account here of the effects of taxation and the relevant discount factor. A few candidates applied a very strict interpretation of the information given and depreciated the machinery over four years, rather than three. They were not penalised for this.

Part 5.2 of the question required discussion of the timings of the cash inflows from the contract. It was not done well. Too many candidates produced general points and didn't supplement their conclusions with relevant workings.

Part 5.3 of the question was done well and most candidates were able to identify the main advantages of a business combination. Part 5.4 was not answered well in most cases. Too many candidates were unable to identify the correct approach and, therefore, the relevant figures to work with.

As with part 5.3 part 5.5 of the question was done well and most candidates were able to identify the main advantages/disadvantages of cash offer/share-for-share exchange.

---

6 Horton plc (June 2009)

Marking guide

				Marks
6.1	(a)	Calculation of capital allowances	3	
		Calculation of NPV	1	
				4
	(b)	Scenario 1	1	
		Scenario 2	4	
		Scenario 3	5	
		Scenario 4	2	
				12
	(c)	Characteristics of finance leases	3	
		Characteristics of operating leases	3	
		Reasons why leasing might be a preferred source of finance:		
		1 mark per valid point	max 2	8
6.2	(a)	Calculations for:		
		1 year cycle	1	
		2 year cycle	1	
		3 year cycle	1	
		Annual equivalent cost, 0.5 marks per cycle	1.5	
		Conclusion	0.5	
				5
	(b)	1.5 marks per valid issue discussed	max 6	
				35

6.1 (a) **Project 3**

Capital Allowances

Cost	3,000,000

20X9 WDA $\dfrac{540,000}{2,460,000}$ @ 21% = 113,400

20Y0 WDA $\dfrac{442,800}{2,017,200}$ @ 21% = 92,988

20Y1 WDA $\dfrac{363,096}{1,654,104}$ @ 21% = 76,250

20Y2 WDA $\dfrac{297,739}{1,356,365}$ @ 21% = 62,525

Proceeds $\dfrac{1,000,000}{}$
Bal. All. 356,365 @ 21% = 74,837

Year	0	1	2	3	4
	(2,886,600)	(1,407,012)	3,826,250	3,812,525	3,824,837
	1	0.909	0.826	0.751	0.683
PV	(2,886,600)	(1,278,974)	3,160,483	2,863,206	2,612,364
NPV	£4,470,479				

(b) **Scenario 1:**

With no capital rationing, all projects yielding a positive NPV should be accepted.

Therefore, accept 100% of Projects 1, 3 and 4.

Scenario 2:

With capital rationing of £4.5m at T_0 and divisible projects, the NPV per £ invested needs to be calculated for each project:

Project 1: 2,676,600/2,400,000 = £1.12 (Rank 2)

Project 2: (461,700)/2,250,000 = Negative

Project 3: 4,470,479/3,000,000 = £1.49 (Rank 1)

Project 4: 2,016,250/2,630,000 = £0.77 (Rank 3)

Project 5: (45,250)/3,750,000 = Negative

So with £4.5m to invest, accept 100% of Project 3 (£3m) and 62.5% of Project 1 (£1.5m).

Scenario 3:

Under this scenario Project 2 will never be accepted as it yields a negative NPV and consumes funds in the year of capital rationing. However, Project 4 will always be accepted as it yields a positive NPV and generates funds in the year of capital rationing.

Of the remaining projects:

Project 1: 2,676,600/750,000 = £3.57 (Rank 1)

Project 3: 4,470,479/1,500,000 = £2.98 (Rank 2)

Project 5: Negative NPV

However, although Project 5 has a negative NPV of £45,250 it does release £1,050,000 at T_1. The question that needs to be asked, therefore, is whether the negative NPV is outweighed by the return on these released funds if Project 5 is undertaken.

Without Project 5, capital available = £300,000 + £750,000 (from Project 4) which means Horton can accept 100% of Projects 1 and 4, and 20% of Project 3 to yield an overall NPV of £5,586,946.

If Project 5 is undertaken, capital available = £300,000 + £750,000 (from Project 4) + £1,050,000 (from Project 5) which means Horton can accept 100% of Projects 1, 4, 5 and 90% of Project 3 (£1.35m) to yield an overall NPV of £8,671,031. So this latter solution maximises shareholder wealth.

Scenario 4:

With indivisible projects, the potential portfolios of investments possible with capital of £5.25m are as follows: Project 1 OR Project 3 OR Project 4 OR Projects 1 and 4

The NPVs generated by these four possibilities are:

Project 1: 2,676,600

Project 3: 4,470,479

Project 4: 2,016,250

Projects 1 and 4: 4,692,850

Therefore, the projects that should be undertaken are Projects 1 and 4.

Note. 99.9% of candidates attempting this question proceeded on the basis set out above, which takes account of the revised NPV for Project 3 calculated in part 6.1(a) – £4,470,479 – but which retains the original Project 3 cash outlays as (£3m) in T_0 and (£1.5m) in T_1, thereby reflecting the practical reality that Horton would have to spend these sums before receiving the benefit of the capital allowances calculated in part 6.1(a).

However, it should be noted that full credit was given to any candidate who used the revised Project 3 cash outlays of £2,886,600 in T_0 and £1,407,012 in T_1.

Taking this approach would have the following impact on the calculations:

In Scenario 1, no impact.

In Scenario 2, Project 3 would now yield an NPV per £ invested of £1.55 (still Rank 1) and 67.2% of Project 1 could now be undertaken (up from 62.5%)

In Scenario 3, Project 3 would now yield an NPV per £ invested of £3.18 (still Rank 2); without Project 5, 21.3% of Project 3 could now be undertaken (up from 20%); and this would now yield an overall NPV of £5,646,036; with Project 5, 95.9% of Project 3 could now be undertaken and this would now yield an overall NPV of £8,936,936.

(c) The differences between finance leases and operating leases can be summarised as follows:

A finance lease transfers substantially all the risks and rewards of ownership of an asset to the lessee (ie. the lessor does not retain these risks and rewards). One lease will exist for the whole or major part of the useful life of the asset – with ownership possibly passing to the lessee at the end of the term, possibly at a 'bargain price' or a peppercorn rent is paid during a secondary lease period. The lessor does not usually deal directly in the type of asset leased. The lease cannot usually be cancelled and if it is the lessee usually has to pay a penalty that equates to liability for all outstanding payments due under the lease agreement. The substance of the transaction is the purchase of the asset by the lessee, financed by a loan from the lessor.

With an operating lease the lease period will be less than the useful life of the asset and the lessor will depend on the subsequent leasing or eventual sale to cover his outlay and generate a profit. The lessor may very well carry on a trade in the particular type of asset leased. The lessor is normally responsible for repairs and maintenance. The lease can sometimes be cancelled at short notice. The substance of the transaction is the short-term rental of the asset by the lessee.

The reasons why leasing might be a preferred source of finance are as follows:

(1) Tax: the tax effects of owning an asset compared to using one under a lease are different and can lead to a preference for leasing as a source of finance.

(2) Capital rationing: firms, in particular small firms, who may encounter difficulties raising conventional loan finance, are effectively able to use the asset acquired as security to overcome such potential funding problems.

(3) Cash flow: leasing means avoiding the large cash outlay at the outset. Lease payments will be predictable which aids business planning.

(4) Cost of capital: the implicit cost of borrowing in the lease can be lower than that in a conventional bank loan.

(5) Flexibility: examples such as ease of arrangement; lower payments in early stages; combining other elements into overall package – service, insurance, secondary lease terms.

6.2 (a) Calculation of NPVs of each potential replacement cycle:

1-year cycle:

$$(11,000) + \{7,000 \times 0.909\} + \{(6,600) \times 0.909\} = £(10,636)$$

2-year cycle:

$$(11,000) + \{4,200 \times 0.826\} + \{(6,600) \times 0.909\} + \{(7,600) \times 0.826\} = £(19,808)$$

3-year cycle:

$$(11,000) + \{1,800 \times 0.751\} + \{(6,600) \times 0.909\} + \{(7,600) \times 0.826\} + \{(9,200) \times 0.751\} = £(28,834)$$

The annual equivalent costs are:

1-year cycle: $(10,636)/0.909 = £(11,701)$
2-year cycle: $(19,808)/1.736 = £(11,410)$
3-year cycle: $(28,834)/2.487 = £(11,594)$

Therefore the advice to the managing director should be to replace the new company cars after two years.

(b) Weaknesses of the method

- The analysis in part 6.1(a) ignores price changes of all descriptions. A change in the price of a new car, for example, could easily alter the conclusion. The same would be true for all of the input factors.

- The approach taken assumes that replacement will take place with an identical car. The car may be replaced with an improved model. Horton may conclude that it no longer has a need for such a car. In practice it seems unlikely that cars are replaced with identical models on a continuing basis.

- The timing of the cash outflows on new cars could be an issue in practice, ie making payments every fourth year may cause less of a cash flow problem than every third year.

- The effects of taxation have been ignored in this analysis.

Examiner's comments:

Candidates generally coped well with the calculation of capital allowances in the opening section of part 6.1 and it was a rare script that failed to pick up full marks (where this did happen, it was most commonly due only to arithmetical slips of the pen). With the four capital rationing scenarios most candidates were able to identify the correct projects to pursue in scenario 1. However, in scenario 2 there were weaker candidates who simply failed to use the ranking methodology based on NPV per £ invested. Weaker candidates also found scenario 3 rather challenging, overlooking the need to consider Project 5 in spite of its negative NPV in view of the cash released in the second period. Most candidates coped well with scenario 4. Most candidates picked up high marks on the technical knowledge part of the lease discussion, but scored less strongly on the whole in discussing the relative merits of leasing over outright purchase. Another notable feature was that some candidates tended to answer the question with their 'financial reporting' hat on rather than their 'financial management' hat – the examination is a test of candidates' knowledge of the financial management learning materials.

Most candidates found little to trouble them in the standard replacement analysis question in part 6.2.

7 Oxidian plc (December 2010)

		Marks
7.1	Calculation of capital allowances	2
	Calculation of balancing allowance	2
	Conclusion on when to dispose	1
		5
7.2	Investment	1
	Capital allowances	1
	SG contribution	1
	Lost M contribution	2
	Development	2
	Redundancy	1
	Salaries	1
	Tax	1
	Working capital	2
	Discount factors	0.5
	Omission of market research costs	1
	Recommendation to proceed	0.5
		14
7.3	Conflict between objectives	2
	Directors adopting multiple stakeholder perspective	1
	Difference in risk appetite	2
	Short-term perspective by directors	1
	Dividends versus retentions	1
	Information asymmetry	1
		Max 6
		25

7.1

			Tax Effect at 21%
		£	£
20X0	Cost	900,000	
	WDA (18%)	162,000	34,020
		738,000	
20X1	WDA (18%)	132,840	27,896
		605,160	
20X2	WDA (18%)	108,929	22,875
		496,231	
20X3	WDA (18%)	89,322	18,758
		406,909	
EITHER			
20X4	Disposal	150,000	
	Bal. All	256,909	53,951
OR			
20X4	WDA (18%)	73,244	15,381
		333,665	
20X5	Disposal	150,000	
	Bal. All	183,665	38,570

Disposal should not be delayed until 20X5 – identical capital allowances arise under each option but the larger positive cash flow in 20X4 under the first option means disposal in 20X4 should be selected as the preferred option.

7.2	20X0 £	20X1 £	20X2 £	20X3 £	20X4 £
Investment	(900,000)				150,000
Capital allowances	34,020	27,896	22,875	18,758	53,951
SG contribution (W1)		412,500	660,000	825,000	412,500
Lost M contribution (W2)		(135,000)	(216,000)	(270,000)	(135,000)
Development	(20,000)				
Redundancy	60,000				(80,000)
Salaries		(90,000)	(90,000)	(90,000)	(90,000)
Tax (21%)	(8,400)	(39,375)	(74,340)	(97,650)	(22,575)
Working capital (W3)	(52,500)	(31,500)	(21,000)	52,500	52,500
Net cash flow	(886,880)	144,521	281,535	438,608	341,376
df	1.000	0.909	0.826	0.751	0.683
Present value	(886,880)	131,370	232,548	329,395	233,160
NPV	39,593				

As the NPV is positive, it is recommended to proceed with the investment.

WORKINGS

(1) **SG contribution = (Annual demand × £55)**

(2) **Lost M contribution**

20X1 7,500 × 100 = 750,000 × 30% = 225,000 × 60% = 135,000
20X2 12,000 × 100 = 1,200,000 × 30% = 360,000 × 60% = 216,000
20X3 15,000 × 100 = 1,500,000 × 30% = 450,000 × 60% = 270,000
20X4 7,500 × 100 = 750,000 × 30% = 225,000 × 60% = 135,000

(3) **Working capital required is 0.1 × 0.7 × SG sales revenue**

20X0 0.1 × 0.7 × 750,000 = 52,500 Cash flow = (52,500)
20X1 0.1 × 0.7 × 1,200,000 = 84,000 Cash flow = (31,500)
20X2 0.1 × 0.7 × 1,500,000 = 105,000 Cash flow = (21,000)
20X3 0.1 × 0.7 × 750,000 = 52,500 Cash flow = 52,500
20X4 0.1 × 0.7 × Nil = Nil Cash flow = 52,500

7.3 There may be a conflict between the shareholders' required pursuit of wealth maximisation by directors and the directors' actual pursuit of managerial objectives (pay, job security, prestige, power, working conditions).

Directors adopting a multiple stakeholder perspective as opposed to a pure shareholder perspective.

A difference in risk appetite between shareholders and directors – shareholders viewing risk from the perspective of their portfolio of investments, whilst the perspective of directors may be purely based on the firm. This may, for example, lead to directors raising less debt than is optimal for shareholders.

A short-term perspective by directors (possibly created by their remuneration mechanism) versus a long-term perspective expected by shareholders.

- Dividends versus retentions.
- Issues around information asymmetry.

Examiner's comments:

Overall, candidates found this question much to their liking, with many very high marks being recorded. It is clear that most candidates are very well drilled in the mechanics of NPV calculations and have a firm grasp of the principles involved.

Most well-prepared candidates scored full marks on part 7.1. However some weaker candidates lost their way towards the end of the calculation through a misunderstanding of how to deal accurately with the balancing allowance. Some candidates recorded only the final tax effects in their answers without setting out in full the capital allowances from which those tax effects arose – credit was, however, given for clearly correct underlying calculations.

Many strong responses were again in evidence on part 7.2. Indeed, there were many instances of full marks being achieved. Where this was not the case, the following were the most common errors – errors in the calculation of both the lost contribution and the working capital requirements due to overlooking the need to include appropriate adjustments eg. 0.7 in the latter calculation; miscalculation of the relevant development cost; incorrectly including the sunk cost; failure to bother doing the discounting or to make a final recommendation.

Instances of full marks were, in contrast, much less common on part 7.3. Weaker candidates were often restricted to making just one or two of the above points and too often they failed to develop the point in a way that illustrated their full grasp of the point being made.

8 Broadham Hotels Ltd (December 2001)

Marking guide

		Marks
8.1	Annual cost	4
	Money terms	2
	PV of expected cost	1
	Annual fee	2
	Workings	4
		13
8.2	1 mark per point	max 4
8.3	1 mark per point	max 5
		22

8.1 Determination of the minimum annual payment

Expected value of the loss of the rooms

Since at the two lowest levels of demand occupancy would not be affected by the Septo proposal, the expected value of lost bookings will be as follows.

$$[(420-400) \times 0.3] + [(440-400) \times 0.2] + [(460-400) \times 0.1] = 20 \text{ rooms per night}$$

Annual cost (at 1 July 20X2 prices) = $20 \times 50 (1 - 10\%) \times 360 = £324,000$

In 'money' terms

Year ending 30 June			£	Net of tax £	Factor (see below)	PV £
20X3	$£324,000 \times 1.03$	=	333,720	263,639	0.883	232,793
20X4	$£324,000 \times 1.03^2$	=	343,732	271,548	0.779	211,536
20X5	$£324,000 \times 1.03^3$	=	354,044	279,695	0.688	192,430
20X6	$£324,000 \times 1.03^4$	=	364,665	288,085	0.607	174,868
20X7	$£324,000 \times 1.03^5$	=	375,605	296,728	0.536	159,046
			Present value of expected cost			970,673

Let F = Annual Septo fee

F + 2.957F − (3.493F × 0.21) = 970,673

F = £301,127

(The annual fee is receivable on 1 July 20X2 and on 1 July of each of the four subsequent years. Tax is payable on 30 June 20X3 and on 30 June of each of the four subsequent years.)

WORKING

Discount factors	$1 + m$	$= (1 + r) \times (1 + i)$		
	M	$= (1.10 \times 1.03) − 1$		
		$= 0.133$		
Factor for 1 year	$= \dfrac{1}{1.133}$	$= 0.883$		
Factor for 2 years	$= \dfrac{1}{1.133^2}$	$= 0.779$		
Factor for 3 years	$= \dfrac{1}{1.133^3}$	$= 0.688$		
Factor for 4 years	$= \dfrac{1}{1.133^4}$	$= 0.607$	2.957	= 4 year annuity factor
Factor for 5 years	$= \dfrac{1}{1.133^5}$	=	0.536	
			3.493	= 5 year annuity factor

8.2 Information that should have been brought into the annual payment determined in 8.1

Possible information that could have been brought into the determination of the annual payment includes the following.

- The possible effect on room sales of the loss of the top floors (view and security etc).

- The possible loss of sales as a result of customers not attempting to book a room because of the likelihood that the hotel will be full.

- The possible room sales to Septo if the proposal does not go ahead; Septo's staff will have to stay somewhere locally.

- The likely loss of ancillary sales eg restaurant sales.

8.3 Discussion of the advisability of the proposal from Septo's perspective

Septo is seeking to have 'in house' an activity that most businesses would 'outsource'. It involves Septo in an activity that seems well outside its core activity and, presumably, its area of expertise.

This could be expensive and risky as it turns a variable type of cost (paying by room/night as needed) into a fixed cost. How often will Septo need all 100 rooms?

Five years is a long time to commit to use a facility like this.

It also has an adverse cash flow profile, since the annual fee is payable in advance.

On the other hand, Septo has the opportunity to control quality and style. It could prove to be much cheaper than taking rooms by the night, provided that Septo were able to make good use of the facility.

Examiner's comments:

Generally the performance on this question, particularly on requirement 8.1, was disappointing. This is difficult to understand because the scenario is straightforward and well defined in the question.

In part 8.1 candidates were asked to use NPV to identify the fixed annual fee that a business needs to pay a hotel to make the hotel owners indifferent between letting out a significant part of the hotel as a block and letting the rooms available in the normal way.

This was generally not well answered, with relatively few correct answers. Many candidates failed to recognise that the effective cost to BH of leasing 100 rooms to Septo, all other things being equal, was the expected loss of room lettings. Since BH would still have 400 rooms available, it was only its inability to meet demand above that number that would represent a cost of a deal with Septo. These candidates tended to calculate the cost of the arrangement to BH by taking the expected value of the entire projected demand.

Many candidates who correctly recognised the incremental nature of the cost, failed to recognise that at the two lowest levels of projected demand the Septo arrangement would not affect matters. Having identified the ENPV of the lost rooms, some candidates experienced difficulties in converting this to a fixed annual fee. Some simply divided by five, some treated the fee as being receivable at year ends and some ignored tax on the fee.

Part 8.2 asked candidates to state and explain any information, not taken into account in 8.1 that should have been included. Generally this requirement was well answered. There were plenty of good, obvious points to be made and most candidates made sufficient of them to score well.

Part 8.3 asked candidates to discuss whether, from the point of view of the potential lessee, the proposed arrangement seems a good idea. Generally this was not well answered. Septo is contemplating taking 'in house' a normally 'outsourced' activity, yet few candidates picked up this area of discussion. A number of candidates made points that were simply not justified, such as saying that a possible deal with BH would be cheaper for Septo than booking rooms as it needed them. Without knowing the fee that BH would accept and much else besides, it is simply not logical to make such an assertion.

9 ProBuild plc (June 2013)

Marking guide

		Marks
9.1	Best case scenario:	
	Plant and equipment	2
	Capital allowance	2
	Operating cash flow	2
	Tax	1
	Working capital	2
	Discount factor and NPV	2
	Worst case scenario:	
	Capital allowance	2
	Operating cash flow	1
	Tax	2
	NPV	1
		17
9.2	Discussion of uncertainty and risk	6
		6
9.3	Discussion of real options	6
		6
		29

9.1 *Best case scenario*

	20X3	20X4	20X5	20X6	20X7
Plant & Equipment	(1,500,000)				100,000
Capital Allowance (W1)	84,000	67,200	53,760	43,008	144,032
Operating Cash Flow (W2)		1,173,000	1,196,460	1,220,389	1,244,797
Tax (28%)		(328,440)	(335,009)	(341,709)	(348,543)
Working Capital (W3)	(163,200)	(3,264)	(3,329)	(3,396)	173,189
	(1,579,200)	908,496	911,882	918,292	1,313,475
Discount Factor (W4)	1	0.9337	0.8636	0.7911	0.7250
	(1,579,200)	848,263	787,501	726,461	952,269
NPV	£1,735,294				

Worst case scenario

	20X3	20X4	20X5	20X6	20X7
Plant & Equipment	(1,500,000)				100,000
Capital Allowance (W1)	84,000	67,200	53,760	43,008	144,032
Operating Cash Flow (W2)		499,800	509,796	519,992	530,392
Tax (28%)		(139,944)	(142,743)	(145,598)	(148,510)
Working Capital (W3)	(97,920)	(1,958)	(1,998)	(2,038)	103,914
	(1,513,920)	425,098	418,815	415,364	729,828
Discount Factor (W4)	1	0.9337	0.8636	0.7911	0.7250
	(1,513,920)	396,914	361,689	328,594	529,125
NPV	£102,402				

WORKINGS

(1) **Capital Allowances (£)**

20X3	Cost	1,500,000
	WDA	$300,000 \times 28\% = 84,000$
		1,200,000
20X4	WDA	$240,000 \times 28\% = 67,200$
		960,000
20X5	WDA	$192,000 \times 28\% = 53,760$
		768,000
20X6	WDA	$153,600 \times 28\% = 43,008$
		614,400
20X7	Disposal	100,000
		$514,400 \times 28\% = 144,032$

(2) **Operating Cash Flows**

Best Case Scenario: $2,000,000 - (500,000 + 350,000) = 1,150,000$

20X4:	1,173,000	$(1,150,000 \times 1.02)$
20X5:	1,196,460	$(1,150,000 \times 1.02^2)$
20X6:	1,220,389	$(1,150,000 \times 1.02^3)$
20X7:	1,244,797	$(1,150,000 \times 1.02^4)$

Worst Case Scenario: $1,200,000 - (360,000 + 350,000) = 490,000$

20X4:	499,800	$(490,000 \times 1.02)$
20X5:	509,796	$(490,000 \times 1.02^2)$
20X6:	519,992	$(490,000 \times 1.02^3)$
20X7:	530,392	$(490,000 \times 1.02^4)$

(3) **Working Capital**

Best Case Scenario:

20X3:	$(2,000,000 \times 1.02 \times 0.08) = (163,200)$
20X4:	$(2,000,000 \times 1.02^2 \times 0.08) - 163,200 = (3,264)$
20X5:	$(2,000,000 \times 1.02^3 \times 0.08) - 166,464 = (3,329)$
20X6:	$(2,000,000 \times 1.02^4 \times 0.08) - 169,793 = (3,396)$
20X7:	173,189

Worst Case Scenario:

20X3: $(1,200,000 \times 1.02 \times 0.08) = 97,920$
20X4: $(1,200,000 \times 1.02^2 \times 0.08) - 97,920 = (1,958)$
20X5: $(1,200,000 \times 1.02^3 \times 0.08) - 99,878 = (1,998)$
20X6: $(1,200,000 \times 1.02^4 \times 0.08) - 101,876 = (2,038)$
20X7: $103,914$

(4) **Discount Factor**

20X4: $1/(1 + 0.05)(1.02) = 0.9337$
20X5: $1/(1 + 0.05)(1 + 0.06)(1.02^2) = 0.8636$
20X6: $1/(1 + 0.05)(1 + 0.06)(1 + 0.07)(1.02^3) = 0.7911$
20X7: $1/(1 + 0.05)(1 + 0.06)(1 + 0.07)^2(1.02^4) = 0.7250$

9.2 Decisions are usually said to be subject to uncertainty if the possible outcomes of a decision are known but the probabilities attaching to each possible outcome are unknown.

Decisions are usually said to be subject to risk if, although there are several possible outcomes of a decision, these outcomes as well as the respective probabilities attaching to each of these possible outcomes are known.

The calculations undertaken in part 9.1 have been made under conditions of uncertainty as the directors do not have details of the probabilities attaching to the two scenarios. So they need to establish such probabilities and then calculate expected values for each variable (the arithmetic mean of possible outcomes weighted by the probability of each outcome).

9.3 The concept of 'real options' relates to the strategic implications attaching to undertaking a particular project - the value of such 'real options' would not ordinarily be included in a traditional NPV calculation – consideration of 'real options' leads to a revised decision model:

Project Value = Traditional NPV + the value of any 'real options'

Two obvious 'real options' applicable to Brixham's acquisition of Cabin are:

(1) Follow-on option: for example, the opportunity to add further acquisitions in due course to gain the benefits of increased economies of scale/market share

(2) Growth option: for example, the opportunity to broaden the range of services on offer in due course.

Examiner's comments

The first question on the paper was a standard investment appraisal question, supplemented by tests of technical knowledge and its practical application. For the most part, candidates scored strongly on the first part of the question, the majority clearly being well-drilled in the quantitative techniques involved in this part of the question. Equally apparent was that the majority of candidates were ill-equipped in terms of simple technical knowledge to pick up full or even high marks in the second and third parts of the question, with many scripts scoring zero or at most very low marks on both parts.

In the first part of the question, probably the most common error was inaccurate calculation of the inflation-adjusted discount factors. However, there were many instances of full marks.

The second part of the question was a straightforward test of knowledge of elements from the Learning Materials, but many candidates were completely unacquainted with them and consequently there was much waffling and little accuracy and substance to many of the candidates' responses. In the final part of the question, many candidates were completely unaware of what a 'real option' was in an investment decision-making context, with many candidates incorrectly interpreting 'real' as meaning after taking account of the effects of inflation, thereby betraying their lack of study of the Learning Materials. The last part of the question was of a different character to the second part in that it was not merely looking for technical knowledge, but also the application of that knowledge to the scenario in the question and weaker candidates too often simply presented theory rather than practical application.

10 Frome Lee Electronics Ltd (September 2008)

10.1

	T_0 £'000	T_1 £'000	T_2 £'000	T_3 £'000
Plant	(400.000)			60.000
Tax saved (W1)	15.120	12.398	10.167	33.715
Working capital (W2)	(32.000)	(5.000)	(3.000)	40.000
Sales (W2)		320.000	370.000	400.000
Materials		(52.000)	(64.000)	(70.000)
Labour		(26.000)	(32.000)	(35.000)
Other variable costs		(12.000)	(14.000)	(16.000)
Fixed overheads		(11.000)	(11.800)	(12.700)
Tax on profit (W3)		(45.990)	(52.122)	(55.923)
Total Cash Flows	(416.880)	180.408	203.245	344.092
Discount factor (W4)	1.000	0.925	0.855	0.783
PV	(416.880)	166.877	173.774	269.424
NPV	193.195			

Comments:

The NPV is positive and so Frome should proceed with the investment as shareholder value is enhanced.

WORKINGS

(1)

Cost	400.000	328.000	268.960	220.547
WDA @ 18%	(72.000)	(59.040)	(48.413)	160.547
WDV	328.000	268.960	220.547	60.000
Tax saved @ 21%	15.120	12.398	10.167	33.715

(2)

Working capital increment	32,000	5,000	3,000	(40,000)
Working capital total	32,000	37,000	40,000	
Sales (WC total × 10)		320,000	370,000	400,000

(3)

Sales (W2)	320,000	370,000	400,000
Total costs	(101,000)	(121,800)	(133,700)
Taxable profits	219,000	248,200	266,300
Tax payable @ 21%	(45,990)	(52,122)	(55,923)

(4)

Discount factor	(1/1.05/1.03)	0.925		
	(1/1.05/1.03/1.05/1.03)		0.855	
	(1/1.05/1.03/1.05/1.03/1.05/1.04)			0.783

10.2 Inflation has to be taken properly into account so that the correct NPV is calculated. Inflation will have a negative effect on the real value of money and an investor will need to be compensated for that loss of value. As a result it is important to match real cash flows with real interest/discount rate. This method can be problematic and so it is preferable, if possible, to match money (nominal) cash flows, ie actual cash flows, with an inflated discount rate. This discount rate is calculated as follows: $(1+m) = (1+r) \times (1+i)$, where m = money rate, r = real rate and i = inflation rate.

10.3 The cost of capital is the cost of funds that a company raises and uses, and the return that investors expect to be paid (commensurate with the risk exposure) for putting funds into the company and therefore is the minimum return that a company must make on its own investments, to earn the cash flows out of which investors can be paid their return.

If a company calculates its cost of capital at too high a figure then it is likely to reject investment opportunities that it should be taking on (ie would provide a positive NPV).

In contrast if it sets the cost of capital at too low a level then it is likely to take on investment opportunities that it shouldn't be taking on (ie those with negative NPVs).

Both of these outcomes would be detrimental to shareholder value.

10.4 **Follow-on**

Launching the Pink 'Un would give Frome an opportunity to launch further models at a later date. By investing in this first model, Frome effectively has the right to 'follow-on'. It is a call option.

Abandonment

Frome has budgeted to sell the capital equipment for £60,000 in September 20Y1. It may be that the three year project does not go as well as hoped and the company might then wish to abandon it and sell the assets earlier than anticipated. This would be a put option.

These two real options could be taken account of by Frome's management and would affect their decision regarding the project, which is otherwise only appraised by calculating its NPV.

The revised decision model becomes: Project worth = traditional NPV + value of any options.

Examiner's comments:

This question scored the highest average mark for the paper and was done very well.

Part 10.1 was relatively straightforward and most candidates scored high marks. The main errors were candidates inflating the cash flows (unnecessarily) or getting the discount factor to t_2 and t_3 incorrect.

Part 10.2 was done reasonably well, but too few candidates were able to adequately explain the reasons for their approach to inflation.

Most candidates failed to explain the meaning of the cost of capital in part 10.3. Otherwise it was done well.

Part 10.4 was generally done well and those candidates who scored well here explained the real options in the context of the question.

11 Farmshoppers Ltd

Marking guide

		Marks
NPV	1 mark per point	
SA	1 – 2 marks per point	
EV	1 – 2 marks per point	max 13

Notes on three techniques used in investment appraisal

NPV

The following points could be included:

- NPV is directly linked to the generally accepted, shareholder wealth maximisation objective

- It takes all of the relevant information into account

- The cost of financing the project is accounted for in such a way that it is only while the project uses the funds that the cost is charged to the project

- By using the opportunity cost of capital, the project is directly compared with competing demands for funds

- The level of risk can be accounted for in a logical way through a risk-adjusted discount rate

- It is generally accepted as the appropriate way of assessing investment projects.

Sensitivity analysis (SA)

This is a technique for assessing the riskiness of a project by asking how much each of the input factors to the decision could vary, in an adverse direction, from the original estimate, before it would cause the project to be non-viable (negative NPV).

The advantage of the approach is that it gives the decision-maker a feel for the input factors to which the outcome of the project would be particularly sensitive. This could lead to a reassessment of the project. Steps might be able to be taken to make the decision-maker more confident as to the actual outcome for the sensitive input factors. For example, if there were fears regarding a rise in the price of a raw material, it might be possible for some forward purchasing to take place.

The problems with the approach include the following:

- It provides only subjective signals that can be difficult to interpret in many cases.

- It is difficult to assess relative sensitivities: two factors may appear equally sensitive, yet their different natures could easily mean that their sensitivities are not at all similar.

- It is rather a 'static' technique: only one variable is considered at a time, but in practice usually more than one factor turns out to be different from the original estimate.

Scenario building is an extension of SA, where the possibility that various input factors could vary from their predicted values is considered. This is most easily achieved by modelling the project on a spreadsheet. Assessment can be made of various scenarios, including a worst case one. Scenario building does not solve the 'subjective judgement' problem of SA, but it can certainly deal with the 'static' criticism.

Expected value (EV)

The expected value is the average of all of the perceived possible outcomes for the project, weighted according to how likely each possible outcome is. As it is being used in this question, the weighted average value of each input is established and one single expected value is deduced for the NPV of the project.

Decision-making can be difficult where there is a vast array of possible outcomes, some favourable, others adverse. With a single EV the decision-maker has a single value on which to make a decision.

The problems with EV include the following:

- Difficulty in ascribing probabilities to various outcomes for each of the input factors.

- As it is being applied in the question, the EV only provides an average and, as with all averaging, information is hidden. The decision-maker would normally find it helpful to know the range and probabilities of the various outcomes for the project.

An alternative approach to that taken in the question would be to identify all of the possible outcomes, ie all of the various combinations of outcomes for each of the input factors. This would enable the decision-maker to know the overall expected value for the project and could also provide information on the dispersion of the various possible NPVs, perhaps by calculating the standard deviation.

A problem here is that in real life the number of possible combinations could be vast. Simulation (Monte Carlo) enables the decision maker to 'sample' this vast population, and to use the sample data to draw conclusions.

Examiner's comments:

Generally this question was rather poorly done, though there were some good answers. This was disappointing because the question dealt with some basic tools of financial decision-making.

Candidates were required to explain, in layperson's terms, NPV, sensitivity analysis and expected values, all in the context of a major investment decision by a small business. Many answers lacked depth and failed to explain the issues in simple, non-technical terms. A particularly disappointing aspect to many answers was that they gave the impression that the candidates concerned did not have a clear grasp of the issues themselves. Many answers were more concerned with the technical process of calculating NPV etc, than with explaining the principles involved and how the calculated figures could be helpful to a decision-maker.

12   CAPM and project appraisal

Marking guide

	Marks
12.1 2 marks per paragraph	max 14
12.2 1 mark per point	max 4
	18

12.1 Notes for the divisional manager

Discounting

Discounting of future cash flows is a technique used to place less value on cash flows which are received further into the future. This reflects the fact that our investors would rather receive money now than in the future. This preference for money now, which is known as the time value of money, is increased if there is inflation in the economy, as investors also need to be compensated for the buying power of their money being reduced in the future.

Therefore the discount rate is a combination of both the time value of money and inflation. Even if inflation is negligible, cash flows still need discounting to reflect the time value of money.

Discount rate

Finding the correct discount rate can be a difficult exercise and this is where the capital asset pricing model (CAPM) can be very useful.

CAPM looks at the returns paid on shares on the stock market compared to the risk or variation in returns of those shares. Because investors in general are risk averse, they will expect a higher average return by way of dividends and capital gains to compensate for a higher risk.

The logic then follows that if shareholders can earn a given return on the stock market for a certain level of risk, then any projects which we may undertake must at least satisfy that target return.

Where CAPM is special, however, is in the way it considers risk. A company or project looked at on its own may have a very high level of risk. However, if it is added to the shareholders' portfolio of investments, some of that risk will be removed or diversified away.

This is because two different causes of the total risk of a company can be identified.

Systematic risk   –   Due to the economy, such as interest rates, exchange rates, etc which affect all companies

Unsystematic risk – Due to events specific to a company, such as new product developments, fires, strikes, etc

Systematic risk cannot be diversified away; however, the unsystematic risk will cancel out across companies, as bad events in one company are evened out by good events in another.

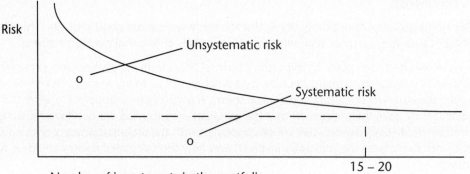

Therefore as shareholders suffer only systematic risk if they hold a wide-ranging or well-diversified portfolio, a company only needs to pay a return based on that risk.

CAPM measures the systematic risk as a beta. A beta of 1 indicates that the company has the same level of risk as the average of all UK shares, called the market portfolio. A beta of 0.5 would indicate that it has only half the risk of the market portfolio, and therefore does not need to give such a high return.

This can be expressed in the following equation.

Required return = $R_f + \beta (R_m - R_f)$

Where R_f = return on risk-free investments such as treasury bills
        R_m = average return on the market portfolio.

The beta for this type of industry can be readily found in a book published by the London Business School, as companies in the same industry share the same risk of economic variables.

Payback

Payback is a good technique in that it uses earlier cash flows which are more certain and useful if a company is short of cash. However, it has the following drawbacks:

- It ignores the time value of money
- It ignores cash flows after the payback period
- It does not measure the change in shareholder wealth
- Target paybacks are chosen subjectively.

The technique of using discounted cash flows, although more complicated, overcomes all of these problems.

Optimistic

	t0 20X1 £	t1 20X2 £	t2 20X3 £	t3 20X4 £
Machine	(480,000)			0
Tax saved on m/c	18,144	14,878	12,200	55,578
Contribution (W5)		399,300	399,300	399,300
Fixed costs		(140,000)	(140,000)	(140,000)
Tax on extra profit (W6)		(54,453)	(54,453)	(54,453)
Working capital	(50,000)			50,000
Total cash flows	(511,856)	219,725	217,047	310,425
Discount factor 10%	1.000	0.909	0.826	0.751
PV	(511,856)	199,730	179,281	233,129
NPV	100,284			

Average NPV $\dfrac{(55,259)+100,284}{2}$ = **£22,513**

OR

Overall expected sales = (9,700+12,100)/2=10,900 units

	t0 20X1 £	t1 20X2 £	t2 20X3 £	t3 20X4 £
Machine	(480,000)			0
Tax saved on m/c	18,144	14,878	12,200	55,578
Contribution (@£33)		359,700	359,700	359,700
Fixed costs		(140,000)	(140,000)	(140,000)
Tax on extra profit (W7)		(46,137)	(46,137)	(46,137)
Working capital	(50,000)			50,000
Total cash flows	(511,856)	188,441	185,763	279,141
Discount factor 10%	1.000	0.909	0.826	0.751
PV	(511,856)	171,293	153,440	209,635
NPV	22,512			

Positive NPV. Shareholder wealth increased. Therefore proceed.

WORKINGS

(1)

	t0 £	t1 £	t2 £	t3 £
Cost/WDV	480,000	393,600	322,752	264,657
WDA @ 18%	(86,400)	(70,848)	(58,095)	(264,657)
WDV	393,600	322,752	264,657	0
Tax @ 21%	18,144	14,878	12,200	55,578

(2) **Annual contribution**	£33/unit × 9,700 units =	£320,100
(3) **Annual fixed costs**	£300,000 - £160,000 =	£140,000
(4) **Annual tax on extra profit**	(£320,100 - £140,000) × 21% =	£37,821
(5) **Annual contribution**	£33/unit × 12,100 units =	£399,300
(6) **Annual tax on extra profit**	(£399,300 - £140,000) × 21% =	£54,453
(7) **Annual tax on extra profit**	(£359,700 - £140,000) × 21% =	£46,137

13.2 If inflation is taken into account then money (inflated) cash flows will be matched against NBL's money cost of capital, which is 15.5% (1.10 × 1.05)

(1) **Contribution** – there will be no effect on the NPV of the investment as both the cash inflows (annual contribution) and the cost of capital will have been inflated by 5% per annum, which will produce the same present value (allowing for small rounding differences) in each relevant year.

	t1	t2	t3	Total
'Real' cash flow (W2)	£320,100	£320,100	£320,100	
'Real' discount factor (10%)	(1/1.10)	(1/1.10²)	(1/1.10³)	
'Real' Present Value	£291,000	£264,545	£240,496	£796,041

	t1	t2	t3	Total
'Money' cash flow (inflated)	£336,105	£352,910	£370,556	
'Money' discount factor	(1/1.155)	(1/1.155²)	(1/1.155³)	
'Money' Present Value	£291,000	£264,545	£240,496	£796,041
NPV difference				0

(2) **Working capital** – the NPV will be affected by the impact of inflation on the working capital investment as there will be incremental increases to the working capital in the three years of the project and there will be an inflated working capital figure at the end of the project.

	t0	t1	t2	t3	Total
'Real' cash flow [see (a)]	(50,000)	0	0	50,000	0
'Real' discount factor (10%)	1.000	(1/1.10)	(1/1.10²)	(1/1.10³)	
'Real' Present Value	(50,000)	0	0	37,566	(12,434)
	t0	t1	t2	t3	Total
'Money' cash flow	(50,000)	(2,500)	(2,625)	55,125	0
'Money' discount factor (15.5%)	1.000	(1/1.155)	(1/1.155²)	(1/1.155³)	
'Money' Present Value	(50,000)	(2,164)	(1,968)	35,777	(18,355)
NPV difference					(5,921)

So the total impact of 5% annual inflation on contribution and working capital will be an NPV figure that is £5,921 lower.

Examiner's comments:

This question had the highest average mark on the paper and most candidates scored high marks.

This question tested the investment decisions element of the syllabus. The scenario was that of a manufacturer wishing to introduce a new product to the market and therefore needing to make a major capital investment.

In part 13.1 for 18 marks candidates were presented with a lot of information, as in a typical NPV setting, and were required to calculate the NPV of the proposal. The question was unusual in that candidates had to calculate the level of customer demand by using expected values. In addition, this demand was constrained by the fact that the new equipment had a maximum level of output. Despite this intricacy, candidates could secure a good mark here if they followed the key elements of an NPV calculation. Part 13.2 for 6 marks required candidates to explain the implications for their NPV calculation in part 13.1 if the contribution and working capital figures were adjusted to take account of a 5% annual inflation rate.

In part 13.1 most errors related to the expected values calculation with only a small minority of candidates getting it right. Many candidates ignored the production constraint completely. Despite these errors the majority of candidates scored high marks.

In part 13.2 the contribution figure was generally inflated accurately, but too many candidates only adjusted the final working capital figure, without taking account of the incremental annual changes. Also, too many candidates failed to make use of a money (inflated) discount rate, which suggests a real lack of understanding of the impact of inflation on cash flows.

14 Newmarket plc (Sample paper)

		Marks
14.1	Discount factor	1
	Equipment cost	1
	Incremental unit costs	2
	Incremental salary	1
	Market research fee	1
	Tax	2
	Writing down allowance	2
	Sale proceeds	1
	Price calculation – revenue	1
	Price calculation – tax on revenue	1
	Price calculation – equation	1
	Price calculation – selling price	1
		15
14.2	1 mark per point	max 6
14.3	1 mark per point	max 6
14.4	Existence of real options	1
	Follow on options	2
	Abandonment options	2
	Timing option	2
	Growth option	2
		max 8
		35

14.1 The schedule of relevant cash-flows and present values (in £) would be as follows:

Year	Item	CF	10% df	PV
0	Equipment purchase	(750,000)	1.000	(750,000)
1-5	Incremental unit costs (W1)	(170,000)	3.791	(644,470)
1-5	Tax re: unit costs	35,700	3.791	135,339
1-5	Incremental salary	(35,000)	3.791	(132,685)
1-5	Tax re: incremental salary	7,350	3.791	27,864
1	Market research fee	(10,000)	0.909	(9,090)
1	Tax re: market research fee	2,100	0.909	1,909
0	WDA (W2)	28,350	1.000	28,350
1	WDA	23,247	0.909	21,132
2	WDA	19,063	0.826	15,746
3	WDA	15,631	0.751	11,739
4	WDA	12,818	0.683	8,755
5	WDA	47,892	0.621	29,741
5	Sale proceeds	50,000	0.621	31,050
				(1,224,620)

Alternative presentation (also in £)

	0	1	2	3	4	5
Cost	(750,000)					50,000
Fee		(10,000)				
Inc.Costs		(170,000)	(170,000)	(170,000)	(170,000)	(170,000)
Salary		(35,000)	(35,000)	(35,000)	(35,000)	(35,000)
Tax		45,150	43,050	43,050	43,050	43,050
WDA	28,350	23,247	19,063	15,631	12,818	47,892
Net	(721,650)	(146,603)	(142,887)	(146,319)	(149,132)	(64,058)
10%	1	0.909	0.826	0.751	0.683	0.621
PV	(721,650)	(133,262)	(118,025)	(109,886)	(101,857)	(39,780)

Total PV = (1,224,460) difference due to rounding discount factors

If we set price equal to P

1-5	Revenue	2,000P	3.791	7,582P
1-5	Tax re: revenue	(420)P	3.791	(1,592)P
				5,990P

Therefore: **5,990P – 1,224,620 = 300,000**
5,990P = 1,524,620
P = £254.53

To the nearest £, Newmarket would need to charge a minimum unit price of £255

WORKINGS

(1) **Incremental unit costs**

Incremental unit cost:	£	
Labour (4 hours @ £12 per hour)	48.00	incremental
Components	32.00	incremental
Loan interest	0.00	dealt with via df
Depreciation	0.00	not a cash-flow
Energy costs	5.00	incremental
Share of Newmarket's fixed costs	0.00	not incremental
	85.00	

£85.00 × 2,000 = £170,000

(2) **Writing Down Allowances**

Year end		£	Tax effect @ 21% (£)	Year
30 June 20X2	Purchase	750,000		
	WDA @ 18%	(135,000)	28,350	0
		615,000		
30 June 20X3	WDA @ 18%	(110,700)	23,247	1
		504,300		
30 June 20X4	WDA @ 18%	(90,774)	19,063	2
		413,526		
30 June 20X5	WDA @ 18%	(74,435)	15,631	3
		339,091		
30 June 20X6	WDA @ 18%	(61,036)	12,818	4
		278,055		
30 June 20X7	Sale proceeds	50,000		
	Balancing allowance	228,055	47,892	5

14.2 1. Sensitivity analysis:

A way of incorporating alternative forecasts into project evaluation

Involves taking each uncertain forecast and calculating the change in the variable necessary for the NPV of the project to fall to zero

Formula: Sensitivity = NPV of project/PV of cash-flows subject to uncertainty × 100

2. Simulation (scenario analysis):

Allows the effect of more than one variable changing simultaneously to be assessed

Monte Carlo simulation, for example, makes use of random numbers and probability statistics to evaluate projects armed with a more detailed insight into the nature of risks and returns

[Reference to expected values would also be rewarded with up to three marks]

14.3 Systematic risk:

Also known as market risk

It is that element of risk that cannot be eliminated by diversification

It affects all markets within the economy systematically

Examples in this (or any such scenario) would be changes in macroeconomic variables, for example, changes in interest rates, inflation rates, capital allowances or other tax rate changes

Non-systematic (unsystematic) risk:

Also known as unique or specific risk

It is that element of risk that can be eliminated by diversification

It is related to factors that affect the return on individual investments in unique ways

Examples in this scenario would be a decrease in demand for the product below projections, unexpected actions of competitors or an increase in component costs

14.4 NPV only considers the cash flows associated with the NL500 project. It is possible that the project is worth more than the target NPV of £300,000 because of the existence of real options associated with the project.

Follow on options

Launching the NL500 gives an opportunity to launch a second (and third and so on) version of the lawnmower that could be very profitable (or not). The right to invest in later versions is a call option.

Abandonment option

If the NL500 is a failure then management can terminate the project early and sell the equipment, giving them a put option.

Timing option

It may be possible to delay the introduction of the NL500, particularly if the demand estimates are uncertain, effectively a call option. The longer the possible delay the more valuable the option. Newmarket would need to protect its position, eg from a competitor establishing a strong market position, by using patents.

Growth option

If the NL500 is more successful than envisaged, Newmarket have the (call) option to expand production facilities ie the opposite of the abandonment option.

Examiner's comments:

Rather surprisingly, this was the lowest scoring question on the paper, which is not something we normally associate with the investment appraisal question, albeit on a paper with a relatively high pass rate of 88%. The final stage of part 14.1 of the question proved beyond many candidates, who up until that point had generally coped well with the standard demands of the question. Parts 14.2 and 14.3 proved relatively straightforward for well-prepared candidates, but the failure of many weak candidates to complement their learning of technique with the acquisition of basic knowledge led to many of them often sacrificing all 12 of the marks available on these parts of the question.

Overall, the performance in part 14.1 of the question was strong, although where errors were made the most common ones related to the inclusion and timing of the fee payment, the inclusion of irrelevant costs and an inability to use the net present value calculation to accurately address the final stage of the question.

For the most part, well-prepared candidates scored full marks in part 14.2, but there were still a surprising number of scripts that missed the opportunity to score strongly, often veering off course into other areas of the syllabus, notably derivatives, which were not relevant to the precise requirements of the question.

Although part 14.3 covers an element of the syllabus that is tested relatively infrequently, the majority of candidates coped well with it, although there were still a significant number of weaker scripts that displayed a complete misunderstanding of the terms and that were, consequently, unable to apply them meaningfully to the scenario in the question.

15 Grimpen McColl International Ltd (September 2012)

	Marks
15.1 Equipment cost and residual value	0.5
Tax saving	2
Income	0.5
Materials and labour	1
Overheads	2
Lost contribution	1
Tax on extra profit	2
Working capital	2
Discount factor	1
Conclusion	1
	13
15.2 Calculation of decrease	2
Minimum value of second instalment	1
	3
15.3 1 mark per point	max 5
15.4 Annual surplus from year 4	1
Tax	1
Perpetuity factor	1
Discount to PV	1
	4
15.5 1 mark per point	max 5
	30

15.1

	20X2 Year 0 £'000	20X3 Year 1 £'000	20X4 Year 2 £'000	20X5 Year 3 £'000
Machinery	(30,000)			5,000
Tax saving (W1)	1,134	930	763	2,424
Income	10,000			85,000
Materials and labour (W2)		(7,280)	(8,653)	(10,124)
Overheads (W3)		(2,600)	(3,245)	(3,937)
Lost contribution (W4)		(4,200)	(4,410)	(4,631)
Tax on extra profit (W5)	(2,100)	2,957	3,425	(13,925)
Working capital (W6)	(5,000)	(1,240)	(1,331)	7,571
Total Cash Flows	(25,966)	(11,433)	(13,451)	67,378
8% factor	1.000	0.926	0.857	0.794
PV	(25,966)	(10,587)	(11,528)	53,498
NPV	5,417			

As the NPV is positive GMI should proceed with the investment as this will enhance shareholder wealth.

WORKINGS

(1)

	Year 0 £'000	Year 1 £'000	Year 2 £'000	Year 3 £'000
Cost of machinery	30,000	24,600	20,172	16,541
WDA @ 18%	(5,400)	(4,428)	(3,631)	(11,541)
WDV/sale	24,600	20,172	16,541	5,000
Tax saving @ 21% (WDA × 21%)	1,134	930	763	2,424

ICAEW

(2)

	Year 0 £'000	Year 1 £'000	Year 2 £'000	Year 3 £'000
Materials and labour		(7,000)	(8,000)	(9,000)
Inflation @ 4% pa		× 1.04	× 1.04^2	× 1.04^3
		(7,280)	(8,653)	(10,124)

(3)

Overheads (excluding Head office costs)		(2,500)	(3,000)	(3,500)
Inflation @ 4% pa		× 1.04	× 1.04^2	× 1.04^3
		(2,600)	(3,245)	(3,937)

(4)

		£'000	£'000	£'000
Lost contribution		(4,000)	(4,000)	(4,000)
Inflation @ 5% pa		× 1.05	× 1.05^2	× 1.05^3
		(4,200)	(4,410)	(4,631)

(5)

Income	10,000			85,000
Materials and labour		(7,280)	(8,653)	(10,124)
Overheads		(2,600)	(3,245)	(3,937)
Lost contribution		(4,200)	(4,410)	(4,631)
Profit/(loss)	10,000	(14,080)	(16,308)	66,308
Tax @ 21% on profit/(loss)	(2,100)	2,957	3,425	(13,925)

(6)

	Year 0 £'000	Year 1 £'000	Year 2 £'000	Year 3 £'000
Total investment (money terms)	5,000			
£6,000 × 1.04 (year 1)		6,240		
£7,000 × 1.04^2 (year 2)			7,571	0
(Increase)/decrease in WC	(5,000)	(1,240)	(1,331)	7,571

15.2 For NPV to fall to zero then the second instalment will need to fall by:

	£
£5,417,000/0.794/0.79 =	(8,635,972)
Estimated second instalment =	85,000,000
Minimum value of the second instalment	76,364,028

15.3 GMI's money cost of capital already takes into account GMI's estimated inflation rate. So if the cash flows are inflated at the same rate then the correct NPV will be calculated.

If the South American inflation rates are higher than predicted then inflate further the money cost of capital and the estimated cash flows. NPV will not be affected.

However, for the WDA, equipment resale and the second instalment, the NPV will fall as the money discount rate rises. These are in money terms already.

15.4

	£'000
Annual income from 20X6 (Year 4)	5,000
Annual costs from 20X6	(3,000)
Annual surplus from 20X6	2,000
Less tax @ 21%	(420)
	1,580
Perpetuity factor (1.08/1.03)	4.85%
PV of future cash flows at Year 3 [end 20X5] (£1,580/4.85%)	32,577
Discount to PV (from Year 3 [end 20X5])	× 0.794
PV of future cash flows (minimum selling price of the maintenance contract)	25,866

15.5 Political risk is the risk that political action will affect the position and value of a company.

Candidates' discussion should be based on the following possible risks:

- Quotas/tariffs/barriers imposed by the overseas government
- Nationalisation of assets by the overseas government
- Stability of the overseas government
- Political and business ethics
- Economic stability/inflation
- Remittance restrictions
- Special taxes
- Regulations on overseas investors.

Examiner's comments:

This question was a good discriminator between those students who have learned the calculations and underlying theory by rote and those who really understand the topic.

In general, in part 15.1, a fairly standard NPV calculation, most candidates scored high marks. The most common errors were made with regard to working capital investment and the corporation tax flows.

Part 15.2 was done reasonably, but a surprising number of candidates forgot to take taxation into account in their calculations.

The discursive nature of part 15.3 caught out many candidates - they failed to adequately explain the impact of using an erroneous inflation rate and therefore to demonstrate that they fully understood this part of the syllabus. A common error made by candidates was to forget that revenue from the project was fixed.

Part 15.4 was done poorly and too few candidates were able to adequately deal with the discounting techniques required.

16 Wicklow plc (December 2008)

Marking guide

		Marks
16.1 Capital allowances	3	
Revenue	3	
Material costs	2	
Lost contribution	3	
Labour	2	
Working capital	4	
Tax	1	
NPV calculation	1	
Maximum		18
16.2 Calculation of selling price sensitivity	4	
Calculation of cost of equity sensitivity	3	
		7
16.3 PV of tax shield	2	
APV calculation	2	
		4
16.4 2 marks per valid point		
Maximum		6
		35

	20X8	20X9	20Y0	20Y1	20Y2
Investment	(2,000,000)				200,000
Capital allowances (W1)	75,600	61,992	50,833	41,683	147,891
DH revenue (W2)		11,725,000	14,147,000	15,561,000	15,561,000
DH material costs (W3)		(6,365,000)	(7,679,800)	(8,447,400)	(8,447,400)
Duo lost contribution (W4)		(2,500,592)	(3,016,824)	(3,318,208)	(3,318,208)
Additional labour (W5)		(167,500)	(202,100)	(222,300)	(222,300)
New manager	35,000	(40,000)	(40,000)	(40,000)	(60,000)
Working capital (W6)	(941,700)	(194,625)	(113,625)		1,249,950
Taxation (21%)	(7,350)	(556,901)	(673,738)	(741,949)	(737,749)
NCF	(2,838,450)	1,962,374	2,471,746	2,832,826	4,373,184
df (8%)	1	0.926	0.857	0.794	0.735
DCF	(2,838,450)	1,817,158	2,118,286	2,249,264	3,214,290

NPV £6,560,548

The recommendation to the directors should, therefore, be to proceed with the 'Heritage' version of the Duo cooker.

WORKINGS

(1) **Capital Allowances**

20X8	£		£
Cost	2,000,000		
WDA (18%)	360,000	× 21% =	75,600
20X9	1,640,000		
WDA (18%)	295,200		
20Y0	1,344,800	× 21% =	61,992
WDA (18%)	242,064		
20Y1	1,102,736	× 21% =	50,833
WDA (18%)	198,492		
20Y2	904,244	× 21% =	41,683
Proceeds	200,000		
Bal. Allowance	704,244	× 21% =	147,891

(2) **DH Revenue**

20X9: $1,500(0.65) + 2,000(0.35) = 1,675 \times £7,000 = £11,725,000$

20Y0: $1,800(0.65 \times 0.7) + 2,000(0.65 \times 0.3) + 2,200(0.35 \times 0.6) + 2,500(0.35 \times 0.4) = 2,021 \times £7,000 = £14,147,000$

20Y1 and 20Y2: $110\% \times 2,021 = 2,223 \times £7,000 = £15,561,000$ p.a.

(3) **DH Material Costs**

Unit sales × £3,800
20X9: 1,675 units = £6,365,000
20Y0: 2,021 units = £7,679,800
20Y1 and 20Y2: 2,223 units = £8,447,400 p.a.

(4) **Duo Lost Contribution**

The effective lost contribution on each Duo = £6,500 - £3,516 = £2,984 as the labour cost and fixed overheads will still be incurred

20X9: 838 × £2,984 = £2,500,592
20Y0: 1,011 × £2,984 = £3,016,824
20Y1 and 20Y2: 1,112 × £2,984 = £3,318,208 p.a.

(5) Additional Labour Costs

The standard Duo product will simply provide half of the labour required to manufacture the 'Heritage' version of the product.

20X9: 1,675 units × 8 = 13,400/2 = 6,700 × £25 = £167,500
20Y0: 2,021 units × 8 = 16,168/2 = 8,084 × £25 = £202,100
20Y1 and 20Y2: 2,223 units × 8 = 17,784/2 = 8,892 × £25 = £222,300 p.a.

(6) Working Capital

	Next Year's Sales Value	15%
DH:		
20X8	11,725,000	(1,758,750)
20X9	14,147,000	(2,122,050)
20Y0	15,561,000	(2,334,150)
20Y1	15,561,000	(2,334,150)
20Y2	0	0
Duo:		
20X8	(5,447,000)	817,050
20X9	(6,571,500)	985,725
20Y0	(7,228,000)	1,084,200
20Y1	(7,228,000)	1,084,200
20Y2	0	0
Net effect:		
20X8	(941,700)	
20X9	(194,625)	
20Y0	(113,625)	
20Y1	0	
20Y2	1,249,950	

16.2 (a) To calculate the sensitivity of changes in sales price, it is assumed sales quantity is fixed and then the relevant cash flows from part 16.1 are considered.

	20X9	20Y0	20Y1	20Y2
DH revenue	11,725,000	14,147,000	15,561,000	15,561,000
Tax on revenue	(2,462,250)	(2,970,870)	(3,267,810)	(3,267,810)
Cash flow	9,262,750	11,176,130	12,293,190	12,293,190
df (8%)	0.926	0.857	0.794	0.735
Present value	8,577,307	9,577,943	9,760,793	9,035,495

Total present value = £36,951,538

Sensitivity = 6,560,548/36,951,538 = 17.8%

This means selling price can fall by 17.8% to £5,754 before the decision to invest would change.

(b) To calculate the sensitivity to the cost of equity, an IRR is required, using the net cash flows from part 16.1.

NCF	(2,838,450)	1,962,374	2,471,746	2,832,826	4,373,184
df (15%)	1	0.870	0.756	0.658	0.572
DCF	(2,838,450)	1,707,265	1,868,640	1,864,000	2,501,462

NPV = 5,102,917

IRR for this project = 8 + (6,560,548/(6,560,548 − 5,102,917))(15 − 8) = 39.5%

The cost of equity would need to increase to 39.5% (an increase of almost 400% from its current level) before the investment decision would change.

16.3 The NPV calculated in 16.1 above at £6,560,548 is for an ungeared firm.

The PV of the tax shield (interest = £2m × 0.05 = £0.1m) is calculated as follows:

Time	£ per annum	df @ 5%	PV (£)
1–4	0.1m × 0.21 = 0.021m	3.546	74,466

Therefore the adjusted present value = £6,560,548 + £74,466 = £6,635,014.

16.4 The APV technique is based upon the assumptions of Modigliani and Miller with tax.

That means that issues that may affect the attractiveness of debt finance are not reflected in the technique:

- Direct and indirect costs of bankruptcy
- Agency costs and covenants
- Tax exhaustion
- Perfect market assumptions eg. risk-free debt.

To the extent that any of these assumptions do not hold true, the APV methodology will not take account of all the potential implications of increased debt within a firm's capital structure.

There is also a question mark over the appropriate rate at which to discount the tax shield.

Examiner's comments:

Most candidates found section 16.1 of the question to their liking. The initial calculation of expected values proved largely unproblematic, but common errors among weaker candidates were incorrect calculation of the lost contribution from the existing product and an inability to calculate accurately the net working capital impact of the project. In this latter regard, a surprising number of candidates correctly calculated the impact of the new product, but then failed to deduct the off-setting impact of the existing product. It was also apparent that a significant number of candidates appear to believe that it is an effective time-saving tactic not to bother with the calculation of discount factors and/or the actual discounting of cash flows and simply to say that if the resultant NPV was positive their recommendation would be to accept the project (or vice versa). Given that marks were explicitly available for both the discount factors and the discounting process itself, this was a potentially costly omission.

Section 16.3, along with section 16.4, proved to be effective discriminators between stronger and weaker candidates. Many weaker candidates were unable to make any meaningful attempt, some simply believing that what was required was to discount the net cash flows calculated in section 16.1 at a discount factor of 5%. Common errors among candidates who were able to adopt the correct approach were to use an incorrect annuity factor in the calculation or to use the post-tax cost of debt, but for well prepared candidates this proved to be easy marks.

Section 16.4 polarised performance, although unlike in section 16.3 it was the majority rather than the minority of candidates who struggled. The question required candidates to think laterally across the syllabus to establish the link to underlying theory. However, many candidates resorted simply to listing all they knew about the limitations of issues such as WACC and CAPM.

Performance overall was relatively strong on this question with the majority of candidates scoring well in the first section, although the adjusted present value sections of the question served to polarise performance.

17 Beaters Ltd (December 2000)

Marking guide

		Marks
17.1 Sensitivities:		
(a) Discount rate	2½	
(b) Annual volume	2½	
		5
17.2 Sensitivities as % of estimate	4	
Input factors: 1½ – 2 marks each	7	
		11
		16

17.1 Estimation of the sensitivities of other factors

(a) **Discount rate**

NPV – 50,000 + [2,000 (20 – 6 – 5 – 2)]AF = 0

(Where AF = annuity factor for zero NPV)

$$AF = \frac{50,000}{7 \times 2,000} = 3.571$$

Looking at the annuity table for six years, 3.571 falls almost exactly halfway between 15% and 20%, ie about 17.5%.

(b) **Annual volume**

NPV – 50,000 + [V (20 – 6 – 5 – 2)]3.784 = 0

(Where V = annual volume for zero NPV)

$$V = \frac{50,000}{7 \times 3.784} = 1,888 \text{ units per annum}$$

17.2 Comments on the NPV and the sensitivity analysis

It would be helpful to look at the sensitivities expressed as a percentage of the original estimate.

		Difference expressed as a percentage of the original estimate
Cost of machine	$\dfrac{52,938 - 50,000}{50,000}$	5.9
Selling price	$\dfrac{20.00 - 19.60}{20.00}$	2.0
Material cost	$\dfrac{6.40 - 6.00}{6.00}$	6.7
Labour cost	$\dfrac{5.40 - 5.00}{5.00}$	8.0
Variable overheads	$\dfrac{2.40 - 2.00}{2.00}$	20.0
Sales life	$\dfrac{6.00 - 5.50}{6.00}$	8.3
Discount rate	$\dfrac{17.50 - 15.00}{15.00}$	16.7
Annual sales volume	$\dfrac{2,000 - 1,888}{2,000}$	5.6

This is clearly a risky project: the NPV is positive but it is relatively small (less than 6% of the initial investment). Though in theory an NPV above zero is enough to justify taking on the investment, particularly when the discount rate already allows for risk, it looks particularly risky. The length of the project (six years) raises problems of predicting cash flows in later years.

Taking each input factor in turn:

Cost of machine

Though this looks to be one of the most risky factors, in fact it is relatively risk free. If the price of the machine were to rise above the estimate, this fact would be known before the company need commit itself to the project.

Selling price and sales volume

The project seems very vulnerable to either or both of these turning out to be lower than estimated, particularly sales volume. This is a luxury product and may well be one subject to the vagaries of taste and fashion. Management may believe that it should carefully re-examine the premises on which the price and volume estimates were made. It might be worth undertaking some further market research to assess the reliability of the estimates.

Material and labour costs

The project also looks vulnerable to these two factors. Again, the basis of the estimates could be re-examined. Each of these costs involves a financial rate and a quantity of usage (eg grammes of material, minutes of labour). Both of these could be looked at again. In theory, it might be possible to determine one of these variables by buying call options on the raw material or agreeing future contracts with the supplier. This will increase costs since the counterparty to the option or the supplier will take on the risk and will require an incentive to do so.

Variable overheads

These look fairly safe.

Discount rate

There is a reasonable margin of safety here, though real financing costs over six years could vary.

Sales life

Again a small safety margin, particularly when looking more than five years into the future.

Annual sales volume

Yet another high risk area.

Sensitivity analysis (SA) has the advantage of enabling the decision-maker to gain good insights to the project and what could cause it to fail. It suffers from two weaknesses as a decision-making tool. It gives the decision-maker no clear guidelines on how to proceed; and it considers only one variable at a time.

Scenario building takes SA a stage further by considering various plausible outcomes for each input factor in combination.

The fact that the rate used to discount the projected cash flows has a significant risk premium attached to it, implies that the riskiness of the individual factors has already been accounted for. The risk of a project is the risk that estimates used in the assessment of the project prove not to be as accurate.

Examiner's comments:

Probably less than 50% of candidates scored full marks for 17.1, despite it being relatively easy, particularly since the investment returns represented an annuity. In 17.2 many candidates failed to discuss the sensitivities more than very superficially, despite a clear requirement in the question to comment on this. Many candidates seemed reluctant to do more than to repeat the points in their study material on the strengths and weaknesses of sensitivity analysis, when they were required to go further and relate it to the circumstances of the question.

In 17.2 candidates were required to comment on the NPV and sensitivities given in the question and the two sensitivities calculated in 17.1. They were also asked how the managers might reach a decision on the project. Though there were some excellent answers to this requirement that scored full marks, there was a tendency to be limited and superficial. Only a minority of candidates went through the eight input factors and discussed their sensitivities and possible reaction by the managers. Candidates tended to be stronger on the arguments for and against the use of sensitivity analysis.

18 Air Business Ltd (September 2013)

Marking guide

			Marks
18.1	Old aircraft	1	
	Tax cost	2	
	New aircraft	1	
	Tax saved	2	
	Extra profit	4	
	Tax	1.5	
	Working capital	2	
	TCF	0.5	
	PV	1	
	Negative NPV and advise not to proceed	1	
			16
18.2(a)	Extra income needed in Y3	2	
	Estimated trade-in-value in Y3	1	
	Trade-in value required to break even	1	
			4
(b)	Pre-tax extra profit	1	
	Tax	1	
	Discount factor and NPV	1	
	Sensitivity	1	
	Advice based on calculation	1	
			5
18.3	Theory – including 2 marks for drivers	5	
	Practical	5	
			10
			35

18.1

	Y0 £	Y1 £	Y2 £	Y3 £
Old aircraft	760,000			
Tax cost (W1)	(159,600)			
New aircraft	(3,000,000)			600,000
Tax saved (W2)	113,400	92,988	76,250	221,362
Extra profit (W3)		566,475	594,799	624,539
Tax (W4)		(118,960)	(124,908)	(131,153)
Working Capital (W5)	(80,000)	(4,000)	(4,200)	88,200
TCF	(2,366,200)	536,503	541,941	1,402,947
8% factor	1.000	0.926	0.857	0.794
PV	(2,366,200)	496,801	464,443	1,113,939
NPV	**(291,017)**			

Negative NPV and so don't proceed as shareholders' wealth would fall

WORKINGS

(1)

	Y0 £
WDV b/f	0
Balancing charge	760,000
Sale proceeds	760,000
Tax due (balancing charge × 21%)	159,600

(2)

	Y0 £'000	Y1 £'000	Y2 £'000	Y3 £'000
Cost/WDV	3,000.000	2,460.000	2,017.200	1,654.104
WDA @18%	(540.000)	(442.800)	(363.096)	(1,054.104)
WDV/sale	2,460.000	2,017.200	1,654.104	600.000
Tax saving (WDA × 21%)	113.400	92.988	76.250	221.362

(3)

	Y0 £	Y1 £	Y2 £	Y3 £
Current profit	987,500			
Estimated profit	1,527,000			
Increase	539,500			
× 1.05		566,475		
× 1.05 =			594,799	
× 1.05				624,539

(4)

	Y0 £	Y1 £	Y2 £	Y3 £
Extra profit (W3)		566,475	594,799	624,539
Tax @ 21%		(118,960)	(124,908)	(131,153)

(5)

	Y0 £	Y1 £	Y2 £	Y3 £
Extra working capital	£80,000	× 1.05		
		£84,000	× 1.05	
			88,200	
Increment	(£80,000)	(4,000)	(4,200)	88,200

18.2(a)

£291,017/79%/0.794	£463,950	Extra income needed in Y3
	£600,000	Estimated trade-in value in Y3
	£1,063,950	Trade-in value required to break even (NPV = 0)

(b)

	Y1 £	Y2 £	Y3 £
Pre-tax extra profit	566,475	594,799	624,539
less: Tax at 21%	(118,960)	(124,908)	(131,153)
Post-tax extra profit	447,515	469,891	493,386
8% factor	0.926	0.857	0.794
PV	414,399	402,697	391,748
Total NPV			1,208,844

Sensitivity: £291,017/£1,208,844 =   **24.1%**

Thus post-tax profits would need to increase by 24.1% for the project to be taken on, ie where NPV = 0

18.3 Theory

Shareholder value analysis (SVA) concentrates on a company's ability to generate value and thereby increase shareholder wealth. SVA is based on the premise that the value of a business is equal to the sum of the present values of all of its activities. SVA posits that a business has seven value drivers:

	Relevance to ABL figures
1. Life of projected cash flows	**Three year projection – so relevant in part but not to infinity**
2. Sales growth rate	**Not used – no growth rate other than inflation**
3. Operating profit margin	**Yes, relevant. Margin and fixed costs used**
4. Corporate tax rate	**Yes, relevant**
5. Investment in non-current assets	**Not used as in usual SVA approach (% of change in sales)**
6. Investment in working capital	**Not used as in usual SVA approach**
7. Cost of capital	**Yes, a discount rate of 8% was used**

The value of the business is calculated from the cash flows generated by drivers 1-6 which are then discounted at the company's cost of capital (driver 7). A terminal/residual value is also calculated to cover the period from the end of competitive advantage to infinity. This can create major problems with estimating a PV of future cash flows. However, SVA links a business' value to its strategy (via the value drivers).

Practical

Some of the information in 18.1 is relevant to a SVA calculation (see relevance column in bold above), but 18.1 is looking at a specific investment (three new aircraft) - no terminal/residual value has been calculated, ie the PV of future cash flows once the period of competitive advantage lapses.

Examiner's comments

This question had the lowest average mark on the paper.

This was a three-part question that tested the candidates' understanding of the investment decisions and valuation element of the syllabus.

In the scenario an airline company was considering whether or not to proceed with the purchase of three new aircraft. In addition its management was concerned that the company might be the subject of a takeover bid and wanted guidance. Part 18.1 for 16 marks was a fairly traditional NPV calculation and required candidates to deal with capital allowances (including the trade-in of old aircraft), incremental cash flows with regard to contribution and fixed costs, inflation and working capital. Part 18.2 for nine marks tested candidates' ability with sensitivity analysis, ie how sensitive was the investment to changes in (a) the trade-in value of the aircraft and (b) the incremental profits arising. Part 18.3 for ten marks examined candidates' understanding of shareholder value analysis (SVA) and to what extent the NPV calculations in part 18.1 could be employed if the company was the subject of a takeover bid.

Part 18.1 was generally answered well, but too few candidates were able to correctly calculate the incremental change in contribution and fixed costs. Not many candidates scored full marks with regard to the balancing charge arising on the sale of the old aircraft. A majority of candidates failed to calculate the working capital figures correctly.

In part 18.2(a), when testing the sensitivity of the NPV with regard to the trade-in value of the old aircraft, few candidates took into account the impact of taxation/capital allowances.

In part 18.2(b), candidates generally did better when calculating the sensitivity of the incremental profits, but their interpretation of the results was often rather weak.

Part 18.3 was not done well, even the theoretical aspects of SVA, which should have been straightforward. Too many candidates explained the value drivers and how the company's value could be increased as these changed. There were few attempts to explain the relevance of SVA to candidates' calculations in part 18.1.

19 Investment portfolios

		Marks
19.1 2 marks per paragraph	max	4
19.2 2 marks per paragraph	max	4
19.3 2 marks per paragraph	max	4
		12

19.1 Unsystematic risk

Unsystematic risk may be defined as the risk attached to a specific investment, in contrast to systematic risk, which is the overall market risk. As such, it is possible by the compilation of a portfolio of investments to eliminate unsystematic risk through diversification. The investor who only holds one security will therefore bear a total risk, made up of the systematic risk of the market and the unsystematic risk of the investment itself.

Hence it is incorrect to argue that he need only be concerned with the unsystematic risk of that security. On the other hand, he may well be concerned about the unsystematic risk of the security, because of the fact that it is that portion of the risk which is present simply because he holds only one, rather than a portfolio of investments.

19.2 Total risk

In holding a portfolio of investments, the rational investor will assemble the portfolio in such a way as to minimise the risk associated with the portfolio. This means that in a large portfolio it is possible to diversify away the unsystematic risk completely.

The total risk to the investor under such circumstances is only the systematic risk of the market itself. The total risk to an investor in a number of securities may therefore be made up of only systematic risk, or systematic plus unsystematic risk, depending on the extent to which the portfolio is diversified.

19.3 Market rate of return

In deciding whether to add an investment to a portfolio, the investor should determine the effect of the extra investment on the overall risk of the portfolio. If the effect is to reduce the overall risk then, assuming that the investor does seek to minimise risk, the investment should be undertaken.

An investment yielding a rate of return less than that of the market is one which is of relatively low risk or possibly risk-free; it would therefore be appropriate to add such an investment to a currently high-risk portfolio as a means of reducing the overall level of risk. It is not relative return but the effect on risk which should determine the investment decision.

20 Sunday newspaper article (June 2003)

Marking guide

	Marks
2 marks per paragraph	max 19

It is true that management need to be concerned with all of the 'stakeholders' in the business. This may mean that managers need to balance 'maximisation of shareholders' wealth' (MSW) with the objectives of others.

It can be argued that the welfare of other stakeholders is not inconsistent with MSW. Normally, unless other stakeholders are getting, at least, a fair deal from the business, this will be at odds with MSW. For example, if suppliers are being treated unfairly by the business, they will seek ways to avoid dealing with the business. This may not be open to them in the short-term, but in the longer-term it probably will be, and this will be to the disadvantage of shareholders.

Once MSW is accepted as the key objective, NPV is the only totally logical approach to business investment decision-making. This is because the NPV is the net increase in wealth caused by the investment.

Investments give rise to various outflows of cash that have the effect of reducing the shareholders' wealth and inflows, which have the opposite effect. Were all of these flows to occur simultaneously, assessing investments would be simple; net inflows would represent an increase in wealth and net outflows the opposite. In practice, the various cash flows do not occur simultaneously but at various points in time, often at points wide apart. Since investors do not view £1 receivable next year as being as valuable as £1 receivable today, a direct comparison between total inflows and total outflows cannot be made.

Discounting enables the various effects on wealth to be assessed on a common basis. All of the cash flows are converted to their value at the same point in time, normally the present time, and the net effect on wealth assessed. None of the other popular investment appraisal techniques looks specifically at wealth.

IRR is the average return on the investment over its lifetime, taking account of the fact that, typically, cash will be flowing into and out of the investment project at various times over its life.

The key weakness of IRR is that it is a rate of return and, as such, it is not directly concerned with wealth. It would always indicate that a large percentage return on a small investment is preferable to a smaller percentage return on a large investment, when it is quite possible for the latter to have a more favourable effect on shareholders' wealth. Thus using IRR does not necessarily lead to undertaking investments that make shareholders richer, though it should not make them poorer.

It is fair to say that IRR typically gives the same signals as NPV, so its use will tend to lead to wealth maximising investments, but NPV should always lead to the correct decision if MSW is accepted.

CAPM (capital asset pricing model) is a device for deriving investors' required returns from an investment. It says that the expected return is the risk-free rate plus a risk premium. The risk premium depends on the average risk premium for all risky investments and the level of risk of the investment under consideration, relative to the average.

Theory and evidence suggest that investors can only expect a premium relating to systematic risk, ie the risk arising from factors that tend to be common, though differentially severe, to most risky investments. Specific risk, because it can be, and in practice is, diversified away, does not attract a risk premium.

It would not be correct to ignore the risks of the particular investment under consideration, but it is logical to ignore the specific risk. Often when using CAPM to derive a discount rate for use with NPV, an average risk premium for businesses engaged exclusively in the activity of the particular investment is used. This is logical because all investments in a particular area of business can be expected to have a similar level of systematic risk.

WACC and CAPM are not in conflict. WACC simply takes account of the required returns of the various providers of a business's finance. CAPM is a means of deriving the cost of each of these elements. So logically WACC could use CAPM-derived required returns, averaging them according to how important they are, by value, to the business.

WACC, if it is based on the business's own data, is an average rate of return for all the business's activities, some of which will be more risky than others. This may well provide an inappropriate rate for NPV discounting or comparison with the IRR.

In theory (Modigliani and Miller – ignoring taxes) shareholders' wealth is not affected by the approach taken to financing the business (equity or debt). Since debt is relatively low risk, lenders expect lower returns than equity holders, but the existence of debt increases the shareholders' risk and the net effect on shareholders' wealth is nil.

This theory was revised by MM who said that if account is taken of the fact that interest on debt is tax deductible, increasing amounts of debt reduce the average cost of capital and make shareholders wealthier.

In practice there is a limit to the amount of debt finance a business can take on because high levels of debt expose it to the risk of incurring the costs of financial distress (bankruptcy). In practice there seems to be some level of debt financing that balances the benefits of tax relief against the potential costs of bankruptcy. This will vary from business to business depending on such things as the nature of their commercial activities.

It does not cost anything to retain profit, in the sense of costs of making a share issue. In that sense loan stock issues are relatively cheap and share issues relatively expensive, particularly public issues.

Retained earnings certainly have cost in terms of returns required by the shareholders. These shareholders incur an opportunity cost if their profits are retained instead of being paid to them as dividends. Naturally they expect to be compensated for this cost. Since their funds are being invested in the same business as the original share capital, they expect similar returns.

Examiner's comments:

Candidates were asked to comment on some statement made to them on corporate investment and financing by a person. The question, both implicitly and explicitly, made it plain that the person had little understanding of such matters. Most candidates were able to deal competently with the technical issues in the question and some were able to explain them in simple, everyday language. Unfortunately most seemed unable to avoid using unexplained jargon and to make the points in simple language. To be able to do this is an extremely valuable skill for a professional accountant. It also is an area that provides the examiner with a helpful means of assessing whether candidates really understand the technical points – only those who really understand a point are able to explain it to others in simple language.

21 Daniels Ltd (March 2007)

Marking guide

		Marks
21.1 (a) Reasoning: 1 Figures: 1	2	
(b) Method and figures: 2 Ranking: 1	3	
(c) Method: 1 Calculations: 2 Conclusions and reasoning: 2	5	
		10
21.2 Reasoning: 2 Conclusion: 1 NPV: 1		4
21.3 Calculations: 4 Limitations: 2		6
21.4 PV calculations: 3 Conclusion and reasoning: 2		5
		25

21.1 (a) No capital rationing, so choose all projects with a positive NPV, ie:

	NPV
	£'000
Bristol	577
Swansea	2,856
Tiverton	1,664
Total	5,097

(b) Capital rationing of £8m on 31/5/X7 (t_0). Rank according to NPV/£ invested:

	Bristol	Cardiff	Gloucester	Swansea	Tiverton
	£'000	£'000	£'000	£'000	£'000
NPV (£'000)	577	(1,309)	(632)	2,856	1,664
Investment t_0	4,150	3,870	6,400	5,000	4,600
NPV/£	0.139	n/a	n/a	0.571	0.362
Rank	3			1	2

Therefore choose all of Swansea (£5m investment) and 65.2% (£3,000/£4,600) of Tiverton:

	NPV
	£'000
Swansea (100%)	2,856
Tiverton (65.2%)	1,085
Total	3,941

(c) No capital rationing at t_0 but only £500,000 available at t_1:

Bristol	Positive NPV and negative funds in t_1	So consider further
Cardiff	Negative NPV and negative funds in t_1	So ignore
Gloucester	Negative NPV and positive funds in t_1	So consider further
Swansea	Positive NPV and negative funds in t_1	So consider further
Tiverton	Positive NPV and positive funds in t_1	So accept unconditionally

If Gloucester is ignored, because it has a negative NPV, then there is £1,790,000 (£500,000 + 1,290,000 [Tiverton]) available at t_1.

Thus choose Swansea (higher ranking than Bristol) and do 68.6% (£1,790/£2,610) of it. Thus the total NPV would be:

	£'000
Tiverton	1,664
Swansea (68.6% × £2,856,000)	1,959
	3,623

Alternatively, if Gloucester is considered and its positive t_1 cash flow utilised then there is £3,560,000 capital available (£1,790,000 + £1,770,000) at t_1.

Based on the same ranking, for t_1 choose 100% Swansea and use the balance (£950,000) to fund Bristol, ie (higher ranking than Bristol) and do 73.6% (£950/£1,290) of it. Thus the total NPV would be:

	£'000
Tiverton	1,664
Swansea (100%)	2,856
Bristol (73.6% × £577,000)	425
Gloucester	(632)
	4,313

Thus it is preferable if the Gloucester project is taken on as this produces the higher total NPV.

21.2 Capital rationing of £9m in t_0, but projects not divisible:

Only choose the projects with positive NPVs, ie Bristol, Swansea or Tiverton. The highest NPV is generated from Swansea (and is higher than Bristol and Tiverton added together). Thus the NPV would be £2,856,000.

21.3

	£	£	PV factor	PV (£)	PV factor	Eq. Ann Cost (£)
Replace vans after one year						
t_0 Cost of van		(12,400)	1.000	(12,400)		
t_1 Maintenance costs	(4,300)					
Resale value	9,800					
		5,500	0.909	5,000		
				(7,400)	0.909	(8,140)
Replace vans after two years						
t_0 Cost of van			1.000	(12,400)		
		(12,400)				
t_1 Maintenance costs		(4,300)	0.909	(3,909)		
t_2 Maintenance costs	(4,800)					
Resale value	7,000					
		2,200	0.826	1,818		
				(14,491)	1.735	
						(8,352)
Replace vans after three years						
t_0 Cost of van		(12,400)	1.000	(12,400)		
t_1 Maintenance costs		(4,300)	0.909	(3,909)		
t_2 Maintenance costs		(4,800)	0.826	(3,965)		
t_3 Maintenance costs	(5,100)					
Resale value	5,000					
		(100)	0.751	(75)		
				(20,349)	2.486	(8,185)

Thus the cheapest option for Daniels is to replace the vans every year as this produces the lowest Equivalent Annual Cost (EAC). However it should be noted that this is by no means a clear decision, as a three-year cycle produces only a slightly higher EAC.

Limitations

* Changing technology, leading to obsolescence, changes in design
* Inflation – affecting estimates and the replacement cycles
* How far ahead can estimates be made and with what certainty?

Note. A further limitation is the ignoring of taxation, which the candidates were told to do.

21.4 The PV of the two investments should be considered:

Original situation

	Cash Flow	10% factor	PV
Year 1–7	190,000	4.868	925,000

Proposed change

	Cash Flow	10% factor	PV
Year 1	925,000	0.909	840,825

The NPV is higher if Daniels maintains the current cash flow profile and so is better off not accepting Kithill's proposal. The IRR might be higher by accepting, but the NPV is the key measure and should be followed.

Examiner's comments:

This question was based on (a) investment appraisal with capital rationing and (b) replacement analysis. Both of these elements, whilst comprehensive and technical, were straightforward and most candidates did well. In addition there was a small final part to the question which required candidates to compare, in effect, net present value and internal rate of return.

As expected most candidates scored full marks for part 21.1(a).

Part 21.1(b) was also done well, and most candidates demonstrated how to rank the projects on the basis of NPV/£ invested.

Part 21.1(c) was answered satisfactorily and a good number of scripts demonstrated how to deal with capital rationing in the second year of the projects.

Part 21.2 was answered well, and most students were able to make the right decision.

Part 21.3 was also answered well and a good number of students scored full marks for it.

In the final part of the question, part 21.4, a majority of candidates gave the correct advice, although few were able to produce the exact relevant cash flow.

22 Adventurous plc (December 2013)

		Marks
22.1	Contribution	3
	Fixed costs	1
	Rent	1
	Tax	1
	Plant and equipment	1
	Tax saved on CAs	2
	Working capital	2
	Discount factor	1
	NPV	1
	Negative NPV and reject	1
	Not include sunk costs in NPV	1
		15
22.2(a)	PV of factory annual rent after tax	1
	Sensitivity	1
	Extent rent must fall	1
	(b) IRR	2
	Sensitivity	1
	Sensible comments on the sensitivities	1
		7
22.3	Problem if gearing changes	1
	APV model is suitable	1
	Base case value	1
	Adjustments to base case	1
	Maximum	3
22.4	Effect on value	1
	Possible political measures taken by government	3
	Strategies to limit effects	3
	Maximum	5
22.5	Follow on options	1.5
	Abandonment options	1.5
	Timing options	1.5
	Growth options	1.5
	Maximum	5
		35

22.1

	Year				
	0	1	2	3	4
	£'000	£'000	£'000	£'000	£'000
Contribution (W1)		15,450	16,709	18,071	19,544
Fixed costs		(3,090)	(3,183)	(3,278)	(3,377)
Rent	(1,000)	(1,000)	(1,000)	(1,000)	0
Operating cash flow	**(1,000)**	**11,360**	**12,526**	**13,793**	**16,167**
Tax	210	(2,386)	(2,630)	(2,897)	(3,395)
Plant and Equipment	(50,000)				15,000
Tax saved on CAs (W2)	1,890	1,550	1,271	1,042	1,597
Working Capital (W3)	(1,500)	(122)	(133)	(142)	1,897

		Year			
	0	1	2	3	4
	£'000	£'000	£'000	£'000	£'000
Net cash flow	**(50,400)**	**10,402**	**11,034**	**11,796**	**31,266**
Discount factor (10%)	1	0.909	0.826	0.751	0.683
Present Value	(50,400)	9,455	9,114	8,859	21,355
Net Present Value	**(1,617)**				

Decision: negative NPV therefore reject the project

Note. Not including sunk costs in the NPV

WORKINGS

(1) **Contribution = £295 – £170 = £125**

Year		£'000
1	$120,000 \times £125 \,(1.03)$	15,450
2	$120,000 \times (1.05) \times £125 \times (1.03)^2$	16,709
3	$120,000 \times (1.05)^2 \times £125 \times (1.03)^3$	18,071
4	$120,000 \times (1.05)^3 \times £125 \times (1.03)^4$	19,544

(2) **Capital allowances**

Year	Cost/WDV	CAs @18%	Tax @21%
	£'000	£'000	£'000
1	50,000	9,000	1,890
2	41,000	7,380	1,550
3	33,620	6,052	1,271
4	27,568	4,962	1,042
5	22,606		
Sale	(15,000)	7,606	1,597

(3) **Working capital**

Year 1 $1,500 \times 1.05 \times 1.03 = 1,622$
Year 2 $1,622 \times 1.05 \times 1.03 = 1,755$
Year 3 $1,755 \times 1.05 \times 1.03 = 1,897$

22.2 (a) The present value of the factory annual rent after tax is (£'000):

$1,000(1 - 0.21) \times 3.487 = 2,754.73$ Round to 2,755.

Note. 3.487 = 1 + The annuity factor for 3 years at 10%.

The sensitivity is found by: NPV/PV of annual rent = -1,617/2,755 = -0.587 or -58.7%

The rent must fall by 58.7%.

(b) The internal rate of return of the project must be calculated. The net present value of the project at 5% = £5,435,000.

The internal rate of return is: $10 - \left(\dfrac{1,617}{1,617 + 5,435} \times 5 \right) = 8.9\%$

The WACC would have to fall by (8.9 – 10)/10 = 0.11 or 11%

(Marks available for sensible comments on the sensitivities.)

22.3 A major assumption of the WACC/NPV model is that the gearing of a company will not change as a result of taking on projects and that the projects are financed from a pool of funds made up of debt and equity.

If the gearing of Adventurous changes materially as a result of taking on the project it is no longer appropriate to use the WACC/NPV model.

M & M argued that in a world with tax changing the capital structure may cause the cost of capital to alter.

The appropriate project appraisal model to use is Adjusted Present Value (APV).

APV is calculated discounting the ungeared cash flows using the cost of equity of Adventurous as if it were ungeared; this is the base case value of the project.

The base case value is then adjusted for the present value of the tax shield on loan interest and any costs associated with raising finance for the project.

22.4 The risk is that political action will reduce the value of the project.

The measures that a foreign government might use include: Quotas; Tariffs; Non-tariff barriers; Restrictions; Nationalisation; Minimum shareholding; Blocked funds.

Strategies that can be used to limit the effects of political risk include: Negotiations with the host government; Insurance; Production strategies; Management structure.

22.5 NPV only considers the cash flows associated with the bicycle computer project. It is possible that the project may be worthwhile as a result of the real options associated with it.

These are:

Follow on options – Adventurous has the opportunity at the end of four years to continue production of the bicycle computer. This might be profitable or not. This is a call option.

Abandonment options – If the bicycle computer is not popular and is a failure Adventurous has the right to terminate the project early and sell the equipment. This is a put option.

Timing options – It may be possible for Adventurous to delay the production of the bicycle computer and wait until the rumours about the rival company are either dispelled or are based on fact. This is a call option.

Growth options – The rumours of the new GPS system also create growth options. Adventurous could invest and hope that the new GPS system does not materialise. Wait and see if the GPS system comes to market but competitors might take a lead and not wait.

If the new bicycle computer is successful and demand is greater than estimated Adventurous may expand production. This is a call option.

Examiner's comments

This was a five-part question that tested the candidates' understanding of the investment decisions element of the syllabus.

The question was based on a scenario where the company was intending to launch a new product and set up a manufacturing facility in the UK. The question covered NPV analysis, inflation, relevant and irrelevant cash flows, working capital requirements and capital allowance calculations. Part 22.1 for fifteen marks required candidates to calculate, using money cash flows, the net present value of the project and advise the board of the company as to whether it should proceed. Part 22.2 for seven marks required candidates to calculate and comment upon the sensitivity of the project to two of the inputs to the NPV analysis. Part 22.3 for three marks required candidates to describe a different project appraisal methodology to WACC/NPV. Part 22.4 for five marks required candidates to consider the political risk of setting up the manufacturing facility overseas and how the company might limit its effects. Part 22.5 for five marks required candidates to identify and comment upon the 'real options' available to the company.

Part 22.1 was well answered, however candidates did not always pay full attention to the timing of cash flows and when they should be increased for price inflation and growth in turnover.

In part 22.2, weaker candidates had some difficulty since the project produced a negative NPV. Candidates should be prepared to apply their knowledge to projects that have either a negative or positive NPV.

Part 22.3 was well answered with most candidates identifying APV as the alternative methodology to use.

In part 22.4, most candidates were able to identify political risk, however few were able to state how to limit its effects.

In part 22.5, most candidates were able to identify the real options available to the company; however a disappointing number of candidates did not refer to the scenario of the question.

23 Headington Ltd (December 2006)

	Marks
23.1 Calculations: 1 per line. Conclusion: 1	max 11
23.2 Calculations: 1 per line. Conclusion: 1	max 5
23.3 1 mark per point	max 3
	19

23.1

				Year		
	0	1	2	3	4	5
	£	£	£	£	£	£
Opportunity cost		(89,250)	(93,713)	(98,398)	(103,318)	(108,484)
Extra revenue (EV)		816,480	857,304	900,169	945,178	992,437
Variable costs		(408,240)	(428,652)	(450,085)	(472,589)	(496,219)
Fixed costs		(89,250)	(93,713)	(98,398)	(103,318)	(108,484)
Taxable CF		229,740	241,226	253,288	265,953	279,250
Tax (21%)		(48,245)	(50,657)	(53,190)	(55,850)	(58,643)
Tax on WDAs (W)	28,350	23,247	19,063	15,631	12,818	31,590
Investment	(750,000)					127,628
NCF	(721,650)	204,742	209,632	215,729	222,921	379,825
df (10%)	1	0.909	0.826	0.751	0.683	0.621
DCF	(721,650)	186,110	173,156	162,012	152,255	235,871
NPV	£187,754					

The investment is financially viable and from that perspective should proceed.

Note. Omission of the sunk cost in respect of the market research.

WORKING

Time		£	@ 21% £
0	Cost	750,000	
	Writing-down allowance (18%)	(135,000)	28,350
		615,000	
1	Writing-down allowance (18%)	(110,700)	23,247
		504,300	
2	Writing-down allowance (18%)	(90,774)	19,063
		413,526	
3	Writing-down allowance (18%)	(74,435)	15,631
		339,091	
4	Writing-down allowance (18%)	(61,036)	12,818
		278,055	
5	Proceeds (100,000 × 1.05^5)	(127,628)	
		150,427	31,590

23.2 The net after-tax present value of the contribution is as follows.

		Contribution £	Tax payment (21%) £	Cash flow £	Df £	PV £
Year	1	408,240	85,730	322,510	0.909	293,162
	2	428,652	90,017	338,635	0.826	279,713
	3	450,085	94,518	355,567	0.751	267,031
	4	472,589	99,244	373,345	0.683	254,995
	5	496,219	104,206	392,013	0.621	243,440
					Total	1,338,341

The NPV of the investment is £187,754, so the present value of the contribution can reduce by this amount before the NPV becomes negative. In other words, the present value can fall by 14.0% (187,754/1,338,341 × 100).

23.3 The reservations in respect of the figures used in the calculation of the net present value of the investment would be as follows.

- The presumed stability of the inflation rate, the discount rate and the tax rate

- The accuracy of the discount rate used – we are not told how it has been derived nor whether the impact of this project on the firm's cost of capital has been considered

- The accuracy of the estimates for residual value of equipment and incremental fixed costs

- While the expected value of revenue calculation is based to some degree on probabilities, they are subjective and the calculation is not based on a full probability distribution

- The presumption that the opportunity cost will be valid for a five-year term

- The presumption of a stable contribution/sales ratio throughout the five-year term

Examiner's comments:

A generally well answered question with overall performance entirely satisfactory. There was nothing in the first part that was out of the ordinary in terms of this sort of question, but the second part of the question proved beyond many candidates and is clearly a part of the syllabus that warrants closer attention by candidates.

Overall, performance on part 23.1 of the question was strong. Among the weaker candidates the most common errors were a failure to even attempt to inflate the relevant figures, omission of either the opportunity cost or the incremental fixed costs, incorrect calculation of the final year writing down allowance, using an incorrect discount factor by adjusting the 10% figure given when it was already confirmed as a money cost of capital and not commencing the tax savings in the correct year.

Part 23.2 of the question proved to be a major discriminator between stronger and weaker candidates, with many picking up full marks but many others showing that they had no grasp at all of where to even start to address the question. Between these two extremes, the most common error was to omit tax in the calculations.

The most common failing in part 23.3 was to make too few observations. Such questions as this usually give rise to a potentially wide range of issues and it is often advisable to double the marks available to give a good indication of the number of different (and relevant) points that need to be made to earn full marks.

24 Hawke Appliances Ltd (September 2014)

		Marks	
24.1 (a)	New machine	1	
	Tax relief	2	
	Old machine	0.5	
	Tax due	1	
	Sales, materials, unskilled labour, lost contribution	5.5	
	Tax on extra profits	1	
	Working capital	2	
	Discount factor	0.5	
	NPV	0.5	
	Advise to proceed as NPV is positive	1	
	State market research fee is not a relevant cash flow as it is sunk	1	
			16
(b)	Sensitivity of sales price	3	
	Sensitivity of sales volume	4	
			7
24.2	Asset value	1	
	P/E with current earnings	1	
	P/E with one year of growth	1	
	Future cash flows/earnings	2	
	Dividend valuation	1	
	Reasons why acquisitions do not benefit bidding firm	4	
	Compare cash and shares	4	
		Max	12
			35

24.1 (a)

	Y0 £'000	Y1 £'000	Y2 £'000	Y3 £'000
New machine	(4,500.000)			1,000.000
Tax relief (W1)	170.100	139.482	114.375	311.043
Old machine	220.000			
Tax due (W2)	(29.400)			
Sales (W3)		8,060.000	15,926.560	7,845.926
Materials (W4)		(2,756.000)	(5,445.856)	(2,682.801)
Unskilled labour (W5)		(1,456.000)	(2,877.056)	(1,417.329)
Lost contribution (W6)		(2,288.000)	(4,521.088)	(2,227.231)
Tax on extra profits (W7)		(327.600)	(647.338)	(318.899)
Working capital (W8)	(806.000)	(786.656)	808.063	784.593
Total cash flows	(4,945.300)	585.226	3,357.660	3,295.302
12% discount factor	1.000	0.893	0.797	0.712
PV	(4,945.300)	522.607	2,676.055	2,346.255
NPV	**599.617**			

The NPV is positive and so the investment should go ahead as it will enhance shareholder wealth

The market research fee is not a relevant cash flow as it is sunk/committed (candidates needed to state this to get the mark and not just ignore).

(1)

£'000	£'000	£'000	£'000	£'000
Cost/WDV	4,500.000	3,690.000	3,025.800	2,481.156
WDA @ 18%/Bal. allowance	(810.000)	(664.200)	(544.644)	(1,481.156)
WDV/sale	3,690.000	3,025.800	2,481.156	1,000.000
Tax on WDA @ 21%	170.100	139.482	114.375	311.043

(2)

	£'000
WDV b/f	80.000
Balancing charge	140.000
Sale proceeds	220.000
Tax due on bal. charge @ 21%	(29.400)

(3)

		£'000	£'000	£'000
Sales units		50,000	95,000	45,000
Selling price/unit		£155 × 1.04	£155 × 1.04^2	£155 × 1.04^3
Sales		8,060.000	15,926.560	7,845.926

(4)

		£'000	£'000	£'000
Sales units		50,000	95,000	45,000
Material cost/unit		£53 × 1.04	£53 × 1.04^2	£53 × 1.04^3
Materials		2,756.000	5,445.856	2,682.801

(5)

		£'000	£'000	£'000
Sales units		50,000	95,000	45,000
Unskilled cost/unit		£28 × 1.04	£28 × 1.04^2	£28 × 1.04^3
Unskilled costs		1,456.000	2,877.056	1,417.329

(6)

		£'000	£'000	£'000
Sales units		50,000	95,000	45,000
Lost contribution/unit ([£96-£74] x 2)		£44 × 1.04	£44 × 1.04^2	£44 × 1.04^3
Variable costs		2,288.000	4,521.088	2,227.231

(7)

		£'000	£'000	£'000
Extra profit (sales less materials, unskilled labour, lost contribution)		1,560,000	3,082.560	1,518.565
Tax at 21%		327.600	647.338	318.899

(8)

	£'000	£'000	£'000	£'000
Sales	8,060.000	15,926.560	7,845.926	
Sales increment	8,060.000	7,866.560	(8,080.634)	
Working capital at 10%	(806.000)	(786.656)	808.063	784.593

(b)

		£'000	£'000	£'000
Sales		8,060.000	15,926.560	7,845.926
Discount rate at 12%		× 0.893	× 0.797	× 0.712
PV of sales		7,197.580	12,693.468	5,586.299
Total PV of sales	25,477.347			
less: Tax at 21%	(5,350.243)			
	20,127.104			
Sensitivity of sales price	599.654			
	20,127.104			

$$= 3\%$$

ICAEW

Sensitivity of sales volume

Contribution (£30 × 50 × 1.04)	£1,560.000		
Contribution (£30 × 95 × 1.04 × 1.04)		£3,082.560	
Contribution (£30 × 45 × 1.04 × 1.04 × 1.04)			£1,518.565
Discount rate at 12%	× 0.893	× 0.797	× 0.712
PV of contribution	1,393.080	2,456.800	1,081.218
Total PV of contribution	4,931.098		
less: Tax at 21%	(1,035.531)		
	3,895.568		
Sensitivity of sales volume	599.461		
	3,895.568		
	= 15.3%		

24.2 (1) Possible values for Durram

Asset value (book value) =	£3.6m
P/E – with current earnings – 11 × £0.7m =	£7.7m
P/E – with one year of growth – 11 × (£0.7m × 1.05) =	£8.1m
Future cash flows/earnings (12% discount rate) for PV of future cash flows	
(£0.7m × 1.05)/(12%-5%) =	£10.5m
Dividend valuation (no growth) – £0.7m/12% =	£5.8m

(2) Reasons why acquisitions do not benefit the bidding firm

The price paid is too high and synergies go to the target shareholders.

Lack of fit within the existing group of companies, so cost savings and synergies are not as great as forecast.

Transaction costs – underwriting, legal fees etc - are expensive and reduce any gains made.

Talented staff in the target company may leave.

The takeover/merger may be because of management hubris rather than an increase in shareholder value.

The subsidiary is too small and does not warrant the management time required.

Conglomerate discount may exist, ie the individual parts of the business are worth more than the group as a whole.

(3) Is it better to pay with cash or shares?

Paying in cash

This is more attractive to the target shareholders as the value is certain, but there may be personal tax implications.

This may cause liquidity problems for the bidding firm and so it may be necessary to increase its gearing.

Lower transaction costs will arise with a cash purchase.

Paying with shares

There will be a dilution of ownership and any gains made will now be shared with the target shareholders.

Examiner's Comments

This question had the highest average mark on the paper. Candidate performance was very good.

This was a four-part question that tested the candidates' understanding of the investment decisions and valuation element of the syllabus.

In the scenario a UK manufacturer of household appliances was planning (1) the development of a new product and (2) the possible purchase of an electrical goods retailer. Part 24.1(a) for 16 marks required candidates to advise the company's board, based on an NPV calculation, whether the proposed product manufacture should proceed. Candidates were required to deal with relevant cash flows, tax allowances and costs, inflation and working capital. In part 24.1(b)) for seven marks they had to calculate the sensitivity of their calculations to changes in the proposed selling price and estimated sales volumes. Part 24.2 was worth twelve marks and required candidates to calculate a range of values for the target retailer and then provide guidance for the board on the inherent dangers of buying another company and the best method with which to pay for it, ie cash or shares

In part 24.1(a) most candidates scored well. The main weakness evident was the opportunity cost calculation, which was either completely ignored (by the weakest candidates) or halved instead of doubling the lost volume. Also many candidates included calculations regarding skilled labour, which was not a relevant cost. A number of candidates failed to calculate the balancing charge arising on the sale of the old machinery.

Part 24.1(b) was generally done well, but a disappointing number of candidates used contribution rather than sales revenue in their first set of sensitivity calculations.

In part 24.2 candidates coped well, as expected, with the book value and P/E methods of valuation, but many were unsure of themselves (as in previous papers) when valuing the company based on discounted cash flows. A high proportion of candidates struggled with the reasons for the failure of acquisitions, but in general the cohort was stronger when explaining the implications of buying in cash or shares.

---

25 Rossendale Hotels plc (December 2014)

	Marks
25.1 NPV calculation:	
Expected sales	1.5
Contribution Year 1	0.5
Contribution Years 2-4	2.5
Fixed costs	1
Tax	1
Vehicles and equipment (0.5 marks for each year)	1
Tax saved on CAs (0.5 marks for each year)	2.5
Working capital	2.5
Continuing value	1.5
PV factor 10%	1
Discounting/NPV	1
	16
25.2 Sensitivity calculation:	
Contribution (0.5 if sales)	1
Tax	1
Continuing value	1
Discounting	1
Sensitivity	1
Conclusion and reasoning	2
	Max 5
25.3 1 mark per relevant point	3
25.4 2 marks per well explained point	Max 5
25.5 Advantages and disadvantages:	
Demerger	3
Sell-off	3
MBO	3
	Max 6
	35

25.1

Probability	Sales £m	Pro × Sales £m
0.4	25	10
0.4	130	52
0.2	105	21
Expected Sales		83

Contribution = £ 83 m × 15% = £12.45 m in 20X5 £s already

Nominal discount rate = $(1.07) \times (1.03) - 1 = 10\%$ (or 10.21%)

	0 £m	1 £m	2 £	3 £m	4 £m
Contribution		12.45	14.38	16.61	19.18
Fixed Costs		(5)	(5.15)	(5.3)	(5.46)
Operating cash flows		7.45	9.23	11.31	13.72
Tax 21%		(1.56)	(1.94)	(2.38)	(2.88)
After tax operating cash flows		5.89	7.29	8.93	10.84
Vehicles and Equipment	(10)				2

Tax saved on Cash	0.38	0.31	0.25	0.21	0.53
Working Capital	(5)	(0.78)	(0.9)	(1.03)	7.71
Continuing value					108.4
Net cash flows	(14.62)	5.42	6.64	8.11	129.47
PV factors a t 10%	1	0.909	0.826	0.751	0.683
Present value	(14.62)	4.93	5.48	6.09	88.43
NPV	90.31				

CAs and Tax saved.

	Cost/WDV	CA	Tax
0	10	1.8	0.38
1	8.2	1.48	0.31
2	6.72	1.21	0.25
3	5.51	0.99	0.21
4	4.52		
Sale	-2	2.52	0.53

Contribution:

Year 2: 12.45 x 1.10 x 1.05 = £14.38m
Year 3: 14.38 x 1.10 x 1.05 = £16.61m
Year 4: 16.61 x 1.10 x 1.05 = £19.81m

Working capital:

Year 1: 5 × 1.1 × 1.05 – 5 = £0.78m
Year 2: 5.78 × 1.1 × 1.05 – 5.78 = £0.90m
Year 3: 6.68 × 1.10 × 1.05 – 6.68 = £1.03m
Year 4: £7.71m
Continuing value: 10.84 × 10 = £108.4 m

25.2

	1	2	3	4
Sensitivity	£m	£	£m	£m
Contribution X (1– 0.21)	9.84	11.36	13.12	15.15
Continuing value				151.5
	9.84	11.36	13.12	166.65
PV factors a t 10%	0.909	0.826	0.751	0.683
Present Value	9	9	10	114
Total present value	142			
Sensitivity				
90.31/142	63.4%			

A fall in sales of £83 million to: 83(1 – 0.634) = £30.12 million.

As there is a 40% chance that the sales will be £25 million the management of Rossendale should consider how this will be viewed by the markets if Inside&Out were to be listed, or by a potential buyer.

25.3

Inside&Out could be valued by reference to a multiple such as a p/e ratio. A proxy company would have to be chosen that has similar operating characteristics to Inside&Out. This multiple could be adjusted to take into account that Inside&Out is a division of Rossendale and a not listed company.   3

25.4 Appropriate reasons for divestment in Rossendale's circumstances include:

Lack of fit – Inside&Out is a diversification from Rossendale's core activities and the divestment will allow the firm to concentrate on developing its hotel chain. This would particularly be the case if the division's size is making increasing demands on senior management's time.

Conglomerate discount – a belief that the individual parts of the business can be worth more than the whole. This is sometimes expressed as 5 – 1 = 5!

Liquidity – divestment by way of a sale will provide funds for further expansion of the hotel chain or to pay down debt.

25.5

(a) A demerger (or spin-off) into two listed companies – Advantages include: no change in ownership, since shareholders will hold shares in two separate businesses; shareholders can enjoy the growth prospects of both companies; the two companies will have separate corporate identities and shareholders can choose whether they wish to realise their investment in one or other of the businesses; the spin-off may avoid the problem of conglomerate discount; it may avoid the takeover of the whole business by separating a particularly attractive part of the business. The major disadvantage is that the demerger will not result in any cash inflows for Rossendale.

(b) A sell-off has the advantage that it will provide cash that can be invested in the development of the hotel chain. The disadvantages include: the shareholders of Rossendale will no longer be able to participate in the future growth potential of Inside&Out; it may be difficult to find a buyer and to agree on the price, especially with the uncertainty attached to the projected sales.

(c) A management buyout (MBO) – The same advantages and disadvantages apply to an MBO as to a sell-off. However the major advantage is that Rossendale may have a willing buyer that has knowledge of Inside&Out. The management team will have knowledge of the risks and uncertainties attached to the business and may be more willing to take the risk than a third party buyer. The management team may also be keen to safeguard their jobs. However the management team may have difficulty raising the funds to buy the division.

Examiner's comments

This was a five-part question that tested the candidates' understanding of the investment decisions element of the syllabus. The scenario of the question was that a company wished to restructure by the divestment of a division. Part 25.1 of the question required candidates to value the division being divested. Part 25.2 of the question required candidates to calculate the sensitivity of the division's value to certain inputs into the valuation model. Part 25.3 of the question required candidates to outline another valuation technique that could be used to value the division. Part 25.4 of the question required candidates to discuss the possible reasons for the divestment of the division. Part 25.5 of the question required candidates to discuss whether the advantages and disadvantages of different methods that could be used for the divestment:

Part 25.1 was well answered by the majority of students. The valuation was to be carried out using NPV analysis and the question was designed to give 7 or 8 basic marks, however some errors that many candidates made were: incorrect adjustments for price increases, inflation and growth; incorrect working capital computations; discounting nominal cash flows with a real cost of capital; incorrect continuing value computations.

In part 25.2 quite poor attempts were made by a lot of students. There were many basic errors were made in the sensitivity computations: using sales instead of contribution; omitting tax; incorrect application of the formula for sensitivity; no interpretation of the results and no, or little, reference to the probability distribution of sales.

In part 25.3, quite poor answers were made and many students suggested valuation methods were inappropriate for the valuation of a service company, or just gave a list of all valuation techniques. It was disappointing to see students use this part of the question to write about SVA which gained no marks.

Part 25.4 was reasonably well answered. However weaker students only mentioned lack of fit.

In part 25.5 it was evident that many students only had a superficial knowledge of this area of the syllabus.

26 Premier Transport Group plc (March 2015)

	Marks
26.1(a) Bus Hiring:	
Fares	1.5
Fuel costs	1.5
Other costs	2.5
Tax	1
Discounting	1
Bus purchase:	
Bus purchase	0.5
Bus sale	0.5
Tax relief of buses	2
Fares	0.5
Fuel costs	0.5
Other costs	0.5
Tax	1
Discounting	1
Ignore depreciation	1
Recommend bus hire as NPV is higher	1
	16
(b) Change required in NPV	1
Adjustment required for tax relief on CAs	1
Adjustment required for time value of money	1
Sale price per bus	1
	4
(c) IRR of bus purchase scheme:	
IRR approximation	2
Advantages and disadvantages – 1 mark per relevant point	Max 3
	5
26.2 Equivalent annual running cost:	
Deluxe	2
Mid-range	2
Economy – three year cycle	2
Economy – six year cycle	3
Recommendation	1
	10
	35

26.1 (a)

Bus Hiring	Year to 30/4/X5 £	Year to 30/4/X6 £	Year to 30/4/X7 £	Year to 30/4/X8 £
Fares (W1)		936,768	2,340,900	3,661,168
Fuel Costs (W2)		(444,960)	(473,586)	(534,999)
Other Costs (W3)		(766,850)	(869,232)	(955,536)
Taxation (W4)		57,759	(209,597)	(455,833)
Net Cash flow after taxation	0	(217,283)	788,485	1,714,800
10% factor	1.000	0.909	0.826	0.751
PV	0	(197,510)	651,289	1,287,814
NPV	1,741,593			

Bus Purchase	Year to 30/4/X5	Year to 30/4/X6	Year to 30/4/X7	Year to 30/4/X8
Bus (purchase)/Sale	(1,600,000)			400,000
Tax relief on buses (W5)	60,480	49,594	40,667	101,260
Fares		936,768	2,340,900	3,661,168
Fuel Costs		(444,960)	(473,586)	(534,999)
Other Costs (W3)		(406,850)	(509,232)	(595,536)
Taxation (W6)		(17,841)	(285,197)	(531,433)
Net cash flow after taxation	(1,539,520)	116,711	1,113,552	2,500,460
10% factor	1.000	0.909	0.826	0.751
PV	(1,539,520)	106,090	919,794	1,877,845
NPV	**1,364,209**			

Ignore depreciation as it is not a cash flow.

The bus hiring scheme produces the higher NPV and so should be chosen as this will enhance shareholder wealth more.

WORKINGS

	Year to 30/4/X5 £	Year to 30/4/X6 £	Year to 30/4/X7 £	Year to 30/4/X8 £
W1				
Fares (April 20X5 prices)		918,400	2,250,000	3,450,000
Inflate at 2% pa		× 1.02	× (1.02)^2	× (1.02)^3
'Money' fares		936,768	2,340,900	3,661,168
W2				
Fuel costs (April 20X5 prices)		432,000	446,400	489,600
Inflate at 3% pa		× 1.03	× (1.03)^2	× (1.03)^3
'Money' fuel costs		444,960	473,586	534,999
W3				
Other costs (April 20X5 prices)		755,000	840,000	905,000
less: Hire costs (8 × £45,000)		(360,000)	(360,000)	(360,000)
		395,000	480,000	545,000
Inflate at 3% pa		× 1.03	× (1.03)^2	× (1.03)^3
'Money' Other costs		406,850	509,232	595,536
plus: Hire costs		360,000	360,000	360,000
Total other costs		766,850	869,232	955,536
W4				
'Money' fares (W1)		936,768	2,340,900	3,661,168
'Money' fuel costs (W2)		(444,960)	(473,586)	(534,999)
Total other costs (W3)		(766,850)	(869,232)	(955,536)
Taxable profit/(loss)		(275,042)	998,082	2,170,633
Tax (payable)/due @ 21%		57,759	(209,597)	(455,833)
W5				
Bus purchase/WDV	1,600,000	1,312,000	1,075,840	882,189
WDA @ 18%/Bal. All'ce	(288,000)	(236,160)	(193,651)	482,189
WDV/sale	1,312,000	1,075,840	882,189	400,000
Tax (21% × WDV/BA)	60,480	49,594	40,667	101,260
W6				
'Money' fares (W1)		936,768	2,340,900	3,661,168
'Money' fuel costs (W2)		(444,960)	(473,586)	(534,999)
'Money' other costs (W3)		(406,850)	(509,232)	(595,536)
Taxable profit/(loss)		84,958	1,358,082	2,530,633
Tax payable @ 21%		(17,841)	(285,197)	(531,433)

Part 26.1(a) was well answered by most candidates and they showed a good understanding of relevant cash flows and the impact of inflation and taxation. The most common mistakes made by candidates here were (1) not multiplying the hire cost by eight [years] and (2) not inflating the cash flows correctly (ie not compounding the inflation adjustment).

(b) Change required in NPV (£1,741,593 – £1,364,209)   £377,384

Adjustment required for tax relief on capital allowances (£377,384/79%)   £477,701

Adjustment required for time value of money (£477,701/0.751)   £636,087

Total sale price of buses would need to be £636,087 higher, ie   £79,511 each

Sale price per bus would need to be (£50,000 + £79,511)   £129,511

(c) IRR of bus purchase scheme

NPV @10%   £1,364,209

Rework cash flows at 20%:

	£	£	£	£
Net cash flow after tax	(1,539,520)	116,711	1,113,552	2,500,460
20% factor	1.000	0.833	0.694	0.579
PV	(1,539,520)	97,220	772,805	1,447,766
NPV	**£778,271**			

IRR approximation 20% + ((£778,271/(£1,364,209 – £778,271)) × 10%) 33%

IRR takes into account cash flows and the time value of money. It represents a break-even point, so an exact cost of capital is not needed. It's easier to use and communicate practically.

However, it may give conflicting advice to that given by NPV (which is technically superior)

26.2

		£	£
Deluxe	Initial cost (Year 0)		(260,000)
	Annual running costs	(57,000)	
		×	
	Year 6 annuity factor (@ 10%)	4.355	
		(248,235)	
		(508,235)	

Equivalent annual running cost   (£508,235)/4.355   (116,701)

Mid-Range	Initial cost (Year 0)	(210,000)	
	Annual running costs	(54,000)	
		×	
	Year 4 annuity factor (@ 10%)	3.170	
		(171,180)	
		(381,180)	

Equivalent annual running cost   (£381,180)/3.170   (120,246)

Economy

Three year cycle	Initial cost (Year 0)		(160,000)
	Annual running costs	(70,000)	
		×	
	Year 3 annuity factor (@ 10%)	2.487	
		(174,090)	
		(334,090)	

Equivalent annual running cost   (£334,090,180)/2.487   (134,334)

Economy

Six year cycle	Initial cost (Year 0)		(160,000)
	Annual running costs (Y1-Y3)	(70,000)	
		×	
	Year 3 annuity factor (@ 10%)	2.487	

		(174,090)
		(334,090)
plus: Repair costs at Year 3 (£90,000 × 0.751)		(67,590)
plus: Running costs (Y4-Y6) (£85,000 × 2.487 × 0.751)		(158,758)
		(560,438)

Equivalent annual running cost	(£560,438)/4.355	(128,688)

Thus the cheapest replacement cycle is for the Deluxe coach and, ignoring any other factors, this coach type should be purchased.

Examiner's comments

This question had the highest average mark on the paper. Candidate performance was very good.

This was a four-part question that tested the candidates' understanding of the investment decisions element of the syllabus.

In the first part of the scenario (16 marks) a UK transport company had to choose (using the NPV approach) whether to hire or purchase extra buses to operate on new bus routes. Candidates, as an employee of the company, had to advise its board. They were given estimated incremental income and cost flows and had to take account of inflation rates and corporation tax implications. Secondly, for four marks, they were required to calculate the sensitivity of that decision to the trade-in value of new buses. For a further five marks they were asked to estimate the IRR of the bus purchase proposal and to explain the advantages and disadvantages of the IRR method of investment appraisal. Finally, for ten marks, candidates were tested on their understanding of replacement analysis. Here the company had to choose between three types of coach and candidates were required to advise the board as to which was the most cost effective method of replacing its coaches:

Part 26.1(a) was well answered by most candidates and they showed a good understanding of relevant cash flows and the impact of inflation and taxation. The most common mistakes made by candidates here were (1) not multiplying the hire cost by eight [years] and (2) not inflating the cash flows correctly (ie not compounding the inflation adjustment).

Overall, part 26.1(b) was poorly done. Most candidates used NPV/PV cash flows, which doesn¹t work when there's a balancing allowance involved, which was the case here.

In part 26.1(c), candidates' performance here was very variable. A positive NPV at 10% means that the discount rate should go up not down for the next NPV calculation. Weaker scripts demonstrated a poor use of the IRR extrapolation formula and very poor understanding of the advantages/disadvantages of the IRR approach.

Candidates' answers to part 26.2 were also very variable. Many scored full marks, but many failed to discount the cash flows and/or divide by the annuity factor. A lot of candidates couldn't calculate the NPV of the extended life (Economy coach) correctly. A significant minority of candidates wasted time by calculating annuity factors that were already there for them in the tables supplied.

27 Bluesky Entertainments plc (June 2015)

	Marks
27.1 NPV Calculation:	
Expected Sales	1
State market research should be excluded as it is a sunk cost	1
Contribution	2
Fixed costs	1
Tax at 21%	1
Property, Plant and Equipment (0.5 marks for each year)	1
Land	0.5
Tax saved on CAs (0.5 marks for each year)	2.5
Working capital	2.5
Continuing value	1.5
PV factor 10%	0.5
Discounting	0.5
Positive NPV therefore accept	1
	16
27.2 Sensitivity calculation:	
Contribution (0.5 if sales)	1
Tax	1
Continuing value	1
Discounting	1
Sensitivity	1
Conclusion and reasoning	2
	Max 5
27.3 2 marks per well explained point	Max 4
27.4 2 marks per well explained point – essential to consider size	Max 4
27.5 1 mark per relevant point	Max 3
27.6 1 mark per relevant point	3
	35

27.1

	t0	t1	t2	t3	t4
Contribution		134.64	144.91	155.96	167.85
Fixed Costs		(90.00)	(93.60)	(97.34)	(101.23)
Operating cash flows		44.64	51.31	58.62	66.62
Tax 21%		(9.37)	(10.78)	(12.31)	(13.99)
After tax operating cash flows		35.27	40.53	46.31	52.63
Property, plant and equipment	(500.00)				120.00
Land	(40.00)				80.00
Tax saved on Ca's	18.90	15.50	12.71	10.42	22.27
Working Capital	(35.00)	(2.67)	(2.87)	(3.09)	43.63
Continuing value					473.67
Net cash flows	(556.10)	48.10	50.37	53.64	792.20
PV factors at 10%	1.00	0.91	0.83	0.75	0.68
Present value NPV	(556.10)	43.72	41.61	40.28	541.07
	110.58				

Positive NPV, therefore accept

Note. If the resale value of the land is not included marks will still be awarded on the basis that there is a continuing value and therefore the same site, and therefore land, will not be replaced

Expected sales and contribution

Probability (p)	Visitors million	Sales £million	p x Sales £million
0.5	12	408	204.00
0.3	9	306	91.80
0.2	6	204	40.80
Expected Sales	9.9 × £34 =		336.60

Sales revenue is £34 per visitor.

For stating that the market research of £100,000 should not be included as it is a sunk cost

Contribution in year 1 = £336.6 × 0.40 = £134.64 million.

Contribution in year 2 = £134.64 × 1.05 × 1.025 = £144.91 million

Contribution in year 3 = £144.91 × 1.05 × 1.025 = £155.96 million

Contribution in year 4 = £155.96 × 1.05 × 1.025 = £167.85 million

Continuing value = 52.63 × 9 = £473.67 million

Working capital

Year 1 = (-35 x 1.05 x 1.025) – 35 = £-2.67 million

Year 2 = (-37.67 x 1.05 x 1.025)- 37.67 = £-2.87 million

Year 3 = (-40.54 x 1.05 x 1.025) – 40.54 = £-3.09 million

Year 4 = 40.54 + 3.09 = £43.63 million

27.2

Sensitivity

	t1	t2	t3	t4
Contribution X (1 – 0.21)	106.37	114.48	123.21	132.60
Continuing value				1193.40
	106.37	114.48	123.21	1326.00
PV factors at 10%	0.91	0.83	0.75	0.68
Present value	97.00	95.00	93.00	906.00
Total present value	1191.00			120.00

Sensitivity =
110.28/1191 = 9%

A fall in sales of £336.6 million to: 336.6(1-0.09) = £305.35 million will result in a zero NPV.

There is a 50% chance that sales will be less than £305.35 million. The management of Bluesky will have to consider whether it is willing to accept this level of risk. Especially since a competitor is likely to enter the market.

27.3

Underseaworld has already identified a site to launch its operations in the UK, therefore this will increase the uncertainty of the Waterworld project revenues. In the circumstances Bluesky might consider waiting to start the project until the decision regarding the planning permission that Underseaworld has applied for has been made. The real option regarding the decision to delay the start of the Waterworld project is a Timing option.

Bluesky could start the project at time zero and has the option to abandon the project should Underseaworld commence their project and erodes the profitability of Waterworld.

Bluesky also has the option to continue after four years, this is a Follow-on-option.

Bluesky could expand facilities at the new site, or open new sites, this is a Growth option.

Only 2 need be discussed

27.4

Bluesky has an equity market capitalisation of (£9m/0.10) x £12 = £1,080 million. The Waterworld project requires and investment of (£500+£40+£35) = £575 million. This is over half the current market capitalisation. Raising this amount of finance might affect the company's gearing and financial risk. The Waterworld project is also a diversification from Bluesky's current operations, which will affect its business systematic risk.

Simply adding a 'fudge figure' of 2% to the current WACC of the company is not appropriate and the finance director of Bluesky should consider:

- How to accurately measure the systematic risk of the Bluesky project. This can be achieved by adjusting the cost of equity by using an equity beta from a comparable company that reflects the systematic risk of the project. However gearing adjustments may have to be made.

- The size of the Waterworld project may mean that Bluesky's gearing will materially change and it would not be appropriate to use the WACC/NPV project appraisal methodology. Instead it would be more appropriate to appraise the Waterworld project using the Adjusted Present Value model.

27.5

Assuming that the UK stock market is semi-strong form efficient and reacts instantaneously to public information, when Bluesky makes an announcement in the Stock Market regarding the Waterworld project the share price will immediately reflect the new information.

The increase, or decrease, in price will depend on whether the markets have confidence that the project will indeed be successful.

Assuming that the markets believe this project will be successful, the share price will increase by: (£110.58/90) = 123p per share. Giving a new share price of £12 + £1.23 = £13.23.

However several factors might mean that the price is below £13.23, the presence of the Underseaworld expansion into the UK and the size of the project may make the markets cautious.

27.6

The suggestion that close family members of the board should buy shares in Bluesky before the announcement about the Waterworld project is made is highly unethical, since they will be supplied with price sensitive information that has not yet been made public. It is also insider trading and illegal.

Examiner's comments

This was a six-part question that tested the candidates' understanding of the investment decisions element of the syllabus. The scenario of the question was that a company is expanding its operations by diversifying and opening a new entertainment facility:

Part 27.1 was well answered by most students. The project appraisal was to be carried out using NPV analysis and the question was designed to give up to ten basic marks, however some errors that many candidates made were: incorrect adjustments for inflation and growth; treating the contribution as 60% of sales instead of 40%; incorrect working capital computations; calculating capital allowances on the value of the land; discounting the cash flows at 8% rather than 10%; incorrect continuing value computations; not discounting the continuing value; omitting to comment that the market research is a sunk cost and should not be included in the NPV analysis.

In part 27.2, many basic errors were made in the sensitivity computations: using sales instead of contribution; omitting tax; incorrect application of the formula for sensitivity; no, or little, reference to the probability distribution of sales.

In part 27.3, it was disappointing to note that in this section many students did not refer to the scenario of the question and made no mention of the competitor that might be entering the market. Students would be well advised to ensure that they relate answers to the scenario of the question and not just brain dump everything that they know about real options. At this level we do not provide superfluous information in the questions.

Part 27.4 was reasonably well answered. However it was disappointing to note that some students suggested that the IRR should be used as the discount rate. It was also disappointing that not many students related the size of the project to the market capitalisation of the company and the potential implications for the gearing of the company and the type of project appraisal technique that could be used. Few students mentioned that the project was a diversification and that the systematic risk of the new project should be reflected in the discount rate.

In part 27.5, many students adjusted the current share price by the NPV per share of the project. However the explanations as to whether the actual share price would equal their figure were varied. Few students mentioned the EMH and/or the LSE's reaction to the public announcement about the project. It was also disappointing that, again, few students related their answers to the scenario of the question and mentioned the competitor that is likely to come into the market. Also the project was a diversification, which might also affect the LSE's confidence in the future of the company and therefore the share price.

Part 27.6 was well answered by the majority of candidates. However it is a little worrying that some weaker candidates thought that as long as the board members did not buy shares themselves, it was acceptable to advise family members to buy shares in advance of the public announcement about the project.

28 Silverdale plc (June 2015)

		Marks
28.1 Forecast Income Statement:		
Revenue	0.5	
Direct costs	2	
Indirect costs	0.5	
Interest – (0.5 for each financing option)	1	
Taxation – (0.5 for each financing option)	1	
Dividend – (0.5 for each financing option)	1	
Forecast Balance Sheet:		
Non-current assets	1	
Inventory	0.5	
Trade receivables	0.5	
Cash (0.5 marks for each financing option)	1	
Ordinary shares (1 mark for each financing option)	2	
Share premium	1	
Retained earnings (0.5 marks for each financing option)	1	
Debentures (0.5 marks for each financing option)	1	
Trade payables	0.5	
Dividends payable	0.5	
Redemption yield:		
2 PVs	2	
IRR calculation	1	
		18
28.2 (a) Gearing (0.5 marks each for current value, and after each financing option)	1.5	
Interest cover (0.5 marks each for current value, and after each financing option)	1.5	
Earnings per share (0.5 marks each for current value, and after each financing option)	1.5	
		Max 4
(b) 2 marks per well explained point – essential to consider debt capacity, and effect on the debenture issue	13	
Conclusion	1	
		Max 10
(c) Current ratio before expansion	0.5	
Current ratio after expansion for rights issue and debenture issue	1	
Current ratio approaching industry average	1	
Silverdale unable to finance expansion beyond May 20X7 if it wants to maintain current ratio	1	
If rights issue used - spare debt capacity could be used to finance further expansion plans	0.5	
		Max 3
		35

28.1 Forecast Income Statement for the year ended 31 May 20X6

	Rights Issue £'000	Debenture Issue £'000
Revenue (£780,000 x 1.15)	897,000	897,000
Direct costs (see working)	544,920	544,920
Indirect costs (£225,000 + £12,000)	237,000	237,000
Operating profits	115,080	115,080
Interest	4,200	
Interest (£4,200 + £75m x 9%)		10,950
Profit before tax	110,880	104,130
Taxation	23,285	21,867
Profit after tax	87,595	82,263
Dividend (declared)	43,798	41,131

Direct costs: (£468,000 – £36,000) x 1.16 + ((£144,000 + £75,000) x 0.20) = £544,920

Forecast Balance Sheet at 31 May 20X6

	Rights Issue £'000	Debenture Issue £'000
Non-current assets		
Plant and Machinery (NBV)		
(£144,000 + £75,000) x 0.80	175,200	175,200
Current Assets		
Inventory (£60,000 + £15,000)	75,000	75,000
Trade receivables (£130,000 x 1.15)	149,500	149,500
Cash (Balancing figure)	54,095	48,763
	278,595	273,263
	453,795	448,463
Capital and reserves		
50p Ordinary shares (see working)	48,000	40,000
Share premium	67,000	----------
Retained earnings (£81,000 + £43,797)	124,797	----------
Retained earnings (£81,000 + £41,132)	----------	122,132
	239,797	162,132
Non-current liabilities		
7% Debentures at par value	60,000	60,000
9% Debentures at par value	----------	75,000
	60,000	135,000
Current liabilities		
Trade payables (£95,000 x 1.16)	110,200	110,200
Dividends payable	43,798	41,131
	153,998	151,331
	453,795	448,463

Rights Issue: Issue price 586p x 0.80 = 469p. The number of shares to be issued will be:

£75m/469p = 15.99m say 16m. The nominal value is: 16m x 50p = £8m. The share premium is £75m - £8m = £67m.

The redemption yield of the current 7% debentures is:

Time	Cash flow £	Factors at 5%	P.V. £	Factors at 10%	P.V. £
0	(95)	1.000	(95.000)	1.000	(95.000)
1	7	0.952	6.664	0.909	6.363
2	7	0.907	6.349	0.826	5.782
3	107	0.864	92.448	0.751	80.357
NPV			10.461		(2.498)

RY = 5 + (10.461/10.561+2.498) x 5 = 9%

The redemption yield and coupon of the new debenture issue at par will therefore be 9%.

28.2 (All in £m)

	Gearing	Interest cover	Earnings per share
Current	49.6% (£60/£121)	20.71 (£87/£4.2)	81.8p (£65.412/80)
After:			
Rights issue	25% (£60/£239.797)	27.4 (£115.08/£4.2)	91.2p (£87.595/96)
Debenture issue	83% (£135/£162.132)	10.51 (£115.08/£10.95)	102.8p (£82.263/80)

28.2 (b) Financing the expansion with a rights issue:

The rights issue will result in the issue of a further 16 million ordinary shares which is 20% (16/80) of the existing shares in issue. There will be a dilution of control for those shareholders who do not take up their rights. Shareholders will be encouraged by the increase in earnings per share from 81.77p to 91.2p.

The gearing ratio by book values after the rights issue and expansion of 25% is a significant reduction in the gearing from the present level of 49.6%. Since the industry average gearing is 50% it could be argued that Silverdale would be under geared. However this would leave unused debt capacity of £60 million, which could be used for further expansion. WACC may be higher than necessary as the company may be away from the optimal gearing level. It may be more appropriate to consider market values rather than book values for the gearing calculations.

The increase in the interest cover to 27.4 from 20.71 reduces the financial risk. This also points to unused debt capacity and is substantially above the average for the industry of 20.

Financing the expansion with a debenture issue:

There will be no control issues with a debenture issue. The increase in the earnings per share to 102.8p from 81.77p may encourage the shareholders but might not be reflected in the share price due to the increased financial risk of the company.

The gearing ratio by book values after the debenture issue and expansion of 83% is a significant increase in the gearing from the present level of 49.6% and the industry average gearing of 50%. This may have a detrimental effect on Silverdale's share price and also its ability to find institutions willing to invest in the debentures. The increase in gearing is likely to reduce the company's credit rating, which would result in investors in the debentures requiring a higher yield to maturity. It may therefore be necessary to issue the debentures at a discount, and/or to increase the coupon. Silverdale's WACC may increase.

The decrease in the interest cover 10.51 from 20.71 is a significant decrease from the current level and is substantially below the industry average of 20. This increases the financial risk of the company and is likely to have a detrimental affect on the company's share price and credit rating.

Conclusion

The rights issue results in what might be regarded as an unacceptably low gearing ratio when compared to the industry average. Whereas the debenture issue results in a gearing ratio that likely to be regarded as unacceptably more than the industry average. It would be worth the finance director of Silverdale exploring the possibility of raising the finance from both a debenture issue and a rights issue in such proportions to maintain the company's current gearing ratio.

This would also ensure that the interest cover does not fall to unacceptably low levels

Note. Capital structure theory, M & M, scores zero.

28.2 (c) Before the expansion Silverdale has a current ratio of 1.24:1.(£190m/£153m).

The current ratio after the rights issue and expansion would be 1.81:1 (£278.595m/153.998m) for the rights issue and also 1.81 (£273.263m/£151.331m) for the debenture issue. This is a significant increase from the present level of 1.24:1 and will ensure that the company has sufficient working capital for its expansion plans.

The current ratio is now approaching the industry average.

Hence, if Silverdale wishes to maintain a current ratio near to the industry average it will not be able to finance further expansion beyond 31 May 20X7 from cash surpluses at 31 May 20X6.

However if a rights issue is used to finance the expansion to 31 May 20X6 there will be spare debt capacity that could be used to finance further expansion plans.

Examiner's comments

This was a four-part question that tested the candidates' understanding of the financing options element of the syllabus. The scenario was that a company that is planning its expansion over the next two years is uncertain about how to raise the finance that will be required. The choice of finance being either a rights issue or an issue of debentures:

Part 28.1 was quite well answered with many students presenting reasonable projected income statements and balance sheets. Common errors were incorrect calculation of the interest for the debenture issue; omission of the existing debt after the debenture issue; incorrect calculation of the nominal value of the new shares to be issued for the rights issue; omission of the share premium.

In part 28.2(a), the examining team were shocked at the inability of students to calculate some basic ratios. Common errors were: Ignoring the definition of gearing which was given in the question as debt/equity, instead many candidates calculated debt/(debt + equity). Subsequent comparisons with the industry average gearing calculated using debt/equity were, therefore, meaningless. In some cases excluding retentions from the book value of equity; when calculating interest cover dividing interest into profits after tax, sales or even retentions. In some cases inverting the ratio; when calculating EPS using profits after dividends. In some cases dividing the profits after tax by the balance sheet value of the equity and not the number of shares in issue.

In part 28.2(b), the evaluation of the two potential methods of financing the expansion was very disappointing. When you have three sets of ratios and also industry averages the team are left a little puzzled as to how students can exclude any numerical analysis in their answers especially since the question had been set to bring out marked differences in the ratios under each financing alternative. Also a number of students took the opportunity to simply brain dump all they know about Modigliani and Miller's theory on capital structure, this did not achieve any marks as it was irrelevant to the question asked.

Again answers to part 28.2(c) of the question were disappointing, this is simple analysis. The company wishes to maintain a current ratio approaching the industry average and, again, it was surprising that many students did not take the time to calculate the current ratio under each scenario. It was alarming to note how many students thought that retentions equal cash.

29 Bradford Bedwyn Medical plc (March 2014)

		Marks
29.1 (a) Dividend/share	1	
Current accounting rate of return	1.5	
Proportion of profits retained	1	
Growth rate	0.5	
k_e	1	
k_d	2	
IRR	2	
WACC	2	
Maximum		10
(b) Market risk premium	1	
Cost of equity via CAPM	1	
WACC	1	
		3
29.2 Limitations of Gordon growth model	3	
		3
29.3 Ungeared beta	1	
Geared beta	1	
Cost of equity via CAPM	1	
Cost of new debt	1	
WACC	2	
Explanation	3	
		9
29.4 Discussion of issues	5	
	(max 2 for traditional and M&M)	5
29.5 Share buy back	5	
		5
		35

29.1 (a) **Cost of equity**

Dividend/share for year to 28/2/X4	£1,493/34,600 =	£0.0432

Dividend growth rate = g = r × b   r = current accounting rate of return
b = proportion of profits retained

Current accounting rate of return =   Earnings/Opening Equity Capital Employed

(£4,977/[£65,984 – £3,484]) =   r = 8%

Proportion of profits retained   Retained profits/Earnings
£3,484/£4,977   b = 70%

Thus the growth rate (g) = 8% × 70% = **5.6%**

$k_e =$ $\dfrac{d_1}{MV} + g$ $\dfrac{£0.0432 \times 1.056}{£2.45} + 0.056 =$ **7.5%**

$k_d =$

Year	Cash Flow	5%	PV	10%	PV
0	(104.00)	1.000	(104.00)	1.000	(104.00)
1-5	6	4.329	25.97	3.791	22.75
5	100	0.784	78.40	0.621	62.10
			0.37		(19.15)

Thus IRR is approx. 5% (fractionally higher). So $k_d =$ 5% (1-0.21) = 3.95%

WACC

		Market value		
Equity	34,600 × £2.45	84,770	7.5% × 84,770/93,714	6.78%
6% debentures	£8,600 × 104/100	8,944	3.95% × 8,944/93,714	0.38%
		93,714		WACC = 7.16%

(b)

Market risk premium =	(8.6% – 2.1%)	6.50%
BBM's beta is equity beta so no adjustment required		0.9
BBM's risk premium =	(6.5% × 0.9)	5.85%
plus: Risk free rate		2.10%
Cost of equity via CAPM		7.95%

WACC

	Market value		
Equity	84,770	7.95% × 84,770/93,714	7.19%
6% debentures	8,944	3.95% × 8,944/93,714	0.38%
	93,714		WACC = 7.57%

29.2 The Gordon growth model is a simple model of dividend behaviour. In particular:

The growth rate (g) must be less than the cost of equity (k_e). Otherwise the share price will be infinitely high. To maintain such a high growth rate to perpetuity is impossible. Companies are likely to experience periods of varying growth rates for which sophisticated models have been developed.

In addition the model:

Relies on accounting profits
Assumes that b and r are constant
Can be distorted by inflation
Assumes all new finance is from equity or gearing is held constant

29.3

Beta of the new market =		1.90
Ungeared beta of the new market =	1.9 × (83/(83 + [17 × 79%])	1.63
BBM's geared beta for the new market =	1.63 × ([84.770 + (8.944 × 79%)]/84.770)	1.77

BBM's cost of equity:

BBM's risk premium =	(6.5% × 1.77)	11.51%
plus: Risk free rate		2.10%
Cost of equity via CAPM		13.61%
Cost of new debt	(8% × 79%)	6.32%

WACC

	Market value		
Equity	£84,770	13.61% × 84,770/93,714	12.31%
6% debentures	£8,944	6.32% × 8,944/93,714	0.60%
	£93,714	WACC =	12.91%

BBM's current WACC figure (part 29.1 above) is 7.16% – 7.57%, depending on the method of calculation. It would be unwise to use this figure (approx. 7%) when appraising the diversification.

This is because the company will be working in a new market and its systematic risk (a key tenet of the CAPM) will change. This new market has a beta of 1.9, whereas BBM currently uses a beta of 0.9.

Were BBM to underestimate its WACC figure it would overestimate the NPV of the planned diversification. The cost of new debt is higher.

29.4 Gearing and systematic business risk have both changed. To get WACC one needs the MV of equity which includes the NPV of the project. To get NPV one needs WACC. So it's a circular argument. One could use APV to overcome this.

BBM cannot use the cost of the new debt after tax as the required return of the shareholders would be ignored. Neither can it use its risk adjusted cost of equity (as this ignores debt finance raised).

It can't use the risk adjusted WACC figure from part 29.3 because BBM's gearing level will have changed (it's an all-debt issue) – the WACC to be used then depends on the reaction to the increased gearing (U-shaped under traditional and M&M 1963 with market imperfections). If however there was a subsequent issue of equity planned which would re-establish the current gearing level, then the risk adjusted WACC from 29.3 could be used.

29.5 Normally a share buy-back returns money to shareholders and enables a company to use surplus cash when there are no investment opportunities with a positive NPV available. It doesn't appear to be the case here as the company is issuing debt.

If BBM made a large dividend payment then this would be contrary to company dividend policy. It might have an adverse effect on the company's share price - uncertainty created if larger dividend is not maintained in future.

A buy-back would reduce the number of shares in the market and this will mean that BBM's earnings per share and market value per share may increase depending on the reaction to the change in gearing – see below.

A buy-back could change control eg remove the influence of an unwelcome shareholder by buying their shares.

A share buy-back would increase BBM's gearing, which might, if BBM is below its optimal level of gearing, lead to an increase in BBM's share price via a reduced WACC.

A buy-back gives a capital gain subject to CGT rather than a dividend subject to income tax.

Examiner's comments

This question had the second highest average mark on the paper. Candidate performance was very variable.

It was a five-part question that tested the candidates' understanding of the financing options element of the syllabus.

In the scenario a medical equipment manufacturer was planning to raise additional funding to support a diversification into a new market. Part 29.1 for 13 marks required candidates to calculate the company's current weighted average cost of capital (WACC) figure using (a) the Gordon growth model and (b) CAPM. Part 29.2 for 3 marks asked them to explain the limitations of the Gordon growth model. In part 29.3 [9 marks], they were required to re-calculate and explain the WACC figure that should be used when appraising the company's diversification plans. The assumption in this scenario was that the funding raised would be in the same debt: equity ratio as currently exists. Part 29.4 for 5 marks asked candidates to discuss how the company would determine its WACC figure if the funding raised would all be in the form of debentures. In part 29.5 [5 marks] candidates had to explain the implications of using the funds raised for a share buy-back rather than a diversification.

In part 29.1(a) many candidates did well, as expected, but a disappointing number of them were unable to calculate the dividend growth rate ($g = b \times r$) and a lot of candidates used (erroneously) the cum-interest value of the debentures when calculating the cost of debt, despite there being numerous examples of these calculations in the study materials.

In part 29.1(b), when calculating WACC using CAPM, many candidates correctly established the cost of equity, but then failed to calculate a WACC subsequently.

Few candidates knew the limitations of the Gordon model for part 29.2. This was straightforward and a better understanding was expected.

In part 29.3, many candidates were able to correctly de-gear and re-gear the beta figure as required, but too many used book values when re-gearing (incorrect). Also a vast majority of candidates only did calculations in this part despite the explicit requirement to explain their reasoning.

For part 29.4, this has been asked regularly in the past, ie the issues in determining a WACC, but it was, overall, done poorly.

In part 29.5 too few candidates recognised that the share buy-back financed by a debt issue would increase gearing. Many candidates argued that gearing would decrease and, disappointingly, many confused the buy-back with a rights issue.

30 Liteform plc (December 2012)

Marking guide

	Marks
30.1 Current ex-dividend price per share	1
Calculation of r	1
Calculation of b	1
Calculation of g	1
Cost of equity	1
Cost of loan stock IRR style layout	2
Calculation of cost of loan stock	1
Calculation of WACC	2
	10
30.2 1 mark per valid point	max 8
30.3 1 mark per valid point	max 5
	23

30.1 **Cost of equity:**

	t
Current price per share cum-dividend	4.58
Current price per share cum-dividend	(0.27)
Current price per share ex-dividend	4.31

$$k_e = \frac{d_0(1+g)}{P_0} + g$$

We cannot calculate g using the average growth in dividends as we have not been provided with sufficient information. So the Gordon Growth Model (g = r × b) must be used:

r = 2,106,000/(13,359,000 − 972,000) = 0.17
b = 972,000/2,106,000 = 0.46
Therefore g = 0.17 × 0.46 = 7.8%

Therefore $k_e = \dfrac{0.27 \times 1.078}{4.31} + 0.078$

Cost of equity = 14.6%

Cost of loan stock:

	£	Df 5%	PV	Df 10%	PV
t_0	(85.10)	1	(85.10)	1	(85.10)
$t_1 - t_{10}$	7	7.722	54.05	6.145	43.02
t_{10}	105	0.614	64.47	0.386	40.53
			33.42		(1.55)

Cost of loan stock = 5% + 33.42/(33.42 + 1.55) × (10 – 5)% = 9.78%

Post-tax cost of loan stock = 9.78 × (1 – 0.21) = 7.73%

The weighted average cost of capital - MVs are (4.2m × £4.31) and (1.819m × £0.851):

$$= \frac{(18,102,000 \times 0.146) + (1,547,969 \times 0.0773)}{(18,102,000 + 1,547,969)} = 14.1\%$$

30.2 1. The Gordon Growth Model:

In its use of ARR, it relies upon accounting profit figures as opposed to cash-flows
It assumes that both r and b will remain constant
ARR can be distorted by inflation if assets remain valued at historic cost
The model assumes all new finance comes from equity (or gearing remains constant)

2. The Dividend Valuation Model:

The model assumes that the value of shares derives solely from dividends, which is untrue
The model assumes either that dividends do not grow or will grow at a constant rate
The model assumes share prices are constant, but they are subject to constant fluctuation
The model ignores future income growth

30.3 The dividend growth rate might change in future
All projects have different business risk so each should have a risk-specific discount factor
Market values might change in future
The tax rate might change in future
The gearing ratio might change in future
Other sources of finance might emerge in future

Examiner's comments:

The opening part of the question was generally well-answered although weaker candidates made common mistakes in mis-calculating the constituent elements (r and b) of the Gordon growth model. However, overall performance here was strong.

In the second part of the question, either through a lack of attention to the precise question being asked or, more probably we suspect, an inability to answer that precise question, a good number of candidates simply chose to write about the assumptions and weaknesses in calculating a WACC rather than the assumptions and weaknesses in calculating the cost of equity as the question precisely called for. Many weaker candidates consequently lost a good number of marks on a part of the question which carried just over one third of the total marks for the question.

Overall performance in part 30.3 was strong.

31 Seager Forest Scientific plc (March 2011)

		Marks
31.1	Calculation of dividend growth rate	1.5
	Calculation of cost of equity	1.5
	Calculation of cost of redeemable debt	3
	Calculation of cost of irredeemable debt	1
	Calculation of market values of equity and debt	3
	Calculation of WACC	1
		11
31.2	Relevant discussion	max 4
31.3	Profit before tax	1
	Debenture interest	2
	Taxation	1
	Earnings per share under equity issue	1
	Earnings per share under debt issue	1
		6
31.4	Calculations of EPS under different scenarios	2
	Relevant discussion on issue prices under each scenario	3
		5
31.5	Semi-strong efficient discussion	4
31.6	1 mark per relevant point	max 5
		35

31.1

Dividend % in 20X0/X1 =	£12m/£300m =	4% (ie 2p)
Dividend % in 20W9/X0 =	3.7% (ie 1.85p)	
Dividend/share 20X0/X1 =	12m/600m =	£0.02
Dividend growth rate =	4%/3.7% (or 2/1.85) = 1.081 =	8.1%
Cost of equity =	$\dfrac{(d1)}{MV} + g = \dfrac{(£0.02 \times 1.081)}{£1.24} + 8.1\% =$	9.84%

Cost of redeemable debt

Year	Cash Flow	5% factor	PV	10% factor	PV
0	(96.00)	1.000	(96.00)	1.000	(96.00)
1-3	7.00	2.723	19.06	2.487	17.41
3	100.00	0.864	86.40	0.751	75.10
			NPV 9.46		NPV (3.49)

IRR = 5% + [5% × (9.46/(9.46+3.49))] = 8.65%

Post-tax = 8.65 × (1 − 0.21) = 6.83%

Cost of irredeemable debt = [9% × (1 − 21%)]/£94 = 7.56%

WACC

		£m
Total market value of equity = 600m × £1.24 =		744.000
Total market value of redeemable debt = 120m × 96/100 =		115.200
Total market value of irredeemable debt = £80m × 94/100 =		75.200
Total market value		934.400

WACC	Weighted cost of equity	9.85% × £744.000/£934.400 =	7.83%
	Weighted cost of redeemable debt	6.83% × £115.200/£934.400 =	0.84%
	Weighted cost of irredeemable debt	7.56% × £75.200/£934.400 =	0.61%
			9.28%

31.2 SFS's long term funding has a current market value of £934.400 million. It plans to raise an additional £110m which represents an 11.8% increase on that current market value. This is a relatively small increase and so it reasonable to use the existing WACC as the hurdle rate. However, SFS will be using the new funding to expand its product range and its foothold in new geographical markets. This may mean that the level of risk changes and a different hurdle rate should be used to appraise the investment. CAPM should be considered as a means of establishing the hurdle rate. Were the funding to be raised using debt, it should be noted that the cost of the new debt represents the risk to the lenders and not that of the project.

31.3 **SFS Income Statement for the year to 30 April 20X2**

		Equity issue £m	Debt issue £m
Profit before Interest and Taxation (£84.1m × 1.08)		90.828	90.828
Less debenture interest (W1)		(15.600)	(22.200)
Profit before Taxation		75.228	68.628
Less taxation @ 21%		(15.798)	(14.412)
Profit after Taxation		59.430	54.216
Earnings per share (EPS)	(£59.430m/700m)	8.49p	
	(£54.216m/600m)		9.04p

WORKING

	£m
Interest cost of existing debt [(7% × £120m) + (9% × £80m)]	15.6
Interest cost of new debt (6% × £110m) =	6.6
	22.2

31.4

The current EPS (20X0/X1) =	£54.110m/600m	9.02p
EPS after 1 for 6 rights issue =	(£59.430m/700m)	8.49p
EPS after 1 for 8 rights issue =	(£59.430m/675m)	8.80p
EPS after 1 for 10 rights issue =	(£59.430m/660m)	9.00p

EPS will be lower in all three cases above. A 1 for 10 issue (ie fewest extra shares in issue) would give the best EPS result of the three.

However a 1 for 10 rights issue (60m extra shares) would mean that the issue price would be £1.83/share (£110m/60m). As the current market value is only £1.24/share then the rights issue would not be successful.

Similarly a 1 for 8 rights issue (75m extra shares) would mean that the issue price would be £1.47/share (£110m/75m). At this price, again the rights issue would not be successful.

A 1 for 6 rights issue (100m extra shares) would mean that the issue price would be £1.10/share (£110m/100m). This is not a massive discount (11%) on the current market value and it may be that a smaller multiple (1 for 5) might be needed, even though the impact on the EPS would be negative.

31.5 The efficient market hypothesis is concerned with the information-processing efficiency of markets, eg the valuation of shares in a stock market.

Assuming that SFS is operating in a semi-strong efficient market, then once the information about the new funds and investment becomes public knowledge (eg via a press release) then the market price of SFS' shares is likely to change as the information is assessed by the users of that market.

If the market believes that a positive NPV will accrue from the investment then, in all likelihood, the share price will increase.

31.6 There are a number of observed behavioural effects, which question the validity of the efficient markets hypothesis (EMH).

These behavioural effects include overconfidence by investors in their own ability, leading them to ignore warning signs about company performance and for example not sell their shares when a company makes an announcement about poor financial performance as would be expected under EMH.

A further significant effect occurs where investors ignore the bigger picture and concentrate on one small area of performance, such as that of one particular share. This is known as narrow framing.

Another important effect is that of extrapolative expectations, where investors expect rising prices to keep rising, this effect is thought to contribute to stock market bubbles.

Overall, despite these behavioural tendencies meaning that investors do not necessarily act rationally in all circumstances, the UK Stock Market can be seen as relatively efficient with the odd anomaly rather than not being efficient at all.

Examiner's comments:

This question had the second highest average mark on the paper.

It tested candidates' understanding of sources of finance and was divided into six sections.

In part 31.1 most candidates did well and were able to score good marks across the various elements of the WACC calculation. However, the dividend growth calculations were, in general, poor. Too many candidates used the [g = b × r] approach (not relevant here). Also too few candidates were able to calculate the future dividend/share and, when calculating the cost(s) of debentures, many used the wrong market values. A disappointing number of candidates used book values (rather than market values) to weight-average the WACC elements.

In part 31.4 too many candidates' answers were rather general and didn't produce sufficient figures to illustrate the key points. A lot of candidates failed to recognise that the rights issue price would be adversely affected by choosing the higher multiples outlined in the question.

32 Penny Rigby Fashions plc (September 2011)

		Marks
32.1	Market value of ordinary shares	1
	Market value of preference shares	1
	Market value of irredeemable debentures	1
	Calculation of WACC	1
		4
32.2	Ordinary dividends	1.5
	Preference dividends	1.5
	Debenture interest	1.5
	Proof of WACC	0.5
		5
32.3	Explanation of hurdle rate	3
	Explanation that failure to meet hurdle rate means value declines	2
		Max 4
32.4	Earnings per share	1
	Price earnings ratio	1
	Gearing ratio	1
	Calculation of earnings	
	Profit before interest and tax	0.5
	Interest	1.5
	Corporation tax	1
	Preference dividends	1
	Ordinary dividend	1
		8
32.5	Growth rate should represent future growth	1.5
	But commonly use past measures: dividends per share	1.5
	Or Gordon growth model	1.5
	0% growth means no capital growth	1.5
		6
		27

32.1

Type of Capital		Market Capitalisation (£)
Ordinary shares (50p)	(£4m/£0.50) × £2	16,000,000
Preference shares (25p)	(£0.8m/£0.25) × £0.80	2,560,000
Irredeemable debentures	£1.4m × 110/100	1,540,000
		20,100,000

Ordinary shares	10.50%	× £16,000/£20,100	8.358%
Preference shares	8.75%	× £2,560/£20,100	1.114%
Irredeemable debentures	4.17%	× £1,540/£20,100	0.319%
Weighted Average Cost of Capital			9.791%

32.2

	£
Ordinary dividends = £16m × 10.5% (or 0.105 = d/2; d = 0.21 × 8m)	1,680,000
Preference dividends = £2.56m × 8.75% (or 0.0875 = d/0.80; d = 0.07 × 3.2m)	224,000
Debenture interest = £1.54m × 4.17% (or 0.0417 = I(1-t)/110; I(1-t) = 4.587 × 0.014m)	64,218
	1,968,218

£1,968,218 / £20,100,000 = 9.792% (difference due to rounding)

32.3 The hurdle rate (WACC) is:

(a) The cost of funds that a company raises and uses, and the return that investors expect to be paid for putting funds into the company and therefore is

(b) The minimum return that a company must make on its own investments, to earn the cash flows out of which investors can be paid their return.

If the company does not achieve this hurdle rate on its investments then it will be investing in projects that produce a negative net present value and the value of the company (and the wealth of the shareholders) will decline.

32.4

Earnings (see Workings below)	£1,980,000	
Ordinary shares in issue	8 million	
Earnings per share	(£1,980,000/8,000,000)	£0.2475
Price earnings ratio	£2.00/£0.2475	8.08
Gearing ratio = $\dfrac{\text{Fixed Return Capital}}{\text{Total Long term Capital}}$	$\dfrac{£2.56m + £1.54m}{£20.1m}$	20.4%

Profit before interest and tax – see Workings below

WORKINGS (working upwards)	£
Profit before interest and tax	2,871,162
Less interest (£1.54m × 4.17% / 0.79)	(81,289)
Profit before tax	2,789,873
Less corporation Tax (£2,204,000 × 21/79)	(585,873)
Profit after tax	2,204,000
Less preference dividends (£2.56m × 8.75%)	(224,000)
Earnings	1,980,000
Less ordinary dividends (£16m × 10.5%)	(1,680,000)
Retained Profits (given)	300,000

32.5 Key points regarding dividend growth:

It should be future growth – forecasts, strategy, retentions etc – but often use past ie past dividends per share or the Gordon growth model.

0% growth means constant share price with no capital growth. The return is just dividend yield.

Examiner's comments:

This question had the lowest average mark on this paper and caused problems for a large number of students.

Most candidates scored full marks in part 32.1, but a surprising minority could not calculate the number of shares and debentures.

Part 32.2 was poorly done although a minority of candidates did secure full marks. The majority however were unable to work to an unknown figure which isn't the cost of capital (as this was given in the question). This was surprising as candidates would have learnt the formulae required or, in the case of the Dividend Valuation Model, it was given in the formulae sheet. Also many OT's in the learning materials require candidates to work backwards towards an answer, as was required here.

In part 32.3 many candidates knew about the desirability and impact of positive NPV's, but could not explain what a WACC actually is, ie a required rate of return.

Part 32.4 was in general answered very poorly indeed. Too many candidates treated retained earnings and earnings as the same figure. A significant minority added ordinary and preference share prices for the P/E calculation. The majority could not work backwards, up through the Income Statement, despite this appearing in the learning materials.

In part 32.5 virtually no-one considered future forecasts. When past dividend growth rates and the Gordon model were used few candidates noted the assumption that past growth = future growth. The significance of the company's 0% dividend growth rate was poorly answered. The question was couched in terms of returns but few candidates spotted that there would be no capital return on the current share price.

33 Personal investment (June 2003)

	Marks
Banks and building societies	2
Shares	3
Company profits and dividends	3
Buying and selling shares	3
Risk and return	1
Sainsco	2
Diversification	2
Total available	16
Maximum	14

Banks and building societies

When you put money into a bank (or building society), you are lending money to it. It uses this cash to make loans to other people and businesses. The bank will pay you interest on your deposit to encourage you to do so. It charges interest to those to whom it lends. On this aspect of its business the bank makes a profit from this. You are a customer of the bank and the reward (interest) that you get is not linked to the profit that the bank makes.

There are only limited government-backed guarantees, but in general the major UK banks and building societies provide a very safe deposit for your money. At the same time the rates of interest are very low. This partly reflects the fact that returns are safe. Risk and return tend to be linked.

Interest rates are low at present, by historical standards, but they reflect low expectations of price inflation. In reality you are probably not much worse off by having your funds in a bank deposit account now than you were a few years ago.

Shares

When you buy shares in a company, you become a part owner of that business. The benefits that you get from ownership depend entirely on how profitable the company is.

Shares are slices of the ownership of the company. When you buy shares through the Stock Exchange you are buying them from some person or investing institution (like an insurance company) that has decided to sell its stake, or part of it, in the ownership of the company. You merely replace the previous owner of the shares as a part owner of the company.

Sometimes companies expand by inviting investors to buy new shares that it issues. Here investors would be buying new shares rather than 'second hand' shares from an existing shareholder.

Company profits and dividends

As already said, shareholders share in the profits made by the company in proportion to how many of the total shares they own individually. Most companies whose shares are available to buy through the Stock Exchange reinvest much of their profits in an attempt to generate greater future profits for their shareholders. Most of them also pay part of the profit as a cash dividend to their shareholders, according to how many shares each owns.

Dividends are not guaranteed. If a company makes no profit there would usually be no dividend, though companies are allowed to pay dividends using funds generated from previous years' profits. Even where profits are good, the directors may feel that reinvesting all of those profits and not paying any dividend will serve the shareholders' best interests.

In theory, the dividend should be dependent on the amount of funds available and the investment opportunities available to the business. If there are lots of profitable opportunities, no dividend would be payable. The larger, better known companies, like Sainsco, usually pay part of their profit as a dividend, partly because they know that many, perhaps most, of their shareholders need a regular stream of cash. Companies seem reluctant to fail to pay any dividend. They seem to pay fairly steady dividends from one year to the next, with relatively small increases from time to time. Whether the company pays a dividend or not, the profits generated belong to the shareholders; so, if they are not getting a dividend, the value of their shares should be increasing.

When you buy your shares you will have to pay the current market price. That price will depend on general expectations of the future economic prospects for the company concerned. This, in turn, will depend on such things as the perceived quality of the management, the future market for the product or service that the company sells etc. No one knows what will happen in the future, but the price of a share at any moment should represent the consensus view on what the share is worth taking account of the prospects for the company. There is strong evidence that the price of a share at any time is a fair representation of its fair value according to the information available.

Share prices alter on a minute-to-minute basis, according to investors' perceptions of their fair value. This means that when you come to sell your shares, they may not be worth as much as you hope, or even as much as you paid for them.

Risk and return

The rewards of share ownership are a combination of the dividends received plus any increases (less any decreases) in the price of the shares. There are no guarantees. History shows that on average investing in shares yielded significantly higher returns than putting your money in the bank. Despite this, over particular short periods and with the shares of particular companies, investment in shares has been less rewarding than bank interest.

Sainsco

Evidence shows that newspaper tips and advice of any 'experts', on individual shares, are not worth following and that they will only be correct by chance. If Sainsco is a well-run company with a profitable future, neither the newspaper tipster, nor you will be the only people to notice this. This information will already be reflected in the share price. This is not to say that Sainsco does not represent a good investment, but if the shares of all companies are fairly priced, then this will be equally true of all of them. Share prices reflect expected returns.

Eggs and baskets

You would be ill-advised to put all of your money into the shares of one company. Evidence shows that spreading your funds between 15 or more different shares can eliminate some of the risk of owning shares. If the amount of funds that you have to invest is small, it may be uneconomic, in terms of agents' fees, to spread your investment funds so thinly.

In this case it is possible to achieve this risk diversification by pooling your funds with those of other small investors. Funds (unit trusts etc) are available for this. The disadvantage of this is that the managers of the funds take a fee out of your investment for running the funds. These fees vary from fund to fund, so it may be valuable to shop around.

Examiner's comments:

This question was well answered, in general, though many candidates displayed an inability to explain the issues in simple terms.

Candidates were asked to comment on some questions asked, about investing in shares relative to putting money in a bank deposit account, by a friend who clearly has no understanding of the issues involved. Most candidates were able to deal competently with the technical issues, but seemed unable to explain them in simple terms. There were some honourable exceptions to this and some answers were expressed in an appropriate manner. A surprisingly consistent error was a failure to say that investing in shares and putting money in a bank deposit account are not just of different risk, but are fundamentally different in nature. Many candidates dealt with this as if equity investment is like putting money in the bank, only more risky.

Sheridan plc (September 2004)

		Marks
Introduction	3	
Rights issue	4	
Loan stock / bank loan	5	
Recommendation	2	
Maximum		14
Total available		12

Briefing notes

A substantial investment such as that proposed may be seen as increasing the business risk of the company, despite the fact that the company being acquired operates in the same sector. This could increase the required return of both shareholders and lenders.

Issuing more debt could reduce the average cost of capital, although an expansion of this size, funded entirely by debt, could push up the cost of capital rather than reduce it.

The company may well be below its optimal capital gearing level at the present time and while the precise optimal level is a matter of judgment (based on likely market response to particular capital structures), forming that judgment must take account of Sheridan's current level of gearing as well as the sector average.

With regard to the comments by Director C, in theory gearing makes no difference to the wealth of shareholders in the absence of taxes (M&M) – cheaper loan finance has a positive impact that is precisely cancelled out by the higher returns required by shareholders in the face of higher risk.

However, taking account of the tax deductibility of loan interest, gearing favours shareholders, although at higher levels of gearing the risk of non-servicing of interest commitments could impact adversely on shareholder wealth via liquidation. Gearing policy, therefore, appears to be about striking a balance between the benefits of tax relief and the potential costs of bankruptcy.

Rights issue

This is relatively cheap to issue and not as difficult to price compared to a public issue.

If fully taken up it will not change the control of the company and existing shareholders will retain all the benefits of the acquisition.

There would, however, be no benefit from cheaper debt finance.

Investors need not lose out if they do not wish to participate as they can sell their rights (market efficiency will dictate a price at which they will not lose out). Existing investors will only lose if they neither take up nor sell their rights.

Equity is rather more expensive than loan finance as investors expect higher returns than they do for loans, given that the returns are more risky and paid after the payments to lenders.

The comment made by Director A is somewhat illogical – market efficiency theory (and evidence) suggests that whatever the current share price, it represents the best unbiased estimate of a share's worth based on available evidence.

Unlike interest, dividends are not, in theory, a fixed commitment.

Loan stock or bank loan

Either would be cheaper to raise and service relative to equity, as it offers a fixed income to providers, which is paid ahead of equity shareholders and for which they are prepared to accept a lower level of return. However, it is often seen as more risky than equity.

With regard to the comments of Director B, the driver of EPS or share price is not how a project is financed but the nature of the project itself – as long as it has a positive net present value it will generate returns for shareholders over and above their required minimum return and should therefore increase both earnings and share price.

The use of debt finance instead of equity should result in a lower overall average required rate of return and, correspondingly, a higher share price.

This is a large acquisition for the company, so serviceability of additional debt would be a key issue. There is also, often, an obligation to redeem loan stocks.

High gearing may increase the perceived risk, thereby increasing the interest rate demanded by lenders and, unlike dividends, interest is a fixed commitment.

Another issue to consider is whether the loan stock would be secured or unsecured, which could, in turn, have an impact on the interest cost.

With regard to the comments of Director D, a bank loan may well require good security and come with a series of restrictive covenants. This raises the question of whether the company has sufficient unused debt capacity in its assets.

Lenders have contractual rights to interest and redemption payments, but loan interest is tax deductible, which makes it cheaper than equity.

Recommendation

Probably a mixture of rights issue and debt – the precise balance being based on estimated calculations of the likely impact on the overall cost of capital.

Examiner's comments:

There was a tendency for a minority of candidates to 'dump' everything they knew that was remotely linked to the topic under discussion, rather than to apply what they knew to providing useful, practical advice to directors which reflected the specifics of the question. In addition, a minority of candidates addressed each of the specific points made by the four directors but then provided no more discussion in accordance with the requirements of the question.

35 Nash Telecom (December 2003)

Marking guide	

	Marks
35.1 1 mark per point	3
35.2 1 mark per point	4
35.3 1 mark per point	4
35.4 Up to 2 marks for each reasoned point	5
35.5 1 mark per point	3
	19

35.1 Rights issues

A rights issue is an issue of new shares for cash to existing shareholders in proportion to their existing holdings.

The ex-rights price is the price at which the shares will settle after the rights issue has been made.

Underwriting is the process whereby, in exchange for a fee, an institution or group of institutions will undertake to purchase at the issue price any securities not subscribed for by the public.

35.2 Theoretical ex-rights price

The theoretical ex-rights price = $\dfrac{\text{Market value of shares pre-rights issue} + \text{rights proceeds}}{\text{Number of shares ex-rights}}$

Calculation of the theoretical ex-rights price

		€
Current holding	20 shares at €20 each	400
Rights issue	16 shares at €15.5 each	248
Total new holding	36 shares worth	648

So theoretical ex-rights price = €18 (€648 ÷ 36) as stated in the newspaper.

However, it is possible that the actual price may be higher or lower than the theoretical figure, depending on market expectations about the prospects for the business.

35.3 Effect on wealth

You should consider a number of factors in deciding whether to take up the rights issue.

- Whether you wish to continue in the company for the long term (as its recent performance has been poor and it has run up a debt mountain).

- Whether you want to maintain your holding at the same proportionate level. (If you give up your rights, you will effectively have half the proportionate holding).

- Whether you have the money to subscribe for the rights issue.

- The market price for selling the rights.

In theory, this is the financial effect on your uncle of him subscribing or not subscribing for the rights issue.

		€	€
Uncle's current holding (say 200 shares) is worth (200 × €20)			4,000
(1)	If uncle takes up the rights		
	New holding is worth ((200 + 160) × €18)	6,480	
	Less Cost of new shares (160 × €15.5)	(2,480)	
	Net effect		4,000
(2)	If uncle sells the rights		
	Holding is now worth (200 × €18)	3,600	
	Plus Sale of rights (160 × (€18 – €15.5))	400	
	Net effect		4,000
(3)	If uncle does nothing		
	Holding is now worth (200 × €18)		3,600

Thus in situations (1) and (2) above uncle 'breaks even', ie his wealth remains the same (€4,000). If he chooses to do nothing (situation (3)), however, he will lose €400 (€4,000 – €3,600).

However, in practice the company might well sell the rights on your uncle's behalf and reimburse him with the difference (€400).

35.4 Reducing debts

Nash Telecom seems to have considered debt-based options. Other possibilities might include the following:

- Make a public issue of shares – this would dilute the control of existing shareholders. This would also be expensive. However, existing lenders would be encouraged, as gearing will be declining.

- Negotiate the conversion of (substantial) loans into equity – this dilutes existing shareholders' interests and eliminates right of lenders to repayment.

- Seek to be taken over by a large company with limited debts, ie to produce a combined company with a reasonable debt to equity relationship – this reduces risks for existing shareholders and for employees.

- Seek a venture capitalist investment – this dilutes the existing shareholders' interests; and there is continuing uncertainty about long-term ownership for both employees and shareholders.

- Divestment, ie sell off assets and raise cash to reduce debt. This subsequent lack of assets might well affect the company's performance, and a sale and leaseback arrangement might be preferred.

- Seek Government finance to re-structure the company and/or to support specific operations – this increases the Government's stake in the future of the business.

35.5 WACC

The cost of equity is generally deemed to be greater than that for debt. This is not least because of the tax advantages of debt (since the interest payments get tax relief). In addition debt holders normally require a lower rate of return, as the level of return is fixed and the company is obliged to pay it.

So, it is probable that the weighted average cost of capital would increase with the shift from debt to equity, but it would depend on whether the company is close to (or even above) its optimal level of gearing.

Interest rates are currently relatively low, but Nash Telecom would need to pay higher than market rates due to its high level of debt.

However, Modigliani and Miller originally concluded that a company's weighted average cost of capital should not be affected by its capital structure. They argued that, as a company's level of debt increased the cost of equity would increase in direct proportion, thus cancelling out the effect of the cheaper debt. Subsequently they developed their theory to show that in the presence of corporation tax it is advantageous to issue debt.

Examiner's comments:

This question was based around a recent real life situation and parts 35.1 to 35.3 tested candidates on rights issues. Parts 35.4 and 35.5 looked at long-term finance more generally – asking candidates for alternatives to the rights issue and then testing their ability to explain the effects on the company's WACC of this scenario.

In part 35.1 candidates were asked to explain the meaning of the terms 'rights issue', 'ex-rights' and 'underwriting'. It was answered well and many candidates scored full marks.

In part 35.2 candidates were asked to explain how the 'theoretical ex-rights price' had been calculated. Candidates demonstrated a good understanding and again many scored full marks.

Part 35.3 required students to advise a shareholder on whether or not to take up the rights issue. This was done less well and many students failed to deal with this in sufficient depth (eg the investor could also sell the rights).

In part 35.4 candidates were asked to explain the ways in which the company might reduce its debt mountain. There were plenty of marks available and it was answered well by most candidates, although far too many candidates suggested borrowing more money in order to reduce the debt mountain.

In part 35.5 candidates were asked to discuss the possible effects on the company's weighted average cost of capital of increasing equity and reducing borrowings. A good answer required candidates to consider the traditional theory regarding WACC and to contrast this with the Modigliani and Miller (M&M) theories. Although this was answered well in general, there was some confusion as to how the M&M approach would affect the WACC in practice.

36 Battlesbridge Roberts plc (March 2013)

			Marks
36.1	Cost of equity	3	
	Cost of preference shares	1	
	Cost of redeemable debt using IRR	3	
	Calculation of WACC	4	
			11
36.2	Explanation of preference to use WACC	6	
			6
36.3	Price of redeemable debenture stock	3	
			3
36.4	CAPM calculation	5	
	Advice based on calculation	3	
			8
			28

36.1

Cost of equity (k_e) $\quad d_0 = \dfrac{£6.48m}{27m} \qquad\qquad = £0.24/\text{share}$

$$\frac{(d_1)}{MV} + g \qquad \frac{(£0.24 \times 1.06)}{£4.56} + 6\% \qquad = 11.58\%$$

Cost of preference shares (k_p) $\quad \dfrac{£0.07}{£1.18} \qquad = 5.93\%$

Pre-tax cost of redeemable debt (k_d)

Year	Cash Flow	5% factor	PV	10% factor	PV
0	(93.00)	1.000	(93.00)	1.000	(93.00)
1-3	4.00	2.723	10.89	2.487	9.95
3	100.00	0.864	86.40	0.751	75.10
			NPV 4.29		(7.95)

IRR = 5% + [5% × (4.29/(4.29+7.95))] = 6.75%

Post-tax cost of debt = 6.75% × (1 − 0.28) = 4.86%

WACC

	£m
Total market value of equity = 27m × £4.56 =	123.120
Total market value of preference shares = 2.8m × £1.18	3.304
Total market value of redeemable debt = 4.6m × 93/100 =	4.278
Total market value	130.702

WACC			
	Weighted cost of equity	11.58% × £123.120/£130.702 =	10.91%
	Weighted cost of irredeemable debt	5.93% × £3.304/£130.702 =	0.15%
	Weighted cost of redeemable debt	4.86% × £4.278/£130.702 =	0.16%
			11.22%

36.2 The cost of capital (hurdle rate) is:

- The cost of funds that a company raises and uses, and the return that investors expect to be paid for putting funds into the company and therefore is

- The minimum return that a company must make on its own investments, to earn the cash flows out of which investors can be paid their return.

The cost of equity is ignored in the calculation so the hurdle rate (5.5%) is too low. If the company does not achieve this hurdle rate on its investments then it will be investing in projects that produce a negative net present value and the value of the company (and the wealth of the shareholders) will decline.

So the cost of capital is an opportunity cost of finance – it is the minimum return that investors require. If they do not get this return, they will transfer some or all of their investment elsewhere. So when shareholders invest in a company the returns that they can expect must be sufficient to persuade them not to sell some or all of their shares and invest somewhere else.

The yield on their investment is, therefore, the opportunity cost to the investors of not investing elsewhere. Thus current market prices must be used to establish the costs of the various elements of long term capital. Nominal (historic) values are irrelevant. Market values also reflect the importance (ie weighting) of the different forms of finance which the 50:50 in the 5.5% rate suggested does not.

The tax relief on debt interest is also ignored.

36.3 Cost of redeemable debt (k_d)

Year	Cash Flow	7% factor	PV
1	(93.00)	1.000	(92.51)
2-3	2.88	1.808	5.21
3	100.00	0.873	87.30
		NPV	0.00

The MV of the debt at 31 March 20X4 will equal the PV of the future cash flows, ie: (£5.21 + £87.30) = £92.51

36.4 The Capital Asset Pricing Model (CAPM) is a method of calculating the cost of capital of an organisation and is based on the premise that investors require a premium for systematic risk (SR). The major assumptions are that:

There is a linear relationship between the return of individual companies and the average return of all securities in the market.

Individual securities will be more or less risky than the market average in a fairly predictable/measurable way over time.

The measure of this relationship can be developed into a beta factor – (ß) – for individual securities.

ß is a measure of a share's volatility in terms of market risk.

CAPM states that unsystematic risk (UR) can be eliminated by diversification. Therefore the average portfolio return depends on: (a) changes in the average market return and (b) the ß of shares in the portfolio.

Excess return = difference between the market return and the risk-free return.

CAPM equation: Rs – Rrf = ß(Rm – Rrf) or Rs = Rrf + ß(Rm – Rrf)

s = an individual share, rf = a risk-free investment, m = market average

CAPM can be used to calculate the cost of equity (an alternative to the Dividend Growth Model) and this can then be used in a WACC calculation.

The resultant WACC would be applied as the cost of capital in an NPV calculation.

Examiner comments

This question had the lowest average mark on the paper.

This was a four-part question that tested the financing element of the syllabus. In the scenario a company wished to establish its WACC figure for employment in its planned large scale investments. Candidates were therefore required to calculate a WACC figure and demonstrate a good understanding of WACC's relevance and usefulness.

Part 36.1 for eleven marks asked candidates to calculate the company's WACC. Part 36.2 was worth six marks and required candidates to explain why the WACC from part 36.1 would be preferable to an alternative figure put forward by the company's directors. Part 36.3 for three marks asked candidates to calculate a market price for debenture stock based on a given market yield. Finally, part 36.4 for eight marks required candidates to explain the CAPM and how it relates to the NPV approach of investment appraisal. Part 36.1 should have been reasonably straightforward for all candidates, but parts 36.2 to 36.4 would have been good discriminators.

Part 36.1 was generally answered very well, but a surprising number of candidates were unable to calculate the cost of preference shares correctly - typically they used a post-tax dividend figure. Also many candidates were unable to calculate the cost of redeemable debentures because they didn't use the correct current market price or the correct future (post-tax) interest receipts.

Surprisingly, many candidates did poorly in part 36.2. A key issue was that by using the wrong WACC (hurdle rate) the company would make poor investment decisions. Too few candidates addressed this. Thus many answers were far too general and failed to demonstrate a real understanding of what WACC means.

Part 36.3 was answered very poorly indeed and only a small minority of candidates indicated a real understanding here.

Part 36.4 was also disappointing and a large number of candidates failed to explain how the CAPM fits into the NPV approach to investment appraisal. WACC is used as a discount rate to calculate the NPV of an investment. CAPM is used as a means of calculating the WACC.

37 Turners plc (June 2014)

		Marks
37.1 (a)	Ke	1
	Kd	3
	Loans	1
	WACC	3
		8
(b)	Retentions rate	2
	Shareholders' return	1.5
	Growth	0.5
	Ke	1
	WACC	1
		6

37.2 Degearing equity beta	1.5
Regear asset beta	1.5
Ke	1
State discount rate should reflect systematic risk	1
State discount rate should reflect financial risk	1
	6

37.3 Weighted average beta of enlarged group	1
Ke	1
WACC of enlarged group	1
Implications	3 (Capital structure theory; max 2 marks)
	6

37.4 Diversification plans	5 (max 3 for EMH)
	5

37.5 Project appraisal methodology and discount rate	4
	4
	35

37.1 (a) The current WACC using CAPM is calculated as follows: Ke = 2 + 0.60 (8-2) = **5.6%**

Calculation of Kd

The cost of the debentures the cost can be calculated using linear interpolation

		5%		1%	
T0	(108)	1	(108)	1	(108)
T1-4	6	3.546	21.276	3.902	23.412
T4	100	0.823	82.3	0.961	96.1
			(4.424)		11.512

IRR = 1%+ (11.512/11.512 + 4.424)(5 – 1)=**3.89%** × (1 – 0.21) = **3.1%** after tax

Loans have an after-tax cost of 4(1 – 0.21) = **3.16%**

Market values:

Equity 233m/0.10 × 276p =	**£6,431m**
Debentures 1,900m × 108/100 =	**£2,052m**
Loans	**£635m**
Total market values	**£9,118m**

WACC = (5.6% × 6,431 + 3.1% × 2,052 + 3.16% × 635)/ 9,118 = 4.9%

(b) The current WACC using the Gordon growth model is calculated as follows:

Calculating growth using the formula r × b.

Retentions rate:

Dividends = share price × dividend yield = 276p × 4.2% = **11.6p**

Dividend payout ratio = dividend/ EPS = 11.6/25 = 46.4% ∴ Retentions = 1 – 0.464 = 0.536 or **53.6%**

Shareholders return is calculated as follows:

Profit after tax (PAT) = EPS × number of shares in issue = 25p × 233/0.10 = **£582.5m**

Return = PAT/opg shareholders funds = 582.5/(**5,263** – (**2,330** × **£0.134***)) = 11.77%

*EPS – Dividend: 25p – 11.6p = 13.4p

Growth = r × b = 0.1177 × 0.536 = 0.063 or **6.3%**

Ke = (Do(1 + g)/Po) + g = (11.6(1 + 0.063)/276) + 0.063 = **10.77%**

Kd and market values as in (a)

WACC = (10.77% × 6,431 + 3.1% × 2,052 + 3.16% × 635)/9,118 = **8.51%**

37.2 The cost of equity should be adjusted to reflect the systematic risk of the new project. The beta factor for the holiday travel industry should be adjusted for gearing. Degearing the equity beta, ßa = 1.40/(1+(3(1-0.21)/5) = **0.95**

Gear up the asset beta to reflect Turners' gearing

ße = 0.95 × (1 + (2,687(1-0.21)/6,431) = **1.26**

The Ke should be = 2 + 1.26 (8 – 2) = **9.56%**

With regard to the WACC to be used for the project students should state that the discount rate should reflect the **systematic risk of the project** and the **financial risk of the company**.

37.3 If the diversification goes ahead the cost of equity will reflect the systematic risk of both divisions.

The weighted average beta of the enlarged group = 1.26 × 0.10 + 0.6 × 0.90 = **0.666**

Ke = 2 + 0.666(8-2) = **6.00%**

The WACC of the enlarged group will be:

(6% × 6,431 + 3.1% × 2,052 + 3.16% × 635)/9,118 = **5.15%**

The implications of a permanent change in the company's WACC from 4.9% to 5.15% are less clear. An increase in the WACC is usually associated with reductions in value, on the other hand assuming that the new project has a positive net present value this could result in an increase in the market capitalisation.

37.4 The diversification plans may not be welcomed by the market. Portfolio theory tells us that rational shareholders would hold a well-diversified portfolio and that they might not welcome the company diversifying. Conglomerate companies often trade at a discount.

37.5 Students should mention that if the gearing changes dramatically then it is not suitable to use WACC/NPV to appraise the project. Instead APV should be used.

The discount rate will be that of an all equity company using the ßa of 0.95 to reflect the systematic risk. The discount rate will be = 2 + 0.95(8 – 2) = 7.7%.

This will be used to calculate the base case NPV. This will then be adjusted for the benefits and costs of the actual way that the project has been financed.

Examiner's comments

This was a six-part question that tested the candidates' understanding of the financing options element of the syllabus. The scenario of the question was that a company was considering diversifying its activities. The diversification was to be financed in such a way that the gearing of the company remained unchanged. Part 37.1 of the question required candidates to calculate the current WACC of the company using CAPM and also the Gordon growth model. Part 37.2 of the question required candidates to calculate, using CAPM, the cost of equity to be included in the WACC that should have been used to appraise the new project. Part 37.3 of the question required candidates to calculate the overall WACC of the company after the diversification. Part 37.4 of the question required candidates to discuss whether the company should diversify its operations. Part 37.5 of the question required candidates to discuss how the project should have been appraised assuming that there was a major change in financial gearing of the company. Also candidates were required to calculate a discount rate that should have been used in these circumstances.

Part 37.1 (a) was designed to give a basic eight marks to build on and was set at a textbook level with no tricks or complications. However, weaker candidates lost many of these marks by: completely ignoring the cost of a bank loan (2 marks) or not deducting tax (1 mark); incorrect calculation of the cost of the redeemable debentures, incorrect interpolation calculations, incorrect coupon and timing (3 marks), correct interpolation but no tax adjustment (1 mark); incorrect equity beta or correct beta but error in computation (1 mark).

Part 37.1 (b) was a discriminator as expected, however many candidates demonstrated poor knowledge of what a dividend yield is, many students multiplying earnings by the dividend yield.

In part 37.2, again many basic errors were made: eg degearing using market values but regearing using book values, even though the formulae sheet states market values on the key to the formulae and despite the examiner's comments regarding March 2014, omitting tax completely from the computations and poor mathematical ability using beta equations. Also no explanation of what candidates were doing threw away 2 marks in this section.

Part 37.3 was well answered by many candidates. However in the discursive part of their answers some candidates mainly discussed capital structure theory.

Part 37.4 had very mixed responses but flexible marking allowed candidates to pick up 2 to 3 marks.

In part 37.5, most candidates mentioned APV but many did not calculate the discount rate needed.

38 Middleham plc (Sample paper)

	Marks
38.1 Earnings in 20W8	1
Dividend in 20W8	1
Dividend growth rate	1
Dividend per share in 20X2	1
Current ex-dividend share value	1
Cost of equity	1
Cost of preference shares	1
Cost of debentures – two present values calculated	2
Cost of debentures – IRR calculation	1
WACC calculation	3
	13
	max 5
38.2 1 mark per point	
38.3 Ungear industry beta	2
Regear using Middleham's data	2
CAPM calculation	1
1 mark per assumption	3
	max 7
38.4 1 mark per point	max 5
38.5 Forms of efficiency (1.5 marks for each)	4.5
Stock exchange regarded as semi-strong form efficient	1
Market reacts to press announcement if semi-strong form	1.5
Market does not react to press announcement if strong form	1.5
	max 5
	35

38.1 Cost of equity capital:

Earnings in 20W8 = £0.35 × 6,400,000 = **£2,240,000**
Dividends in 20W8 = £2,240,000 × 40% = **£896,000**
Dividend growth rate: $896,000 \times (1+g)^4$ = £1,088,000
$\qquad\qquad (1+g)^4$ = 1,088,000/896,000 = 1.2143
$\qquad\qquad 1+g$ = $\sqrt[4]{1.2143}$ = 1.0497
$\qquad\qquad$ **g = 5%**

Dividend per share in 20X2 (d_0) = £1,088,000/6,400,000 = **17p**
Current ex-dividend share value = £1.42 – £0.17 = **125p**
Using the dividend growth model: k_e = $d_0(1 + g)/p_0 + g$
$\qquad\qquad$ = 17(1.05)/125 + 5%
$\qquad\qquad$ = **19.3%**

Cost of preference share capital: = 2.5p/20p
$\qquad\qquad$ = **12.5%**

Cost of debentures:

Year	Cash Flow	10% df	PV	Cash Flow	1% df	PV
0	(105)	1.000	(105.00)	(105)	1.000	(105.00)
1-10	7	6.145	43.02	7	9.471	66.30
10	100	0.386	38.60	100	0.905	90.50
		NPV	(23.38)		NPV	51.80

IRR = 1% + 51.8/75.18 × 9 = **7.20%**

Post-tax = 7.20 × (1 – 0.21) = 5.7%

Weighted Average Cost of Capital:

	Cost	Total Mkt. Value (£'000)	WACC
Equity	19.3%	8,000	15.2
Preference shares	12.5%	560	0.7
Debentures	5.7%	1,575	0.9
		10,135	16.8

Thus the Weighted Average Cost of Capital = **16.8%**

38.2 If this weighted average cost of capital of 16.8% is used in the appraisal of the proposed investment then the following assumptions must be recognised and if these assumptions do not hold then the WACC figure has serious limitations if used as a discount factor:

Historical proportions of debt and equity are to remain unchanged
Business risk is to remain unchanged
The finance raised is not project specific
The project is small in size relative to the size of the company

Other factors are:
Is the dividend growth rate sustainable given the lack of track record?
There could be other sources of finance that have not been considered
Future tax rate changes will affect the cost of debt and so the WACC
Will the redeemable debentures be replaced by similar funds in 10 years?

38.3 (a) Ungear the equity beta of the industry

$1.3 = ß_a(1 + (1(1 - 0.21)/1))$
$ß_a = 0.7263$
regear using Middleham's gearing from part 38.1 (prefs are treated as debt)
$ß_e = 0.7263(1 + (2,135(1 - 0.21)/8,000))$
$ß_e = 0.879$
Cost of equity capital $= R_f + ß(R_m - R_f) = 6 + 0.879 (14 - 6) = $ **13.0%**

(b) Key assumptions comprise:

(1) The objective of the company is to maximise the wealth of shareholders
(2) All shareholders hold the market portfolio (they are fully diversified)
(3) Shareholders are the only participants in the firm.

38.4 The increased risk created by issuing more debentures is a financial or gearing risk. The traditional view of gearing is that at low levels of gearing a company's WACC will decrease (because debt is cheaper than equity) - this will cause the value of the company to rise.

However, as gearing becomes a greater proportion of total long term funds, the cost of debt will start to increase and WACC will rise too, and the value of the company will fall.

The view of Modigliani and Miller (1963) is that a company's WACC, and therefore value, is not affected by the level of gearing other than through the effects of tax relief and that this leads to a fall in WACC and a corresponding increase in the value of the company.

However, at very high levels of gearing bankruptcy costs, tax exhaustion and agency costs can all cause the cost of debt to increase and, as with the traditional theory, the WACC will start to rise and the value of the company fall.

38.5 The are three levels of market efficiency:

- Weak form – share prices reflect information about past price movements and future price movements cannot be predicted from past movements (Chartism/technical analysis).

- Semi-strong form – share prices incorporate all publicly available information rapidly and accurately. The market cannot be beaten by analysing publicly available information.

- Strong-form – share prices reflect all information whether published or not. Insider dealing has no value.

The London Stock Exchange is generally regarded as at least semi-strong efficient.

If the stock market is semi-strong efficient then Middleham's share price should rise (+ NPV project) or fall (–NPV) when the project is announced to the market eg in the newspaper, press release etc.

If the stock market is Strong-form efficient then Middleham's share price should remain unaltered as the +NPV or –NPV will already be reflected in the share price ie. as soon as the decision is made (unlikely).

Examiner's comments:

A generally very well answered question which was the second highest scoring question on the paper.

A very common error on this relatively straightforward cost of capital question was a failure to follow the instructions in the question – many candidates chose to use the Gordon growth model rather than the dividend growth model – an easy way to lose marks. Other common errors were an inability to accurately calculate the dividend growth rate from the data provided, errors in calculating market values in the final WACC calculation and in calculating the cost of debt a number of candidates betrayed basic misunderstanding by firstly applying one discount rate that produced a negative NPV and then choosing a larger rather than smaller discount rate for their second choice.

Parts 38.2 to 38.5 were generally well answered.

39 Better Deal plc (March 2010)

Marking guide

				Marks
39.1	(a)	Dividend growth rate	1	
		Cost of equity	1	
		IRR	3	
		Market value of equity	1	
		Market value of debt	1	
		WACC	1	
	(b)	Cost of equity	1	
		WACC	1	
				10
39.2		New market ungeared beta	2	
		Better Deal's geared beta	2	
		Cost of equity	1	
		Cost of debt	1	
		WACC	1	
		Reasoning for approach – 1 mark per point	Max 4	
				11
39.3		1 – 2 marks per relevant point		Max 8
39.4		Key theories regarding dividend policy	3	
		Additional comments	Max 3	
		Relating theory to the scenario	Max 3	
				Max 6
				35

ICAEW

39.1 (a)

Dividend per share 20Y0 (29.5m/165m) =   17.9 pence

Dividend growth rate = $\sqrt[4]{(29.5/25.2)} - 1 =$ 4% p.a.

Cost of equity = $\dfrac{d1}{MV} + g$ $\dfrac{(£0.179 \times 1.04)}{£2.65} + 4\% =$ 11%

Cost of debt

Year	Cash Flow	5% factor	PV	10% factor	PV
0	(98.00)	1.000	(98.00)	1.000	(98.00)
1-4	8.00	3.546	28.37	3.170	25.36
4	100.00	0.823	82.30	0.683	68.30
			NPV 12.67		NPV (4.34)

IRR = 5% + (12.67/(12.67+4.34)) × (10% − 5%) = 8.72%
Post-tax = 8.72 × (1 − 0.21) = 6.89%

WACC

	£m
Total market value of equity = (£82.5m/£0.50) × £2.65 =	437.250
Total market value of debt = £340m × 98/100 =	333.200
Total market value	770.450

WACC = (11% × 437.250/770.450) + (6.89% × 333.200/770.450) =   9.22%

(b)

Cost of equity = (1.1 × (11.4% − 5.2%)) + 5.2% =	12.02%
Cost of debt (as above)	6.89%
WACC = (12.02% × 437.250/770.450) + (6.89% × 333.200/770.450) =	9.8%

39.2

New market geared beta =   1.5

New market ungeared beta = $\dfrac{1.5 \times 64}{(64 + (31 \times 79\%))} = \dfrac{1.5 \times 64}{88.49} =$ 1.08

Better Deal's geared beta = $\dfrac{1.08 \times (£437.25m + (£333.2m \times 79\%))}{£437.25m} =$ 1.73

So, cost of equity = (1.73 × (11.4% − 5.2%)) + 5.2% =   15.9%

Cost of debt = 9% × 79% =   7.11%

WACC = (15.9% × £437.25m/£770.45m) + (7.11% × £333.2m/£770.45m) =   12.1%

It would be unwise to use the existing WACC (9.22%) as Better Deal's plan involves diversification and therefore a change in the level of systematic risk. Thus a new WACC must be calculated. Systematic risk is accounted for by taking into account the beta of the petroleum market and this is then adjusted to eliminate the financial risk (level of gearing) in that market. The resultant ungeared beta is then 're-geared' by taking into account the level of gearing of the new funds being raised. Using this, the WACC can be calculated.

39.3

CAPM theory is based on the fact that there is one factor that affects the expected return on a security (or portfolio) and that is systematic risk. This measure of risk is given by the equity beta of a security (or portfolio).

Multiple factor models are based on the idea that other factors will also determine the return as there are other aspects of risk attached to securities, not just the market portfolio. Arbitrage pricing theory states that there are many factors, but it does not state what these factors are.

Some models have been developed which actually state factors, such as the French and Fama model, which stated that the size of the company (size) and the difference between book and market values of the shares (value) would also influence the level of returns.

Since their original model, the momentum has been added as a fourth factor which shows the difference in returns between shares that are increasing in value and those that are decreasing in value.

Multiple factor models have been designed to get around the problem caused by the simplicity of the CAPM, but they are complex to understand and the factors are difficult to identify and quantify.

39.4 Key theories regarding dividend policy:

(1) Traditional view
(2) Modigliani and Miller theory
(3) Residual theory

The key points of these should be expanded to attract a good mark.

Additional areas for comment:

(1) Dividend signalling
(2) Clientele effect
(3) Pecking order

Candidates will also have been given credit for covering these topics.

Credit would also be given for (1) relating, where possible, dividend theory to the Better Deal scenario and (2) producing a cohesive answer.

Examiner's comments:

Most candidates scored well on this question and it had the highest average mark in the paper.

It was based on a supermarket operation and covered the topics of cost of capital and dividend policy. Part 39.1 was worth 10 marks and required candidates to calculate the company's WACC based on (a) the dividend growth model and then (b) the CAPM model.

Part 39.2 was worth 11 marks and tested the candidates' understanding of geared and ungeared betas and required them to calculate the relevant cost of capital for the company to use if it diversified its operations into a new product range. Part 39.4 made up 6 marks and candidates had to explain the relationship between a company's dividend policy and the value of its shares.

Part 39.1(a) was pretty straightforward and candidates generally did well. However, a number of them were unable to calculate the rate of dividend growth correctly and a disappointing number of candidates calculated the cost of redeemable debentures as if they were irredeemable.

As expected, most candidates scored full marks for the calculation in part 39.1(b).

Part 39.2 was more difficult, but many candidates scored well here. However, key errors made were (1) book values rather than market values were used when re-gearing beta and (2) too few candidates calculated the new WACC figure as required.

Part 39.4 was done well and candidates who produced a well-rounded answer will have scored high marks.

40 Havant Hall Ltd (June 2011)

Marks

40.1	Retention rate	1
	Return on capital	1
	Current dividend	1
	Cost of equity	1
	Justification of use of dividend valuation model	1
	Justification of use of Gordon growth model	1
	Justification for using current cost of equity	1
	Justification for using recent share valuation	1
		Max 7
40.2	1 – 2 marks per relevant point made	Max 7
40.3	Rights issue:	
	No change in control	1
	Flexible nature of dividend payments	1
	Reaction of existing shareholders	1
	Unlisted status unattractive	1
	No listing and reporting requirements	1
	AIM listing:	
	Increased marketability	1
	Cost involved	1
	Dilution of control	1
		8
40.4 (a)	One mark per advantage	6
(b)	One mark per assumption	3
		Max 7
40.5	One mark per valuation method	Max 6
		35

40.1 Cost of equity = $D_0(1+g) / P_0 + g$

Where g = rb

Retention rate (b) = 489/922 × 100 = 53%

Return on capital (r) = 922/(4,250 – 489) = 24.5%

g = 0.53 × 0.245 = 13%

D_0 = 433/2,000 = 21.65p

P_0 = 400p

Cost of equity = 21.65(1.13)/400 + 0.13 = 0.191 = 19.1%

The dividend valuation model has been used to calculate the cost of capital because there is no debt within current liabilities so the firm is all-equity financed.

The dividend growth rate uses the Gordon growth model, which can be justified by the figures being consistent with previous years and likely to continue in future.

The proposed expansion is into related activities with no consequent change in business risk and so the current cost of equity capital is appropriate.

£4 per share is a recent valuation and is therefore approximate to current market value.

40.2 The dividend valuation model makes several assumptions which are unlikely to hold in reality.

One assumption is that shares have value because of the dividends paid. Some companies choose a low (or no dividend) payout policy and attract investors who prefer capital gains. Companies that do not pay dividends do not have zero value to their shares.

The dividend growth rate is unlikely to be constant and short-term variations in the growth rate would change the value of the shares.

The retention rate and return on capital are based on historic data, which may differ from the likely future values due to various factors such as economic conditions and investor confidence.

Also the data used within the model contributes to its limitations. For example, Havant Hall is a limited company and the share price used here is an estimation by the company auditors at a point in the last year. The share price may have changed since then, but as there is no active market for the shares this value is difficult to quantify.

In addition the dividend growth rate is more likely to be linked to future earnings growth rather than past dividend growth. The growth in earnings will determine the growth of dividends. For example if earnings grow at a slower rate than dividends, the company will eventually run out of funds to pay the dividends. Similarly, if dividend growth is less than earnings growth then the company will start to accumulate surplus funds.

40.3 1. A rights issue:

No change in control if fully taken up by existing shareholders (but not if not taken up)

Flexible nature of dividend payments as opposed to a fixed interest commitment

How will existing shareholders **react** and do they have **access to the required funds**?

Any new shareholders might find the firm's **unlisted status unattractive**

No listing and reporting requirements

2. AIM listing:

Increased **marketability** of shares (exit route for owners)

Listing and reporting requirements

Cost involved

Dilution of control

40.4 (a) HH would obtain finance at a lower rate of interest than on an ordinary bank loan, provided that the firm's prospects were considered to be good post-expansion.

This might encourage future outside investors with the prospect of a future share in profits.

This would also introduce an element of short-term gearing, with potential beneficial cost of capital implications.

If the debt was subsequently converted it would also avoid subsequent redemption problems.

If the debt was subsequently converted it would enable HH to issue equity relatively cheaply.

There may be an argument that a convertible loan would come with fewer covenants than a bank loan.

(b) The revised debt/equity ratio is not to be changed in future.

The firm's operating and business risk is not to be changed in future.

The new finance is not project specific.

40.5 Historic cost (book) valuation (the balance sheet value of equity)

Net realisable value of assets less net realisable value of liabilities (market value)

Replacement cost (the cost of setting up such a business from scratch)

Income-based approaches:

- The present value of future cash flows
- Use of the P/E ratio of similar quoted firms (P/E ratio × earnings)
- Dividend valuation method

Examiner's comments:

This question that combined the cost of capital, sources of finance and firm valuation elements of the Financial Management syllabus was the question that candidates found by far the most challenging.

The first part of the question required candidates to calculate a firm's cost of equity using the dividend valuation method (incorporating the Gordon growth model). Whilst elements of the calculation were invariably done accurately, weaker candidates often struggled to calculate accurately a return on capital figure to underpin the calculation of the annual dividend growth rate and there was great variability in the quality of responses to the second section of this part of the question, which called for a discussion of assumptions underlying the methodology employed in calculating the cost of equity.

The third part of the question required candidates to identify and discuss the issues surrounding two potential non-debt sources of finance (rights issues and AIM) with regard to a firm's proposed expansion. A key aspect of examination technique often came to the fore here – not answering the question set. Weaker candidates insisted on comparing equity to debt rather than one form of equity raising with another. Well prepared candidates, however, coped easily with the question.

Weaknesses in many candidates' technical knowledge were also exposed in the fourth part of the question which required candidates to discuss the advantages of convertible loans over a bank loan. This part of the question was not, overall, well answered, which is surprising as it was very much a 'knowledge' question with only limited analytical demands being placed on candidates.

The final part of the question required candidates to identify valuation methods that the firm's accountants may have employed in providing a recent share valuation. Generally candidates scored well on this part of the question.

41 Puerto plc (December 2013)

			Marks
41.1	Operating profit	1	
	Interest	1	
	Taxation	1	
			3
41.2	Market capitalisation	0.5	
	Market value of debt	0.5	
	Gearing 30 November	0.5	
	No. of shares issued to SMC	0.5	
	Total no. of shares in issue	0.5	
	Market capitalisation of new share price	1	
	Market value of debt	1	
	Gearing 1 December	0.5	
			5
41.3	Relevant discussion	9	
			Max 5
41.4	Cost of equity	1	
	Cost of debt	1	
	WACC at 30 November	1	
	Degear the equity beta	2	
	Regear the asset beta	2	
	Cost of equity	1	
	Cost of debt	1	
	WACC after 1 December	1	
			10
41.5	Relevant discussion	7	
			Max 6
41.6	Relevant discussion	10	
			Max 6
			35

41.1 Income Statement for the year to 30 November 20X4

	£'000
Operating profit (2,280 + 3,000)	5,280
Interest (24,000 × 6% + 6,000 × 7%)	(1,860)
Profit before tax	3,420
Taxation @ 21%	(718)
Profit after tax	2,702

41.2

Gearing (debt/equity) by market values at 30 November 20X3:
Market capitalisation: 492 million x 10p = £49.2 million
Market value of debt: £68 million + £6 million = £74 million
Gearing 74/49.2 = 150%

Gearing (debt/equity) by market values after the restructuring on 1 December 20X3:
Number of shares in issue:
Issued to SMC (£68/4) × 30 = 510 million.
Total number of shares in issue = 492 + 510 = 1,002 million.
Market capitalisation at the new share price (10p × 1.35 = 13.5p): 1,002 × 13.5p = £135.27 million.
Market value of debt: Secured bank loans £6 million + Risky Bank £24 million = £30 million.
Gearing 30/135.27 = 22.18%

41.3

Profitability: Puerto has been loss making and the purchase of the additional vehicle leasing business will make the business profitable.

Financial risk: The interest cover of Puerto before the restructuring is less than one. This increases to 5,280/1,860 = 2.8 after the restructuring which appears to be reasonable and should give the markets and stakeholders some comfort.

The 150% gearing of Puerto at 30 November is far in excess of the industry average of 25% which means that the company is in serious risk of bankruptcy. This improves to 22% after the restructuring which is below the industry average and should give the markets and stakeholders confidence. However this is only the case if the share price does increase to 13.5p. Puerto may be in danger of breaching SMC's covenant if the share price does not reach 13.5p. If the share price remains at 10p the gearing will be:

Market capitalisation: 1,002 x 10p = £100.2 million
Debt £30 million
Gearing 30/100.2 = 30%

A gearing ratio of 30% breaches the Risky Bank plc covenant and, depending on the action taken by Risky Bank plc, could cause problems for Puerto. Any other sensible comment will be awarded marks.

41.4 **The WACC of Puerto at 30 November 20X3:**

Ke = 2.8 + 2.13 × 5 = 13.45%
Kd = 7% (non-convertible loans) and
3% (convertible loans)

Note. Since Puerto is not paying tax at this date no adjustment for tax is necessary.
WACC using the weightings previously calculated:
(13.45% × 49.2 + 7% × 6 + 3% × 68)/(49.2 + 74) = 7.37%

The WACC of Puerto at 1 December 20X3 immediately after the restructuring:

Ke. Since the financial risk of Puerto has changed the equity beta will have to be adjusted to the new gearing level:

Degear the equity beta (Note. no tax adjustment is necessary since Puerto is not paying tax prior to the restructuring): $ßa = 2.13/(1 + (74/49.2)) = 0.8506$

Regear the asset beta to calculate Puerto's new equity beta (Note. Puerto is now paying tax and tax adjustments are therefore necessary): $ße = 0.8506 (1+(30(1-0.21)/135.27)) = 0.9996$

$Ke = 2.8 + 0.9996 × 5 = 7.798\%$

Kd (1-tax) (Note. Puerto is now paying tax): 7%(1-0.21) = 5.53% and 6%(1-0.21) = 4.74%

WACC = (7.798% × 135.27 + 5.53% × 6 + 4.74% × 24)/(135.27 + 24 + 6) = 7.27%

41.5 Prior to the restructuring Puerto had a very high level of gearing at 150% compared to the industry average of 25%. Consequently the cost of equity reflected this extreme level of financial risk.

The traditional view of gearing is that at lower levels of gearing a company's WACC will decrease - this will cause the value of the company to rise. However, as gearing becomes a greater proportion of total long term funds, the cost of debt will start to increase and WACC will rise too, and the value of the company will fall.

The view of Modigliani and Miller (1963) is that a company's WACC and therefore value is not affected by the level of gearing other than through the effects of tax relief and that this leads to a fall in WACC and a corresponding increase in the value of the company. However, at Puerto's very high level of gearing bankruptcy costs, tax exhaustion and agency costs can all cause the cost of debt to increase and, as with the traditional theory, the WACC will start to rise and the value of the company fall.

Now Puerto has a more normal level of gearing at 22% the WACC should now remain around 7.27%. Any other sensible comment will be awarded marks.

41.6 Prior to the restructuring Puerto is very highly geared at 150% and is also not profitable. The various stakeholders' reaction to the restructuring is likely to be:

Shareholders: Shareholders have limited liability and may be tempted to take risks. However in this case the shareholders have not received dividends since 2008 and the share price has only recently risen. This may be because the industry has stabilised but also may be in anticipation of a restructuring. Shareholders are likely to welcome the restructuring since there is a very real possibility of increasing their wealth through dividend income and capital gains. However the shareholders may be concerned about the change in control due to the new shares issued to SMC.

SMC: SMC was in a very vulnerable position before the restructuring since interest cover was below one and there was a very real possibility of the company being unable to meet interest payments. Since the loan was unsecured SMC would be uncertain as to how much it might receive if Puerto was wound up. Converting their loan to equity means that with the company now profitable there is a very real chance of them realising their investment.

Risky Bank plc: Risky Bank plc are secured and since the interest cover is now more substantial at 2.8 and gearing is below the industry average, assuming a share price of 13.5p, the company is on a sound financial footing. The same comments apply to the original secured bank loans.

Employees: Employees should welcome the restructuring since the company now has a much more certain future and they will feel more confident about keeping their jobs.

Suppliers: Suppliers will also welcome the restructuring since Puerto will now be more likely to continue and they will not lose the business that it creates for them.

Customers: Customers of Puerto will be pleased that the company is now on a sound financial footing and that it will be able to provide them with services in the future.

Government: Puerto will now be paying tax.

Any other sensible point will be given marks.

Examiner's comments

The scenario of this question was that a company had been in difficulty and was considering a reconstruction, whereby debt would be converted to equity. The company would then purchase an additional business opportunity, which would be financed by new borrowings.

Part 41.1 for three marks required candidates to restate the income statement in twelve months' time assuming that the reconstruction went ahead. Part 41.2 for five marks required candidates to calculate the gearing ratio, by market values, both before and immediately after the reconstruction. Part 41.3 for five marks required candidates to comment upon the financial health of the company both before and after the reconstruction. Also candidates had to consider a covenant imposed by the providers of the finance for the new business. Part 41.4 for ten marks required candidates to calculate, using the CAPM, the WACC of the company both before and after the reconstruction. This involved adjusting the equity beta for gearing and consideration of taxation. Part 41.5 for six marks required candidates to consider, with reference to relevant theories, how the reconstruction would affect the WACC in the long term. Part 41.6 for six marks required candidates to consider the likely reaction to the reconstruction of various stakeholders in the company.

Part 41.1 was well answered by the majority of candidates. However it was disappointing to see that some candidates did not really demonstrate a full understanding of the scenario and also included the interest in the income statement for the loan which had been converted to equity.

The majority of candidates answered part 41.2 well, however some candidates failed to understand the scenario and showed gearing increasing rather than decreasing, whereas a correct interpretation of the facts would show a substantial decrease.

Part 41.3 was reasonably well answered, however those who had misinterpreted the question scored poorly.

In part 41.4, many candidates did not take account of the fact that the company was not paying tax until after the reconstruction. When taking into account the effect of the change in gearing on the equity beta, weaker candidates showed that they need to practise gearing adjustments.

In part 41.5, a lot of candidates gave a generic answer and did not relate to the scenario of the question.

Part 41.6 was well answered and many students identified a sufficient number of stakeholders.

42 Efficient markets hypothesis

	Marks
42.1 Explanation of the hypothesis	1
Each form of hypothesis: 1 mark × 3	3
	4
42.2 Max 3 marks per statement	max 8
	12

42.1 Three forms of EMH

The efficient market hypothesis considers how efficient the market is at impounding in prices information available to investors. Three possible levels of efficiency have been postulated.

Weak form

A market is weak form efficient if all the information which has been gleaned from a security's past price movement has been reflected in the current market value of that security.

Semi-strong form

A market is semi-strong form efficient if all publicly-known information about a company, including its plans, together with information about the security's past price movements, is reflected in the current market value of that security.

Strong form

A market is said to be strong form efficient if the current market value of a security reflects all relevant information, including information which is supposedly secret to the company.

42.2 Stock market efficiency

One of the principal assumptions underlying financial management is that the market value of a security is based upon investors' expectations of future earnings derived from that security, and that those earnings are discounted at the investors' required rate of return. Expectations of future earnings are based upon information available in the market.

First statement

The first view given in the question is stating that having released information regarding a company's earnings, this has resulted in a revision of investors' expectations. In this situation this has led to an increase in the market value of the security because the information was favourable – actual earnings being better than market expectations.

Because this high return was experienced over two or three days following the announcement, it suggests that the market transmission mechanism is not perfect. Had it been perfect there would have been no time delay: all investors would have received the information at the same time and acted upon it.

This scenario is characteristic of a semi-strong form efficient market, in that investors are revising their expectations regarding future earnings as soon as the information is publicly known, although as stated there is a time delay. Having acted upon this information, a new equilibrium is achieved over a period of two to three days following the announcement.

Second statement

Implicit in the second view is that a professionally-managed portfolio may give a return which is no better than that which can be achieved by a naive investor, because both have access to the same information.

This may accord with the view that the market is strong form efficient, all investors having access to all relevant information. Therefore no party is in a more favourable position relative to the other party, and neither party can make a gain.

It is also consistent with semi-strong efficiency, ie fund managers do not have access to better (inside) information.

Third statement

This suggests that it is possible to earn abnormal returns by adopting a strategy ('buy just before the fiscal year end and sell a week or so later'), which is based on information contained in the past time series. This implies inefficiency. The fact that there is an identifiable cause does not eliminate the inefficiency. If the market were weakly efficient, arbitrageurs would eliminate the excess return at the start of the fiscal year by creating buying pressures for the under-priced shares being sold at the end of the previous fiscal year.

43 Abydos plc

Marking guide

	Marks
43.1 Capital allowances/tax saving	2
Base case NPV	3 – 4
Financing side effects	2 – 4
Give credit for technique	max 10
43.2 Reward sensible discussion. Bonus mark for mention of real options	max 6
	16

43.1 Expected APV

To calculate the base case NPV, the investment cash flows are discounted at the **ungeared cost of equity,** assuming the corporate debt is risk free (and has a beta of zero).

$$\beta_a = \beta_e \frac{E}{E + D(1-t)}$$

$$= 1.4 \times \frac{0.6}{0.6 + 0.4(1 - 0.21)} = 0.917$$

The ungeared cost of equity can now be estimated using the CAPM:

$$K_{eu} = 5 + 0.917 (12 - 5)$$
$$= 11.42\% \text{ (say, approximately 11\%)}$$

Capital allowances

These are on the £10 million part of the investment that is non-current assets (not working capital or issue costs).

Year	Value at start of year	Capital allowance 18%	Tax saving 21%
	£'000	£'000	£'000
1	10,000	1,800	378
2	8,200	1,476	310
3	6,724	1,210	254
4	5,514	993	209

Financial Management: Answer Bank

Year	0	1	2	3	4
	£'000	£'000	£'000	£'000	£'000
Pre-tax operating cash flows		3,000	3,400	3,800	4,300
Tax @ 21%		(630)	(714)	(798)	(903)
Tax savings from capital allowances		378	310	254	209
Investment cost	(11,500)				
Issue costs					
After tax realisable value					4,000
Net cash flows	(11,500)	2,748	2,996	3,256	7,606
Discount factor 11%	1.000	0.901	0.812	0.731	0.659
Present values	(11,500)	2,476	2,433	2,380	5,012

The expected base case net present value is **£801,000**.

Financing side effects

Issue costs

£1m, because they are treated as a side-effect they are not included in this NPV calculation.

Present value of tax shield

Debt issued by project = £5m

Annual tax savings on debt interest = £5m × 8% × 21% = £84,000

PV of tax savings for 4 years, discounted at the gross cost of debt 8%, is:

£84,000 × 3.312 = £278,208

$$\left(\frac{1}{0.08} \left(1 - \frac{1}{1.08^4} \right) = 3.312 \right)$$

	£'000
Adjusted present value	
Base case NPV	801
Tax relief on debt interest	278
Issue costs	(1,000)
	79

The adjusted present value is **£79,000**

43.2 Validity of the views of the two directors

Sales director

The sales director believes that the **net present value** method should be used, on the basis that the NPV of a project will be reflected in an **equivalent increase in the company's share price**. However, even if the market is efficient, this is only likely to be true if:

- The financing used **does not create a significant change** in gearing (finance ratio ≠ current gearing so gearing may change)

- The project is **small relative to the size of the company**

- The project **risk is the same** as the company's average operating risk (but different line of business)

Finance director

The finance director prefers the **adjusted present value method**, in which the cash flows are discounted at the ungeared cost of equity for the project, and the resulting NPV is then adjusted for financing side effects such as issue costs and the tax shield on debt interest. The main problem with the APV method is the **estimation** of the various **financing side effects** and the **discount rates** used to appraise them. The ungearing process assumes risk free debt (5%) which it isn't as it costs 8%.

Problems with both viewpoints

Both methods rely on the restrictive assumptions about capital markets which are made in the capital asset pricing model and in the theories of capital structure. The **figures used** in CAPM (risk-free rate, market rate and betas) can be difficult to determine. **Business risks** are assumed to be **constant**.

Neither method attempts to value the possible **real options** for abandonment or further investment which may be associated with the project.

44 Wiggins plc (December 2014)

			Marks
44.1	Cost of equity	1	
	IRR	2	
	Post-tax cost of debt	1	
	WACC	2	
			6
44.2	Issue price	2	
	Total nominal value	1	
	Reasons for different yield – 1 mark per relevant point	2	
			5
44.3	Number of new shares	1	
	Rights price	0.5	
	Discount on current share price	0.5	
	TERP	2	
	1 mark per discussion point	2	
			Max 5
44.4	General disadvantages	3	
	Current position:		
	Gearing	0.5	
	Interest cover	0.5	
	If debt is issued:		
	Gearing	0.5	
	Interest	1	
	Interest cover	0.5	
	With rights issue:		
	Gearing	0.5	
	No change in Interest cover	0.5	
	Up to 2 marks per relevant point	Max 4	
	Recommendation	1	
			Max 10
44.5	Up to 2 marks per well explained point		Max 5
44.6	Up to 2 marks per well explained point:		
	CAPM only takes into account market risk, other factors are present		
	Arbitrage pricing model		
	Famma and French		
			Max 4
			35

ICAEW

44.1

The cost of equity = 2% + 1.2 × 5% = 8%
The cost of debt will be the internal rate of return (IRR) of the 4% debenture less tax relief.

The IRR is calculated as follows:
The ex-interest price of the debentures = £108 – £4 = £104

Timing years	Cash Flow £	Factors at 1%	PV £	Factors at 5%	PV £
0	(104)	1	(104)	1	(104)
1-4	4	3.902	15.61	3.546	14.18
4	100	0.961	96.10	0.823	82.30
			7.71		(7.52)

IRR = 1 + (7.71/(7.71+7.52)) × 4 = 3.03%
Kd = 3.03(1 – 0.21) = 2.39%

Market values:

Equity 360 million × £5.6 = £2,016 million
Debt £300 million × 104/100 = £312 million
WACC = (8% × 2016 + 2.39% × 312)/(2016+312) = 7.25%

44.2

The issue price is:

Timing years	Cash Flow £	Factors at 5%	PV £
1-10	3	7.722	23.17
10	100	0.614	61.40
		Issue price	84.57

The total nominal value will be: £200/0.8457 = £236.5 million.

Possible reasons for the yield of 5% on the new debentures being greater than the 3.03% yield on the current debentures are: expectations of higher interest rates in the future since the new debentures mature in 20Y4 rather than 20X8 for the current debentures; higher risk; market appetite for the issue (price to succeed); the increase in Wiggins's financial risk.

44.3

(a) A 1 for 8 rights issue will require 360/8 = **45** million new shares to be issued.

The price per share = £200 million / 45 million = **£4.44**

A discount on the current market price of: 5.60-4.44/5.6 = **21% (or £1.16)**

The theoretical ex-rights price is:

	Number of shares	Value per share £	Number x Value £
Existing shares	8	5.60	44.80
New shares	1	4.44	4.44
Total shares	9	Total value	49.24

Theoretical ex-rights price = £49.24/9 = **£5.47**.

(b) The actual share price will depend on the market's reaction to the rights issue eg fully taken up and whether the proceeds are invested in positive net present value projects. If we were told the net present value of the projects this could be incorporated in the theoretical ex-rights price of £5.47 giving a more realistic estimate of the actual share price post rights issue.

44.4

General advantages and disadvantages are:

Equity: The advantage of a rights issue is that there will be no increase in gearing or

reduction in interest cover. However the disadvantages are cost, timing and dilution of control if the rights are not taken up. The rights issue may also fail to be successful; however this can be mitigated by the issue being underwritten. **(debt = converse so no more marks)**

In the circumstances of Wiggins plc the two alternatives would have the following effects on gearing and interest cover:

Current position:

Gearing = £312 / £2016 = **15.5%**
Interest cover = £239 / £12 = **20** times

If debt is issued:

Gearing = £312 + £200 / £2016 = **25%**
Interest cover =
Interest = £12 + (£236.5 × 0.03) = **£19.1** Interest cover based on current earnings = £239/£19.1 = **12.5** times.

With a rights issue:

Gearing = £312 / (£2016 + £200*) = 14%

No change in interest cover (based on current earnings)

*Rounding

In both cases the figures would be affected by the additional earnings from the new investments and any change in the share price.

The rights issue slightly reduces the gearing from 15.5% to 14%, this may not be desirable since Wiggins's gearing is well below the average for the sector of 30%. Interest cover at 20 times is well above the industry average of 11, this is a very safe margin. This analysis indicates that Wiggins has spare debt capacity.

The debenture issue increase Wiggins's gearing to 25% which is still below the industry average of 30%. The interest cover of 12.5 times is now much closer to the industry average of 11 times. The effect on Wiggins's share price and also the cost of debt is hard to predict, however having a gearing ratio and interest cover close to the industry averages may be welcomed by the markets and shareholders.

Having regard to the gearing and interest cover comments above the debenture issue is likely to be preferred since it is quicker and less costly than a rights issue.

44.5

Wiggins's long term funding currently has a market value of £2328 million and the company plans to raise £200 million which represents an increase of 9% on that current market value.

This is a small increase and it is reasonable to use the existing WACC as the hurdle rate. However since the new finance will be used to invest in some projects in a different industry sector than current operations, the discount rate will have to be adjusted to reflect the systematic risk of those projects.

It would not be appropriate to use the individual cost of each source. Regarding equity, the company is financed from a pool of funds and WACC should be the hurdle rate. Regarding debt, the cost of debt represents the risk to the lenders and not that of the projects

44.6

The CAPM specifies that the only risk factor that should be taken into account is the market risk premium. Subsequent empirical research has shown that there may be other factors in addition to market risk premium that explain differences in asset returns, such as interest rates and industrial production.

Two models which analyse returns on multiple factors are:

The arbitrage pricing model (APM). APM uses four key factors to analyse returns, these factors are: unanticipated inflation; changes in the expected level of industrial production; changes in the risk premium of bonds; unanticipated changes in the term structure of interest rates. The model works in a similar way to the CAPM in that it assumes that investors are fully diversified. A beta for each factor is calculated and applied to the risk premium.

Famma and French identified two factors in addition to the market portfolio that explain company returns namely size and the ratio of book value to market value. Again a beta factor Is calculated and applied to the risk premium. The model has been augmented with the addition of a fourth factor namely the momentum factor.

Examiner's comments

This was a six-part question that tested the candidates' understanding of the financing options element of the syllabus.

The scenario of the question was that a company was planning its capital expenditure programme and was discussing how best to raise the additional funds required, either by debt or equity.

Part 44.1 of the question required candidates to calculate the current WACC of the company. Part 44.2 of the question required candidates to make some calculations in relation to a debenture issue and to discuss certain practical aspects of the debenture issue. Part 44.3 of the question required candidates to make some calculations regarding rights issues and to discuss certain practical aspects of rights issues. Part 44.4 of the question required candidates to discuss the advantages and disadvantages of the two alternative sources of funds (debt or equity) and to discuss which would be most appropriate for the company. Part 44.5 of the question required candidates to discuss the hurdle rate that should be used to appraise the projects that the new capital is to be invested in. Part 44.6 of the question required candidates to discuss alternatives to the CAPM:

In part 44.1 there were some disappointing attempts at this part of the question which has been examined many times before, common errors were: deducting the risk free rate from the market risk premium; adjusting the beta factor for gearing when not required to do so; incorrect computation of the market value of debt; incorrect computation of the yield to maturity of the existing debenture; no deduction of tax from the cost of debt.

In part 44.2 answers were disappointing since this has been asked before. Candidates were required to calculate the issue price for the new debentures, they were given the coupon, the redemption value, which was at par, the redemption date and the yield to maturity. They then had to calculate the nominal value of the total debt to be issued. Common errors were: calculating the YTM when it was given in the question; no grossing up to arrive at the total nominal value; deducting tax from the yield to maturity in the question; no discussion of why the YTM on the new issue was different to that of the existing debentures. However the better candidates gained full marks on this section.

Part 44.3 was well answered by most students. However weaker students were calculating the discount that the rights issue represents as the difference between the current share price and the theoretical ex-rights price.

In part 44.4 it was disappointing to see many candidates not using the information given in the question regarding the industry average interest cover and gearing. Many candidates made the following errors: providing a discussion, and diagrams, of M & M's theory on capital structure; just a general discussion of debt and equity with no reference to the scenario of the question; no reference to the industry averages; incorrect gearing calculation; incorrect interest cover calculations, often using after interest and sometimes after tax profits; no conclusion.

Part 44.5 was not well answered with many students not considering the scale of the new finance raised in proportion to the current market values of equity and debt. Weaker students suggested that the individual cost of each source of funds should be used as the hurdle rate.

Part 44.6 was not well answered with many students only discussing the weaknesses of the CAPM.

45 Perryfield Paper plc (March 2015)

		Marks
45.1 Cost of equity	2.5	
Cost of preference shares	1.5	
Cost of irredeemable debentures	2.5	
WACC	1.5	
		8
45.2 1 mark per relevant point		4
45.3 1 mark per relevant point		7
45.4 Interest	1	
Redemption	1	
PV of future cash flows	1	
Total funds raised	1	
		4
45.5 1 mark per relevant point		5
45.6 WACC and gearing	2	
Effect of buy-back on PP's WACC	5	
		7
		35

45.1

Cost of equity (ke)	$\dfrac{£4,976,400 \times 1.02}{£63,800,000} + 2\%$	9.96%
Cost of preference shares (kp)	$\dfrac{£313,400}{£5,400,000}$	5.80%
Cost of irredeemable debentures (kd)	$\dfrac{(£405,000 \times 79\%)}{£14,175,000}$	2.26%

WACC	Market Value (£'000)	Cost	WACC
ke	63,800	9.96% × 63,800/83,375	7.62%
kp	5,400	5.80% × 5,400/83,375	0.38%
kd	14,175	2.26% × 14,175/83,375	0.38%
Total	83,375		8.38%

So, based on the figures given, PP's WACC figure is approximately 8.4%

45.2 PP's WACC (8.4%) is higher than the 6.5% figure currently used and this should be used as a hurdle rate in investment appraisal. Otherwise PP could be taking on projects that have an IRR of more than 6.5%, but less than 8.4%. To do so would mean that PP's shareholders' wealth would decline as these projects would produce negative NPV's.

45.3 The Capital Asset Pricing Model (CAPM) is an alternative method of calculating the cost of equity. As such it can be used within the WACC calculation.

The CAPM assumes that investors are diversified, ie they have diversified specific risk away. Thus it takes account of systematic risk only and measures the systematic risk of investments. This risk is measured as an index (beta). The beta index of a security is applied to the risk premium of the market portfolio (equity shares). The risk premium is the rate of return from the market portfolio less rate of return from risk-free securities. Thus, with the CAPM, a higher beta (systematic risk) index will mean a higher cost of equity.

Overall part 45.3 was poorly answered. Too many candidates just explained how the CAPM equation works or just wrote out what was on the formulae sheet without working through the underpinning logic. Also a disappointing number of candidates answered the wrong question, ie they explained how to de-gear/re-gear using a similar quoted company, beta and new project.

45.4 Selling price of redeemable debentures

Year		Cash flow (£)	5% factor	PV (£)
1-4	Interest	4.00	3.546	14.18
4	Redemption	100.00	0.823	82.30
	PV of future cash flows at a yield of 5% pa			96.48
Total funds raised = £9m × 96.48%				£8.68m

45.5 Share buy-back and implications

A company buys back its equity from shareholders. It is often used when there is no other use for surplus cash funds available, eg (a) no investments available that have positive NPV's or (b) no wish to alter company's dividend policy (via a special dividend).

Control implications – control is maintained if the buy-back is in proportion to existing shareholdings. However a buy-back can be used to remove an awkward shareholder.

Tax implications – income tax would be due on dividends (eg special dividend) whereas CGT would be due on a buy-back.

45.6 WACC and gearing

A buy-back reduces equity and so PP's gearing ratio would increase.

The effect of the buy-back on PP's WACC:

Consider the theories – traditional view, M&M 1958 and 1963

Consider the modern view – optimum gearing level (maximisation of company value) is a balance between the benefits of the tax shield and bankruptcy costs. The impact on PP's WACC (and value) depends on where its optimum gearing level is.

Examiner's comments

This question had easily the lowest percentage mark on the paper, which was disappointing as some basic finance concepts were examined here.

It was a six-part question that tested the candidates' understanding of the financing options element of the syllabus.

It was based around a paper manufacturing company which needed to make a range of financing calculations and decisions. Part 45.1 of the question (for eight marks) required candidates to calculate the company's current WACC figure. In part 45.2 they were then asked to explain whether this figure should be used rather than the company's current WACC. Part 45.3 was worth seven marks and here candidates had to discuss the logic underpinning the CAPM and explain how it can be used to calculate the WACC. For part 45.4 candidates were required to calculate the market price of redeemable debentures, having been given the required yield figure. This was worth four marks. The last two parts of the question dealt with share buy-backs. In the scenario the company was considering a buy-back and in part 45.5, for five marks, candidates were asked to explain the how it works and its implications for shareholders. Finally, for seven marks, part 45.6 required candidates to discuss how the buy-back would affect the company's gearing and its WACC:

In part 45.1, most candidates scored well here, but in the weaker scripts candidates divided by cost not market value when calculating the cost of preference shares and debentures.

In part 45.2, candidates scored well if they explained the implications of using the wrong discount rate (WACC) for project NPV's (and shareholder wealth). A minority of candidates failed to do this adequately.

Overall part 45.3 was poorly answered. Too many candidates just explained how the CAPM equation works or just wrote out what was on the formulae sheet without working through the underpinning logic. Also a disappointing number of candidates answered the wrong question, ie they explained how to de-gear/re-gear using a similar quoted company, beta and new project.

For part 45.4, this, in effect required candidates to work backwards through a cost of debt calculation. A good number were able to do it, but, sadly, far too many were not.

Parts 45.5 and 45.6 were generally well done and most candidates were able to demonstrate an understanding of the workings and implications of a share buy-back.

46 Worsley plc (June 2010)

Marks

46.1	Forecast Income Statements:		
	Revenue	1	
	Operating costs (excluding depreciation)	1	
	Depreciation	1	
	Finance costs	1	
	Tax	2	
	Dividends	1	
	Forecast Balance Sheets:		
	Non-current assets	1	
	Inventories	1	
	Receivables	1	
	Cash	1	
	Ordinary share capital	0.5	
	Retained earnings	1	
	Debentures	1	
	Payables	1	
	Bank overdraft	1	
	Forecast Cash Flow Statements:		
	Profit before tax	0.5	
	Depreciation	0.5	
	Increase in inventories	1	
	Increase in receivables	1	
	Increase in payables	1	
	Purchase of non-current assets	0.5	
	Tax paid	0.5	
	Dividends paid	0.5	
			21
46.2 (a)	1 mark per method. Up to 2 marks per well explained point		max 6
(b)	1 mark per valid point		max 5
			32

46.1 Forecast Income Statements for the years ending 31 March

	31 March 20X1 £'000	31 March 20X2 £'000
Revenue	65,059	70,264
Operating costs (excluding depreciation)	51,480	53,539
Depreciation	875	875
Operating profit	12,704	15,850
Finance costs	1,200	1,200
Profit before tax	11,504	14,650
Tax (W1)	2,297	3,012
Profit after tax	9,207	11,638
Dividends	2,951	3,128
Retained profit	6,256	8,510

WORKINGS

1 **Tax**

Profit before tax	11,504	14,650
Add back depreciation	875	875
Less capital allowances	(1,440)	(1,181)
Taxable profits	10,939	14,344
Tax @ 21%	2,297	3,012

Forecast Balance Sheets as at 31 March

	31 March 20X1 £'000	31 March 20X2 £'000
ASSETS		
Non-current assets	35,975	35,100
Inventories	9,922	9,922
Receivables	9,759	10,540
Cash (balancing figure)	–	7,449
TOTAL ASSETS	55,656	63,011
EQUITY AND LIABILITIES		
Ordinary share capital	16,700	16,700
Retained earnings	18,738	27,248
Debentures	8,000	8,000
Payables	7,629	7,935
Bank overdraft (balancing figure)	1,638	–
Dividends	2,951	3,128
TOTAL EQUITY AND LIABILITIES	55,656	63,011

Forecast Cash Flow Statements for the years ending March

	31 March 20X1 £'000	31 March 20X2 £'000
Profit before tax	11,504	14,650
Depreciation	875	875
Increase in inventories	(902)	–
Increase in receivables	(723)	(781)
Increase in payables	293	306
Purchase of non-current assets	(8,000)	–
Tax paid	(2,297)	(3,012)
Dividends paid	(2,784)	(2,951)
Net cash flow	(2,034)	9,087
Cash balance brought forward	396	(1,605)
Cash balance carried forward	(1,638)	7,449

46.2 (a) (1) Management buy-out: a new company acquires either the trade and assets or the shares of the subsidiary to be sold, with the purchase usually funded by a mix of debt and equity provided by the managers (equity), venture capital providers (debt and equity) and other financiers (debt)

(2) Management buy-in: as above, but with purchase by a group of external managers

(3) Spin-off (demerger): shareholders are given shares in the new entity pro rata to their shareholdings in the parent company – there is no change in ownership; with separate legal identities established; used to avoid the problems of the conglomerate discount; sometimes used as a defence against takeover of the entire business

(4) Trade sale: to another company

(b) The ICAEW code of ethics for professional accountants in public practice has express provisions to provide guidance in this instance.

The first step is to have **procedures in place to recognise a conflict of interest** exists. This involves a combination of formal and informal processes to highlight a practice's clients, work and potential work for those clients, and any potential conflicts that may arise. A nominated partner/compliance officer (or committee of partners in larger practices) may act as a central point for gathering this information.

The second step is to **make all parties aware of the potential conflict**, outline a plan for dealing with the potential conflict and to **obtain written consent** from all parties that they are aware of the situation and processes for managing the conflict and are happy to proceed.

Potential safeguards include:

- The use of **different partners and team**s for the two clients, each having separate internal reporting lines.

- All necessary **steps are taken to prevent the leakage of confidential information** between the two teams.

- **A regular review of the situation by a senior partner or compliance officer** not directly or personally involved with either client. The more 'distanced' this senior partner's proximity to the client and the engagement teams the better.

- **Advise the clients to seek additional independent advice** if appropriate.

Ultimately, the firm needs to feel confident that an objective, reasonable interpretation of the steps taken would be that the situation has been fairly managed. If it does not appear feasible to manage the conflict internally, then one or both clients may need to be advised to approach an alternative firm.

The ICAEW have an ethics helpline the accountants could call for further clarification and advice if necessary.

Examiner's comments:

Performance on this second question was also good, although the average mark of 65.6% indicates that candidates did not find it as much to their liking as the opening question.

In the first section of the question the main errors made by weaker candidates were in the following areas:

(1) An inability to correctly calculate the tax figure in the Income Statement – very often weaker candidates simply calculated this from the profit before tax figure rather than taking account of both the depreciation and the capital allowances in the calculation.

(2) A failure to use the cash/overdraft figure as the balancing item in the Balance Sheet – it was also surprising how many candidates chose to put an overdraft in the current assets section of the Balance Sheet.

(3) Incorrect calculation of the payables figure due to misinterpretation of the available information.

(4) Failure to include, on many occasions, tax and dividends in the Cash Flow Statement.

It seemed that weaker candidates had failed to prepare themselves adequately for a question on this new aspect of the syllabus and had placed too much reliance on their knowledge from earlier papers rather than studying the Financial Management learning materials closely which would have rendered this question quite straightforward as it mirrored closely the style of question used in the learning materials.

Most candidates coped well with the demands of the second part of the question, although weaker candidates too often simply listed a number of divestment options without actually describing the nature of the options in each case.

47 Wentworth plc (December 2006)

		Marks
47.1 1 mark per reason	max	5
47.2 1 mark per point	max	6
47.3 1.5 marks per paragraph	max	6
47.4 1.5 marks per paragraph	max	5
		22

47.1 The potential reasons are as follows:

(1) The existence of limited investment opportunities due, for example, to the maturity of existing product lines or a downturn in the market for the company's goods or services.

(2) Traditionally strong cash flows generated by the business.

(3) To signal confidence in the future of the company, thereby raising the company's stock market rating (and facilitating future financing) as well as impacting positively on the share price.

(4) The knowledge that an actual or potential shareholder clientele prefers a high dividend payout policy.

(5) As a discipline on their managers (thereby addressing the classic agency problem), who will more often have to seek out funds from the market to fund investment and, therefore, be called upon to justify proposals to potential investors, rather than simply being able to rely on the use of internally generated funds.

(6) The 'bird in the hand' theory – the company may be persuaded that the market will value more highly a firm that pays dividends and issues shares to finance a new investment, than one that uses retentions.

47.2 This refers to the theory of dividend policy irrelevance, first developed by Modigliani and Miller (M&M) in 1961. They showed the irrelevance of dividends in a world without taxes, transaction costs or other market imperfections. M&M showed that if a company has a set investment and borrowing policy, the source of equity finance (retained earnings or new issues of equity) had no impact on shareholder wealth – the gain or loss to existing shareholders is the same whether a reduction in dividend (retained earnings) or a new issue of shares was used to finance an investment. Therefore, the dividend decision was irrelevant. In other words, if a change in dividend policy leaves the present value of future dividends unchanged, then that policy must be irrelevant. It does not matter when the dividends occur, provided that their present value is maximised.

47.3 In practice there are a number of reasons why those directors who feel that dividend policy is not an irrelevance may have a point. The practical risks involved in changing an established dividend policy comprise:

(1) It is argued that companies attract a clientele of investors who favour their current dividend policy for tax, cash flow and other reasons. Any change in policy could cause this clientele to dispose of their shares, in turn causing the share price to fall.

(2) Dividends resolve uncertainty, such that investors may prefer high payout policies, as they regard future capital gains as uncertain. If investors are rational they will perceive future dividends and gains to be equally risky, but evidence suggests they tend not to be fully rational, preferring a current dividend to a cut and the promise of future increased dividends.

(3) Similarly, in the absence of perfect information, dividends will be used as information signals by shareholders of future earnings and dividends. In the short term, a share price might fall as a result of a dividend cut to finance an investment, since investors might have incomplete information regarding the new investment and may consequently revise downwards their future dividend expectations. This may also affect the firm's cost of capital.

(4) Any change in dividend policy may adversely affect either investors (eg tax) or the firm (eg share price fall).

47.4 Shareholders who are faced with a dividend cut which is not their preference can 'manufacture' a dividend by selling shares or conversely, can purchase shares out of dividend income to cancel out, to a certain extent, the effect of the dividend.

The company could use the option of a scrip dividend, where shares are issued as dividend rather than cash. This would enable the company to maintain its current level of dividend whilst conserving liquidity, although the extent to which this might be achieved would depend on the precise terms of the scrip dividend on offer. A scrip dividend can either be in one of two 'normal' forms 1) for example, a 1 for 10 scrip dividend in place of the usual cash dividend – this would maximise liquidity preservation; or 2) a choice between cash or scrip dividend – which would conserve liquidity only to the extent that shareholders opt for the scrip dividend; or it can be undertaken in its 'enhanced' form, where a choice would be given between a cash dividend and an enhanced scrip dividend, to encourage uptake of the scrip option and therefore encourage liquidity preservation.

This strategy, therefore, would, to some extent, address both the risks inherent in an absolute change (cash reduction) in dividend policy, whilst maintaining the actual level of the dividend and preserving liquidity.

Lesser credit was also given for suggestions to pass or reduce the dividend (or to adopt a residual dividend policy that would lead to either of these options), accompanied by clear communication to the market of the reasons behind the decision.

Examiner's comments:

Many candidates did not score as strongly as they might have done due to a failure to respond with answers of sufficient breadth, ie many candidates were able to respond to a particular part of a question with, for example, two entirely valid, but basic, points where four or five were actually sought for full marks.

Many candidates scored only half marks on part 47.1. Signalling and clientele effects were invariably known, but many candidates failed to go beyond those two points. Even writing at some length on them did not enable candidates to overcome the lack of breadth in their response.

In part 47.2 the vast majority of candidates displayed a firm grasp of the theory and explained it well. A good number of candidates, however, then wasted time going beyond the theory asked for in the question to bring in issues that they then repeated in the next part of the question where they belonged. Whilst no marks were lost for this, it is not good practice as it simply imposes time pressure of the candidate's own making.

Part 47.3 was another example of candidates often knowing the signalling and clientele effects but not providing any of the further points that would have provided the necessary breadth of response for full marks.

Part 47.4 of the question was only correctly answered by a very small minority of candidates. The ideal answer would have focused on the scrip dividend and its characteristics and implications. Credit was given for those candidates who suggested options such as reductions in or passing of the dividend, but not for the many other common suggestions, not least because they were not actually dividend strategies. These other suggestions included leasing, rights issues, bonus issues, and issues of cumulative preference shares.

48 Biddaford Lundy plc (March 2012)

	Marks	
48.1 Total funds calculations	1	
Total geared funds	1	
Gearing calculation	2	
One mark per relevant point	max 5	
		9
48.2 Rights issue calculations	2	
Theoretical ex-rights price	1	
Value of a right per new share	1	
		4
48.3 Current EPS	1	
Current P/E ratio	1	
Interest savings	2	
New EPS	1	
New P/E ratio	1	
Reduction in EPS	1	
Relevant discussion	max 3	
		10
48.4 Amended EPS	1	
Ordinary shares required	1	
Number of shares in rights issue	1	
Rights issue price	1	
Relevant discussion on rights issue success	2	
	max 6	
48.5 1 – 2 marks per relevant point made	6	
		35

48.1 Gearing level

	Par value £m		Market value £m
Ordinary share capital (50p)	67.50	(135m × £2.65)	357.75
Retained earnings	73.20		
7% Preference share capital (£1)	60.00	(60m × £1.44)	86.40
4% redeemable debentures (20X7)	45.00	(45m × 0.9)	40.50
Total funds	245.70		484.65
Total geared funds (£m)	105.000		126.90
Gearing % 1 (Gearing/Total Funds)	42.7%		26.2%
Or			
Gearing % 2 (Gearing/Equity)	74.6%		35.5%

Traditional view

Loan finance is cheap because (a) it's low risk to lenders and (b) loan interest is tax deductible. This means that as gearing increases, WACC decreases.

Shareholders and lenders are relatively unconcerned about increased risk at lower levels of gearing.

As gearing increases, both groups start to be concerned - higher returns are demanded and so WACC increases.

Thus, WACC decreases (value of equity increases) as gearing is introduced. It reaches a minimum and then starts to increase again. This is the optimal level of gearing.

Modigliani and Miller (M&M) view

Shareholders immediately become concerned by the existence of any gearing.

Ignoring taxes, the cost of 'cheap' loan finance is precisely offset by the increasing cost of equity, so WACC remains constant at all levels of gearing. There is no optimal level - managers should not concern themselves with gearing questions. M&M '58 position $V_g = V_u$.

Taking taxation into account, interest is cheap enough to cause WACC to fall despite increasing cost of equity. This leads to an all-debt-financing conclusion. M&M '63 position $V_g = V_u + DT$ (Tax shield).

Modern view

M&M are probably right that gearing is only beneficial because of tax relief.

At high levels of gearing, investor worries about the costs of the business going into enforced liquidation ('bankruptcy') become significant and required returns (both equity and debt) would increase at high levels of gearing.

Conclusion - a business should gear up to a point where the benefits of tax relief are balanced by potential costs of bankruptcy and interest rate increases - here WACC will be at a minimum and value of the business at a maximum.

Presumably the directors feel that the current level of gearing is beyond the optimum ie where the WACC is minimised and the company's value is maximised (perhaps because as an engineering company its operational risk is very high and gearing adds additional financial risk). Alternatively, they are incorrectly looking at the book value gearing ratio, as the market value ratio doesn't look particularly bad.

48.2

			£m
Value of current ordinary shareholding	135m	£2.65	357.750
Rights issue (135m/9) (£45m × 60%)	15m	£1.80	27.000
Theoretical ex-rights values	150m	£2.565	384.750

Theoretical ex-rights share price [TERP] (£384.75m/150m)	£2.565
Value of a right (£2.565 – £1.800) per new share	£0.765
OR per existing share £0.765/9 =	£0.085

48.3

Current earnings per share (EPS) £32.4m/135m		£0.240
Current P/E ratio	£2.65/£0.24	11.04
		£m
Current earnings figure		32.400
Savings on debenture interest (£45m × 60% × 4% × 79%)		0.853
Amended earnings figure		33.253
New EPS	£33.253m/150m	£0.222
New P/E ratio (using TERP)	£2.565/£0.222	11.55

The earnings per share figure will fall by 7.5% (from £0.240 to £0.222).

The proposed rights issue will, as the board suggests, cause a dilution of the EPS figure as the additional shares issued have a greater negative impact than the interest saved from the debenture redemption. Whilst in theory (TERP) the market price of BL's ordinary shares will fall, at least initially, it is very difficult to predict what will happen to the market value of the shares in practice. As gearing is being reduced the market may react favourably (ie there would be a share price increase). However, based on market values the gearing level is currently not high (26.2% or 35.5%), and so the market may react negatively (ie there would be a share price decrease) if it considers that insufficient use is being made of the tax savings that gearing affords.

48.4 Current earnings per share (EPS)	£32.4m/135m	£0.240
Amended EPS (with a 5% reduction)	£0.24 × 95%	£0.228
New earnings figure		£33.253m
Thus required total ordinary shares ex-rights	£33.253/£0.228	145.846m
New shares to be issued via rights	145.846m − 135.000m	10.846m
Rights issue price per share	£27.000m/10.846m	£2.49

This rights issue price is only £0.16 less than the current market value, ie a 6% discount and this is likely to be an insufficient inducement for shareholders. As a result the issue would fail to raise the £27m of funds required for the debenture redemption.

48.5 Issue costs are a significant part of a rights issue. They have been estimated at around 4% on £2m raised but, as many of the costs are fixed, the percentage falls as the sum raised increases.

Shareholders may react badly to firms who continually make rights issues as they are forced either to take up their rights or sell them, since doing nothing decreases their wealth. They may sell their shares in the company, driving down the market price.

Unless large numbers of existing shareholders sell their rights to new shareholders there should be little impact in terms of control of the business by existing shareholders.

Unlisted companies often find rights issues difficult to use, because shareholders unable to raise sufficient funds to take up their rights may not have available the alternative of selling them if the firm's shares are not listed. This is less likely to be a concern for a listed company like Biddaford Lundy.

Examiner's comments:

This question was, overall, done poorly and produced the weakest set of answers in the examination.

In general, part 48.1 was not done well. The book value of equity often excluded retained earnings. When calculating the market value, a majority of candidates included retained earnings in the equity figure. Very few of them could calculate the gearing ratio correctly – far too many included preference shares as equity. In the discursive part of the answer, some candidates made no reference to the theories on capital structure at all and some referred to the 'Modigliani and Miller traditional theory'. Disappointingly, very few candidates made reference to the ratios that they had calculated (ie high/low gearing level etc).

Answers to part 48.2 were better and the most common mistake was to confuse the market value and the book value of debt when calculating the redemption figure.

Part 48.3 was very poorly answered. The vast majority of candidates ignored the reduction in interest post-redemption. Also far too many candidates restricted their discussion to a consideration of the impact of the rights issue on the shareholders' wealth. This was not relevant to the question which was about gearing.

In part 48.4 there were some good attempts, but often candidates' answers just consisted of identifying a 5% fall in EPS.

49 Duofold plc (March 2004)

				Marks
49.1	Ex-rights price		1	
	Price to sell rights		1	
	Option 1		1.5	
	Option 2		1.5	
	Option 3		1.5	
				Max 6
49.2	Value combined		1	
	Value alone		1	
	Conclusion		1	
	Justifications		2	
				5
49.3	1 mark per point		4	
	M&M assumptions		2	
				6
				17

49.1 Mr Jones' options

Ex-rights price of the company's ordinary shares

$$\frac{(10m \times £1.80) + £5m + £2m}{10m + 5m} = £1.6666$$

He could reasonably sell his rights for £1.6666 – £1.00 = 66.66p

Option 1: Take up his rights

		£
Wealth prior to the rights issue	= 2,000 × £1.80	3,600.00
Wealth post the rights issue	= 3,000 × 1.6666	4,999.80
Less Cost of rights issue	= 1,000 × 1.00	(1,000.00)
		3,999.80

He is therefore £399.80 better off as a result of taking up his rights.

Option 2: Sell his rights for 66.66p

		£
Wealth prior to the rights issue	= 2,000 × £1.80	3,600.00
Wealth post the rights issue	= 2,000 × £1.6666	3,333.20
Plus Proceeds of sale of rights	= 1,000 × 66.66p	666.60
		3,999.80

He is therefore £399.80 better off as a result of selling his rights.

Option 3: Do nothing

		£
Wealth prior to the rights issue	= 2,000 × £1.80	3,600.00
Wealth post the rights issue	= 2,000 × £1.6666	3,333.20

He is therefore £266.80 worse off as a result of doing nothing.

49.2 Maximum price

The maximum that should be paid for the competitor is as follows.

Value of Duofold plc and target combined $\frac{£6.8m}{0.10} = £68m$

Value of Duofold plc on its own $\frac{£4.2m}{0.12} = £35m$

So the maximum that Duofold plc should pay is £33m.

The usual justifications for an acquisition are as follows.

(1) Synergy (from issues such as administrative savings, economies of scale, shared investment, leaner management structures and access to under-utilised assets).

(2) Risk reduction (reflected in reduced WACC).

(3) Reduction in or elimination of competition (as well as market access).

(4) Vertical protection (via acquisition of a supplier, distributor or customer).

(5) Increased shareholder wealth arising from any of the above.

49.3 Dividend policy

Dividend policy irrelevance is as follows.

- Modigliani and Miller (M&M) (1961) showed that dividends are irrelevant in a world without taxes, transaction costs or other market imperfections.

- M&M showed that the dividend decision is irrelevant, since financing a project by either paying a dividend and issuing shares or not paying a dividend has the same impact on shareholder wealth.

- Although the dividend decision was shown to be irrelevant, dividends themselves were not considered irrelevant – the view is simply that if a change in dividend policy leaves the present value of future dividends unchanged, then the dividend policy must be irrelevant.

- If a shareholder prefers income to capital gains they can 'manufacture' dividends by selling shares with no loss of wealth (M&M).

- However, M&M's argument depends on a perfect capital market, and once the assumptions are relaxed it can be shown that in the real world dividend policy is relevant due to the following.

  (1) Transaction costs (that will reduce shareholder wealth in 'manufacturing' dividends).

  (2) Taxation (which may lead to a preference on the part of individual investors for income or capital gains).

  (3) Dividends acting as information signals (in the absence of perfect information, ie shareholders may not be aware of a particular positive NPV project).

  (4) Dividends being (irrationally) perceived as resolving uncertainty (future capital gains are viewed as uncertain).

  (5) Dividends having a clientele effect (attracting investors who favour a particular dividend policy for tax, cash flow or other reasons).

Examiner's comments:

Most candidates found this question relatively straightforward, with many high marks being awarded. To gain full marks in part 49.3, however, once again required the full development of answers, rather than merely a listing of justifications.

Part 49.1 was well answered by most candidates, although it was a little surprising that a number of scripts provided calculations for the first two options while ignoring those for the third option. Some candidates clearly knew what the calculations would reveal in terms of the theoretical effect on the investor's wealth but, having stated the theory, chose to ignore the instruction in the question and provided no calculation at all.

Part 49.2 was well answered by most candidates. Most candidates found this part of the question straightforward, although, again, weaker candidates stated the theory without actually doing the calculation.

Part 49.3 was well answered by most candidates who clearly had a sound grasp of theory in this area.

50   Portico plc (December 2004)

		Marks
General points	4	
Dividend policy factors	5	
Director comments	3	
Different preferences	3	
Agency problem	3	
Total available		18
Maximum		16

Notes on dividend policy for a company in Portico's position

In theory, companies should make all investments available to them that increase shareholder value (ie all positive NPV investments, when discounted at the shareholders' opportunity cost of capital). Any funds remaining after undertaking such investments should be distributed to shareholders as dividends so that the shareholders can invest them as they see fit. The dividend decision is, therefore, a residual decision. As a company's share price is the PV of its future dividends, shareholders should be indifferent about how the PV is made up (ie the size of each year's dividend).

One point of view is that individual shareholders who dislike a particular dividend policy can adjust the cash flows to suit their own needs. They can do this by 'creating' dividends through the sale of shares or conversely they can buy more shares to cancel the effect of dividends. One drawback to this strategy, however, is the question of transaction costs in the real world.

However, in practice, Portico's dividend policy will be affected by a number of other issues than purely its own investment policy.

Dividend signalling. In reality, shareholders do not have perfect information concerning the future prospects of the company, so the pattern of dividend payments actually functions as a key indicator of likely future performance (increased dividends is taken as a signal of confidence which causes estimates of future earnings to increase, so increasing the share price, and *vice versa*). This supports the argument for the relevance of dividend policy and the need for a stable (and increasing) dividend pay-out.

Preference for current income (as displayed by certain of the private shareholders referred to by Director B). This implies that many shareholders will prefer companies which pay regular dividends and will, therefore, value their shares more highly.

Clientele effect. Investors may be attracted to firms by their dividend policy, for example, because it suits their particular tax position. Major changes in dividend policy may well upset particular clienteles who may then sell their shares, so pushing down the share price. While this may be off-set by other clienteles buying the shares and boosting the share price, the climate of uncertainty concerning long-term dividend policy often depresses the share price.

Cash. Shortage of cash can affect dividend policy, although money may be borrowed to fund a dividend payment to avoid negative signalling effects. In summary, companies should establish a dividend policy which is stable, which sets a stable, rising dividend per share, and which sets the dividend at a level below anticipated earnings to provide for new investment (avoiding the need for new share issues) and to provide a cushion if an unexpected fall in earnings is experienced. Excess earnings over investment needs and normal dividends can be returned to shareholders via a special dividend or used to repurchase the firm's shares.

Director A's comments reflect the dividend valuation model but overlook the issues of both the funds available to a company and the investment calls on the company in any given year. Furthermore, Modigliani and Miller showed that, in the absence of taxes and transaction costs, dividends are irrelevant to the value of a company. In principle, it does not matter when dividends occur, provided that their PV is maximised. Furthermore, transaction costs somewhat undermine the director's comments on raising new finance.

Director B's comments are illustrative of the clientele effect as discussed above.

Addressing the issue of differing shareholder preferences

The way in which a company will try to address the issue of differing preferences of different groups of shareholders depends on the current mix of shareholders (which the company must remain aware of at all times), what other similar companies do, and the effect that changes in dividend payout have had on the share prices of similar companies in the past. It is vital that the company makes clear to shareholders what its long-term dividend policy is, why any changes in dividend policy are being made and what the likely effect will be on shareholder value of any future proposed investments.

In reality, the aspirations of the new management team may mitigate against the family shareholders' desire for dividend payments as required and so the only way ahead is to communicate a planned, long-term dividend policy even if this means driving away those family shareholders.

The relationship between a company's dividend policy and the 'agency problem'

This is apparent in the way that managers/directors do not necessarily act in the best interests of shareholders. Shareholders may seek to keep some control over their money by insisting on high pay-out ratios (in line with Director A's comments), thereby forcing managers/directors wanting new funds for investment to justify why the investment is sound. However, there is an agency cost here in the form of the cost of the new share issue.

Managers/directors may, therefore, be motivated to adopt a low dividend pay-out policy which circumvents this need to justify projects by creating retained earnings which can be used to fund new projects. Even if they do this, however, there may still be an agency cost for shareholders in that managers may invest in empire building projects rather than in those that maximise shareholder wealth. In addition, an over-reliance on retentions can lead to dividend cuts which upset shareholders, depress the share price and increase the cost of equity.

Examiner's comments:

This was a question which candidates found very challenging, although this does mask the fact that strong candidates were still able to score high marks. Weaker candidates struggled, in particular, with the third requirement, often making little or no attempt to explore the relationship between dividend policy and the agency problem, and certainly failing to identify the potential agency costs involved. Similarly, responses by weaker candidates to the second requirement often lacked any practicality. It was in these latter sections that most marks were lost.

51 Cern Ltd (December 2012)

		Marks
51.1 (a)	Freehold land and property adjustment	1
	Investments adjustment	1
	Preference shares adjustment	1
	Debentures adjustment	1
	Net assets value per share	1
	Calculation of dividend per share	1
	Choice of yield	0.5
	Valuation per share	1
	Non-marketability discount	0.5
	Calculation of average EBIT	1
	Calculation of profit after tax	1
	EPS	1
	Choice of P/E ratio	0.5
	Valuation per share	1
	Non-marketability discount	0.5
		13
(b)	Basic weaknesses of net asset, dividend yield and P/E valuations	2
	Other issues - 1 mark per point	5
		Max 4
(c)	1 mark per point	Max 4
51.2	Calculation of each possible replacement cycle – 2.5 marks	10
		31

51.1 (a)

Net asset valuation:	£
Intangibles	900,000
Freehold land and property	4,500,000
Plant and equipment	3,600,000
Investments	1,350,000
Inventory	540,000
Receivables	1,080,000
Cash	180,000
	12,150,000
Less	
Current liabilities	1,080,000
Preference shares	648,000
Debentures	1,980,000
	8,442,000

£8,442,000/3,600,000 = £2.345 per share

Dividend yield valuation:

Dividend in 20X2 = £180,000
Number of shares = 3,600,000
Dividend per share = £0.05

Average dividend yield of other two quoted firms: 3.7% (or the minimum 3.4%)
Valuation = £0.05 / 0.037 = £1.35 (or £0.05 / 0.034 = £1.47)

Less discount to reflect non-marketability (25% - any % will suffice) = £0.34 or £0.37
Valuation = £1.01 per share (or £1.10 per share)

Price/earnings valuation:

Average PBIT = (1,080+440+1,800)/3 = £1,106,667
Less interest 180,000 and tax 194,600 (926,667 × 21%) = PAIT £732,067–43,200 = £688,867
EPS = £688,867/3,600,000 = £0.1914

Average price-earnings ratio of the other two quoted firms: 8.3 (or the minimum 7)
Valuation = £0.1914 × 8.3 = £1.59 (or £1.34)
Less discount to reflect non-marketability (25%) = £0.40 (any % deduction will suffice)
Valuation = £1.19 per share (or £1.00)

(b) In addition to a discussion of basic elements surrounding the weaknesses of net asset valuation (historic cost, omission of internally-generated intangibles) and dividend yield and price/earnings valuations (comparator statistics, unrepresentative annual figures), the following areas were worthy of comment in this specific scenario:

The erratic profits in recent years suggests the earnings value may be somewhat unreliable

Purchasers may prefer a valuation based on the present value of forecast future cash-flows

Given the dividend yield and price/earnings valuations, Cern's directors may prefer to sell off the firm on a break-up basis rather than as a going concern.

Is the discount for non-marketability reasonable?

(c) Synergy: the '2+2=5' effect
Risk reduction via diversification
Removal of a competitor
Vertical integration: safeguard Fenton's position by acquiring a supplier or distributor
Access a new market (possibly overcoming barriers to entry)
The acquisition of skills/knowledge
Speed compared to organic growth
Asset-stripping

51.2

Maximum annual production/sales (units)	300,000	285,000	270,000	255,000
Annual revenue @ £12 per unit (£)	3.60m	3.42m	3.24m	3.06m
Annual variable costs @ £8 per unit	2.40m	2.28m	2.16m	2.04m
Annual contribution	1.20m	1.14m	1.08m	1.02m

One-year replacement cycle:

	Year 0	Year 1	Year 2	Year 3	Year 4
Purchase price	(480,000)				
Scrap value		320,000			
Maintenance costs		(12,000)			
Contribution		1,200,000			
Net cash flow	(480,000)	1,508,000			

NPV (480,000) + (1,508,000 × 0.909) = £890,772/0.909 = **£979,947**

Two-year replacement cycle:

	Year 0	Year 1	Year 2	Year 3	Year 4
Purchase price	(480,000)				
Scrap value			200,000		
Maintenance costs		(12,000)	(14,000)		
Contribution		1,200,000	1,140,000		
Net cash flow	(480,000)	1,188,000	1,326,000		

NPV (480,000) + (1,188,000 × 0.909) + (1,326,000 × 0.826) = £1,695,168/1.736 = **£976,479**

Three-year replacement cycle:

	Year 0	Year 1	Year 2	Year 3	Year 4
Purchase price	(480,000)				
Scrap value				80,000	
Maintenance costs		(12,000)	(14,000)	(16,000)	
Contribution		1,200,000	1,140,000	1,080,000	
Net cash flow	(480,000)	1,188,000	1,126,000	1,144,000	

NPV (480,000) + (1,188,000 × 0.909) + (1,126,000 × 0.826) + (1,144,000 × 0.751) = £2,389,112/2.487 = **£960,640**

Four-year replacement cycle:

	Year 0	Year 1	Year 2	Year 3	Year 4
Purchase price	(480,000)				
Scrap value					10,000
Maintenance costs		(12,000)	(14,000)	(16,000)	(18,000)
Contribution		1,200,000	1,140,000	1,080,000	1,020,000
Net cash flow	(480,000)	1,188,000	1,126,000	1,064,000	1,012,000

NPV (480,000) + (1,188,000 × 0.909) + (1,126,000 × 0.826) + (1,064,000 × 0.751) + (1,012,000 × 0.683) = £3,020,228/3.170 = **£952,753**

Therefore, the directors should change their existing policy of replacing the processing machine every three years to replacing it every year, as that gives the greatest annual equivalent net revenue

Examiner's comments:

Whilst there were many strong responses to the valuation questions, less well-prepared candidates were undoubtedly exposed by the question and were particularly weak in dealing with the technicalities of both the dividend yield and price/earnings valuation techniques. In the second section, whilst many candidates were able to list classic text-book commentary on the respective valuation techniques, far fewer were able to augment this basic analysis with insightful commentary on the relevance of the techniques to the specific scenario set out in the question. The third and final section of the first part of the paper, on take-over motives, was, however, generally very well answered across the board.

The second part of the question was, again, very well answered by the stronger candidates but performance was somewhat polarised as those candidates who had clearly banked on there being a traditional NPV question found their lack of a firm grasp of the replacement methodology exposed. Even some candidates who scored well on the calculations themselves arrived at incorrect conclusions as a result of treating the calculated figures as equivalent annual costs rather than net revenues.

52 Wexford plc (December 2008)

Marking guide

		Marks
52.1 Forecast Income Statement	8	
Forecast Balance Sheet	8	
		16
52.2 Rights issue: Up to 2 marks per valid point	max 7	
Floating rate loan: Up to 2 marks per valid point	max 6	
Report format	1	
		14
		30

52.1 Rights Issue

Forecast Income Statement for the year ending 30 November 20X9

	£'000
Revenue (270 × 1.15)	310,500
Direct costs ((171–19) × 1.18)	179,360
Depreciation (18 + (20% × 25))	23,000
Indirect costs (40 + 10)	50,000
Profit from operations	58,140
Interest	5,000
Profit before tax	53,140
Taxation (21%)	11,159
Profit after tax	41,981
Dividends declared ((22.68/42.66) × 41,981)	22,319
Retained profit	19,662

Forecast Balance Sheet at 30 November 20X9

	£'000	£'000
Non-current assets (carrying amount) (152.59 + 25 – 23)		154,590
Current assets:		
Inventory (35 + 10)	45,000	
Receivables ((49/270) × 310.5)	56,350	
Cash at bank (balancing figure)	43,191	
		144,541
		299,131
Capital and reserves:		
£1 Ordinary shares (50 + 10)		60,000
Share premium (25 – 10)		15,000
Retained earnings (81.41 + 19.662)		101,072
		176,072
Non-current liabilities:		
10% Debentures (repayable 20Y5)		50,000
Current liabilities:		
Trade payables ((43/152) × 179.36)	50,740	
Dividends payable	22,319	
		73,059
		299,131

Floating Rate Loan

Forecast Income Statement for the year ending 30 November 20X9

	£'000
Revenue	310,500
Direct costs	179,360
Depreciation	23,000
Indirect costs	50,000
Profit from operations	58,140
Interest (5 + (25 × 8%))	7,000
Profit before tax	51,140
Taxation (21%)	10,739
Profit after tax	40,401
Dividends declared ((22.68/42.66) × 40.401)	21,479
Retained profit	18,922

Many candidates answered part 53.4 by dealing with ethics in the context of valuing companies, rather than in the context of the promotional campaign. In other words they didn't answer the question.

54 Arleyhill Redland plc (September 2013)

Marking guide

		Marks
54.1 Factors and explanations (1 mark for factor, 1 for explanation):		
Issue costs	2	
Shareholder reactions	2	
Control	2	
Unlisted companies	2	
		Max 4
54.2 Sales	1	
Variable costs	1	
Fixed costs	1	
Debenture interest	2	
Taxation	1	
Dividends	2	
Retained	1	
		9
54.3 Current EPS	1	
Extra shares	1	
New shares in issue	1	
EPS	2	
		5
54.4 Current gearing (book value)	1	
Current gearing (market value)	1	
Gearing ratio (book value)	3	
Gearing ratio (market value)	3	
		8
54.5 Advice on funding	5	
		5
54.6 CLS	2	
Loan stock with warrants	2	
		4
		35

54.1 • Issue costs – these are high compared for equity with debt.

• Shareholder reactions – they may react badly if the firm regularly makes rights issues. They may sell their shares as a result, which will adversely affect the share price.

• Control – should not be affected by a rights issue unless a considerable number of existing shareholders sell their rights.

• Unlisted companies – shareholders may not be able to sell their rights (if unlisted) and so a rights issue would not be practical.

54.2

	Rights issue £m	Debenture issue £m
Sales	65.280	65.280
Less variable costs	(39.168)	(39.168)
Less fixed costs	(8.700)	(8.700)
Profit before interest	17.412	17.412
Debenture interest	(0.930)	(1.770)

Profit before tax	16.482	15.642
Taxation (at 21%)	(3.461)	(3.285)
Profit after tax	13.021	12.357
Dividends	(2.016)	(1.728)
Retained	11.005	10.629

54.3

Current EPS	£0.346	(£9.978m/28,800)
	Rights issue	*Debenture issue*
Extra shares	$\dfrac{£12.0m}{£2.50}$	
	4.8m shares	None
New total shares in issue	28.8m	28.8m
	4.8m	0.0m
	33.6m	28.8m
Earnings per share	$\dfrac{£13.021m}{33.600m}$	$\dfrac{£12.357m}{28.800m}$
	38.8p	42.9p

54.4 Based on DEBT/TOTAL LONG TERM FUNDS

Current gearing (book value)	20.6%	(£15.500/£75.150)
Current gearing (market value)	14.8%	[£15.500/([£3.10 × 28.800] + £15.500)

	Rights issue	*Debenture issue*
Gearing ratio (book value)	$\dfrac{£15.500}{£75.150 + £12.000 + £11.005}$	$\dfrac{£15.500 + £12.000}{£75.150 + £12.000 + £10.629}$
	= 15.8%	= 28.1%
Gearing ratio (market value)	$\dfrac{£15.500}{(33.600 \times £3.30) + £15.500}$	$\dfrac{£27.500}{(28.800 \times £3.30) + £27.500}$
	= 12.3%	= 22.4%

OR

Based on DEBT/TOTAL EQUITY

Current gearing (book value)	26.0%	(£15.500/£59.650)
Current gearing (market value)	17.4%	[£15.500/([£3.10 x 28.800])

	Rights issue	*Debenture issue*
Gearing ratio (book value)	$\dfrac{£15.500}{£59.650 + £12.000 + £11.005}$	$\dfrac{£27.500}{£59.650 + £10.629}$
	= 18.8%	= 39.1%
Gearing ratio (market value)	$\dfrac{£15.500}{(33.600 \times £3.30)}$	$\dfrac{£27.500}{(28.800 \times £3.30)}$
	= 14.0%	= 28.9%

54.5

	Current	*Rights Issue*	*Debenture Issue*
EPS	£0.346	£0.388	£0.429
P/E ratio	8.95	8.52	7.69
Gearing (BV)	20.6% or 26.0%	15.8% or 18.8%	28.1% or 39.1%
Gearing (MV)	14.8% or 17.4%	12.3% or 14.0%	22.4% or 28.9%

EPS increases in both cases. It is highest with debenture issue. However gearing (BV) is now nearly 30%, which might be too high and could have an adverse effect on share price if investors worry

ICAEW

about level of financial risk. If one takes the MV then the gearing level is more moderate (22.4% with issue of extra debt).

Important point regarding share price – £3.30 has been used (as per MC's quote). Is this achievable? The theoretical ex-rights price is £3.01 because of the dilution caused by the rights issue. Thus an extra 29p would need to be added to the actual share price ex-rights, ie the NPV of the expansion would need to be at least 29p per share. If it's a debt issue – would the market react favourably to the increase in gearing?

54.6 Convertible Loan Stock (CLS)

Fixed return securities which may at the discretion of the holder be converted into ordinary shares of the same company.

Loan stock with warrants

Loan stocks which give the holder the right to subscribe at a fixed future date for ordinary shares at a predetermined price. Debt is not converted, but remains as such.

Examiner's comments

This question was generally done very well and had the highest average mark on the paper.

This was a six-part question that tested the candidates' understanding of the financing options element of the syllabus.

In the scenario a manufacturing company was planning to raise additional funding for an expansion of its product range and was considering whether to use equity (via a share issue) or debt (via debentures). Part 54.1 for four marks required candidates to highlight the factors to consider when deciding between a rights issue and a debenture issue. Part 54.2 for nine marks asked them to prepare next year's income statement using both methods of funding. In part 54.3 [5 marks], they were required to calculate the resultant earnings per share figures under both methods. Part 54.4 for eight marks asked candidates to calculate the gearing figures for both schemes (at book value and market value). In part 54.5 [5 marks] candidates had to advise the company's directors of the merits of both schemes, based on their calculations in 54.2 to 54.4 above. Finally, for four marks, in part 54.6 they had to explain the differences between convertible loan stock and loan stock with warrants.

There was a variable performance in part 54.1 and the weakest scripts re-hashed/embellished existing points in the question.

Part 54.2 was very straightforward and most candidates scored full marks. The most common errors were made with the interest and dividend calculations. A disappointing number of students failed to increase the sales and/or variable costs figures correctly.

Part 54.3 was, again, very straightforward and the average mark here reflects that. It was good to see that fewer candidates than previously had (incorrectly) used the retained earnings figure for the EPS calculation.

Part 54.4 was poorly done in general. A majority of students failed to deal correctly with retained profits in the book value and market value calculations for gearing.

Part 54.5 was reasonably well answered, but too few candidates considered the validity of the £3.30 share price (it's only the director's opinion) given in the question.

Part 54.6 tested the candidates' knowledge and there was a wide range of marks here. Few candidates were able to explain how loan stock with warrants operates.

55 Sennen plc (June 2014)

		Marks
55.1 (a) Sales revenue	1	
Operating profit	0.5	
Tax	1	
After tax synergies	1	
Working capital	1	
Additional CAPEX	1	
Free cash flow	0.5	
Present value	1	
Terminal value	2	
Value per share	2	
Advantages and disadvantages	2	
		13
(b) Sensitivity to change in after tax synergies	3	
		3
(c) Operating profit	0.5	
Interest	0.5	
Investment income	0.5	
Tax	0.5	
Share price	1	
Strengths and weaknesses	2	
		5
(d) Relevant discussion	3	
		3
(e) Advice on suitability of each method	8	
		8
55.2 Ethical issues	3	
		3
		35

55.1 REPORT

To: Partner in NWCF
From: Accountant
Date: x – x – xx
Subject: Possible acquisition of Sennen plc

(a)

	Year			
	0	1	2	3
	£m	£m	£m	£m
Sales revenue		21	22.05	23.15
Operating profit		3.15	3.31	3.47
Tax (21%)		-0.66	-0.7	-0.73
After tax synergies		0.53	0.55	0.58
Working capital	-0.21	-0.22	-0.23	-0.24
Additional CAPEX		-0.42	-0.44	-0.46
Free cash flow	-0.21	2.38	2.49	2.62
Present value factor (7%)	1	0.935	0.873	0.816
Present value	-0.21	2.23	2.17	2.14

	£m
Present value of free cash flow years 0 – 3	6.33

	£m
Terminal value: 2.14(1 + 0.02)/(0.07 – 0.02)	43.66

	£m
Enterprise value	49.99
Less debt	-10.00
Add short term investments	2.00
Equity	41.99

Value per share in pence (41.99/17 × 100p)	247

This methodology has the advantage of valuing the free cash flows of the company and is not distorted by accounting policies which can affect other methods. However the valuation is dominated by the terminal value. The methodology is also heavily dependent upon the inputs to the model such as estimating cash flows and growth. For example, reducing the estimated sales growth after the competitive advantage period to, say, 1% would reduce the terminal value to 2.14(1 + 0.01)/(0.07 – 0.01) = £36m a reduction of 45p per share.

(b) The sensitivity of the enterprise value to a change in the after tax synergies: PV of synergies/total value:

	1 £m	2 £m	3 £m
After tax synergies	0.53	0.55	0.58
PV @ 7%	0.5	0.48	0.47

	£m
Present value years 1-3	1.45
Amount in terminal value	9.59
Total present value of synergies	11.04

£11.04m/£51.99m = 21%.

Synergies represent 21% of the value of debt plus equity.

(c) The earnings per share has to be calculated:

	£m
Operating profit £20m × 0.15	3
Less interest £10m × 0.05	(0.5)
Add investment income £2m × 0.03	0.06
Taxable	2.56
Tax at 21%	(0.54)
Profit after tax	2.02
Earnings per share	£2.02m/17m = 11.88p

[NB credit any attempt to calculate prospective EPS rather than historic]

The share price using the p/e ratio for recent takeovers = 11.88p × 17 = 202p

The p/e ratio basis is a market measure and has the advantage of valuing the shares by comparison to other takeovers. However we do not know how comparable to Sennen the other companies are. Also the valuation is based on historic EPS and a more realistic measure might be a prospective EPS.

(d) The range in values is 202p – 247p

The free cash flow valuation can be considered as a maximum value, however the valuation is quite sensitive at 21% to the synergistic savings which may or may not be made and the growth rate of sales in perpetuity.

Both measures offer a premium to the current share price of 160p and the Board of Morgan should feel comfortable offering the shareholders of Sennen a bid premium.

(e) Students should take into account that the company is highly geared and their answers should reflect this. They should consider both the shareholders of Sennen and Morgan in their answers. Some areas that they may mention and expand upon for each method are as follows:

- The ability of Morgan to raise extra funds by borrowing and/or an issue of shares, maybe a rights issue.

- Does Morgan have any cash reserves.

- Dilution of control.

- The tax position of Sennen's shareholders.

- Risk.

55.2 There is a savage conflict of interest with the management team who are party to the MBO also considering making an offer for the company. The management team should be acting in the interests of the shareholders of Sennen and be recommending to the shareholders the best price for their shares. It would be highly unethical for any member of the management team who are party to the MBO to take part in negotiations with Morgan or to make recommendations to Sennen's shareholders.

Examiner's comments

This was a six-part question that tested the candidates' understanding of the investment decisions element of the syllabus. The scenario of the question was that a company had identified a takeover target.

The acquirer has had a policy of expanding by acquisition and, as a result, is highly geared compared to its peers. Also there is a potential bid from the management of the target in the form of a management buyout (MBO). Part 55.1(a) of the question required candidates to use Shareholder Value Analysis (SVA) to value the target. The valuation included after tax synergies, also candidates were required to state the strengths and weaknesses of the valuation method. Part 55.1(b) of the question required candidates to calculate how sensitive the valuation using SVA was to a change in the synergies. Part 55.1(c) of the question required candidates to value the target using p/e ratios and to state the strengths and weaknesses of the valuation method. Part 55.1(d) of the question required candidates to discuss the range of values and whether the acquirer should have offered the target company's shareholders a bid premium. Part 55.1(e) of the question required candidates to discuss the methods that the acquirer could have used to pay for the shares of the target. Part 55.2 of the question required candidates to discuss the ethical position of the members of the MBO team.

In part 55.1(a), the basic discounting was fine with some candidates making the usual timing errors, however the inclusion and computation of the perpetuity flow and discounting it was variable. Few candidates made adjustments to the present value of the free cash flows for the debt and investments. Many candidates wasted time by stating the 7 drivers of SVA, which was not required.

In part 55.1(b), many candidates were able to calculate the present value of the after tax synergies but did not realise that this should then be stated as a percentage of the value calculated in part 55.1(a).

Part 55.1(c) was very disappointing since p/e valuations have been tested several times in the past. Many candidates lost marks by making no attempt to calculate the earnings. Instead a common calculation was to divide the target share price by the p/e ratio given in the question for recent takeovers in the sector and then multiplying the resultant figure back up again: $17 \times eps = 160p$, $eps = 9.41p$, Offer price = $9.41p \times 17 = 160p$!

Part 55.1(d) had reasonable responses. However weaker candidates did not make reference to their range of values calculated in 55.1(a) and 55.1(c).

Part 55.1(e) was quite well answered but weaker candidates did not refer to the offeror being already highly geared compared to its peers.

In part 55.2 many candidates ignored the ethical position of the members of the MBO team.

56 Megagreat plc (June 2002)

	Marks
56.1 Value of Angelic plc share	1½
Value of Megagreat plc share	2
Amount holders receive	1½
Conclusion	1
	6
56.2 1 – 2 marks per point	4
56.3 1 – 2 marks per point	4
56.4 1 – 2 marks per explanation	3
	17

56.1 Evaluation of a takeover offer

Value of an Angelic plc (A plc) share (P_0) $= D_1 / (k_e - g)$

$= 0.37 / (0.12 - 0.05)$

$= £5.29$

Value of a Megagreat plc (M plc) share $= \dfrac{0.43}{1.11} + \dfrac{0.43}{1.11^2} + \dfrac{\left(\dfrac{0.43\,(1.07)}{0.11 - 0.07}\right)}{1.11^2}$

$= £10.07$

The holder of one A plc share will receive $\dfrac{£6 + (3 \times £10.07)}{4} = £9.05$

Therefore, accept the bid.

56.2 Discussion of the limitations of the calculations in 56.2 as the basis of a decision

Possible reasons include the following.

- Lack of confidence in the estimates on which the calculations are based.

- Unwillingness on the part of A plc shareholders to hold M plc shares – dividend policy, level of capital gearing etc and the cost of share dealing charges to move out of M plc shares.

- It looks as if these two companies may have a different risk profile and A plc shareholders may not be happy with this.

- The cash payment may not be appealing to A plc shareholders because of the potential capital gains tax charge to which this may give rise.

56.3 Suggestions on how a target company's share price would tend to move when a takeover offer is announced

If the market were to accept the estimates and believe that the bid would be successful and disregard the factors in 56.2, A plc's share price would tend immediately to move to £9.05.

If the market were to believe that the bid would be successful, but M plc would have to increase its bid to succeed, the price would tend to rise to more than £9.05.

If the market were to believe that the bid would be unsuccessful the A plc share price would tend to remain at its present level.

Changes in market perceptions during the bid period may cause the share price to move around to reflect those changes.

ICAEW

56.4 Suggestions for strategies for growth without making takeovers

Alternatively, growth could be achieved organically by undertaking internally-generated projects, perhaps using retained earnings to finance them.

Another growth strategy might be to 'buy-in' parts of other businesses, perhaps large parts, without going for a full takeover. Buy-ins tend to involve only the assets, whereas takeovers involve the whole of the business including the liabilities.

Examiner's comments:

Though there were many exceptions, candidates generally did not deal well with this question. Many answers failed to score a pass mark.

In part 56.1 candidates were asked to assess a takeover offer. This involved placing values on two different shares, based on the projected levels of dividends. There were relatively few totally correct answers to what was a straightforward dividend-based valuation. Many candidates had problems in dealing with valuing a share where dividends would only start to grow after a short period of static dividends. However, it remained possible to pass the requirement without dealing correctly with this.

In part 56.2 candidates were asked to discuss why individual shareholders might need to look beyond the figures calculated in part 56.1 in reaching a decision on how to react to the takeover offer. This was well answered by most candidates.

In part 56.3 candidates were required to suggest how the target company's share price would tend to react to a particular takeover offer. This was generally not well answered. Despite having figures from part 56.1, candidates tended to discuss this issue in general terms, rather than in the context of the figures calculated in 56.1. The fact that many candidates made errors in their calculations should not have affected their ability to give a good answer.

In part 56.4 candidates were asked for other, non-takeover, strategies to achieve growth. This was well answered.

57 Printwise UK plc (March 2010)

		Marks
57.1	Net assets valuation (historic) per share	1
	Net assets valuation (revalued) per share	2
	Price earnings valuation per share	2
	Marked-down price (PE valuation)	1
	Dividend yield valuation per share	2
	Marked-down price (Dividend yield valuation)	1
	Discounted cash flow valuation per share:	
	Pre-tax cash flows	1
	Taxation	1
	Capital allowances	2
	Disposal of pool (proceeds)	1
	Discount factor	1
	Present value	0.5
	Total present values	0.5
	Potential sale	2
	Final total present values	1
		max 16
57.2	Advantages and disadvantages of each method	max 8
57.3	Explanation of issues regarding purchase by:	
	Cash	3
	Share-for-share exchange	3
	Loan stock-for-share exchange	3
		max 6
		30

REPORT

To: The board of directors
From: An Accountant
Date: x – x – xx
Subject: Possible offer for LSL

57.1 Net assets valuation (historic) per share $\dfrac{£6.3m}{2.1m}$ £3.00

Net assets valuation (revalued) per share $\dfrac{(£6.3m + 15.5m - 11.8m)}{2.1m}$ £4.76

Price earnings valuation per share $\dfrac{£4.4m \times 9}{2.1m}$ £18.86

As LSL is not a quoted company, and its shares are less marketable, this price should be marked down (by, say, 30%), ie (£18.86 – 30%) £13.20

Dividend yield valuation per share $\dfrac{£1.1m/6\%}{2.1m}$ £8.73

As LSL is not a quoted company, and its shares are less marketable, this price should be marked down (by, say, 30%), ie (£8.73 – 30%) £6.11

Discounted Cash Flow valuation per share (W1) $\dfrac{£23.343m}{2.1m}$ £11.12

WORKINGS

(1) Discounted cashflow

	20X1	20X2	20X3	20X4
	£m	£m	£m	£m
Pre-tax cash flows (£m)	4.600	4.300	5.200	5.700
Less corporation tax at 21%	(0.966)	(0.903)	(1.092)	(1.197)
After-tax cash flows (£m)	3.634	3.397	4.108	4.503
Tax saving - capital allowances (W2)	0.136	0.112	0.092	0.000
Disposal of pool (proceeds)				1.985
Total cash flows	3.770	3.509	4.200	6.488
14% discount factor	0.877	0.769	0.675	0.592
Present value	3.306	2.698	2.835	3.841

Total present values (20X1-20X4)	12.680
Plus potential sale in 20X4 (4 × £4.503m × 0.592)	10.663
Final present value of future cash flows	23.343

(2) Capital allowances

	£m	£m	£m	£m
WDV b/f	3.600	2.952	2.421	1.985
WDA @ 18%	(0.648)	(0.531)	(0.436)	(0.000)
WDV/disposal	2.952	2.421	1.985	1.985
Tax saving (WDA × 21%)	0.136	0.112	0.092	0.000

57.2 Explanation of each of the methods (advantages/disadvantages)

Net assets basis (historic) – this is a historic cost and so doesn't have any real merit to it.

Net assets basis (revalued) – as above, but it does take into account the latest asset values. Intangible assets are not easily included in this situation which would mean that an under-valuation would arise.

Price earnings valuation – income based measure, which has advantages over asset-based. However, is it reasonable to take the industry average P/E ratio? How similar is LSL to other printing firms? Also it's based on this year's earnings only.

Dividend yield valuation – income based measure again. Is it reasonable to take the industry average yield? How similar is LSL to other printing firms? Also it ignores dividend growth.

Discounted Cash Flow valuation – this is probably the best method to adopt, ie value a firm by discounting its expected future cash flows. However there are problems with estimating those cash flows – what about synergistic benefits arising from a takeover? Also, what is an acceptable discount rate and for how many years ahead is it reasonable to estimate the cash flows? Finally, the LSL sale value in 20X4 is based on an estimate which makes up 45.6% (£10,663/£23,343) of the total value calculated under this method – how accurate will this be?

57.3 Explanation of issues regarding purchase by:

Cash

Certain amount received
Possible tax issues

Share-for-share exchange

No tax issues immediately
Uncertain amount received
Dealing costs

Loan stock for share exchange

More assured return than with shares
Shareholders may prefer equity

Examiner's comments:

This question had the lowest average % mark in the paper, but overall was done well.

The question was based around the proposed takeover of a private company by a plc. Part 57.1 for 16 marks required candidates to calculate the value (per share) of the private company using a range of methods (five in total). Part 57.2 was worth 8 marks and asked candidates to explain the advantages/disadvantages of using each of those valuation methods. Part 57.3 was worth 6 marks and it tested the candidates' understanding of the various means by which the target company's shareholders could be remunerated for their shares.

Part 57.1 was reasonably straightforward and many candidates scored good marks. However, a number of them struggled to identify the net assets figures as required and quite a few were unable to calculate the dividend yield correctly. In the latter case, too many candidates attempted to use a dividend growth figure in their answers, which was incorrect. The present value (PV) method of valuation was done reasonably well, but too few candidates were able to correctly calculate the capital allowances in full and/or the four year multiple figure as required.

Part 57.2 was generally answered well, but too few candidates produced sufficiently detailed comments on the PV method of valuation.

Part 57.3 was not done as well as expected and too many candidates failed to answer the question, either basing their answer from the plc's point of view or giving a very general answer and failing to apply their knowledge to the scenario.

58 Tower Brazil plc (September 2014)

Marking guide

		Marks
58.1 Theoretical ex-rights price:		
Funds to be raised by rights issue	1	
Market value	1	
TERP calculation	1	
		3
58.2 (a) Current EPS	1.5	
Current earnings plus debenture interest saved	2	
New earnings	1	
New EPS	1	
(b) New EPS if EPS reduces by 10%		
New total shares	1	
Current shares in issues	1	
New shares to be issued	0.5	
Rights issue price/share	0.5	
Rights issue would be unsuccessful as above current market	1	
price	1.5	
		11
58.3 Gearing level (BV)	1	
Gearing level (MV)	2	
Advise whether there is gearing problem	Max 3	
Gearing theory	Max 3	
		9
58.4 Dividend policy and share price	7	
Impact of special dividend	2	
		9
58.5 Ethical implications	3	
		3
		35

58.1 Theoretical ex-rights price

			£m
Funds to be raised by rights issue:	60% × £46,750 × 1.10		30.855

			£m
Current market capitalisation	16.50m	£4.20	69.300
1 for 2 rights issue	8.25m	£3.74	30.855
	24.75m		100.155

TERP =	£100.155/24.75m	£4.05/share

58.2 (a) Current earnings per share

Current earnings per share	(£5.544m − £0.480m)/16.5m	£0.307

		£m
Current earnings figure	(£5.544m − £0.480m)	5,064.000
plus: Debenture interest saved	(£28.050m × 5% × 79%)	1,107,975
New earnings figure		6,171,975

New EPS	£6,171,975/24,750,000	£0.249

(b) If EPS reduces by 10%, then new EPS is £0.307 × (1 − 10%)   £0.2763

New total shares	£6,171,975/£0.2763	22,338m
Current shares in issue		16.500m
New shares to be issued		5.838m
Rights issue price/share	£30.855m/5,838m	£5.29

As this is above the current market price (£4.20) the rights issue would not be successful

58.3

Gearing level (BV)	£54,750/£97,670			56.1%

Gearing level (MV)	Equity MV	£69,300		
	PSC MV	6,400		
	Debt MV (£46,750 × 1.10)	51,425		
		127,125	£57,825/£127,125	45.5%

So gearing at MV is under 50%. Gearing would be a problem if it was causing WACC to rise (tax advantage outweighed by debenture holders and shareholders wanting a higher return) and MV to fall.

Gearing theory – Traditional view/Modigliani & Miller (MM) view/Modern view – balance between tax benefits and bankruptcy costs.

58.4 Dividend policy and share price – Traditional view/MM and irrelevance theory/Modern view – including signaling, clientele effect and agency theory.

Impact of special dividend – the market is not in favour of such dividends generally, ie the share price may well fall as a result, and so it seems to defeat the object of retaining profit for investment.

58.5 Unpublished information of a price sensitive nature should remain confidential, not be disclosed and not be used to obtain a personal advantage

Examiner's comments

This question had the second highest average mark on the paper and the majority of candidates did well enough to 'pass' it.

This was a five-part question that tested the candidates' understanding of the financing options element of the syllabus.

In the scenario the board of a UK manufacturer was concerned about the company's gearing levels. The board is considering either (a) a rights issue to buy back debt or (b) reducing future dividend payments.

In part 58.1 for three marks candidates were required to calculate the company's theoretical ex-rights price. Part 58.2 was worth eleven marks. Half of these were allocated to 58.2(a) which required candidates to calculate next year's EPS figure (based on the fact that some of the debt would have been repaid). Part 58.2(b) required candidates to calculate and explain the implications for the rights issue of restricting the change in the company's EPS to 10%. Part 58.3 for nine marks asked candidates to calculate the company's current gearing levels and then advise the board, with reference to their calculations and generally accepted theory, whether or not the company had a gearing 'problem'. Part 58.4 was a more discursive section and candidates were asked to explain (again with reference to generally accepted theory) the possible impact of a change in dividend policy on the company's share price. Finally, for three marks, part 58.5 tested the candidates' understanding of the ethical implications facing an ICAEW Chartered Accountant when in possession of price-sensitive information

In part 58.1 most candidates scored full marks, but many failed to calculate correctly the market value of the debt being redeemed via the rights issue.

Part 58.2(a) was reasonably well done, but many candidates struggled with (or ignored) the calculation of the adjustment to the interest charge caused by the debenture redemption. Also, as noted in previous papers, many candidates calculated, incorrectly, the earnings figure before preference dividends.

Part 58.2(b) was also reasonably well done, but many candidates tried to adjust the earnings figure rather than, as was required, the number of shares.

In part 58.3 it was the calculation of gearing using market values that caused most problems (again, as in previous papers). A disappointing number of candidates included retained earnings in their market value of equity figure. Most candidates' understanding of the theory of gearing and market value were good, but, in general, there was too little application of this understanding to the actual scenario.

Part 58.4 was mostly done well, but too few candidates gave a sufficient range of points regarding the 'real world' impact of the dividend policy and most candidates ignored the special dividend.

In general part 58.5 was answered well.

---

59 Hildes and Heimer

Marking guide

			Marks
59.1	Asset based valuation	2	
	Earnings based valuation	2	
	DCF valuation	2	
	PE valuation	2	
			8
	Discussion of methods – up to 2 marks per valid point	Max	12
			20
59.2	Up to 2 marks per valid point	Max	5
			30

59.1 REPORT

To: The Directors, Kelly Ltd
From: An Analyst
Date: Today
Subject: Valuation of 50% holding in Kelly Ltd

Contents

1   Terms of reference
2   Summary
3   Basis of valuation
4   Limitations and assumption
5   Appendices

1 Terms of reference

As requested the following report estimates minimum and maximum values for Mr Heimer's stake in Kelly Ltd. A brief explanation of the method of valuation is given.

2 Summary

Various bases of valuation have been used as discussed below. These suggest that the maximum price that might be achieved for a 50% stake in the company would be about £3.1m. Mr Heimer should not accept less than £465,000 which is his share of the underlying asset value of the company. It is important to remember that Kelly is a service company and income based valuations are likely to be more valid than asset based approaches. In reality a bargain will be struck somewhere between the income based valuations and so a price in the range £1.7m – £3.1m would be reasonable.

3 Basis of valuation

Businesses may be valued essentially in two ways: firstly, based on asset value and, secondly, on earnings potential. In applying an asset method an appropriate starting place might be the historical cost balance sheet value of £730,000. However, this value gives little indication of the current market value of the assets, and it is usual to pay greater attention to market values based on break-up or replacement cost assumptions. The open market value of the assets of Kelly Ltd has been established at £930,000, although somewhat less than this would be received due to agents' fees, taxation and other costs of realisation. Mr Heimer's share of this sum would be 50%.

There are two important considerations in using this basis. Firstly, even if the value represents replacement costs rather than break-up value, it should be expected that a going concern valuation should be higher than the cost of assembling the requisite assets. Secondly, where there is a substantial service industry element in the business, market value and asset values are likely to diverge considerably due to the fact that the valuation by a buyer is likely to be based on earnings potential. Such is the case here and thus an earnings basis may be more appropriate.

In using earnings bases the calculation is one of capitalising future earnings streams at an appropriate required rate of return, taking into account growth potential. Capitalisation rates are usually established for private companies by using statistics for quoted companies suitably adjusted. Two methods are adopted to establish the required return in the quoted company. The first is to look at the rate of return implicit in the relationship between share price and dividend expectation, and the second is to short-cut the calculation on the basis that required return and growth expectations are encapsulated in the P/E ratio.

In either set of circumstances it is necessary to look at the current value, what it is currently worth to the vendor, and also on the basis of the revised earnings available to the purchaser due to change he would bring about.

On these bases, using capitalisation by inferred rate of return gives a range for Mr Heimer's holding of £1.66m – £1.90m, whilst use of the P/E ratios gives £2.70m – £3.10m.

Supporting calculations appear in the appendices to this report.

4 Limitations and assumption

All calculations have been carried out on the basis of the total value of the company divided by two. This presupposes a degree of control over the company by the purchaser. However, Mr Hildes' 50% holding would remain and this leaves the underlying supposition in doubt, especially as it may be that the 50% sold could be split between several purchasers.

Were this to be the case it is likely that the purchaser would value the shareholding not directly on the basis of the earnings streams generated but on dividend expectations and perhaps a later capital realisation. If a purchaser were to look at the dividend potential this would give great difficulty. No dividends have been paid for the past five years and if this policy had to be revised, it would clearly have consequences for the retentions policy and hence growth funded by re-investment.

It has been assumed for at least some of the calculations that the growth rate of 8% is sustainable indefinitely which, whilst reflected in the projections for 20X8 (indeed somewhat bettered by them) may be unreasonably high over a long period. Hence the valuations based on capitalisation at an inferred rate of return may need downward revision. This could be compounded by the purchaser taking the view that Mr Heimer's retirement could cause some dip in earnings due to the loss of personal contacts.

The required rates of return employed in earnings based valuation methods have been set at a somewhat lower rate than a comparable quoted company. This assumes that investment in Kelly is of a lower systematic risk. Clearly these figures are vital to the calculations and require further investigation.

In summary, it is clear that these calculations can only provide a range in which a price may be agreed upon. It must be emphasised that this range can be significantly adjusted simply through disparities in negotiating ability between the parties involved, differences in the perceived benefits from sale/purchase, and also the strength of the desire to buy or sell. If Mr Heimer is desperate to sell, and this communicates itself to a purchaser, it may cause a significant reduction in the price achieved.

5 Appendices

(1) **Asset based valuation**

- Historical cost

  £730,000. Therefore, Heimer's holding £365,000.

- Willing buyer/willing seller

	£'000
Historical cost	730
Extra value attributable to land and buildings	200
	930

  Therefore, Heimer's holding £465,000.

(2) **Earnings based valuation**

- Maintainable current earnings

  £276,000

- Maintainable future earnings

  Maintainable future earnings, should Heimer sell out, would be adjusted by savings effect by his replacement with an accountant, thus

	£'000
Present profit before tax	350
Salary saved (Heimer)	75
Accountant's salary	(25)
	400
Taxation at 21%	(84)
Profit after tax	316

(3) Using discounted cash flow techniques

  To value the shareholding, 50% of the total value of the company has been taken. This total value has been obtained by capitalising the earnings stream using an appropriate discount rate (k_e for Kelly Ltd) and taking into account earnings growth at 8%.

  Determination of discount rate

$$k_e = \frac{d_0(1+g)}{P_0} + g$$

$$k_e \text{ (comparable company)} = \frac{0.7 \times 1.07}{6.05 - 0.7} + 0.07 = 21\%$$

k_e (Kelly) = 21% – 4% = 17%

(1) Value of company (status quo)

$$\frac{£276,000 \times 1.08}{0.17 - 0.08} = £3,312,000$$

Therefore, Heimer's holding = £1,656,000

(2) Value of company (Heimer sells)

$$\frac{£316,000 \times 1.08}{0.17 - 0.08} = £3,792,000$$

Therefore, Heimer's holding = £1,896,000

(4) Using P/E ratio

A practical approximation to the discounting model used above is to multiply earnings by a suitable P/E ratio. As Kelly appears to be less risky than the comparative company an increase in the P/E ratio is indicated. An (arbitrary) increase of 40% is therefore applied, ie 14 × 1.4 = 19.6

- Value of company (status quo)

  £276,000 × 19.6 = £5,409,600

  Therefore Heimer's holding = £2,704,800

- Value of company (Heimer sells)

  £316,000 × 19.6 = £6,193,600

  Therefore, Heimer's holding = £3,096,800

59.2 Ways Heimer can realise his investment

The ways in which the objective can be achieved fall into two main areas: purchase of own shares and sales of shares.

Purchase of own shares

This requires cash to be raised within the business. Methods which might be considered could include sale and leaseback of property, or simply mortgage of property, or the issue of loan stock or debentures secured generally on the assets of the company. However, even taking into account the increased value of the land and buildings, it is doubtful whether more than £500,000 could be raised in this fashion; whilst an earnings based valuation of the company may be of the order of £5m – £6m, the providers of debt finance look for security based on tangible assets. This being the case, it is not likely that such a method could provide all the solution to the problem as it will not generate enough cash and would leave the company mortgaged to the hilt with little in the way of assets to pledge in return for any finance seen as necessary for expansion. Thus it will be necessary to consider the sale of all or part of the equity to a third party.

Sales of shares

The pre-requisite is that the continuing company must be a private company and therefore flotation is not a possible method of Heimer realising his holding. In any case the company is rather small, at a maximum capitalised value (based on earnings) of approximately £6m, to be considering this option. The only possibility in this sphere might be the sale of a part of the company to a quoted company on a share-for-share exchange. This is potentially possible as the company is organised in four divisions and if these are reasonably autonomous it may be possible to float these off separately.

Other than this, Heimer's sale of shares can be viewed rather as 'finding a buyer for shares in this type of company'.

Approaching specialist institutions for development capital would be expected. A possible course might be 3i, which provides equity for expansion usually in amounts between £250,000 and £3m to companies engaged in the commercial development of technological innovation. Other similar funds exist.

It should be noted that development capitalists will seek a running yield and therefore the dividend problem noted in part 59.1 of the question may have to be tackled. They will also require an eventual 'exit route' which might ultimately involve 'going public'.

60 Pinky and Perky

Marking guide

			Marks
60.1	Existing share price of Pinky:		
	Calculation of g	1	
	Ex-div MV	1	
	Existing share price of Perky:		
	Calculation of g	1	
	Ex-div MV	1	
			4
60.2	Value of Pinky after takeover:		
	Calculation of g	1	
	Next year's earnings	2	
	Next year's dividend	1.5	
	Disposal of pool (proceeds)	1.5	
			6
60.3	Max price Pinky should pay for Perky		3
60.4	Reasons for buying another company: 1-2 marks per valid point	Max	7
			20

60.1 Existing share price of Pinky plc

$g = r \times b$
$r = 15\%$
$b = 20\%$
$g = 0.15 \times 0.2$
$ = 0.03$

$$\text{Ex dividend market value} = \frac{\text{Next year's dividend}}{k_e - g}$$

$$= \frac{650,000 \times 0.8 \times 1.03}{0.21 - 0.03}$$

$$= £2,975,556$$

$$= 59.5\text{p per share}$$

Existing share price of Perky plc

$g = r \times b$

$ = 0.15 \times 0.8$

$ = 0.12$

$$\text{Ex dividend market value} = \frac{\text{Next year's dividend}}{k_e - g}$$

$$= \frac{240{,}000 \times 0.2 \times 1.12}{0.24 - 0.12}$$

$$= £448{,}000$$

$$= 29.9\text{p per share}$$

60.2 Value of Pinky plc after the takeover

Care must be taken in calculating next year's dividend and the subsequent growth rate. Next year's earnings are already determined, because both companies have already reinvested their retained earnings at the current rate of return. In addition, they will get cost savings of £85,000.

The dividend actually paid out at the end of next year will be determined by the new 35% retention and the future growth rate will take into account the increased return on new investment.

Growth rate for combined firm, $g = 0.17 \times 0.35$

$$= 0.06$$

New cost of equity	$= 20\%$
Next year's earnings	$= 650{,}000 \times 1.03 + 240{,}000 \times 1.12 + 85{,}000$
	$= £1{,}023{,}300$
Next year's dividend	$= £1{,}023{,}300 \times 0.65$
	$= £665{,}145$
Market value	$= \dfrac{665{,}145}{0.2 - 0.06}$
	$= £4{,}751{,}036$

60.3 Maximum Pinky plc should pay for Perky plc

Combined value	$= £4{,}751{,}036$
Present value of Pinky plc	$= £2{,}975{,}556$
Increase in value	$= £1{,}775{,}480$

60.4 Reasons for one company to buy another

Buying another company can be a way of investing in a set of projects which are already up and running. This saves on the time of setting up the project and allows instant access to the new market.

Economies of scale. These can occur if the companies are in the same field, eg reduced advertising and marketing, reduced sales team, combined R&D, etc. They can also occur if they are completely different, eg combining administrative functions such as the accounts department personnel, etc. In addition, there are possible economies on buildings and other fixed assets.

To buy out a competitor and thus increase market share, while possibly being in a position to increase prices without the threat of losing sales to a cut-price alternative.

A cash-rich company might buy a business (often small owner-managed) which has good ideas for products/projects but lacks the resources to develop them.

To buy in expertise and goodwill.

To increase geographical coverage. It is often cheaper and more efficient to buy a company in the area into which you want to expand rather than set up for yourself.

Acquisition of assets (especially intangibles which are difficult to generate).

Diversification.

Tax reasons.

To acquire new technology.

Larger company has increased borrowing powers.

61 Brennan plc

	Marks
61.1 Sales calculations	1.5
Operating profit	1
Tax	1
Working capital investment	1.5
Non-current asset investment	1.5
Discount rate	1
Post year 6 cash flows	1.5
Short-term investments	1
Comment	3
	13
61.2 1 – 2 marks per valid comment	max 7
	20

61.1

	Year					
	1	2	3	4	5	6
Sales (£m) (W1)	212.00	224.72	238.20	252.50	267.65	283.70
Op profit (15%)	31.80	33.71	35.73	37.87	40.15	42.56
Tax at 21%	(6.68)	(7.08)	(7.50)	(7.95)	(8.43)	(8.94)
Working capital investment (W1)	(0.84)	(0.89)	(0.94)	(1.00)	(1.06)	(1.12)
Non-current asset investment (W1)	(1.44)	(1.53)	(1.62)	(1.72)	(1.82)	(1.93)
Free Cash Flows	22.84	24.21	25.67	27.20	28.84	30.57
Factor 9% (W2)	0.917	0.842	0.772	0.708	0.650	0.596
PV	20.94	20.38	19.82	19.26	18.75	18.22

PV of cash flows years 1 – 6 = £117.37m

Post year 6 cash flows (in perpetuity) = 30.57/0.09 × 0.596 = £202.44m

Total SVA value = 117.37 + 202.44 + 2.5 = £322.31m

The majority of the value calculated (63%) comes from the residual value, which is based on the assumption of zero growth in cash flows from year 6. This is highly dependent on the growth being as predicted in the period of competitive advantage.

The SVA value is significantly higher than the market capitalisation of £250 million. This may be caused by the market assuming a lower growth rate or a higher discount rate than those used in the SVA calculation.

WORKINGS

(1)

		Year					
	0	1	2	3	4	5	6
Sales (increasing at 6%)	200.00	212.00	224.72	238.20	252.50	267.65	283.70
Increase in sales		12.00	12.72	13.48	14.29	15.15	16.06
Working capital (7%)		0.84	0.89	0.94	1.00	1.06	1.12
Non-current asset investment (12%)		1.44	1.53	1.62	1.72	1.82	1.93

(2) Discount factor = 3 + 0.75(11 – 3) = 9%

61.2 The current market capitalisation of Brennan is below its net assets value which suggests that Brennan plc may be worth more if it was liquidated. However this assumes that the net book value of assets matches the market value of the assets and this may not be the case in reality. This does give a possible explanation for the low market capitalisation of Brennan, the market may see no future in the company and is already valuing it on a break up basis.

There are other factors which may cause the market to place such an apparently low valuation on Brennan.

The dividend policy offers a relatively low payout of 10%. If there are no plans to reinvest retained earnings then cash balances will be substantial. This could also help to explain the high net assets valuation.

The stock market may be suspicious of the level of control exercised by the founding family. The founding family appears to control the board and also own a substantial number of shares and as such they may be able to dominate the smaller shareholders. The market may view the current management as less able than similar companies due to this family dominance and this affects the valuation.

Brennan is currently all equity funded, which the market may think is inadvisable and does not allow Brennan to exploit the advantage of debt being cheaper than equity due to the tax shield.

62 Lipton plc (December 2010)

Marking guide

		Marks
62.1	Net assets book valuation	1
	Dividend valuation model	2
	Price earnings valuation current	2
	Price earnings valuation forecast	1
	Limitations of net asset valuation	2
	Limitations of dividend valuation model	4
	Limitations of earnings based valuations	4
		16
62.2	Point made about either method (1 mark)	max 8
62.3	Relative advantage of either method (1 mark)	max 6
62.4	1 mark per valid point	Max 5
		35

62.1 Report

To: The board of directors
From: Corporate finance manager
Date: X/X/XX
Subject: Possible valuations of Becal Ltd

(a) Net asset (book) value: £22.5m (the book value of equity).

(b) Dividend valuation = $d_0(1 + g)/(k_e - g)$ = (£0.50 × 1.06)/(0.08 - 0.06) = 0.53/0.02 = £26.50 per share × 750,000 = £19,875,000.

(c) Earnings valuation = P/E ratio × earnings

Current = 618.5/56.25 × (0.765 × 750,000)= £6,308,700, say £6.3m

Forecast = 618.5/56.25 × £2m = £21,991,111 say £22.0m

The net asset value is potentially useful here in view of the high proportion of non-current assets, but even in this scenario its usefulness is limited as a balance sheet is constructed using costs (rather than market values) and usually excludes many valuable intangible assets. Unless the balance sheet reflects the market value of all the firm's assets it will be of limited use as historic cost is not market value. It completely ignores the firm's future potential.

The dividend valuation method is useful for valuing non-controlling interests, but there are problems in respect of estimating future dividends, the future growth rate, the cost of equity and the adjustments to reflect non-marketability with unquoted firms (the adjustments can be somewhat arbitrary). It also uses certain simplifying assumptions – that Becal is a typical firm for its sector and that next year's dividend will be this year's dividend increased by the forecast growth rate; and that past performance is a reliable indicator of future performance. It also ignores any potential post-acquisition synergies.

The earnings-based valuations have a problem with regard to estimating maintainable future earnings. One also has to be aware that accounting policies can be used to manipulate earnings figures. Selecting a suitable p/e ratio to value unquoted firms is also a problem area (again, arbitrary adjustments for non-marketability) – are the listed companies also ungeared? The acquiring firm is also being asked to rely on the target firm's own earnings forecast – how reliable is this forecast (as use of the current year's earnings yields a very different valuation)? Does the eps require adjustment?

62.2 Rights Issue

1   May dilute ownership of existing shareholders, if rights are not exercised
2   More expensive than debt finance (riskier and not tax-deductible)
3   Relatively high issue costs (compared to the loan)
4   May cause a fall in eps (especially in the short-term)
5   Reduced gearing will lower financial risk and anticipated returns
6   Shareholder reaction could be adverse
7   Flexibility of dividend payments compared to a fixed interest commitment

Floating Rate Term Loan

1   Increased gearing may increase financial risk and the cost of equity capital (although this is probably not a major issue in this scenario)

2   No dilution of existing shareholding

3   Cheaper (lower risk and tax deductible)

4   Potential for enhanced eps

5   Potential exposure to interest rate risk with floating rate debt

6   The possible impact of covenants in the loan agreement or security requirements

7   Inflexibility in interest payments

62.3 Relative advantages of organic growth:

1   Costs of growth spread over time/often cheaper than growth by acquisition

2   Rate of change within the firm is likely to be slower (avoids disruption and behavioural and cultural problems – less risky)

3   Synergies anticipated with acquisition often fail to materialise

Relative advantages of growth by acquisition:

1   Synergy (a better rate of return is achieved than would be achieved by the same resources being used independently)

2   Risk reduction via diversification (more stable cash flows as no two firms will have perfectly correlated cash flows), which will reduce the firm's cost of capital and increase its value

3   Competition potentially reduced/eliminated

4   Benefits of vertical integration

5   Quicker method of growth and increase in market share

62.4 A professional accountant in business should have due regard for the interests of shareholders as a whole. However, in addition the professional accountant in business:

- Needs to be aware of and comply with current legislative and regulatory measures concerning an assignment.

- Should prepare all documents in accordance with normal professional standards of integrity and objectivity with a proper degree of care.

Integrity implies honesty and fair dealing, truthfulness and being straightforward. Deliberately and artificially inflating projections is clearly dishonest and untruthful.

Objectivity implies free from bias, conflict of interest or undue influence from others. Inflating the forecast would make them biased as the result of undue influence from others.

Acceding to the request from the shareholders would certainly and clearly be a breach of the ICAEW ethical code, and also quite possibly illegal/fraudulent.

Possible steps to deal with this issue include:

- Discussing the request with a line manager and potentially call the ICAEW Ethics helpline for advice and clarification on the most appropriate course of action.

- Explaining to the shareholders that their request is unethical and quite possibly illegal.

- Taking further advice on whether to report their request elsewhere.

Ultimately the accountant may need to resign if the request persists.

Examiner's comments:

Candidates found this question by far the most challenging on the December 2010 paper, possibly reflecting the fact that this was one of the first instances of a question being solely devoted to the 'valuation' area of the syllabus. The question was a clear indication that candidates can expect such questions to require of them, not only accurate calculations, but also detailed commentary on issues surrounding the various valuation methods. It was in this latter area that weaker candidates were exposed.

Weaker candidates often found even the earnings and dividend valuations beyond them. They also failed to reflect the marks attributed to the second part of part 62.1 in the depth of their responses to that part of the question, often making only a very limited commentary on the issues surrounding each valuation method.

Most well-prepared candidates were able to cope comfortably with part 62.2, although the potential impact on eps was a fairly rare inclusion in candidates' answers. It should be noted that whilst 14 marks appear to be available (with a maximum of 8 to be awarded), in reality this was not the case as 'mirror points' (ie making the same point under each heading eg one is cheaper; one is more expensive) would only earn one mark.

Most well-prepared candidates were also able to cope comfortably with this question, and, indeed, there were many instances of full marks being achieved.

63 Fratton plc (June 2011)

			Marks
63.1	(a)	Forward market:	
		Forward rate	1
		Net receipt	1
		Money market:	
		Euro borrowing	1
		Sterling conversion	1
		Interest	1
		Option market:	
		Type of option	1
		Number of contracts	1
		Premium in euros	1
		Premium in sterling	1
		Scenario 1: Option not exercised	1
		Scenario 1: Sterling receipt	1
		Scenario 2: Option exercised	1
		Scenario 2: Gain on option	1
		Scenario 2: Sterling receipt	1
			14
	(b)	Transaction costs	1
		Exact date does not need to be known	2
		Cannot tailor contracts	1
		Hedge inefficiencies	1
		Limited number of currencies	1
		More complex than forwards	1
			7
63.2	(a)	Buy a 3-6 FRA at a fixed rate	1
		Calculation of amount bank to pay Fratton	1
		Payment on the underlying loan	1
		Net payment on the loan	1
			4
	(b)	Sell three month interest rate futures	1
		Number of contracts	1
		Calculation of gain	1
		Futures outcome	1
		Payment in the spot market	1
			5
			30

63.1 (a) Forward market

Bank sells £ at €1.1856/£

Forward rate = €1.1797 (1.1856 – 0.0059)

So €2,960,000/1.1797 = £2,509,112.49

ICAEW

Money market

To hedge a euro receivable, Fratton needs to create a euro liability which, with interest, will exactly equal the receivable in three months' time:

€2,960,000/1.004 = £2,948,207.17

Convert to £ at spot (1.1856) to give £2,486,679.46

Which with three months' interest at 0.2875% gives £2,493,828.66

Options

Fratton should enter into a call option to buy £ at €1.18/£

Number of contracts = €2,960,000/1.18 = £2,508,475/62,500 = 40.14 = 40 contracts

The premium would be €60,000 (0.024 × 62,500 × 40)

Which at spot would cost £50,654.28 (60,000/1.1845)

Scenario 1:

Spot on expiry €1.12/£ - Exercise price €1.18/£ - intrinsic value: nil – exercise? NO

£ receipt at spot = €2,960,000/1.12 = £2,642,857.14 (net £2,592,202.86)

Scenario 2:

Spot on expiry €1.20/£ - Exercise price €1.18/£ - intrinsic value: €0.02 per £ - exercise? YES

Gain on option of €50,000 (0.02 × 62,500 × 40)

Sell €3,010,000/1.20 = £2,508,333.33 (net £2,457,679.05)

(b) **Advantages:**

Transaction costs of futures should be lower and they can be traded

The exact date of receipt or payment of the foreign currency does not need to be known because the futures contract does not have to be closed out until the underlying transaction takes place (subject only to the expiry date of the futures contract)

Disadvantages:

The contracts cannot be tailored to the user's exact requirements

Hedge inefficiencies are caused by standard contract sizes and basis

Only a limited number of currencies are available with futures contracts

The procedure for converting between two currencies neither of which is the $ is more complex with futures compared to a forward contract

63.2 (a) As a borrower Fratton should buy a 3-6 FRA and can thereby fix a borrowing rate of 2.60%

At 3.00% rates have risen, so the bank will pay Fratton £2,500 (2.5m × {3.00%-2.60%} × 3/12). Payment on the underlying loan will be 3% × 2,500,000 × 3/12 = £18,750

Net payment on the loan: £16,250 (18,750 – 2,500) – an effective rate of 2.60%

(b) Fratton will need to sell three-month £ interest rate futures contracts

Fratton will need to sell 5 contracts (2,500,000/500,000 × 3/3)

Sell at 97.20 and buy at 97.00 for a gain of 0.20%

Futures outcome: 0.20% × 500,000 × 3/12 × 5 = £1,250

Payment in the spot market: 2,500,000 × 3% × 3/12 = £18,750 – £1,250 = £17,500 (=2.80%)

Examiner's comments:

This two-part question combined the interest rate and exchange rate risk management elements of the Financial Management syllabus and was generally well answered by the well-prepared candidates. There is now significant evidence that candidate performance in this relatively new area is increasing to the levels seen in other areas of the syllabus. The average mark achieved was 20.3/30 (67.6%).

The first part of the question required candidates to illustrate how they would hedge foreign exchange risk in the scenario set out in the question using the forward market, the money market and the options market. For the most part, this was well answered although weaker candidates often made fundamental errors in the choice of exchange rate in the first part and then often chose the wrong type of option to hedge the foreign exchange exposure.

Part 63.1 (b) of the question required candidates to discuss the advantages and disadvantages of using futures contracts as opposed to forward contracts to hedge foreign exchange risk. For the most part this posed few problems for stronger candidates.

The second part of the question required candidates to illustrate the use of a forward rate agreement to manage interest rate risk. Again, this was generally well answered and confirmed the continuing improvement amongst most candidates in this area of the syllabus.

The final part of the question required candidates to illustrate the use of interest rate futures contracts to manage interest rate risk. The vast majority of candidates scored well on this question, although the most common omission was the identification of the actual interest rate achieved as a result of the transaction.

64   Dayton plc (December 2011)

			Marks
64.1	(a)	Spot rate in six months' time	1.5
		Net receipt	0.5
	(b)	Forward exchange rate	1.5
		Net receipt	0.5
	(c)	Euro borrowings	0.5
		Sterling receivable	1
		Effective forward rate	0.5
	(d)	Premium	1
		If spot rate is €1.14/£	
		Option not exercised	0.5
		Net receipt	0.5
		If spot rate is €1.20/£	
		Option exercised	0.5
		Net receipt	0.5
	(e)	Explanation of interest rate parity	2
		Calculation of interest rate parity suggested rate	1
	(f)	Economic exposure	1
		Translation exposure	1
	(g)	One mark per strategy	max 4
			18
64.2	(a)	Contract value	1
		Number of contracts	0.5
		Sell futures now	0.5
		Futures gain	1
		Overall position	1
	(b)	Efficiency	1
		Basis risk	1
			6
64.3	(a)	3-9 FRA at 2.69%	1
		Future settlement	0.5
		Interest on loan	0.5
		Net payment on loan	0.5
	(b)	Future settlement	0.5
		Interest on loan	0.5
		Net payment on loan	0.5
			4
			28

64.1 (a) €1.1760/£ × 95% = €1.1172/£
€35,000,000/1.1172 = **£31,328,321**

(b) Bank buys € (sells £) at €1.1760 – 0.0026 = €1.1734/£
€35,000,000/1.1734 = **£29,827,851**

(c) Borrow €35,000,000/1.01 = €34,653,465
Convert €34,653,465/1.1760 = £29,467,232 × (1 + 0.01125) = **£29,798,738**
Effective forward rate = €35,000,000/29,798,738 = **€1.1745/£**

(d) The real cost of the up-front premium is £100,000 × 1.01125 = **£101,125**

If the spot rate is €1.14/£
The amount received at spot is €35,000,000/1.14 = £30,701,754 compared to
£29,914,530 under the option so the option will not be exercised
The net receipt will be **£30,600,629**

If the spot rate is €1.20/£
The amount received at the exercise price is €35,000,000/1.17 = £29,914,530
compared to £29,166,667 at spot so the option will be exercised
The net receipt will be **£29,813,405**

(e) The principle of interest rate parity holds that, when foreign exchange markets are in equilibrium, the forward premium or discount between two currencies is reflective of the interest rate differential between the two countries – differences in interest rates are offset by differences between the spot and forward rates of exchange, such that an investor would be indifferent between investing one currency at that country's interest rate or converting the currency at spot into a second currency and investing that second currency at its country's interest rate, whilst selling the proceeds forward on day one.

Using average spot ({bid+offer}/2)} and average interest rates for 6 months, IRP suggests
$1.17475 \times (1.009375(euro)/1.011875(UK)) = 1.17185$
ie. a forward premium of 1.17475 – 1.17185 = 0.0029 or 0.29 cents
Average premium in data given is 0.30 so IRP very nearly holds (which is why the forward and money market hedges give similar results).

(f) Economic exposure is the risk that longer-term exchange rate movements might reduce a firm's international competitiveness or its value.

Translation exposure is the risk that a firm will incur exchange losses when the accounting results of its foreign branches or subsidiaries are translated into the firm's home currency.

(g) 1 International diversification of sales, production, supplies and finance sources

2 Market and promotional management (balancing market risks and potential)

3 Product management decisions (launch, drop, not launch etc in response to actual and anticipated exchange rate changes)

4 Pricing management decisions (in response to actual and anticipated exchange rate changes)

64.2 (a) Value of portfolio as at 31 December = £48,000,000
Futures price of FTSE 100 index = 4,900 Value of each point = £10
Therefore, value of a contract = **£49,000**
Therefore, number of contracts required is 48,000,000/49,000 = **979.6 say 980 contracts**

Futures position:
In December the investor **sells** 980 September contracts @ 4,900
In September the investor **buys** 980 September contracts @ 4,800
Therefore, the drop in price of the FTSE index futures = 100 points
Value of futures gain = 100 × £10 × 980 = **£980,000**

Overall position in September:
Value of portfolio £46,980,000 Gain on futures £980,000
Overall position **£47,960,000**

(b) Efficiency: gain on futures/loss on portfolio = 980,000/1,020,000 × 100 = **96.1%**
The hedge inefficiency arises due to the incidence of basis risk and rounding the number of contracts to a whole number.

64.3 (a) Fulton needs to use a 3–9 FRA at 2.69%
If the rate is 3.5%, the bank will pay Fulton **£12,150** (£3m × {3.5%-2.69%} × 6/12)
Fulton will pay **£52,500** on its loan at the market rate (£3m × 3.5% × 6/12)
Net payment on the loan is **£40,350** (= 2.69%)

(b) If the rate is 1.5%, Fulton will pay the bank **£17,850** (£3m × {1.5%-2.69%} × 6/12)
Fulton will pay **£22,500** on its loan at the market rate (£3m × 1.5% × 6/12)
Net payment on the loan is **£40,350** (= 2.69%)

ICAEW

Examiner's comments:

Performance on this question was generally satisfactory, although as has been the case in the past, it polarised performance between those with a firm grasp of the material (who scored strongly) and a significant minority who have little grasp at all of the mechanics of the subject.

Requirement 64.1 consisted of several parts. In the first part of the question, the majority of candidates betrayed their lack of understanding of 'depreciation' of a currency - a reduction in its purchasing power, not an increase as most candidates suggested when they multiplied the spot rate by 1.05. Part (b) posed less problems for candidates, although a small number continued to add rather than deduct the forward premium. Part (c) was generally well answered. Part (d) however proved more of a challenge. Disappointingly, many candidates chose to address this question as if they were dealing with a traded option rather than an over-the-counter option. The vast majority of candidates also understated the premium at £100,000. In the following part, there was a generally firm grasp of IRP theory although few scripts gained full marks due to a lack of detail and, very often, a failure to answer the precise question asked. There was a very mixed response to part (f) – for the most part either full marks or none at all, whilst part (g) had very few good answers – too many candidates listed a range of short term measures and scored zero marks.

For part 64.2 a surprising number of candidates calculated the value of a single contract incorrectly. In addition, in the final part of the question too many candidates referred to standardised contract sizes (not an issue in this case) rather than basis risk (which was the issue here). The majority of candidates also calculated the hedge efficiency incorrectly, failing to use the approach adopted in the learning materials.

In part 64.3 some candidates let themselves down by either failing to answer the question, which asked for a calculation of interest cash flows and/or working with full-year rather than six-month figures.

65 Sunwin plc (December 2012)

Marking guide

		Marks
65.1 Type of contract	1	
Value of one contract	1	
Number of contracts needed	1	
Premium	1	
If index rises - abandon	1	
Outcome if index rises	1	
Gain if index falls	1	
Outcome if index falls	1	
		8
65.2 (a) Type of contract	1	
Number of contracts	1	
Futures outcome	1	
Net outcome	1	
Effective interest rate	1	
Hedge efficiency	1	
		6
(b) Type of contract	1	
Number of contracts	1	
Premium cost	1	
Case 1 – exercise	0.5	
Case 1 – futures outcome	1	
Case 1 – effective interest rate	2	
Case 2 – do not exercise	0.5	
Case 2 – effective interest rate	2	
		9
(c) 1 mark per point	Max 3	
		26

65.1 Sunwin requires an option to sell – a December put option with an exercise price of 5,000

Portfolio value = £5.6m Exercise price = 5,000
Value of one contract = 5,000 × £10 = £50,000
Number of contracts required = £5.6m/50,000 = 112 contracts
Premium: 70 points × £10 per point × 112 contracts = £78,400

(a) If the index rises to 5,900, the put option gives Sunwin the right to sell @ 5,000, so the option would be abandoned (with zero value)

Overall position:	£
Value of portfolio	6,608,000
Gain on option	–
Less premium	(78,400)
	6,529,600

(b) If the index falls to 4,100, the put option gives Sunwin the right to sell @ 5,000, so the option would be exercised (value = £9,000 {900 × £10} × 112 contracts = £1,008,000)

Overall position:	£
Value of portfolio	4,592,000
Gain on option	1,008,000
Less premium	(78,400)
	5,521,600

65.2 (a) Sunwin needs to sell a 3-month contract
Number of contracts = 4m/0.5m × 9/3 = 24 contracts

Futures outcome:
Selling at the opening rate of 96 and buying at the closing rate of 95 yields a gain of 1%
Therefore 1% × 0.5m × 3/12 × 24 = £30,000

Net outcome:
Spot market £4m × 4.5% × 9/12 = (£135,000) plus the futures receipt of £30,000 = (£105,000)
Effective interest rate 105,000/4m × 12/9 = 3.5%

Hedge efficiency:
Increase in spot rate = 1.5% so increase in interest = £60,000 (1.5% × 4m) × 9/12 = £45,000
So the hedge efficiency = 30,000/45,000 × 100 = 66.7%

(b) Traded interest rate options on futures:
Sunwin requires a March put option with a strike price of 96.25 (100 – 3.75)
The number of contracts required = 4m/0.5m × 9/3 = 24 contracts @ 0.18%
So the premium = 24 × 0.18% × 0.5m × 3/12 = £5,400

Case 1:

Spot price	4.4%	
Futures price	95.31	
Strike price	96.25	
Exercise?	Yes	
Gain on future		0.94% therefore 0.94% × 0.5m × 3/12 × 24 = £28,200
Borrowing cost at spot	£132,000	
Option	(£28,200)	
Premium	£5,400	
Effective interest rate	£109,200/4m × 12/9 = 3.64%	

Case 2:

Spot price	2.1%
Futures price	97.75
Strike price	96.25
Exercise?	No
Gain on future	–
Borrowing cost at spot	£63,000
Option	–
Premium	£5,400
Effective interest rate	£68,400/4m × 12/9 = 2.28%

(c) (1) The time period to expiry of the option – the longer the time to expiry, the more the time value of the option will be

   (2) The volatility of the underlying security price – the more volatile, the greater the chance of the option being 'in the money', which increases the time value of the option

   (3) The general level of interest rates (the time value of money) – the time value of an option reflects the present value of the exercise price

Examiner's comments:

Following its introduction into the syllabus at the last review, this subject area was initially very challenging for many candidates. However, at this sitting and in a reflection of an emerging trend on the paper in more recent sittings, candidates' grasp of the material appears to get stronger and stronger, so much so that it was this question, rather than the traditional NPV question, that provided many candidates with the basis of their pass on the paper.

Most candidates performed strongly on part 65.1 of this question, although where errors were made they primarily related to incorrect calculation of the number of contracts and the premium.

The only real areas of weakness in most candidates' responses to part 65.2 were in their being unable to effectively calculate hedge efficiency (many candidates simply did not even make an attempt to do so) and in the mis-calculation of time-period adjustments and, consequently, premiums. However, overall candidate strength in this area of the syllabus is pleasing to see.

66 Atherton plc and Tyldesley Inc (June 2010)

				Marks
66.1	(a)	One mark per well explained point	max 5	
	(b)	Not to hedge:		
		Illustration of each outcome using both spot rates	2	
		Forward contract:		
		Forward rate	1	
		Illustration of outcome from forward contract	1	
		OTC option:		
		Type of option	1	
		Exercise the option – illustration of outcome	1	
		Let the option lapse – illustration of outcome	1	
	(c)	One mark per method	max 4	
				16
66.2	(a)	**Scenario 1:**		
		Number of contracts	2	
		Gain per £	1	
		Total gain	1	
		Net cost	1	
		Scenario 2:		
		Loss per £	1	
		Total loss	1	
		Net cost	1	
	(b)	One mark per well explained point	max 2	
				10
				26

66.1 (a) (1) Costs (direct and implicit)

(2) Materiality of the exposure

(3) Attitude to risk may lead the firm to decide to leave the upside potential open

(4) Portfolio effect

(5) If shareholders are fully diversified, their exposure to systematic risk will not be affected, so there will be no benefits for them from hedging

(b) (1) 8,000,000/1.1980 = £6,677,796
(2) 8,000,000/1.1420 = £7,005,254

Forward contract: Forward rate €1.1608
8,000,000/1.1608 = £6,891,799

OTC Option:

Need to sell € so a put option is required at a premium of £1.25 per €100 = £100,000

(1) If spot is €1.1980/£, exercise the option - 8,000,000/1.1750 = £6,808,511, net £6,708,511

(2) If spot is €1.1420/£, let the option lapse - 8,000,000/1.1420 = £7,005,254, net £6,905,254

(c) (1) Appropriate choice of invoice currency

(2) Matching payments and receipts (eg. creating payables and receivables in same currency)

(3) Matching assets and liabilities (eg. creating overdraft borrowing in respect of a receivable)

(4) Leading and lagging payments

(5) Maintaining currency accounts

66.2 (a) Futures price \$1.6436/£ Contract size £62,500 Current spot \$1.6520/£

So needs to buy £20,000,000/62,500 = 320 contracts

Scenario 1:

Buy 320 contracts @	1.6436
In 6 months sell 320 contracts @	1.6610
Gain per £	0.0174
Total gain (320 × 62,500 × 0.0174)	\$348,000
Purchase of £20m in 6 months	\$33,260,000 (20m × 1.6630)
Net cost	\$32,912,000

Scenario 2:

Buy 320 contracts @	1.6436
In 6 months sell 320 contracts @	1.6400
Loss per £	0.0036
Total loss (320 × 62,500 × 0.0036)	(\$72,000)
Purchase of £20m in 6 months	\$32,840,000 (20m × 1.6420)
Net cost	\$32,912,000

(b) (1) Hedge inefficiency caused by basis risk

(2) The fact that the buyer of the contract is tied into buying the £ even if the purchase does not proceed (which appears to be a real possibility) – a currency option would appear to be a much better option in this scenario

Examiner's comments:

The average mark of 65.8% seen on this question was much in line with that of WT2. One pleasing aspect was that there was less polarisation in performance apparent in the responses to the question than has been evident at previous sittings – candidates are clearly more comfortable overall with this area of the syllabus than has previously been the case.

In the opening section of the question most candidates coped well with the identification of reasons why a firm may choose not to hedge its foreign exchange exposure, although attitude to risk was the most frequently omitted item by weaker candidates.

The majority of candidates clearly had a firm grasp of the workings of both forward and option contracts (although there was evidence of continuing confusion amongst weaker candidates of the distinction between a put option and a call option). Most candidates also had a good knowledge of the operational techniques available to a firm to hedge its foreign exchange exposure.

Not surprisingly, weaker candidates found the second section of the question more challenging, with common errors arising in the following areas:

(1) Failure to calculate correctly the precise number of futures contracts required in the scenario outlined in the question;

(2) Confusion regarding whether the futures contracts would be bought or sold;

(3) Confusion between whether gains or losses would arise on the futures contracts;

(4) Failure to recognise that the firm still needs to buy sterling in the spot market at the conclusion of the transaction.

Each of these failings relates to fundamental knowledge in this area of the syllabus and whilst there was a welcome improvement in overall performance on this topic, it is clear that the weakest candidates tend not to have mastered these basics at all and so struggle to pick up marks.

67 Strauss Cook plc (March 2010)

Marking guide

			Marks
67.1	Type of option	1	
	Number of contracts	1	
	Option exercised	2.5	
	Cost of option	1.5	
	Decrease in portfolio value	1	
			7
67.2	Gain on future	2	
	Decrease in portfolio value	1	
	Different values of FTSE 100 index and futures contract	2	
			5
67.3 (a)	Type of option	1	
	Number of contracts	1	
	Interest received	0.5	
	Future trade	2	
	Net interest received	1.5	
(b)	The implications of using an FRA – 1 mark per point	Max 5	
			11
			23

67.1 Strauss Cook would need to buy put option contracts as follows:

$$\frac{£6,300,000}{(4,200 \times £10)} = 150 \text{ contracts}$$

	(a) Portfolio & Index rose		(b) Portfolio & Index fell
Portfolio value at 1 March	£6,375,000		£6,150,000
Option exercised	Not exercised	([4200-4100] ×150 × £10)	150,000
			6,300,000
Cost of option (67 × 150 × £10)	(100,500)		(100,500)
	6,274,500		6,199,500
Current value of portfolio	6,300,000		6,300,000
Decrease in portfolio value	£25,500		£100,500

67.2 (a) Number of contracts = $\frac{£6,300,000}{(4,130 \times £10)}$ = 153 contracts (rounded)

Portfolio value at 1 March	£6,150,000
Gain on future ([4130-4100] × 153 × £10)	45,900
	6,195,900
Current value of portfolio	6,300,000
Decrease in portfolio value	104,100

(b) Not 100% efficient because of basis ie 1 Feb values of FTSE100 index and futures contract are different.

67.3 (a)   Strauss Cook would need to buy March call option contracts as follows:

$$\frac{£2,500,000 \times 6/3}{£500,000} = 10 \text{ contracts}$$

Interest received = £2,500,000 × 4.5% × ½	£56,250
Future trade ([95.80-95.00] × 1/100 × £2,500,000 × 6/12)	10,000
Cost of call option (0.03% × £2,500,000 × 6/12)	(375)
Net interest received	£65,875

(b)   A Forward Rate Agreement (FRA) would allow Strauss Cook to set a fixed rate of interest and is therefore similar to a forward contract. It would run for an agreed period of time, in this case six months. If the actual interest rate is lower than the rate agreed then the bank would pay the lender (Strauss Cook) the difference. If the actual rate is higher then the company would pay the bank the difference. So, in the latter case, an FRA would remove any upside potential for the company.

Options protect against downside (by exercising) but can participate in upside (by abandoning).

Examiner's comments:

This question had the second highest average mark on the paper and again was mostly done well.

It was based on three small scenarios and tested candidates' understanding of risk management for traded share options, stock index futures and traded interest rate options.

Part 67.1 was worth 7 marks and required candidates to calculate the outcome of a company hedging against a fall in the value of its share portfolio using traded index options. Part 67.2 for 5 marks required candidates to hedge the portfolio by using index futures. Part 67.3 made up the remaining 11 marks and was based around a company wishing to invest a large sum of money and to hedge against a fall in interest rates using traded options. Candidates were asked to calculate the outcome of the hedge and then to explain the implications of using an FRA instead.

In part 67.1 most candidates produced good answers. However, a number of them failed to correctly calculate the cost of the option and too few candidates calculated the net outcome of the hedge.

Part 67.2 was also generally well answered, but the common errors were the incorrect calculation of the number of contracts required, and a number of candidates used options rather than futures. In addition too few candidates were able to adequately explain the effectiveness of the hedge.

The numerical element of part 67.3 was done well. Candidates typically lost marks by failing to identify the options correctly, ie that they were March call options. The implications for using an FRA were generally well done.

68 Springfield plc and Woodhouse plc (December 2010)

				Marks
68.1	(a)	Each reason stated (1 mark)	max 5	
	(b)	Calculation of quality spread differential	1	
		Calculation of Springfield's borrowing cost	2	
		Calculation of Faversham's borrowing cost	2	
	(c)	Identification of disadvantaged company and explanation	2	
	(d)	Counterparty, basis, transparency risks (1 mark each)	max 2	
				14
68.2		Date of contract	1	
		Type of option	1	
		Strike price	1	
		Number of contracts	1	
		Calculation of premium	1	
		Whether to exercise at each price	1	
		Outcome of option position	2	
		Amount to borrow	1	
		Net position	1	
		Effective interest rate	1	
				11
				25

68.1 (a) (1) To obtain a lower rate of interest on its preferred type of debt by exploiting the quality spread differential between two counterparties

(2) To achieve a better match of assets and liabilities

(3) To access interest rate markets that might otherwise be closed to the firm (or only accessible at excessive cost)

(4) To hedge interest rate exposure by converting a floating rate commitment to a fixed rate commitment (or vice versa)

(5) To restructure the interest rate profile of existing debts (avoiding new loans/fees)

(6) To speculate on the future course of interest rates

(7) They are available for longer terms than other methods of hedging interest rate exposure

(b) Springfield has a comparative advantage in floating rate borrowing, whilst Faversham has a comparative advantage in fixed rate borrowing – so Springfield should borrow £20m at LIBOR + 2.25%, whilst Faversham should borrow £20m at 5.50%.

The quality spread differential = 1.00% - 0.75% = 0.25% (saving 0.125% each)

Springfield:

Pay LIBOR + 2.25%; Pay Faversham 5.50%; therefore Receive from Faversham LIBOR + 1.375% - net borrowing cost 6.375% (saving 0.125% on its own fixed rate borrowing cost)

Faversham:

Pay 5.50% fixed, Pay Springfield LIBOR + 1.375%, Receive from Springfield 5.50% - net borrowing cost LIBOR + 1.375% (saving 0.125% on its own floating rate borrowing cost)

(c) Springfield will be disadvantaged as it has contracted to make fixed rate payments under the interest rate swap agreement and will, therefore, not see its payments benefit from the reduction in interest rates during the term of the swap agreement.

(d) The risk that the other counterparty to the swap agreement will default on their commitment before completion of the swap agreement

The risk of unfavourable changes in market interest rates after entering into the swap

Transparency risk: the risk that the impact of the swap transaction will be to undermine the clarity and transparency of the firm's financial statements

68.2 Which contract?   March

Which type?	A put option (the right to sell a future)
Strike price?	95.25 (sets a cap at 4.75%, as required)
How many?	6m/500,000 × 6/3 = 24 contracts
Premium?	At 95.25 = 0.12% × 24 × £500,000 × 3/12 = £3,600

Closing prices	(a)	(b)
Benchmark	5.4%	3.1%
Futures price	94.30	96.70

Option market outcome

Strike price (right to sell at)	95.25	95.25
Closing price (buy at)	94.30	96.70
Exercise?	Yes	No
Gain on exercise	0.95%	–
Outcome of option position	£28,500	–
(0.95% × £500,000 × 3/12 × 24)		

Net position

	(a)	(b)
Borrow £6m at benchmark rate	£162,000	£93,000
(£6m × 6/12 × 5.4% or 3.1%)		
Option	(£28,500)	
Premium	£3,600	£3,600
	£137,100	£96,600
Effective interest rate	137,100/6m × 12/6 × 100	96,600/6m × 12/6 × 100
	= 4.57%	= 3.22%

Examiner's comments:

Although the majority of candidates performed well on this question, it was the question that most polarised performance between strong and weak candidates, particularly in the final part of the question.

Too often among weaker candidates, responses were restricted to issues surrounding the type of interest rate achieved (fixed or floating) and the savings in borrowing costs, but the use of interest rate swaps for both hedging and speculation were often overlooked, as was the fact that swaps are the best way of hedging and speculating in the longer term.

The most common error in 68.1 (b) was the failure of candidates to structure the swap around the stated fixed interest leg of the swap – this instruction in the question was often ignored. Also, weaker candidates failed to correctly calculate the potential savings from such a swap.

Question 68.2 polarised performance between those with a firm grasp of the principles and methodology and those who clearly had not studied the learning materials in the required depth. Principal failings among weaker candidates were an uncertainty as to which month's contract to enter into; failure to select a put option; and failure to calculate the premium or number of contracts correctly, invariably due to misunderstanding surrounding the correct adjustments for the number of months involved in each case. This latter point was also relevant to common miscalculations of the effective interest rate. There were also quite a number of instances of candidates failing to select a specific choice of option and using that specific choice to illustrate to management the outcome that could be achieved. Rather, some candidates saw fit to cover every possible course of action by doing calculations for each one, and whilst this did earn some marks where there was evidence that candidates were aware of the methodology, it did not earn full marks as it failed completely to provide any specific advice or recommendation to management as to the precisely appropriate course of action to pursue in the situation set out in the question.

69 Padd Shoes Ltd (March 2014)

			Marks
69.1 (a)	Sterling receipt if rupee weakens by 1%	2	
(b)	Option	2.5	
(c)	Forward contract	2.5	
(d)	Money market hedge	3	
			10
69.2	Relevant discussion	8	
			8
69.3	Government stability	1	
	Political and business ethics	1	
	Economic stability	1	
	Import restrictions	1	
	Remittance restrictions	1	
	Special taxes, regulations for foreign companies	1	
	Trading risks – physical risk, credit risk, liquidity risk etc	1	
	Maximum		5
69.4	Option	2	
	FRA	2	
	No hedge	1	
	Recommendation	2	
			7
			30

69.1

	Sterling receipt at spot rate =		$\dfrac{INR\ 200,000,000}{95.4930}$	**£2,094,394**
(a)	**Sterling receipt if rupee weakens by 1%**	$\dfrac{INR\ 200,000,000}{(95.4930 \times 1.01)}$	$\dfrac{INR\ 200,000,000}{96.4479}$	**£2,073,658**
(b)	**Option** (@ exercise price)	$\dfrac{INR\ 200,000,000}{95.5500}$	£2,093,145	
	Less cost		(£8,000)	
				£2,085,145
(c)	**Forward contract**	$\dfrac{INR\ 200,000,000}{(95.4930 + 0.2265)}$	$\dfrac{INR\ 200,000,000}{95.7195}$	£2,089,438
	Less cost		(£4,500)	
				£2,084,938

(d) Money Market Hedge

Borrow in rupees	$\dfrac{INR\ 200,000,000}{1.012}$	INR 197,628,450	
Convert @ spot rate	$\dfrac{INR\ 197,628,450}{95.4930}$	£2,069,560	
Lend in sterling		£2,069,560 × 1.008	**£2,086,116**

69.2 Padd's directors' attitude to risk is important.

The interest rates and the forward rate discount suggest that the rupee will weaken. A weaker rupee will produce less sterling on conversion, so hedging may be worthwhile.

The worst case scenario from 69.1 is if the rupee weakens by 1% over the next three months.

The MMH (which would give a fixed sterling amount) gives the highest sterling figure, followed closely by the OTC option, with which there is some flexibility for the directors.

The forward contract (which would also give a fixed sterling amount) produces a comparatively poor sterling remittance. It has a high arrangement fee.

Were sterling to remain at spot rate then this would give the best outcome and a strengthening of the rupee would enhance the sterling receipt even more.

69.3 Government stability
Political and business ethics
Economic stability
Import restrictions
Remittance restrictions
Special taxes, regulations for foreign companies
Trading risks – physical risk, credit risk, liquidity risk etc

69.4

LIBOR + 1	4%	7%
Option		
Exercise?	**Indifferent**	**Yes**
Rate	(4%)	(4%)
Premium	(0.75%)	(0.75%)
	(4.75%)	(4.75%)
Annual interest payment (on £8.5m)	(£403,750)	(£403,750)
FRA		
Pay at LIBOR +1	(4%)	(7%)
(Payment to)/receipt from bank	(0.5%)	2.5%
	(4.5%)	(4.5%)
Annual interest payment (on £8.5m)	(£382,500)	(£382,500)
No hedge		
Pay at LIBOR + 1	(4%)	(7%)
Annual interest payment (on £8.5m)	(£340,000)	(£595,000)

If LIBOR is 3% then it's better not to hedge and at 6% the FRA seems to be the cheapest option.

It also depends on the board's attitude to risk.

The FRA eliminates down side risk (rates rising) as well as upside risk (rates falling).

Examiner's comments

The average mark for this question was the highest in the paper, equated to a clear pass and so, overall, was done well.

This was a four-part question that tested the financial risk element of the syllabus.

The scenario was based on a UK footwear manufacturer/exporter and included relevant exchange rates and interest rates. The question tested (a) candidates' understanding of foreign exchange risk management, (b) the more general risks associated with trading overseas and (c) how to hedge against interest rate movements.

Part 69.1 for 10 marks required candidates to calculate (a) the impact of a strengthening of sterling on a proposed export contract and (b) the outcome of three possible hedging strategies for that contract. Part 69.2 was worth 8 marks and here candidates had to advise the company's board as to which hedging technique was preferable (if any), based on their calculations in part 69.1. Part 69.3 for 5 marks asked candidates to advise the company of the risks (non-currency) to consider when trading abroad.

Finally, in part 69.4 for 7 marks, candidates had to recommend whether or not the company, which has borrowed a large amount, should hedge against the impact of interest rate movements on that loan.

Part 69.1 was very similar to past exam questions but despite this many candidates did not get all of the calculation marks available. Typical errors were (a) using a call option rather than a put and (b) ignoring contract costs.

The discussion in 69.2 was, in many cases, brief and very basic for 8 marks.

Part 69.3 was, as expected, answered well.

Part 69.4 caused many students difficulty. Too few of them produced sufficient workings to enable them to produce suitable recommendations.

70 Stelvio Ltd (June 2014)

Marking guide

			Marks
70.1 (a)	**Forward contract:**		
	Forward rates	1.5	
	Cost of payment	0.5	
	Currency futures:		
	Sell £ on futures exchange	1	
	Number of contacts to sell	1	
	Profit	2	
	Net payment	1	
	OTC option:		
	Option premium	1	
	Total cost with interest	1	
	Spot price on 30 Sep	1	
	Cost of payment	1	
			11
(b)	Discussion of advantages and disadvantages	9	
			9
(c)	Explanation of whether to hedge	4	
			4
70.2 (a)	Interest rate differentials	2	
	Rates achieved through swap	2	
	Cash flows	1	
			Max 4
(b)	Difference in interest rates	1	
	LIBOR	1	
			2
			30

70.1 (a) The forward contract:

The forward rates are calculated by deducting the premium from the spot rate:

Spot rates $/£	1.6025
Forward premium	0.0021
Forward rates $/£	1.6004

The payment will cost $940,000/$1.6004 = £587,353

Currency futures:

Since we need to buy $ we will SELL currency futures contracts (ie Selling £ on the futures exchange). The number of contracts to sell: ($940,000/$1.5995)/£62,500 = 9.40 contracts.

Rounding the number of contracts to 9 (or 10)

On 30 September the futures will be closed out and bought at $1.5005. This will result in a profit of ($1.5995 – $1.5005) × (£62,500 × 9) = $55,688.

Net payment ($940,000 – 55,688)/$1.5002 = £589,463

Over the counter call option:

Option premium = ($940,000) × 4p = £37,600
The total cost with interest = £37,600 × (1 + 0.06 × 4/12) = £38,352.
The spot price on 30 September is $/£1.5002 so Stelvio would exercise its option.
The cost of the payment would be ($940,000/$1.6100) + £38,352 = £622,202

(b) The forward contract and futures contracts both lock Stelvio into an exchange rate and do not allow for upside potential.

Forwards:

Tailored specifically for Stelvio
However there is no secondary market
Currency futures:
Not tailored so one has to round the number of contracts
Requires a margin to be deposited at the exchange
Need for liquidity if margin calls are made
However there is a secondary market
OTC currency options:
The options are expensive
There is no secondary market
However the options allow Stelvio to exploit upside potential and protect downside risk

(c) Students should mention interest rate parity, purchasing power parity and expectations theory. The forward rate is an unbiased predictor of the future spot rate. Therefore Fred Hughes (FH) could lose or gain depending on how the spot price moves, he cannot be confident in estimating the exposure. FH's attitude to risk could also be mentioned and that, as Millar once stated, 'not to hedge is to speculate'.

70.2 (a) First it is necessary to calculate the interest rate differentials:

	Stelvio	Zeta	Differentials
Fixed rates	5%	3%	2%
Floating rates	LIBOR + 3%	LIBOR + 2%	1%
	Net differential		1%
	This net differential will be shared		0.5% each

The interest rates that can be achieved through the swap are:

	Stelvio	Zeta
The fixed market rate for Stelvio	5%	–
The floating market rate for Zeta	–	LIBOR + 2%
Less the differential	0.5%	0.5%
Rates achieved through the swap	4.5%	LIBOR + 1.5%

Cash flows would be: LIBOR from Zeta to Stelvio and fixed of 1.5% from Stelvio to Zeta

(b) If LIBOR remains at 0.60% without the swap Stelvio would pay 0.60% + 3% = 3.6%
With the swap Stelvio would be paying 4.5%
LIBOR will have to rise to 4.5% – 3% = 1.5% for the swap to breakeven in interest terms.

Examiner's comments

This was a five-part question which tested the candidates' understanding of the risk management element of the syllabus. In part 70.1 of the question the scenario was that a company had not hedged foreign exchange rate risk before and the managing director was considering using certain techniques to hedge. However he was not convinced that it was necessary and felt that he could estimate his exposure by looking at forward rates. In part 70.2 of the question candidates were required to demonstrate hedging the interest rate risk of a long-term loan.

Part 70.1(a) was well answered by many candidates. However, it was disappointing to note the following common errors made by a large minority of candidates on what should have been very straightforward, well rehearsed calculations which have been examined many times before: using the incorrect rate to calculate the number of futures contracts; making the incorrect decision on whether to buy or sell the contracts at the current date; incorrectly using techniques applicable to interest rate futures when dealing with currency futures; offsetting the gain on futures in $ against the £ payment; omitting the interest on the OTC options premium, which is payable upfront; treating the OTC option as a traded option and in some cases applying the currency futures contract size to the OTC currency option.

Part 70.1(b) was well answered by many candidates, however easy knowledge marks were often missed and it is estimated that 2 to 3 very basic marks were lost by weaker candidates.

In part 70.1(c), weaker candidates only described interest rate parity and purchasing power parity and made no reference to the scenario of the question and the managing director's views. As expected this was a discriminator.

Part 70.2(a) was well answered by many candidates but again weaker candidates lost 2 to 3 basic marks by not being able to calculate the swap gain and revised borrowing rates. These were basic calculations examined many times before.

Part 70.2(b) was well answered by the better candidates and was, as expected, a discriminator.

71 JEK Computing Ltd (September 2014)

			Marks
71.1	Exchange rate % change	1	
	Estimated spot rate 31/12/X4	1	2
			2
71.2 (a)	Sterling receipt at estimated spot rate at 31/12/X4	2	
(b)	Forward contract	2	8
	Money market hedge	3	8
	Option	3	8
			Max 9
71.3	Outcomes	3	8
	MMH and forward contract give best outcomes	3	8
	Advise based on whether JEK is prepared to risk £ weakening	3	8
			Max 8
71.4	Forward exchange contract	2	
	Money market hedge	2	
	Currency option	2	
			6
71.5	Interest rate parity explanation	2	
	Forward rate of exchange and comment	3	
			5
			30

71.1

Exchange rate (€/£)	30 June 20X4	1.1150 – 1.1463
	30 September 20X4	1.1832 – 1.2165
	Change	0.0682 – 0.0702

% change (three months) $\dfrac{0.0702}{1.1463}$ 6.12%

Estimated spot rate at 31/12/X4 1.2165×1.0612 1.2909

71.2 (a)

Sterling receipt at estimated spot rate at 31/12/X4 $\dfrac{€15,109,000}{1.2909}$ **£11,704,237**

(b)

Forward contract $\dfrac{€15,109,000}{(1.2165-0.0020)}$ $\dfrac{€15,109,000}{1.2145}$ £12,440,510

less : Cost $15,109,000 \times £0.002$ (£30,218)

     £12,410,292

Money Market Hedge

Borrow in euros $\dfrac{€15,109,000}{1.0085}$ €14,981,655

Convert @ spot rate $\dfrac{€14,981,655}{1.2165}$ £12,315,376

Lend in sterling $£12,315,376 \times 1.008$ **£12,413,899**

	€15,109,000	
Option (a <u>put</u> option @ exercise price)	$\dfrac{€15,109,000}{1.2150}$	£12,435,391
<u>less</u> : Cost 15,109,000 × £0.012		(£181,308)
		£12,254,083

71.3

Outcomes (in order)	£
Spot rate at 30/9/X4 (as per question)	12,420,000
Money Market Hedge	12,413,899
Forward contract	12,410,292
OTC option	12,254,083
Estimated spot rate at 31/12/X4	11,704,237

The best outcome is if the current spot rate does not alter. The worst is if sterling continues to strengthen at 2% per month and given the lower margin, the contract may make a loss as the receipt would be significantly less than £12.42m. However, interest rates suggest that sterling will weaken (forward rate premium), which would be of benefit to JEK (higher sterling receipt), but the results are all still below the £12.42m.

The MMH and the forward contract give the best outcomes, but the latter has expensive (fixed) costs (£0.002/€). The option has a very high fixed cost (£0.012/€), but it may be that sterling will weaken and it could be abandoned, to JEK's benefit.

If JEK's board is prepared to risk that sterling will weaken then it would be best not to hedge as none of the hedging methods produces £12.42m ie they all result in a reduction of, or elimination of, an already low margin. If not, the MMH would be the best option albeit with a reduced margin but hopefully this can be recovered from the follow-on contracts potentially available.

71.4 Forward exchange contract (FC)

If JEK's bid is not successful, but the company has signed up to a forward exchange contract, then JEK will have an obligation to sell €15.109 in three months' time. It will therefore have to buy that sum of euros, which, if the pound has weakened, will cost an increased amount of sterling.

Money market hedge (MMH)

JEK would have to repay the euro borrowing at 31 December 20X4, but would need to convert this back from sterling.

Any profit or loss on FC or MMH depends on the spot rate on 31 December 20X4.

Currency option - at worst, this would not be taken up, but JEK would incur the £181,308 cost. JEK may exercise option if profitable to do so on 31 December 20X4 – this depends on spot rate at that date.

71.5 The principle of interest rate parity (IRP) means that if an investor places money into a currency with a high interest rate s/he will be no better off after conversion back into their domestic currency using a forward contract than if they had left the money invested at the domestic interest rate.

$$\text{Average spot rate} \times \frac{1 + \text{Average euro interest rate}}{1 + \text{Average sterling interest rate}} = \text{Forward contract rate}$$

$$1.19985 \times \frac{1.0075}{1.00925} = 1.1977$$

Average forward contract premium is 0.00225 and (1.19985 – 0.00225) = 1.1976

As these two rates are almost identical it would appear that IRP is working.

Examiner's comments

The average mark for this question was the lowest in the paper and equated to a marginal 'fail' and so, overall, was not done well.

This was a five-part question that tested the financial risk element of the syllabus.

The scenario was based on a UK computer services company which was tendering for the sale of a euro contract and its board was considering hedging against a weakening of the euro despite having not yet won the tender. The question tested candidates' understanding of (a) foreign exchange risk management and (b) the principle of interest rate parity.

Part 71.1 for two marks required candidates to estimate a future spot rate based on recent changes. Part 71.2 for nine marks required them to calculate the company's sterling receipt from the tender contract based on three hedging strategies. In part 71.3 for eight marks candidates had to advise the company's board as to the advantages/disadvantages of each of the strategies, based on their calculations in part 71.2, assuming that the tender bid was successful. In part 71.4 they had to explain the implications for the company if the tender bid was unsuccessful. Finally, for part 71.5 candidates were required to explain the principles of interest rate parity, making use of the interest and forward contract rates given in the question.

Foreign exchange risk management is regularly tested in the examination, but despite this many candidates did not get all of the calculation marks available. In part 71.1 the weaker scripts failed to calculate the growth rate or applied it (2% per month) once, but not three times as required.

In part 71.2, as expected, most candidates did well, but quite a few used, erroneously, the estimated spot rate from part 71.1 rather than the current spot rate given in the question. Many candidates failed to identify the OTC currency option as a put and many also treated it as a traded option.

Part 71.3 was not done well and too often candidates relied on textbook theory rather than referring to the figures calculated.

In general part 71.4 was also done poorly and too few candidates were able to explain the implications of losing the tender bid.

Overall the responses to part 71.5 were good, but many candidates used annual rather than quarterly interest rates in their calculations.

72 Mayo plc (December 2008)

		Marks
72.1 1 – 2 marks per valid point		max 6
72.2 Calculations	max 2	
Hedging using futures contracts	max 2	
		4
72.3 (a) Number of contracts	0.5	
Target interest receipt	1	
Yield from 3 month deposits	1	
Gains from futures price movement	1.5	
(b) Cash flows: Mayo	2	
Cash flows: Clare	2	
		8
72.4 (a) Interest payments and receipts:		
Mayo	1.5	
Clare	1.5	
(b) Comments	max 2	
		max 4
		22

72.1 Interest rate futures contracts offer a means of hedging against the risk of adverse interest rate movements. If you buy an interest rate futures contract, you buy the entitlement to receive interest; if you sell an interest rate futures contract, you sell the promise to make interest payments. Buying an interest rate futures contract, therefore, equates to lending, whilst selling an interest rate futures contract equates to borrowing.

An interest rate futures contract is effectively a binding, standardised forward rate agreement – similar in effect but with conditions, amounts and terms which are standardised. As a result, they cannot always be matched precisely with a specific interest rate exposure, not least because a number of whole contracts must be bought or sold (based on the standard contract size) and because of the effects of 'basis'.

Interest rate futures contracts represent interest receivable or payable on notional lending or borrowing for a three-month period beginning on a standard future date eg the end of March, June, September or December for LIFFE contracts. The notional period of lending or borrowing starts when the contract expires eg at the end of March or the end of June.

Interest rate futures are priced at 100 – the three-month interest rate contracted for.

In this particular situation, as a depositor (ie. lender) Mayo can hedge against the possibility of interest rates falling by buying 70 March sterling interest rate futures contracts now at the prevailing market price and selling futures on the date that the actual deposit (lending) begins ie. the end of March. If interests rates do fall, Mayo will suffer a loss of interest income on the actual deposit but this will be offset by the gain on the futures contract, whose price will have risen in line with the fall in market interest rates.

72.2 To hedge the deposit, Mayo should buy 70 contracts now and sell 70 contracts at the end of March. If the current deposit interest rate is 4.75%, then Mayo's target interest receipt will be £415,625 (£35m × 4.75% × 3/12).

If the deposit interest rate at the end of March is 3.50% (a fall of 1.25%), the three-month deposit with the bank from the end of March will only yield £306,250 (£35m × 3.5% × 3/12), which is a shortfall of £109,375.

However, assuming that the futures price has converged to equal the spot interest rate at the end of March (ie. the futures price moves from 95.00 to 96.50) this will give Mayo a gain of 1.50%.

The gain from selling 70 interest rate futures contracts at the higher price is £131,250 (£0.5m × 1.50% × 3/12 × 70), which more than compensates for the shortfall in interest on the actual deposit (the excess compensation being due to the effects of 'basis').

72.3 (a) Mayo has a comparative advantage in fixed rate but is looking for a floating rate obligation, whilst Clare has a comparative advantage in floating rate but requires a fixed rate obligation.

The quality spread differential is 0.7% (1.10 – 0.4) so, net of the swap bank's fee, the potential gain from the interest rate swap is 0.5% of which Mayo will take 0.3% and Clare 0.2%.

Therefore, Mayo should raise the debt finance at a fixed rate of 6.00% and pay LIBOR to the swap bank, whilst Clare should raise the debt finance at a floating rate of LIBOR + 1.40% and receive LIBOR from the swap bank.

As a consequence, if Clare then pays a fixed rate of 5.50% on the notional principal of £35m to the swap bank and the swap bank pays just 5.30% to Mayo, the swap bank achieves its fee of 0.2% of the notional principal, whilst Mayo achieves a saving of 0.3% on its current floating rate (LIBOR + 6.00% – 5.30% = LIBOR + 0.7%) and Clare achieves a saving of 0.2% on its current fixed rate (5.5% – LIBOR + LIBOR + 1.4% = 6.90%).

(b) In the first year of the swap agreement, the cash flows of the two companies will be as follows:

Mayo

Interest paid on fixed rate loan:	£2,100,000 (6.00% × £35,000,000)
LIBOR paid to swap bank:	£2,012,500 (5.75% × £35,000,000)
Interest received from swap bank:	£1,855,000 (5.30% × £35,000,000)
Net interest cost:	£2,257,500 which represents a rate of LIBOR + 0.7%

Clare

Interest paid on floating rate loan:	£2,502,500 (7.15% × £35,000,000)
LIBOR received from swap bank:	£2,012,500 (5.75% × £35,000,000)
Interest paid to swap bank:	£1,925,000 (5.50% × £35,000,000)
Net interest cost:	£2,415,000 which represents a rate of 6.90%

72.4 (a) If 12-month LIBOR has fallen by 1.4% and was to stay at that lower level for the remainder of the swap agreement, the annual interest payments and receipts for each company will be as follows:

Mayo

Interest paid on fixed rate loan:	£2,100,000 (6.00% × £35,000,000)
LIBOR paid to swap bank:	£1,522,500 (4.35% × £35,000,000)
Interest received from swap bank:	£1,855,000 (5.30% × £35,000,000)
Net interest cost:	£1,767,500 which still represents a rate of LIBOR+0.7%

Clare

Interest paid on floating rate loan:	£2,012,500 (5.75% × £35,000,000)
LIBOR received from swap bank:	£1,522,500 (4.35% × £35,000,000)
Interest paid to swap bank:	£1,925,000 (5.50% × £35,000,000)
Net interest cost:	£2,415,000 which represents a rate of 6.90% as before

(b) As regards Mayo, the company is now saving annual interest costs of £490,000, so will not regret its entry into the swap agreement. However, with regard to Clare, the company has made no savings in annual interest costs against a background of falling interest rates and so may regret its decision to have entered into the swap agreement.

Examiner's comments:

Performance overall was satisfactory on this question with the majority of candidates scoring well in the first section, although the second half of the question on interest rate swaps served to polarise performance once again.

Most candidates found the 'knowledge' section of the question (section 72.1) to their liking and for the most part good marks were scored.

The strong performance generally continued in section 72.2, although a common error was for some candidates to ignore the figures presented to them (which created an imperfect hedge) and seek to manufacture a position where the gain on the futures contract exactly matched the interest shortfall on the deposit.

Section 72.3, together with section 72.4, acted once again to polarise candidate performance. It was rather disappointing how many candidates were unable to calculate correctly the potential saving from the swap (simply the difference between the fixed rate difference and the floating rate difference), but even more disappointing was how many ignored the instruction in the question (emphasised in bold) that the floating rate leg of the swap was to be set at LIBOR. This information meant that having established where comparative advantage lay, only the fixed rate leg of the swap (5.3% and 5.5%) remained to be calculated, yet weaker candidates often lost most of the marks for this section of the question.

Performance on section 72.4 of the question was, in part, a reflection of accuracy in the previous section, although many candidates were able to grasp the differential impact of the swap on the two firms.

73 Brampton plc (June 2013)

			Marks

73.1 (a) No hedging:
Rates remain unchanged:

H1		1
H2		1

Rates rise to 5.00%

H1		1
H2		1

Rates fall to 1.50%

H1		1
H2		1

(b) Interest rate options:
Cost of premiums:

H1		2
H2		2

Rates remain unchanged:		1

Rates rise to 5.00%:

H1		2
H2		1.5

Rates fall to 1.50%:

H1		1
H2		2.5

(c) Forward rate agreements:
For all three scenarios:

H1		1
H2		1

	20
73.2 Differences between interest rate futures and forward agreements	7
	7
	27

73.1 (a) No hedging

Rates remain unchanged:
H1 - 3.25% × 40m × 6/12 debt = (650,000)
H2 - 3.25% × 70m × 6/12 deposit = 1,137,500
Net interest received = £487,500

Rates rise to 5.00%
H1 - 5.00% × 40m × 6/12 debt = (1,000,000)
H2 - 5.00% × 70m × 6/12 deposit = 1,750,000
Net interest received = £750,000

Rates fall to 1.50%
H1 - 1.50% × 40m × 6/12 debt = (300,000)
H2 - 1.50% × 70m × 6/12 deposit = 525,000
Net interest received = £225,000

(b) **Interest Rate Options**

H1

Take out September put option (right to borrow) @ 96.75 (160 contracts {40m/0.5m × 2})
Premium: 160 × £500,000 × 0.42% × 3/12 = £84,000

H2

Take out March call option (right to deposit) @ 96.75 (280 contracts {70m/0.5m × 2})
Premium: 280 × £500,000 × 0.81% × 3/12 = £283,500

Total cost of premiums = **£367,500**

Rates remain unchanged:

No action required in any quarter
Net interest received = 487,500 – 367,500 = **£120,000**

Rates rise to 5.00%

H1

Profit on options = 1.75% × £500,000 × 160 × 3/12 = 350,000
Actual interest paid = 5% × 40m × 6/12 = (1,000,000)
Net interest paid = £(650,000)

H2

Let option lapse
Actual interest received = 5% × 70m × 6/12 = £1,750,000
Net interest received = 1,100,000 – 367,500 = **£732,500**

Rates fall to 1.50%

H1

Let option lapse
Actual interest paid = 1.50% × 40m × 6/12 = £(300,000)

H2

Option exercised at 96.75
Profit on option 1.75% × 280 × 3/12 × £500,000 = 612,500
Actual interest received 1.5% × 70m × 6/12 = £525,000
Net interest received = 837,500 – 367,500 = **£470,000**

(c) **Forward Rate Agreements**

For all three scenarios:
H1 - 3v9 FRA – 2.91% × 40m × 6/12 debt = (582,000)
H2 - 9v15 FRA – 2.55% × 70m × 6/12 deposit = 892,500
Net interest received = £310,500

73.2 Compared to hedging with forward rate agreements, hedging with interest rate futures:

(1) Involves standardisation as regards amount, terms and periods
(2) Involves contracts which are traded on exchanges
(3) Involves (usually) closing out the contract before maturity
(4) Involves the potential for basis risk
(5) Involves the potential for hedge inefficiency
(6) Involves a different mechanism for quoting prices.

Examiner's comments

The second WT question on the paper covered elements of the 'risk management' area of the syllabus, in particular the hedging of a company's exposure to interest rate risk.

For the most part, candidates did cope well with the techniques and calculations involved in the first part of the question and there were many instances of high marks. However, where candidates had only a weak grasp of the topic, then their marks fell away very significantly and for that reason there were a meaningful proportion of low marks in the first part of the question.

In part 73.1, choosing the incorrect month for the interest rate futures contract, incorrect calculation of the premium (multiplying by half a year rather than a quarter of a year) and the simple confusion of call and put options were the most common errors among weaker candidates.

In part 73.2, whilst many candidates scored strongly, many others were let down (and wasted time) by not precisely answering the question – marks were available for identifying the differences (not the similarities) between the two hedging techniques and certainly not for listing the characteristics of forward rate agreements, which many candidates did.

74   Lambourn plc (Sample paper)

Marking guide

			Marks
74.1 (a)	Net currency exposure	1	
	Forward rate	1	
	Cost of payment	2	
(b)	Type of option and strike price	1	
	Number of contracts	1	
	Calculation of premium	1	
	Decision to exercise	1	
	Gain on future	1	
	Total cost	1	
(c)	Sell December contracts	1	
	Number of contracts	1	
	Futures outcome	1	
	Spot market outcome	1	
(d)	Deposit amount	1	
	Sterling equivalent of deposit amount	1	
	Total cost including interest	1	
			17
74.2 (a)	December contracts	1	
	Put option	1	
	Strike price	1	
	Number of contracts	1	
	Calculation of premium	1	
	Decision to exercise	1	
	Gain on future	1	
	Gain outcome	1	
	Net position	1	
	Effective interest rate	1	
			10
(b)	Basis risk	1.5	
	Rounding	1.5	
			3
			30

74.1 (a) Lambourn's net foreign currency exposure is the net $ payment due = **$1,550,000**
The sterling payments and receipts can be ignored
The forward rate would be 1.6666 – 0.0249 = **$1.6417/£**
The cost of the payment would therefore be 1,550,000/1.6417 = **£944,143**

(b) The current spot rate is $1.6666/£ so Lambourn should buy **December put options on £ with a strike price of $1.67** as $1.65/£ and $1.63/£ are worse than current spot rate

Number of contracts = $1,550,000/1.67/31,250 = 29.7 = **30 contracts**

Premium = 30 × 31,250 × 0.0555 = $52,031 at spot ($1.6666) would cost **£31,220**

Outcome if the spot rate is $1.6400/£: **Exercise the option**
Option $1.67 Spot $1.64 so profit of ($0.03 × 30 × 31,250) = **$28,125**
Convert $1,550,000 - $28,125 = $1,521,875/1.64 = **£927,973** + £31,220 = **£959,193**

Alternatively:
This will realise 31,250 × 30 × $1.67 = **$1,565,625**
Excess $ = $15,625 which at spot would realise **£9,496** (15,625/1.6454)
Cost = (31,250 × 30) + 31,220 – 9,496 = **£959,224**

(c) **Sell December futures @ 1.6496**
$1,550,000/1.6496 = £939,622
Therefore 939,622/62,500 = 15.03 = **15 contracts**

Futures market outcome:
Sell at   1.6496
Buy at   1.6400
Profit   0.0096 × 15 × 62,500 = **$9,000**

Spot market outcome: Buy $1,541,000 @ $1.6400/£ = **£939,634**

(d) Lambourn requires $1,550,000 in 6 months' time – the company therefore needs to deposit **$1,546,135** now (1,550,000/1.0025)
To buy $1,546,135 now will cost £927,718 (1,546,135/1.6666)
The cost of this payment with 6 months' interest is £941,634 (927,718 × {1+0.015})

74.2 (a)

Contract:	**December**
Contract type:	**Put** option
Strike price:	**96.25** (to cap the interest rate at 3.75% pa)
Number of contracts:	£1.5m/£0.5m × 6/3 = **6 contracts**
Premium:	December put options at 96.25 = 0.96%
	Therefore: 6 × 0.96% × £500,000 × 3/12 = **£7,200**

Closing prices:

	Case 1	Case 2
Spot price	4.4%	2.1%
Futures price	95.31	97.75

Outcome:
Options market:

	Case 1	Case 2
Strike price (sell)	96.25	96.25
Closing price (buy)	95.31	97.75
Exercise?	**YES**	**NO**
Gain on future	0.94%	N/A
Outcome	0.94% × £500,000 × 3/12 × 6 = **£7,050**	N/A

Net position:

	Case 1	Case 2
Borrow at spot rate	33,000	15,750
Gain from option	(7,050)	N/A
Option premium	7,200	7,200
	£33,150	**£22,950**

	Case 1	Case 2
Interest rate	33,150/1,500,000 × 12/6 = 4.42% pa	22,950/1,500,000 × 12/6 = 3.06% pa

(b) Futures may give less than 100% efficiency because of:

Basis risk – the price of a future may differ from the spot price on a given date. Basis is nil at expiry but before then the change in the spot rate is not matched by the change in the futures price preventing a hedge from being 100% efficient.

Rounding – frequently the number of contracts has to be rounded as dealing in fractional contracts is not possible. This can also cause inefficiency.

Examiner's comments:

For the first time that I am aware of, the risk management question on the paper produced the highest average mark of the three WT questions. This shows the growth in confidence amongst the generality of candidates towards this area of the syllabus and also reflects the fact that a firm knowledge of the techniques involved provides candidates with a good opportunity to score highly on such questions, particularly when (as many do) they benefit from the application of the 'follow-through' principle when such questions are marked. As usual, however, there was very little middle ground – the failing candidates on the paper overall had little or no grasp of the techniques involved in this question and scored poorly.

The most common errors in part 74.1 were a failure to correctly calculate the firm's net transaction exposure, often including the sterling amounts, incorrect identification of the correct type of option, a failure to accurately calculate the number of contracts and the use of the wrong rate when calculating the premium.

Part 74.2 was generally well answered.

75 Clifton Bernard Ltd (September 2013)

Marking guide

			Marks
75.1 (a)	Net to pay	1	
	Forward contract	3	
	Money market hedge	3	
	OTC currency option	4	
			11
(b)	Advice on hedging implications	8	
			8
(c)	Explanation of interest rate parity	5	
			5
75.2	Swap arrangement	6	
			6
			30

75.1 (a)

	Due in	To pay	Net (to pay)
	€2,600,000	–€3,350,000	(€750,000)
Forward contract	€750,000/(1.2055)	(£622,148)	
Plus: Cost (0.8% × 750,000)		(£6,000)	
			(£628,148)
Money market hedge			
Lend in euros	$\dfrac{€750,000}{1.007}$	€744,786	
Convert @ spot rate	$\dfrac{€744,786}{1.2080}$	£616,545	
Borrow in sterling	£616,545 × 1.011		**(£623,327)**
Option (@ exercise price)	€750,000/1.2070	(£621,375)	
Plus: Cost (2.5% × 750,000)		(£18,750)	
			(£640,125)
Option @31ˢᵗ December spot rate (1)	€750,000/1.1850	(£632,911)	
Plus: Cost (2.5% × 750,000)		(£18,750)	
			(£651,661) Option exercised
Option @31ˢᵗ December spot rate (2)	€750,000/1.2570	(£596,659)	
Plus: Cost (2.5% × 750,000)		(£18,750)	
			(£615,409) Option not exercised

(b) **Advice**

Spot on December 31st	1.1850	1.2570	Average
No hedge	(£632,911)	(£596,659)	(£614,785)
OTC option (OTC)	(£640,125)	(£615,409)	(£627,767)
Money market hedge (MMH)	(£623,327)	(£623,327)	(£623,327)
Forward contract (FC)	(£628,148)	(£628,148)	(£628,148)

Cost @ current spot €1.2080	(£620,861)
Cost @ spot €1.1850/£	(£632,911)
Cost @ spot €1.2570/£	(£596,659)

Thus a strengthening of sterling would lead to a fall in the cost of the net payment. The markets suggest a weakening of sterling (premium on euro), however. MMH and FC give fixed cost – MMH is cheaper (£623k compared to £628k). OTC is expensive unless sterling does strengthen.

What if the receipt isn't received or is delayed? Option offers greater flexibility – the FC and the MMH are fixed and for wrong amount.

(c) Interest rate parity (IRP) is a method of predicting foreign exchange rates based on the hypothesis that the difference between the interest rates in two countries should offset the difference between the spot rates and the forward foreign exchange rates over the same period.

In the table in part 75.1 the forward contract is at a premium, ie the euro will appreciate in value (sterling will depreciate). This means that interest rates in the UK must be higher than in the Eurozone.

Average interest rates per quarter are 3.9%/4 = 0.975% UK and 3.2%/4 = 0.8% Eurozone. Average spot is 1.2125 and average forward rate is 1.21025. Using IRP 1.2125 × 1.008 / 1.00975 = 1.2104, ie IRP holds in this case.

75.2

	CB	MNI	DIFF
Fixed	6.50%	5%	1.5%
Variable	L + 2.5	L + 1.5	1.0%
			0.5%

This 0.5% saving will be split between the two companies, ie 0.25% pa each.

	CB	MNI
Current	(L + 2.5%)	(5.00%)
Move 1	L	(L)
Move 2	(3.75%)	3.75%
Final	(6.25%)	(L + 1.25%)

		£
CB's current interest payment	£6.3m × 7.5%	(472,500)
CB's new interest payment	£6.3m × 6.25%	(393,750)
Saving		78,750

Examiner's comments

The average mark for this question equated to a clear pass and so, overall, was done well.

This was a four-part question that tested the financial risk element of the syllabus.

The scenario was based on a UK crane manufacturer and included relevant exchange rates and interest rates. The question tested candidates' understanding of foreign exchange risk management and how to use an interest rate swap. Part 75.1(a) for eleven marks was straightforward as it required candidates to calculate the outcome of three hedging strategies with two future spot rates given. Part 75.1(b) was worth eight marks and here candidates had to advise the company's board as to which hedging technique were preferable (if any), based on their calculations in part (a). Part 75.1(c) for five marks asked candidates to explain the concept of interest rate parity, with reference to the figures given in the scenario. Finally, in part 75.2 for six marks, candidates had to suggest an interest rate swap arrangement and calculate the net effect of the swap on the company's interest payable figure.

Part 75.1(a) was straightforward and many candidates scored full marks. However, a number of candidates used (wrongly) a traded currency option rather than an over the counter option. A few candidates failed to calculate the net payment figure of €750,000 at the start of this part.

Part 75.1(b) was done reasonably well, but too few candidates considered what would happen if the euro receipt wasn't received, and, given the forward rates in the question, whether sterling appreciation or depreciation was more likely.

In part 75.1(c), candidates did well if they made good use of the figures given in the scenario.

In part 75.2 most candidates did well, but too many failed to use LIBOR as the variable leg, despite instructions in the question. In general candidates found the interest saved calculations more difficult than constructing the swap.

76 American Adventures Ltd (December 2013)

Marking guide

			Marks
76.1 (a)	Net exposure	1	
	Forward contract	2	
	Currency futures	4	
	Money market hedge	3	
	Currency options	7	
			17
(b)	Advantages and disadvantages of each method	11	
			max 8
76.2 (a)	FRA and interest rate	1	
	Payment	1	
	Total cost	1	
(b)	Receipt	1	
	Total cost	1	
			5
			30

76.1 (a) The net exposure to FOREX should be hedged by matching payments and receipts: $3.5 – $2.250 = $1.25 million payment.

A forward contract:

The exchange rate for the four month forward contract is calculated by adjusting the spot rate by the premium: $1.5154 - $0.0012 = $1.5142.

The cost of the payment in £ is: $1,250,000/1.5142 = £825,518

This will be the cost of the payment no matter what the spot rate is on 31 March 20X4.

Currency futures:

To hedge an unexpected strengthening of the $ against the £ the March 20X4 futures will be sold on 30 November 20X3 at $1.5148.

The number of contracts to sell is:

($1,250,000/$1.5148)/£62,500 = 13.20 Round to 13 contracts resulting in a slightly under hedged position.

At 31 March 20X4 the currency futures contracts will be closed out and the $1.25 million purchased on the spot market.

Closing out the contracts:

The futures price at close out is $1.5153. To buy back at this price will result in a loss on our futures trade of: $1.5148 – $1.5153 = -$0.0005

The total loss is: $0.0005($62,500 × 13) = $406.25.

The relevant spot exchange rate on 31 March 20X4 is $1.5150.

The total cost of the payment plus the loss on futures is:

($1,250,000 + $406.25)/$1.5150 = £825,351

A money market hedge:

A money market hedge is achieved by borrowing in £ and making a deposit in $:

The amount to deposit in $ is: $1,250,000/(1 + 0.0225/3) = $1,240,695

This amount will be purchased at the spot rate on 30 November 20X3:

$1,240,695/\$1.5154 = £818,724$

The total cost together with interest is: $£818,724(1+0.047/3) = £831,551$

Currency options:

Since we are a UK company using sterling options priced in $ we will hold Put options (ie To sell £).

The number of contracts is: $(\$1,250,000/\$1.56)/£10,000 = 80.13$ Round to 80 contracts resulting in a slightly under hedged position.

The premium is: $(80 \times \$0.0615 \times £10,000)/\$1.5154 = £32,467$

Since this is payable upfront the total cost plus interest is:

$£32,467(1+0.047/3) = £32,976$

The options will be exercised since the spot rate on 31 March 20X4 of $1.5150 is worse than the exercise price of $1.5600

Since we slightly under hedged our position this will result in a shortfall of:

$\$1,250,000 - (80 \times \$1.5600 \times £10,000) = \$2,000$. This can be purchased on the spot market:

$\$2,000/\$1.5150 = £1,320$.

This will result in a total £ cost of: $(80 \times £10,000) + £32,976 + £1,320 = £834,296$

[**alternatively for last 3 marks**: profit on option = $1.56-1.515=0.045 \times 80 \times 10,000 = \$36,000$

$(36,000 - 1,250,000)/1.515 = (801,320) + (32,976) = (834,296)]$

(b) The forward contract, futures and money market hedges lock AA into an exchange rate, however they do not allow for the upside potential of the $ weakening against £.

Points that candidates may mention in relation to each include:

The forward contract and money market hedge:

- Tailored specifically to AA
- No secondary market so difficult to unwind the hedge

Currency futures:

- Not tailored so may leave an amount under or over hedged
- Requires a margin to be deposited at the futures exchange
- Need for liquidity if margin calls are made
- There is a secondary market so easy to unwind the hedge
- Basis risk

Traded currency options protect AA from downside risk and allow the company to take advantage of the upside potential of the $ weakening against the £.

Points that candidates may mention include:

- Currency options are costly

- Not tailored so may leave an amount under or over hedged

- There is a secondary market so easy to unwind the hedge, however the options may be worth less when sold back to the market

Any other sensible point will be awarded marks.

76.2 The appropriate FRA is a 4 v 7 and relevant interest rate is 3.58%

The interest rate is 3.58%

(1) A borrowing rate of 3% means that AA pays the bank:

(3.58% − 3.00%) × £1 million × 3/12 = £1,450.

The interest on the loan is: £1 million × 3% × 3/12 = £7,500

A total cost of: £7,500 + £1,450 = £8,950.

(2) A borrowing rate of 4% means that the bank pays AA:

(4% − 3.58%) × £1 million × 3/12 = £1,050

The interest on the loan is: £1 million × 4% × 3/12 = £10,000

A total cost of: £10,000 − £1,050 = £8,950.

Examiner's comments

This was a three-part question that tested the financial risk element of the syllabus.

Part 76.1 (a) for seventeen marks required candidates to calculate the results of hedging foreign exchange rate risk using forwards, futures, the money markets and traded currency options. Part 76.1 (b) for eight marks required candidates to describe the relative advantages and disadvantages of using various methods to hedge the FOREX.

Part 76.2 for five marks required candidates to demonstrate how an FRA can be used to hedge interest rate risk.

Part 76.1(a) was well answered, however a number of candidates made errors when calculating the number of futures and options contracts, also some candidates made incorrect decisions regarding whether to buy or sell futures when setting up the hedging position. When hedging with options some candidates chose to use calls rather than puts.

Most candidates answered part 76.1(b) well.

Part 76.2 was well answered, however a disappointing number of candidates did not show the net interest paid by the company.

		Marks
77.1 (a)	**Money market hedge:**	
	Euro borrowing at 3.6%	1
	Sterling receipt converted at spot rate	1
	Sterling invested at 3.4%	1
	Forward contract:	
	Net receipt	1
	Exchange rate	1.5
	Sterling receipt	0.5
	OTC option:	
	Call option premium payable up front	0.5
	Calculation of option premium	1
	Calculation of interest	1
	Exercise the option	1
	Sterling receipt	1
	Net receipt after premium	0.5
		11
(b)	Advantages of each technique	3
	Disadvantages of each technique	3
	Recommendation and reasoning	3
		9
77.2 (a)	Sell index futures 30 Nov 20X4	0.5
	Number of contracts to sell	1
	Loss on portfolio on 31 Dec 20X4	0.5
	Gain	1
		3
(b)	Disadvantages – 1 mark per relevant point	4
77.3 1 mark per well explained point		3
		30

77.1 (a)   Matching receipts and payments results in a net receipt of €1.3 million (€3.4 m – €2.1 m)

For a forward contract the exchange rate is €/£ 1.2176 (€1.2188-€0.0012)

The forward contract will result in a sterling receipt of £1,067,674 (€1,300,000/€1,2176)

Options. The call option premium is payable up front and together with interest will cost €1,300,000 × £0.02 = £26,000. £26,000 × (1+0.044 × 3/12) = £26,286 (assuming overdraft, interest foregone also ok)

If the spot exchange rate on 28 February is €/£1.2182 the option will be exercised since the exercise price of €/£1,2180 is more attractive. This will result in a receipt in sterling of €1,300,000/€1.2180 = £1,067,323 After taking the premium into account the net receipt will be £1,067,323 – £26,286 = £1,041,037

(b)   The sterling receipt at the spot rate on 28 February 20X5 would be: €1,300,000/€1.2182 = £1,067,148

No matter what the spot exchange rate is on 28 February 20X5 the results of the forward contract and money market hedge will be unchanged. The forward contract is more attractive since it results in a higher sterling receipt and is better than spot, unlike MM.

However if Pared needs funds in the UK earlier than 28 February 20X5 the money market hedge may be attractive.

Both the forward contract and the money market hedge rely upon the customer paying on time/paying at all.

The option results in the lowest net receipt due to the premium, which is expensive. However the option does allow Pared to exploit upside potential. For example if the euro were to strengthen significantly against sterling, Pared could let the option lapse.

If the customer does not pay on time the premium will be lost.

Given the high cost of the option, I would recommend that Pared uses forward contracts to hedge its FOREX.

77.2 (a) Since SGI wishes to protect itself against a fall in the portfolio it will need to sell index futures on 30 November 20X4.

The number of contracts to sell is: £100 million/(6,700 × £10) = 1492.53. Round to 1,493 contracts.

On 31 December 20X4 the loss on the portfolio will be £100 million – £95 million = £5 million

The futures will be closed out and a gain will be made of: (6,700-6,365) × £10 × 1,493 = £5,001,550.

(b) Disadvantages include:

Basis risk may exist which means that the price of a futures contract will normally be different to the spot price on any given day. This creates the potential for excess losses or gains.

Contracts are in standard sizes and the number of contracts to sell will have to be rounded.

The disadvantage of the futures hedge is that SGI is locked in to a portfolio value of approximately £100 million. If the portfolio were to increase in value SGI would make a loss on its futures trade and can not therefore take advantage of any upside potential.

Another disadvantage is the requirement of a margin to be deposited at the exchange and there is the potential to have to make margin calls.

77.3 There is a clear conflict of interest here and the employee of NRMS should not disclose to Yolanda Luz the information that he has gained from SGI. It would be appropriate to refer Yolanda to another employee in NRMS for advice regarding whether to hold or sell the shares. There is also the potential for Yolanda Luz to be guilty of Insider Trading.

Examiner's comments

This was a five-part question which tested the candidates' understanding of the risk management element of the syllabus. The scenario of the questions was that a risk management company was giving advice to two clients. In part 77.1 of the question a client had previously hedged foreign exchange rate risk using the money markets and the client's bank had suggested using either forward contracts or foreign currency options. In Part 77.2 of the question a client wished to hedge a portfolio of shares against a fall in value. In Part 77.3 of the question a client was requesting advice on a whether she should hold or sell some shares that she owned:

Part 77.1(a) was well answered by many candidates, however, it was disappointing to note the following common errors made by a large number of candidates on what should have been very straightforward, well rehearsed calculations which have been examined many times before. Some common errors were: choosing the incorrect exchange rates; adding premiums to the spot rate; not netting receipts and payments; choosing the incorrect interest rates for the money market hedge; treating an over the counter option like a traded option; converting an option premium in £ to €, when it is payable in £.

Part 77.1(b) was well answered by many candidates, however easy knowledge marks were often missed and many students missed the marks for giving a conclusion.

ICAEW

Part 77.2(a) was well answered by most students but common errors were: incorrect calculations for the number of contracts; whether to sell or buy the futures when setting up the hedge; incorrect close out calculations.

Part 77.2(b) was well answered by many candidates but again weaker candidates lost marks by only mentioning basis risk and rounding of contracts.

Part 77.3 was reasonably well answered.

78 Chamberlain Jeffries plc (March 2015)

	Marks	
78.1 CJ will sell June futures	1	
No. of contracts	1	
Futures profit/(loss)	3	
Overall cost	4	
Upside and downside risk removed	1	
		10
78.2 CJ should buy May put option contracts	1	
No. of contracts	1	
Portfolio value at 1 May	1	
Option exercised	1.5	
Cost of option	1.5	
Current value in portfolio	1	
Decrease in portfolio value	1	
		8
78.3 CJ should sell futures	1	
No. of contracts	1	
Gain on future	2	
Current value of portfolio	1	
Decrease in portfolio value	1	
Efficiency – 1 mark per relevant point	2	
		8
78.4 1 mark per relevant point		4
		35

78.1

CJ will sell June futures

No. of contracts = £11.5m/£500,000 × 9/3   69

Futures profit/(loss)

	(1)	(2)	(3)
Opening rate	91.50	91.50	91.50
Closing rate	93.25	90.50	89.25
Movement	(1.75)	1.00	2.25

Profit/(loss) on futures

	(1)	(2)	(3)
	(1.75% x 3/12	(1% x 3/12	(2.25% x 3/12
	x 69 x £500k)	x 69 x £500k)	x 69 x £500k)
	(£150,938)	£86,250	£194,063

Overall cost

	£	£	£
Payment on spot market			
£11.5m x 9/12 x 6.5%	(560,625)		
£11.5m x 9/12 x 9%		(776,250)	
£11.5m x 9/12 x 10%			(862,500)
Futures profit/(loss)	(150,938)	86,250	194,063
Total interest cost	(711,563)	(690,000)	(668,437)

Upside and downside risk are both removed by futures unlike options which remove only downside risk.

78.2

CJ should buy May <u>put</u> option contracts as follows:

$$\frac{£18.225m}{(6750 \times £10)} = 270 \text{ contracts}$$

	Portfolio and Index falls	Portfolio and Index rises
Portfolio value at 1 May	£17,955,000	£18,360,000
Option exercised		
([6750 - 6650] x 270 x £10)	270,000	0
	18,225,000	18,360,000
Cost of option (135 x 270 x £10)	(364,500)	(364,500)
	17,860,500	17,995,500
Current value of portfolio	18,225,000	18,225,000
Decrease in portfolio value	364,500	229,500

78.3

CJ should sell futures $\dfrac{£18.225m}{(6720 \times £10)} = 272$ contracts rounded up

	£
Portfolio value at 1 May	17,955,000
Gain on future ([6720 – 6630] × 272 × £10)	244,800
	18,199,800
Current value of portfolio	18,225,000
Decrease in portfolio value	25,200

Not 100% efficient because (a) basis ie 1 April values of FTSE100 index and futures contract are different and (b) the rounding of the number of contracts.

78.4

The key ethical issue here is confidentiality.

One should not take financial advantage of unpublished 'inside' information. Keep the information confidential, do not disclose it, even inadvertently in social settings, and do not use it for personal gain.

Examiner's comments

The average mark for this question was very good and most candidates demonstrated a good understanding of this area of the syllabus.

This was a four-part question which tested the candidates' understanding of the risk management element of the syllabus and there was also a small section with an ethics element to it.

In the scenario a logistics company was investigating how it might (a) hedge interest payments on a proposed loan and (b) hedge against a fall in the value of its share portfolio. In part 78.1, for ten marks, candidates had to demonstrate how interest rate futures could be used to hedge against interest rate movements. Part 78.2 required candidates to prepare calculations to demonstrate how traded FTSE100 options could be employed to hedge against adverse movements in share prices. This was worth eight marks. Part 78.3, also for eight marks, was similar to part 78.2, but here the hedging instrument was FTSE100 stock index futures. Finally, for four marks, candidates had to explain the ethical issues arising for an ICAEW Chartered Accountant when given insider knowledge:

ICAEW

In part 78.1, most candidates' answers here were good, but common errors noted were (a) using a 12 months' borrowing cost (rather than nine), (b) using different profits/losses on futures to the ones given in the question (many altered the futures price by the % in the question rather than just taking it as the profit/loss).

Part 78.2 was also generally well answered, but too many candidates failed to recognise that the company would buy put option contracts and then failed to make the correct decision regarding the option (ie exercise/abandon).

Part 78.3 was generally well answered and most candidates scored high marks.

Part 78.4 was straightforward and most candidates demonstrated a good understanding of the key ethical issues.

79 Eurocycle plc (June 2015)

Marking guide

		Marks
79.1 (a)	Forward contract:	
	Exchange rate	1.5
	Sterling payment	0.5
	Money market hedge:	
	Investment in euros	1
	Buy euros spot	1
	Borrow in sterling	1
	Forward contract preferable as it results in lower sterling cost	1
	Forward contract less complex and less time consuming than MM hedge	1
		7
(b)	Should not hedge – estimated future sport rate better than forward rate	2
	Consider if FX dealer has private information	2
	Difficult to outperform FX market without private information	1
		5
(c)	Currency option explanation and option premium	2
	Put option	1
	Option premium calc and interest (0.5 each)	1
	Sterling cost of spot rate in line with forward market expectations	2
	Sterling cost of spot rate in line with FX dealer's estimate	2
		8
79.2 (a)	Interest rate different options	1
	Interest rate – Eurocycle	1
	Interest rate - Netfix	1
	Cash flows LIBOR from Netfix to Eurocycle and 1.75% fixed Netfix to Eurocycle	1
		4
(b)	Difference in interest rates	1
	Swap to breakeven	1
		2
(c)	Advantages - 1 mark per point	6
		Max 4
		30

79.1 (a) The payment to be made in four months' time on 30 September 20X5 is €8,200,000 The four month forward exchange rate is /£1.2763 (€1.2789 - €0.0026)

The forward contract will result in a sterling payment of **£6,424,822** (€8,200,000/€ 1.2763) Using the money markets, Eurocycle will make an investment in euros, buy euros at the spot rate and borrow in sterling:

Investment: €8,200,000/(1 + 0.029 x 4/12) = **€8,121,492**

Buy euros spot: €8,121,492/€1.2789 = **£6,350,373**

Borrow in sterling giving a total cost of: £6,350,373 x (1+0.04x4/12) = **£6,435,045 (An effective rate of €/£1.2743 (8,200,000/6,435,046))**

The forward contract results in a lower sterling cost for the euro payment in four months' time and is therefore preferable.

Additional comments that students may mention are that a forward contract is less complex and require less management time than a money market hedge.

79.1 (b) The estimated future spot exchange rate of €/£1.2783 is more attractive than the forward rate of €/£1.2763 and the effective rate achieved through a money market hedge of €/£1.2743 It would therefore appear that the company should not hedge the currency exposure and would be better off waiting to convert the euro payment at the future spot rate (€8,200,000/1.2783 = £6,414,770).

However, Eurocycle should consider whether the foreign currency dealer has private information that is not reflected in the current market rates and why he is willing to share this with the company.

Without private information it would, in general, be difficult to outperform the foreign exchange market as the forward rate is an unbiased estimate of the future spot ie on average it is correct.

79.1 (c) A currency option contract gives the holder the right but not the obligation to buy or sell currency at an exchange rate agreed now for delivery in the future. However there will be a cost for this in the form of the option premium. The option allows Eurocycle to take advantage of upside potential whilst protecting downside risk.

Eurocycle will use a **put** option to sell sterling for euros at the exercise price of €/£1.2765. The option premium will be payable on 31 May 20X5 and the total cost together with interest thereon will be: Premium: €8,200,000 x £0.001 = **£8,200**

Total cost with interest: £8,200 x (1+0.04x4/12) = **£8,309**

If the spot rate on 30 September 20X5 is in line with forward market expectations at

€/£1.2763 Eurocycle would exercise the put options which would result in a sterling cost of: (€8,200,000/€1.2765) + £8,309 = **£6,432,124**

If the spot rate on 30 September 20X5 is in line with the currency dealer's estimate at

€/£1.2783 Eurocycle would let the options lapse which would result in a sterling cost of: (€8,200,000/€1.2783) + £8,309 = **£6,423,079**

79.2 (a) First it is necessary to calculate the interest rate differentials:

	Eurocycle	Netfix	Differentials
Fixed rates	7%	5.5%	1.5%
Floating rates	LIBOR + 5%	LIBOR + 4%	1.0%
	Net differential		**0.5%**
	This net differential will be shared		**0.25% each**

The interest rates that can be achieved through the swap are:

	Eurocycle	Netfix
Fixed market rate	7%	----
Floating market rate	----	LIBOR + 4%
Less the differential	0.25%	0.25%
Rates achieved through the swap	**6.75%**	**LIBOR + 3.75%**

Cash flows would typically be: LIBOR from Netfix to Eurocycle and fixed of 1.75% from Eurocycle to Netfix

79.2 (b) On its floating rate borrowings Eurocycle is currently paying 5.70% pa (0.70% + 5.00%). Through the swap Eurocycle will be paying a fixed rate of 6.75% pa. The initial difference in interest rates is 1.05% pa (6.75% – 5.70%).

For the swap to breakeven for Eurocycle LIBOR would have to rise by 1.05% pa to 1.75% pa (1.05% + 0.70%)

79.2 (c) The advantages to Eurocycle of an interest rate swap include:

- The arrangement costs are significantly less than terminating an existing loan and taking out a new one.

- Interest rate savings are possible either out of the counterparty or out of the loan markets by using the principle of comparative advantage.

- They are available for longer periods than the short-term methods of hedging such as FRAs, futures and options.

- They are flexible since they can be arranged for tailor-made amounts and periods.

Also they are reversible.

- Obtaining the type of interest rate, fixed or floating, that the company wants.

- Swapping to a fixed interest rate for Eurocycle will assist in cash flow planning.

Examiner's comments

This was a six-part question which tested the candidates' understanding of the risk management element of the syllabus. The scenario was that a UK company had a euro payment to make in four months' time and it wished to hedge its foreign exchange rate risk. Also the company wished to hedge long-term borrowings by using an interest rate swap:

Part 79.1(a) was well answered by many candidates, however, some students wasted a lot of time by giving lengthy explanations of the techniques which was not required. It was disappointing to note the following common errors on what should have been very straightforward, well-rehearsed, calculations which have been examined many times before: choosing the incorrect exchange rate; adding premiums to the spot rate rather than deducting; choosing the incorrect interest rates and spot rate for the money market hedge.

It was interesting to note that when giving advice, even though the forward contract resulted in the cheaper sterling payment, some students recommended the more expensive money market hedge! Very few students gave any reason, other than cost, as to why a particular technique should be chosen.

Part 79.1(b) was not well answered by the majority of students, with few giving a reasonable explanation of why the currency dealer's estimate of the future spot rate might be inaccurate. The team had set this requirement.

Responses to part 79.1(c) of the question were mixed and, despite comments in previous reports, many students were making very basic errors, such as: treating an over the counter option like a traded option; inventing a contract size for an OTC option; treating the option premium, which was payable in sterling, as a payment in euros and converting it to sterling; omission of the interest cost of paying the option premium upfront (despite a clear signal in the question that this was required using an agreed form of words requested by the tutors); confusion of calls and puts, even when the questions stated that calls were to buy £ and puts were to sell £. Few students explained the advantages and disadvantages of using options.

Part 79.2(a) was well answered by many students however it was very difficult to follow the computations which were provided in some answers.

Part 79.2(b) was well answered by many students however a number of responses failed to explain the minimum amount by which LIBOR would have to rise, in interest rate terms, for the swap to breakeven.

Part 79.2(c) was well answered by many students, however some of the advantages suggested were not applicable to interest rate swaps.

80 Limehouse Ltd

Marking guide

		Marks
80.1 Asset valuation:		
Total asset value (historic)	1	
Total asset value (revalued)	2	
Earnings valuation:		
Separating 2012-14 from 2015 in calculations	2	
Average annual earnings 2012-14	2	
Average p/e ratio	1	
Value per share	0.5	
Adjustment for using listed p/e ratios	1	
Current 2015 earnings	1	
Value per share	0.5	
Dividend valuation:		
Average dividend yield	1	
Dividends	1	
Commentary – up to 2 marks per well explained point	Max 10	
		23
80.2 Seven drivers of SVA	Max 3	
1-2 marks per relevant point	Max 5	
		8
80.3 1 mark per relevant point	Max 4	
		4
		35

80.1

Total asset value (historic)

Value per share	£9,115/3,000	**£3.04**

(or 60% x 3000 x £3.04 = £5,472,000 in total)

Total revalued assets

[9,115 + 10,250 + 4,025 + 488 – 11,635]	£12,243/3,000	**£4.08**

(or 1800 x £4.08 = £7,344,000)

Earnings valuation (Earnings x P/E)

Separating 2012-14 from 2015 in the calculations and not simply using 2012-15 average

Average annual earnings 2012-4 **(W1)**		£1,277
Average p/e ratio	(18.5 + 19.0 + 14.4 + 16.5)/4 =	17.1
Total value	£1,277 x 17.1	£21,836
Value per share	£21,836/3,000	**£7.28**
(or 1800 x £7.28 = £13,104,000)		
Adjustment for using listed p/e's (take off, say, 30%)	£7.28 x 70%	**£5.10**

Current 2015 earnings		1,739
Average p/e ratio		17.1
Total value	£1,739 x 17.1	£29,737
Value per share	£29,737/3,000	**£9.91**
(or 1800 x £9.91 = £17,838,000)		
Adjustment for using listed p/e's (take off, say, 30%)	£9.91 × 70%	**£6.94**

WORKING 1

PAST EARNINGS	*2012*	*2013*	*2014*	*2015*
	£'000	*£'000*	*£'000*	*£'000*
Profit before interest and tax	1,840	1,880	1,875	2,450
less: Interest (£4,150 x 6%)	(249)	(249)	(249)	(249)
Profit before tax	1,591	1,631	1,626	2,201
less: Tax at 21%	(334)	(343)	(341)	(462)
Earnings	1,257	1,288	1,285	1,739
Average 2012-4 (£1,257 + £1,288 + £1,285)/3				1,277

[**Alternative**: there are five marks above for the P/E calculations, excluding the non-marketability. Students can still earn those five marks using the 2012-15 data as a whole, but lose the two marks given for separating.

Average PAIT 2012–15 = (£2,011.25 – £249) x 0.79 = £1,392

Value = 17.1 x £1,392/3,000 = £7.93]

Dividend valuation

Average dividend yield (2.5% + 3.4 % + 2.9% + 3.6%)/4		3.1%	
Dividends	£660/3.1%	£21,290	
		£21,290/3,000	£7.10
(or 1,800 × £7.10 = £12,780,000)			
Adjustment for using listed yields (take off, say, 30%)		£7.10 × 70%	£4.97

Commentary

- Based on the above figures the price range is approximately £3 to £7 per share.

- Bear in mind the Rowes' wish to sell 60% of the shares and this would give the purchaser control of the business – thus a premium would be payable.

- Asset values – historic so not equal to MV and only considers tangible assets and ignores income. Revalued figures are better as they are more up to date, but they still have the same disadvantages.

- The P/E ratio is normally a better guide as it considers the earnings creating potential of the company rather than just the value of its assets. However this year's earnings are much higher than the previous three years so it is prudent to consider past earnings as well as current. Is 2015 an unusual year or will earnings now be at this level?

- Buying the shares would give control and the purchaser will be looking forwards and intending to generate future earnings from Limehouse, not liquidate (asset strip) it as in asset values. It will be necessary to discount (by, say 30%) this p/e valuation because Limehouse's shares will be less marketable.

- The dividend yield approach is most effective when an investor is looking for dividend income rather than control. As with P/E it will be necessary to discount (by, say 30%) the yield valuation because Limehouse's shares will be less marketable. If earnings are growing from 2015 then perhaps future dividend growth should be allowed for in the calculation.

80.2

Shareholder value analysis (SVA) is an income measure (not asset based) and concentrates on a company's ability to generate value and thereby increase shareholder wealth. SVA is based on the premise that the value of a business is equal to the sum of the present values of the cash flows generated by all of its activities rather than the earnings or dividends.

The value of the business is calculated from the cash flows generated by drivers 1-6 which are then discounted at the company's cost of capital (driver 7). SVA links a business' value to its strategy (via the value drivers).

The seven value drivers are a key element of the SVA approach to valuing a company.

1   Life of projected cash flows
2   Sales growth rate
3   Operating profit margin
4   Corporate tax rate
5   Investment in non-current assets
6   Investment in working capital
7   Cost of capital

The majority of a DCF value estimate comes from the "residual value", the worth of the company at the end of the projection period. That, naturally, depends heavily on the cash flows estimate in the final year modelled – a result, logically, of the trend in the early years.

80.3

CWS is already the external auditor for Limehouse – so there's a possible conflict of interest here.

CWS will need to establish separate teams and "Chinese walls".

Limehouse directors may be keen for a low valuation of the company – thus pressure could be applied to CWS re the external audit. There could be intimidation or a self-interest threat.

CWS should behave with integrity.

CWS should behave objectively.

Examiner's comments:

This question had the lowest average mark on the paper. Candidate performance was, in general, poor.

This was a three-part question that tested the candidates' understanding of the investment decisions element of the syllabus and there was also a small section with an ethics element to it. In the scenario the founders of a private UK engineering company were planning to sell their majority shareholding. In part 80.1, for 23 marks, candidates were required to advise the founders of a range of suitable prices for their shareholding and the strengths and weaknesses of each of the valuation methods chosen. In part 80.2, for eight marks, they were required to explain how the Shareholder Value Analysis (SVA) approach to company valuation differs from the methods that they chose in part 80.1. Finally in part 80.3, for four marks, candidates were required to explain the ethical issues facing a firm of ICAEW Chartered Accountants when asked to give valuation advice to the founders of a company for which they also provide an annual external audit.

Part 80.1 was not answered well by most candidates. Many showed a real lack of understanding of how to value a company and a small minority could produce no calculations at all. Very few of them were able to apply their learning to the specific scenario. For example, the vast majority of the candidates said that one of the disadvantages of the P/E approach was that earnings might be erratic, but then made no use of the data in the question which showed exactly that problem. So the candidates' overall performance here was disappointing. This was perhaps the most straightforward set of calculations that the examining team has set on this topic. The errors which stood out because they were so fundamental were:

- Not knowing the basic accounting equation of net assets = equity. Many candidates failed to deduct the debentures in arriving at an equity valuation. A sizeable minority of candidates just used non-current assets as the value, ignoring net current assets and the debentures.

- Using profits before interest and tax (PBIT) as the earnings figure.

- Taking the most recent PBIT figure without question when it was clearly, and deliberately, way out of line with the figures for the previous three years.

- Using the Gordon growth model to calculate a growth rate for dividends which hadn't changed for four years.

Reducing a dividend yield, for the non-marketability of the company's shares, rather than increasing it.

Candidates fared better in part 80.2, but weaker candidates could not identify the seven drivers of value in SVA, nor could they discuss how the technique could be used to value a business.

In general, part 80.3 was done well and the vast majority of candidates produced good answers.

81   Rayner Davies plc

Marking guide

		Marks
81.1	(a) Projected income statements to 31/08/2016 (marks split equally between rights issue and debenture issue):	
	Sales	1
	Variable costs	1
	Fixed costs	1
	Interest	2
	Tax	1
	Dividends	2
		8
	(b) Earnings per share (rights issue)	2
	Earnings per share (debenture issue)	1
		3
	(c) Gearing ratio (rights issue)	2
	Gearing ratio (debenture issue)	2
		4
81.2	1-2 marks per relevant point	Max 7
81.3	1-2 marks per relevant point (EMH must be discussed)	Max 7
81.4	1-2 marks per well explained point (traditional theory and M&M theory must be discussed)	Max 6
		35

81.1 (a)   Projected Income Statements for the year to 31 August 2016

	Rights Issue £'000	Debenture Issue £'000
Sales (£25,800 x 1.20)	30,960	30,960
Variable costs (60% x sales)	(18,576)	(18,576)
Fixed costs (£4,900+ £1,500)	(6,400)	(6,400)
Profit before interest	5,984	5,984
Interest [W1]	(410)	(824)
Profit before tax	5,574	5,160
Tax @ 21%	(1,171)	(1,084)
Profit after tax	4,403	4,076
Dividends [W2]	(3,700)	(3,125)
Retained profit	703	951

WORKINGS

(1)		£'000	£'000
Current interest payment	£8,200 x 5%	410	410
Extra interest from debt issue	£6,900 x 6%	0	414
Total		410	824

(2)		£'000	£'000
Current dividend payment	(£3,125/12,500 = £0.25/share)	3,125	3,125
Extra dividend from rights issue	(£6,900/£3) x £0.25	575	0
Total		3,700	3,125

(b)	Earnings/share (EPS)	£4,403/(12,500 + 2,300)	£0.30
		£4,076/12,500	£0.33

(c)   Gearing ratio

$$\frac{£8,200}{£31,145 + £703 + £6,900} \quad 21.2\%$$

$$\frac{£8,200 + 6,900}{£31,145 + £951 + £6,900} \quad 38.7\%$$

September 2015 exam answers   305

81.2

Current earnings/share	£3,958/12,500	£0.32
Current gearing ratio (book value)	$\dfrac{£8,200}{£31,145}$	26.3%

Rayner's EPS figure worsens with the rights issue (dilution because of extra shares issued), but improves (marginally) with the issue of debt (tax relief on interest a factor here).

However, Rayner's gearing ratio (currently 26.3%) decreases to 21.2% with the equity issue, but increases quite significantly with the extra debt (up to 38.7%). The latter may be considered rather high. Note that the gearing is based on book values rather than market values (MV's) and were MV's to be taken into account the gearing levels would be considerably lower. For example:

Current gearing at MV (assuming debt is quoted at par)	Equity (12,500 x £3.45)	£43,125
	Debt	8,200
		51,325
Gearing ratio at current MV (£8,200/£51,325)		16.0%

The projected income statements show that there is a high level of coverage for interest payments under both options and therefore, the relatively high level of gearing with the debt issue is unlikely to be a problem providing future profits are maintained at the projected level.

81.3

The marketing director feels that the shares are overpriced

However, the efficient markets hypothesis (EMH) holds that stock markets are considered in the main to be efficient, ie all share prices are "fair". Investment returns are those expected for the risks undertaken. Information is rapidly and accurately incorporated into share values. When share prices at all times rationally reflect all available information, the market in which they are traded is said to be efficient. In efficient markets investors cannot make consistently above-average returns other than by chance.

An efficient market is one in which share prices reflect all of the information available. There are three levels of efficiency:

Weak Form - prices only change when new information about a company is made available. There are no changes in anticipation of new information. Information arrives in a random manner (the random walk theory) and so the chartist theory (technical analysis) will not hold up here. The market is efficient in the weak form if past prices CANNOT be used to earn consistently abnormal profits.

Semi Strong Form - prices reflect all information about past price movements and all knowledge that is publicly available/anticipated. The market can anticipate price changes before new information is formally announced. The market is efficient in the semi-strong form if publicly available information (eg historical share prices, dividend announcements) CANNOT be used to earn consistently abnormal profits.

Strong Form - share prices reflect all information about past price movements, all knowledge that is publicly available/anticipated and from insider knowledge available to specialists or experts. The market is efficient in the strong form if all information (private and public) CANNOT be used to earn consistently abnormal profits.

The marketing director feels that investors are irrational

Behavioural finance is an alternative view to the EMH because of investors' irrational tendencies such as :

Overconfidence	Representativeness	Narrow framing
Miscalculation of probabilities	Ambiguity aversion	Positive feedback
Cognitive dissonance	Availability bias	Conservatism

81.4

The danger of radically altering the dividend policy is that Rayner's shareholders will sell their shares and share price will fall. This is the clientele effect. Rayner should establish a consistent policy and stick to it. Dividends also have a signalling effect and a sudden decrease in dividend may well have a negative impact on market confidence in the company.

Reference to main dividend policy theory:

Traditional theory - Shareholders would prefer dividends today rather than dividends or capital gains in future. Cash now is more certain than in the future.

M&M theory - share value is determined by future earnings and the level of risk. The amount of dividends paid will not affect shareholder wealth providing the retained earnings are invested in profitable investment opportunities. Any loss in dividend income will be offset by gains in share price.

Examiner's comments:

This question had the highest percentage mark on the paper and the vast majority of candidates produced answers of a 'pass' standard.

This was a four-part question that tested the candidates' understanding of the financing options element of the syllabus. It was based around a kitchenware manufacturing company which was planning to raise capital to fund an expansion of the business. This capital would be raised either by (a) a rights issue of ordinary shares or (b) an issue of new debentures. Part 81.1 of the question, for 15 marks, required candidates to demonstrate the impact of the two funding options on the company's profits. Within this they were required to calculate the resultant earnings per share (EPS) and gearing figures. In part 81.2 for seven marks, they were then asked to make use of their calculations from part 81.1 to evaluate the impact of the two funding methods on the company and its shareholders. Part 81.3 for seven marks used the scenario to test the candidates' understanding of the Efficient Market Hypothesis (EMH) and behavioural finance. Part 81.4 required candidates to apply their understanding of dividend policy theory to the scenario.

In part 81.1 most candidates got full marks for the equity and debt income statements, although a disappointing number of them failed to calculate correctly the number of additional shares in the rights issue. Also, when calculating the EPS figure, a minority of candidates used, incorrectly, the company's retained earnings or dividends figure. Few candidates scored full marks when calculating the new gearing figures. The main reason for this was that candidates couldn't reflect correctly the impact of the additional £6.9m funds raised in the gearing ratio.

In part 81.2 candidates' discussion of the implications of their calculations from part 81.1 was, generally, very weak. Too few of them compared their predicted EPS and gearing figures to the current figures. Also too many of them allowed their understanding of the M&M theory of gearing to dominate their answers, rather than answering the question asked.

Part 81.3 was generally answered well. Candidates who scored lower marks failed to explain properly (a) the three forms of EMH and/or (b) the key elements of behavioural finance.

Overall, part 81.4 was answered well.

Marking guide

			Marks
82.1 (a)	Does not hedge:		
	Sterling strengthens		1.5
	Sterling weakens		1.5
(b)	Money market hedge:		
	Sterling receipt		1
	Converted at spot rate		1
	Invested at 3.6% p.a.		1
(c)	OTC currency option:		
	Use put option		1
	Receipt in sterling		0.5
	Less option premium		0.5
(d)	Forward contract:		
	Receipt in sterling		1
	Less arrangement fee		1
			10
82.2 1-2 marks per relevant point			Max 9
82.3 Transaction risk			
Economic risk		2	
Translation risk		2	
		2	
			6
82.4 Forward rate agreement		2	
Interest rate futures		2	
Interest rate options		2	
		2	
			Max 5
			30

82.1 (a)

£ strengthens $\dfrac{\$5.3m}{(1.5398 \times 1.05)}$ $\dfrac{\$5.3m}{1.6168}$ **£3,278,080**

£ weakens $\dfrac{\$5.3m}{(1.5398 \times 0.95)}$ $\dfrac{\$5.3m}{1.4628}$ **£3,623,188**

(b) **Money market hedge (MMH)**

Receipt in sterling would be $\dfrac{\$5.3m}{[1+(2.8\%/2)]}$ $\dfrac{\$5.3m}{1.014}$ $5,226,824 borrowed

Converted at spot rate $\dfrac{\$5,226,824}{1.5398}$ £3,394,483

Invested at 3.6% p.a   £3,394,483 × [1 + (3.6%/2)]   **£3,455,583**

(c) **OTC currency option**

A put option would be used (ie at $1.5280/£)

Receipt in sterling would be	$\dfrac{\$5.3m}{1.5280}$		£3,468,586
less: Option premium	5.3m x £0.005	(26,500)	**£3,442,086**

(d) **Forward contract (FC)**

Receipt in sterling would be	$\dfrac{\$5.3m}{(1.5398 - 0.0084)}$ $\dfrac{\$5.3m}{1.5314}$		£3,460,885
less: Arrangement fee 5.3m x £0.003	(15,900)		**£3,444,985**

82.2

Sterling receipt at spot rate	$\dfrac{\$5.3m}{1.5398}$	**£3,442,005**

A weaker £ (using 5% change) gives the highest receipt and vice versa for stronger £

The FC premium suggests a weakening of sterling.

MMH gives best outcome and this is £13k higher receipt than from the option. A rate of $1.5221/£ is break-even point for the option (ie a 1.14% weakening of sterling).

The option gives the company some flexibility unlike the MMH or the FC.

IMT's directors' attitude to risk important.

Other relevant points

82.3

Transaction risk – the risk of adverse exchange rate movements occurring in the normal international trading transactions as in 82.1 above.

Economic risk - the effect of adverse exchange rate movements on the international competitiveness of a company. So sales prices in one currency (customers) could become less competitive whilst costs might become more expensive in another currency (suppliers)

Translation risk – the risk that the company will make exchange losses when the accounting results of its overseas branches are translated into sterling.

82.4

Interest rate risk:

Forward Rate Agreement (FRA) – this is the equivalent of a forward contract on short-term interest rates. It is purchased OTC from its bank. It allows lenders to fix a rate of interest on a future deposit.

Interest rate futures – these are similar to FRA's except that the terms, amounts and periods are standardised. Futures contracts are traded on a futures exchange. Buying an interest rate future equates to investing in debt.

Interest rate options – these grant the buyer of the option the right, but not the obligation to deal at an agreed interest rate at a future maturity date. They allow an organisation to limit its exposure to adverse interest rate movements, while allowing it to take advantage of favourable interest rate movements.

Examiner's comments

The average mark for this question was very good and most candidates demonstrated a good understanding of this area of the syllabus.

This was a four-part question which tested the candidates' understanding of the risk management element of the syllabus. In the scenario a manufacturing company was investigating how it might manage various aspects of its proposed expansion overseas. Part 82.1 for ten marks required candidates to calculate the sterling income arising from a range of hedging techniques applied to a Californian sales contract. In part 82.2 for nine marks, candidates were required to advise the company's board of whether it should hedge those Californian (dollar) receipts. Part 82.3 was worth six marks and required candidates to explain the different types of currency risk that could arise were the company to expand its operations overseas. In part 82.4, for five marks, the company was planning to invest its income from the Californian contract in a UK deposit account in six months' time. Candidates were asked to explain how the company could hedge its exposure to interest rate risk

Most candidates' answers to part 82.1 were good, but common errors noted were
(a) incorrect calculations when strengthening or weakening sterling by 5% eg adding or subtracting 0.05, (b) using a call option rather than a put option and (c) omitting the fee for the forward contract.

Part 82.2's discussion was, overall, reasonable. However, too many candidates, as in Question 80 failed to link their calculations from part 82.1 to their advice, relying in part 82.2 on their understanding of the relevant theory.

Candidates' performance in part 82.3 was very variable and, whilst there were many good answers, too many candidates wrote about other types of risk rather than the currency risk specifically asked about in the requirement and will have scored zero marks.

Part 82.4 was, mostly, answered well, but a lot of candidates suggested an interest rate swap, which would be totally inappropriate in this scenario.

Appendix

The Institute of Chartered Accountants in England and Wales

Professional Level Examination

Financial Management

Formulae and Discount Tables

Formulae you may require:

(a) Discounting an annuity

The annuity factor: $AF_{1 \to n} = \dfrac{1}{r}\left[1 - \dfrac{1}{(1+r)^n}\right]$

Where AF = annuity factor
  n = number of payments
  r = discount rate as a decimal

(b) Dividend growth model:

$$k_e = \dfrac{D_0(1+g)}{P_0} + g$$

Where k_e = cost of equity
  D_0 = current dividend per ordinary share
  g = the annual dividend growth rate
  P_0 = the current ex-div price per ordinary share

(c) Capital asset pricing model: $r_j = r_f + \beta_j(r_m - r_f)$

Where r_j = the expected return from security j
  r_f = the risk free rate
  β_j = the beta of security j
  r_m = the expected return on the market portfolio

(d) $\beta_e = \beta_a\left(1 + \dfrac{D(1-T)}{E}\right)$

Where β_e = beta of equity in a geared firm
  β_a = ungeared (asset) beta
  D = market value of debt
  E = market value of equity
  T = corporation tax rate

Note. Candidates may use other versions of these formulae but should then define the symbols they use.

Discount Tables

Interest rate p.a.	Number of years n	Present value of £1 receivable at the end of n years	Present value of £1 receivable at the end of each of n years
1%	1	0.990	0.990
	2	0.980	1.970
	3	0.971	2.941
	4	0.961	3.902
	5	0.951	4.853
	6	0.942	5.795
	7	0.933	6.728
	8	0.923	7.652
	9	0.914	8.566
	10	0.905	9.471
5%	1	0.952	0.952
	2	0.907	1.859
	3	0.864	2.723
	4	0.823	3.546
	5	0.784	4.329
	6	0.746	5.076
	7	0.711	5.786
	8	0.677	6.463
	9	0.645	7.108
	10	0.614	7.722
10%	1	0.909	0.909
	2	0.826	1.736
	3	0.751	2.487
	4	0.683	3.170
	5	0.621	3.791
	6	0.564	4.355
	7	0.513	4.868
	8	0.467	5.335
	9	0.424	5.759
	10	0.386	6.145
15%	1	0.870	0.870
	2	0.756	1.626
	3	0.658	2.283
	4	0.572	2.855
	5	0.497	3.352
	6	0.432	3.784
	7	0.376	4.160
	8	0.327	4.487
	9	0.284	4.772
	10	0.247	5.019
20%	1	0.833	0.833
	2	0.694	1.528
	3	0.579	2.106
	4	0.482	2.589
	5	0.402	2.991
	6	0.335	3.326
	7	0.279	3.605
	8	0.233	3.837
	9	0.194	4.031
	10	0.162	4.192

ICAEW

Notes

Notes

Notes

Notes